ANTON CHEKHOV

Four Plays
— & —
Three Jokes

ANTON CHEKHOV

Four Plays
— & —
Three Jokes

Translated, with an Introduction and Notes, by
Sharon Marie Carnicke

Hackett Publishing Company, Inc.
Indianapolis/Cambridge

Copyright © 2009 by Hackett Publishing Company, Inc.

All rights reserved
Printed in the United States of America

14 13 12 11 10 09   1 2 3 4 5 6 7

For further information, please address
Hackett Publishing Company, Inc.
P.O. Box 44937
Indianapolis, Indiana 46244-0937

www.hackettpublishing.com

Cover design by Brian Rak
Interior design by Elizabeth L. Wilson
Composition by William Hartman
Printed at Sheridan Books, Inc.

Library of Congress Cataloging-in-Publication Data
Chekhov, Anton Pavlovich, 1860–1904.
 [Plays. English. Selections]
 Four plays and three jokes / translated, with an introduction and notes, by Sharon Marie Carnicke.
   p. cm.
 Includes bibliographical references.
 ISBN 978-0-87220-997-8 (pbk.) —
 ISBN 978-0-87220-998-5 (cloth)
 1. Chekhov, Anton Pavlovich, 1860–1904—Translations into English. 2. Chekhov, Anton Pavlovich, 1860–1904—Correspondence.
 I. Carnicke, Sharon Marie, 1949– II. Title.
 PG3456.A13C365 2009
 891.72'3—dc22   2009012042

The paper used in this publication meets the minimum requirements of American National Standard for Information Sciences—Permanence of Paper for Printed Library Materials, ANSI Z39.48–1984.

Acknowledgments

I would like to thank Gene Nye of Lion Theatre Company (New York) for giving me the opportunity to translate *Three Sisters*. I learned a tremendous amount about Chekhov, translating, and acting from his rehearsals with the company. One performance in particular stands out in my mind: Ron Van Lieu (Yale University) brought depths to Kulygin that I had not seen as potential within the role. In short, Lion gave me the tools I needed for the translations that followed.

In fact, I owe much to all the directors who have staged my translations and the actors in their productions. The directors include John David Lutz (University of Evansville), whose beautiful production of *The Seagull* won for me a translation award from the American College Theatre Festival at the Kennedy Center (Washington, D.C.), and the late John Blankenchip (University of Southern California), who continually supported my work. The actors include Louisa Abernathy (of A/ACT in Los Angeles) and Setrak Bronzian, who taught me the power of physical humor. Because I try to convey in English what I hear in my mind as I read the Russian, I am particularly honored by the émigré directors who have chosen my translations. Among them: Lev Vainstein, who directed *Three Sisters* and then asked me to translate *The Cherry Orchard*, Albert Makhtsier (Theatre in Action in New York), and Eugene Lazerev (formerly of the Moscow Art Theatre).

Additionally, I thank five close colleagues and friends. The émigré movement teacher Edward Rozinsky (Miami, Florida) generously checked my information on pronunciation and the meanings implicit in the characters' names. Mary Joan Negro (Classics Alive and the University of Southern California), R. Andrew White (Valparaiso University), and Leslie Wagner (New York City) offered valuable feedback as I finalized this volume. My friend Patricia Padilla (Los Angeles, California) knew nothing of my contract with Hackett, yet she serendipitously gave me a gift that made work on this publication easier than I could have imagined; she gave me a complete set of Anton Chekhov's works in Russian.

Brian Rak and James Hullett of Hackett Publishing Company invited me to create this volume. Despite numerous productions of

Contents

Acknowledgments	*vi*
Notes on the Translations	*viii*
Source and Transliterations	*viii*
Money and Measures	*viii*
Russian Names	*viii*
Pronunciation	*x*
Introduction: The Riddle of Chekhov the Playwright	xi

Three Jokes
The Bear	3
The Proposal	19
The Anniversary	35

The Major Plays
The Seagull	53
Uncle Vanya	114
Three Sisters	168
The Cherry Orchard	242
A Selected Bibliography in English	*302*

my translations, their appearance in print is due to the efforts of these two creative men, and I am grateful to them.

Finally, I thank a number of my students at the University of Southern California: Rose Leisner, who helped me proof, edit, type, and scan this volume; the members of my freshman seminar (Checking Out Chekhov, fall 2008) who influenced my Introduction and *Uncle Vanya;* and the bachelor of fine arts class of 2009, whose teacher, Mary Joan Negro, used my translations to introduce them to the pleasures of Chekhov's plays.

Notes on the Translations

Source and Transliterations

The plays and letters are taken from A. P. Chekhov, *Polnoe sobranie sochinenii i pisem v tridtsati tomakh* [*The Complete Works and Letters in Thirty Volumes*], Moscow: Nauka, 1974–1984. This edition reprints Chekhov's 1902 revisions, made in connection with the first publication of his complete works by A. F. Marx.

Rather than using a scholarly system for transliterating the Russian alphabet into English, I use more informal conventions that assist readers with the pronunciations of names and words (for example, "Stanislavsky" instead of "Stanislavskii," "Sergeyevich" for "Sergeevich," and "Maria" rather than "Mar'ia").

In my translations, I retain all ellipses used by Chekhov as they appear in the Russian texts. Whenever I elide material from a quotation in my introduction and notes, I use an ellipsis in brackets to mark the place where an abridgement has been made.

Money and Measures

In the Russian monetary system, there are one hundred kopecks in each ruble. I retain these terms, but I recalculate other unfamiliar Russian measures (such as "versts," "desiatins," and "poods") into English equivalents (miles, acres, and pounds).

Russian Names

All names are given as they appear in the Russian texts, because they offer valuable emotional information. Actors, who understand Russian names, can use them effectively in performance.

Formal address in Russian consists of the first name and patronymic, for example, "Anton Pavlovich" (Anton Son-of-Pavel) or "Maria Pavlovna" (Maria Daughter-of-Pavel). When used together, the name and patronymic serve as "Mr.," "Miss," and "Mrs.," signifying the speaker's respect. For example, in *Three Sisters,* the doctor is most often called "Ivan Romanych" (Ivan Son-of-Roman). In his case, respect is as much due to his age as his personal traits and position. When the sisters call Vershinin "Alexander Ignatyevich" (Alexander Son-of-Ignatius), they greet him formally as a guest in their house and pay respect to his military rank.

Rarely do Russians use surnames; these serve primarily to identify a family connection (as in the cast lists), to refer to famous personages (such as authors or actors), or to introduce complete strangers. In *The Seagull*, "Treplev" appears in Konstantin Gavrilovich's passport. The fictional writer "Trigorin" registers as famous, much like the actual novelist "Turgenev," because people refer to them by their last names. When Medvedenko says that "Zarechnaya" will perform in the play planned for that evening, he already treats her as a famous actress. In *Three Sisters*, Vershinin and Andrey introduce themselves to each other with their last names because they are strangers to each other. Sometimes using a last name alone is an insult. In Act IV of *Three Sisters*, Natasha thoughtlessly reveals her disdain for her lover by calling him "Protopopov," only to cover up her gaff by reverting to his first name and patronymic.

First names are used only by one's intimate friends and family. Russian is particularly rich in nicknames (called "pet names" among Russian speakers). These are formed by adding diminutive endings to the first name. These diminutives can be piled onto the name almost endlessly and signify warmth, emotional closeness, and sympathy between people. A first-degree diminutive is common in the family circle ("Masha" for "Maria," "Olya" for "Olga," "Andryusha" for "Andrey," etc.). Second- and third-degree diminutives (two or three endings) show greater and greater warmth ("Mashenka" for "Maria," "Olechka" for "Olga," etc.). My favorite diminutive in Chekhov occurs in *Three Sisters*, when Natasha wheedles her husband into agreeing that his sister Irina should give up her room for their child; she piles three diminutives on top of "Andrey" to create the saccharine-sweet "Andryushchanchik." Diminutives are commonly used with children ("Bobik," not "Bob," and "Sofochka," not "Sofia," in *Three Sisters*). No wonder Chekhov's nannies (like Marina in *Uncle Vanya* and Anfisa in *Three Sisters*) pepper their speech with pet names!

In brackets in the cast lists for each play, I give specific information on the characters' names.

Pronunciation

Unlike English, which uses primary and secondary stresses, Russian stresses only one syllable in each name or word. All other syllables are given equal and minimal weight. To assist with pronunciation, whenever a Russian name or word appears in the text for the first time, I have marked the stressed syllable with an accent. Russian vowels tend to be softer than English vowels. *A* is always "ah," as in "father" ("Máh-sha" for Masha). *E* sounds like "eh," as in "pet" ("Ye-léh-nah" for Yelena). *I* is always "ee," as in "feel" ("Ee-réé-nah" for Irina). The related *y* also sounds like "ee," but a bit shorter ("Cheh-boo-téé-keen" for Chebutykin). *O* resembles "aw," as in "door," never "oh" ("Áwl-gah" for Olga and "Sehmyáwn" for Semyon). *U* is "oo," as in "fool" ("Koo-léé-geen" for Kulygin).

Introduction
The Riddle of Chekhov the Playwright

It is hard to imagine a theatrical tradition without Anton Chekhov. The Russian writer inspires as much passionate enthusiasm as does Shakespeare. Chekhov's insights into human emotions often ring true, even when his audience is unfamiliar with the culture from which he drew his inspiration. One of my undergraduate students would audibly gasp whenever a scene or character struck a surprisingly familiar chord; another more soberly called Chekhov "an author capable of transcending cultures and centuries."[1] After viewing Michael Cacoyannis'

Portrait of Chekhov, 1902.

2002 filmed version of *The Cherry Orchard,* one reviewer wrote: "We are left as always with Chekhov's effortless humanity, the sheer psychological acuity he brought to the loves, hopes and inchoate longings of his characters."[2] An American enthusiast of Chekhov summed it up in this way: "After Shakespeare, [Chekhov]'s the most universal playwright we have."[3]

Fervor for Chekhov can reach extraordinary proportions. Consider the fact that proven playwrights often express their admiration by

---

1. Jennifer Bashian and Kevin Burke, Freshman Seminar: Checking Out Chekhov, University of Southern California, Fall 2008.
2. Kenneth Turan, "The Cherry Orchard," *Los Angeles Times: Calendar Live,* April 5, 2002, http://www.calendarlive.com/movies/Reviews, accessed April 29, 2009.
3. Paul Schmidt, "Translating Chekhov All Over Again," *Dramatists Guild Quarterly* (Winter 1997), 18.

adapting his plays to their own languages and thematic concerns, even when they cannot read Russian. A list of these admirers reads like a *Who's Who* of modern and contemporary drama. Among the Americans are Clifford Odets (with a 1939 version of *Three Sisters*), Tennessee Williams (with an adaptation of *The Seagull* entitled *The Notebook of Trigorin*), Jean Claude Van Itallie (who gave us his versions of Chekhov in the 1960s and 1970s, using French translations to help him), Lanford Wilson (who learned Russian in 1984 specifically to translate *Three Sisters*), and David Mamet (who has adapted most of Chekhov's major plays). Indeed, Chekhov's influence in the United States is so extensive that dramatist Robert Anderson observes, "American playwrights have gone around, trying to be the American Chekhov."[4] British emulators include David Hare, Edward Bond, Pam Gems, Christopher Hampton, and Tom Stoppard, who baldly admits, "I've always felt very envious of Chekhov."[5]

Such enthusiasm translates into frequent and viable Chekhov productions worldwide. Theater directors stage his handful of plays with nearly the same frequency as they do Shakespeare's more prodigious output. Moreover, alongside productions that seek to bring Chekhov's texts to life on their own terms are those that imaginatively reinterpret him. Russia's cherry orchard has been replanted on an antebellum southern plantation in the United States (Joshua Logan's *The Wisteria Trees*) and on a plot of land in South Africa (Janet Suzman's *The Free State*). Sometimes a seagull flies over Ireland (Thomas Kilroy's adaptation of *The Seagull*) or New York's Long Island (Emily Mann's *A Seagull in the Hamptons*). In 2008, 104 years after Chekhov's death, a Broadway revival of *The Seagull* was one of only two productions "to have recouped their New York investments" that year, and this while the New York Stock Market plunged.[6] Laurence Senelick's hefty tome,

---

4. Laurence Senelick, *The Chekhov Theatre: A Century of the Plays in Performance* (New York: Cambridge University Press, 1997), 284.
5. "Stagewrite Productions Archive," *National Theatre Education*, http://www.nt-online.org, accessed August 16, 2002. For more on the phenomenon of playwrights translating Chekhov, see Sharon Marie Carnicke, "Translating Chekhov's Plays Without Russian, or The Nasty Habit of Adaptations," in *Chekhov the Immigrant: Translating a Cultural Icon*, ed. Michael C. Finke and Julie de Sherbinin (Bloomington, IN: Slavica, 2007), 89–100.
6. *The Los Angeles Times: Quick Takes*, "Two Broadway Revivals Recoup" December 9, 2008, http://www.latimes.com/entertainment, accessed December 11, 2008.

Introduction					xiii

The Chekhov Theatre,[7] charts a century of productions in Russia, the English-speaking world, Europe, Scandinavia, and Asia. Paging through this book should be enough to assure the most hardened skeptic of Chekhov's global impact as a dramatist.

However, Chekhov has always endured as much rebuke as praise for his dramatic writing. There are those who dread his plays. Not long ago, I visited the drama section of a large bookstore in Los Angeles. As I browsed, I overheard two young people exclaiming happily whenever they found a play that might provide them with good material for their acting class. "Here's Chekhov," said one. "Oh, no," said the other, "I hate Chekhov!" While putting the book back on the shelf, the first student added, "My friend took a class and they spent the whole term just on Chekhov." "What a nightmare!" the other responded. "I would have dropped that class immediately." These two students are no more unique in their opinion of Chekhov than are those playwrights who model themselves upon him. Extremes of opinion about him can exist side by side in the same auditorium. Rarely does there seem to be any middle ground. Moreover, this riddle of Chekhov as an equally great and awful playwright has persisted for more than one hundred years.

Before attempting to solve the riddle, consider how it came to be. Chekhov's experience as a writer of short stories was entirely different from his career as a playwright; there is little mystery in his meteoric rise to fame in fiction. By 1888, at age twenty-eight, Anton Chekhov had already established himself as the greatest living Russian storyteller, second only to the famous novelist Leo Tolstoy (1828–1910), who was then in his sixties. Chekhov had begun to write at age fourteen. While still in high school he submitted short comedic stories under various pseudonyms to popular magazines. His first publication dates from 1879. As a medical student, he churned out hundreds of stories. In 1883 alone he published ninety. When he graduated, he kept writing at the same furious pace. In 1885 he published more than one hundred stories.

At the end of 1885, Chekhov visited his publisher in Russia's cosmopolitan capital of St. Petersburg. He was astonished to learn that people not only read his stories avidly, but eagerly awaited his next contributions. His readers, it seemed, were taking him seriously as a writer. "If I had known they were reading me like that," he told his eldest brother, "I would not have written on short

---

7. Senelick, *The Chekhov Theatre: A Century of the Plays in Performance* (New York: Cambridge University Press, 1997).

order."[8] Three months later, Chekhov received a long, detailed letter that, he said, "surprised me, as if it were a lighting bolt."[9] The nationally famous author Dmitry Grigorovich had written to tell Chekhov that his "real talent," which "far exceeds other writers of the new generation," could translate into a literary career of significance. "You are, I am sure, meant to write some exceptional, truly artistic works." But Grigorovich also reprimanded the young writer for obviously hasty and careless writing, telling him to "respect" his own talent or risk "commit[ing] the great moral sin of not fulfilling your calling."[10] Chekhov took heed, began to use his real name for publications, slowed the pace of his writing, and perfected the economical and allusive craft by which he created true masterpieces of short fiction. A scant two years later in October 1888, the Russian Academy of Sciences unanimously voted to give him the prestigious Pushkin Prize for literature. In another two years, Chekhov would himself become a member of the Academy.

In tandem with fiction, Chekhov had also been writing plays, but fame as a dramatist came much harder and later. He was attracted to the theater from the first. In high school, his father and teachers forbade him from attending the local theater. Such entertainment, after all, could prove a bad influence on a boy. Chekhov still managed to sneak off to see lascivious French farces and operettas, Russian plays by Nikolay Gogol and Alexander Ostrovsky, Shakespeare's classics, and broadly comic vaudevilles. Among the first books that Chekhov bought were translations of Shakespeare's *Hamlet* and *Macbeth*.[11] By the time Chekhov was eighteen, he had written at least two plays (a serious one, *Fatherless,* and a lost vaudeville, *Why the Hen Clucks*).

When he moved to Moscow for medical school, he built his social life around theater: he attended all kinds of performances, befriended actors of the highest rank, and flirted (and more) with actresses. When he decided to marry in 1901, he chose a leading actress of the Moscow Art Theatre, Olga Knipper. Like his early stories, many of his plays were short "jokes," as he called them.

8. Chekhov to Al. P. Chekhov, January 4, 1886, in A. P. Chekhov *Sobranie sochinenii* [Collected Works], vol. 11 (Moscow: Izdatel'stvo khudozhestvennoi literatury, 1956), 70.
9. Chekhov to D. V. Grigorovich, March 28, 1886, ibid., 79.
10. Grigorovich to Chekhov, March 25, 1886, ibid., 626.
11. Donald Rayfield, *Anton Chekhov: A Life* (New York: Henry Holt, 1997), 59.

Staged widely throughout Russia's provinces, these one-acts provided Chekhov with substantial income, so much that he advised his older brother to sit down and write two or three plays. "A play," he said "is a pension fund."[12]

Despite his early infatuation with theater, Chekhov had also begun to criticize the unconvincing melodramatic claptrap and the histrionic acting that was common on nineteenth-century stages. He wanted plays and acting to be "just as complex and also just as simple as in life. People eat their dinner, just eat their dinner, yet at the same time their happiness is taking shape and their lives are being smashed."[13] Put another way, "In real life people do not spend every minute shooting each other, hanging themselves, or making declarations of love." Instead, "They eat, drink, flirt, talk nonsense."[14] Chekhov began to experiment with dramatic forms that matched his opinions of theater.

In his longer plays, he turns the usual stories of melodrama inside out by putting action-packed events like duels and fires offstage; nothing much seems to happen onstage. This innovation can best be seen by reading a melodrama, like Dion Boucicault's *The Octoroon* (1859), against one of Chekhov's plays, *The Cherry Orchard*. Both tell the same basic story: a widow, whose husband left her with nothing but debts, finds that her property will be sold at auction. Boucicault depicts murder, fraud, and a climactic onstage auction. In contrast, Chekhov shows what happens to people between the big incidents in their lives. Every action-packed event in *The Cherry Orchard*, even the auction, happens offstage. Onstage, the characters only wait for and then react to what has happened elsewhere. We watch them spend time, worry, make plans, have coffee, reminisce, tease, converse, flirt, give a party, and cope with bad news that forever changes their lives. After learning of the auction, the widow collapses into a state of shock, while the buyer of her estate expresses his exultant, yet guilty, joy. Nor does Chekhov end the play with these climactic reactions; instead he follows his characters

---

12. Chekhov to Al. P. Chekhov, February 21, 1899, in A. P. Chekhov *Polnoe sobranie sochinenii i pisem: Pis'ma* [Complete Works and Letters: Letters], vol. 3 (Moscow: Nauka, 1976), 164. Hereafter cited as *Pis'ma* [Letters].

13. Spoken words from 1889, translated by Gordon McVay in *Chekhov's* Three Sisters (London: Bristol Classical Press, 1995), 42.

14. D. Gorodetskii, "Iz vospominanii ob A. P. Chekhove" [Reminiscences of A. P. Chekhov] in *Chekhov i teatr* [Chekhov and the Theater], ed. E. D. Surkov (Moscow: Iskusstvo, 1961), 208–9.

as they pick up their lives, establish new routines, and move on. While Boucicault depicts the external causes that throw lives into turmoil, Chekhov paints the familiar experience of living from day to day. By turning melodrama inside out, he has also effectively redefined the notion of dramatic action as the inner, psychological, often subtle movements of the soul. As one of my students observed, "Chekhov's portrayal of the tedium of life allows the audience to get to the subtleties of the characters and become more personally attached to them."[15]

Chekhov also refuses to sort his characters into easily identifiable heroes and villains as melodrama does; all his characters are in turn admirable and silly, cruel and kind. While writing *Ivanov* in 1887 (his first full-length play to be staged), Chekhov described his approach:

> Contemporary playwrights fill their plays with angels, villains, and clowns. Go find such types anywhere in Russia! However hard you look, you won't find them anywhere except in plays. [. . .] I wanted to do something original: I didn't bring into it one villain, not one angel (although I couldn't resist the clowns).[16]

Another quick look at Boucicault's *The Octoroon* makes Chekhov's point about angels and villains clear: Boucicault's widow has only one flaw; she lacks business experience. As for the buyer of her land, Mr. McClosky has only one admirable trait, his well-trimmed mustaches. They are heroine and villain personified. In *The Cherry Orchard*, Chekhov's widow may lack business sense, but she understands love very well; in fact, her first name, Lyubov, means *love* in Russian. Her nemesis, Lopakhin, may exceed her in business savvy, but he is helpless in regard to affairs of the heart. Neither one is fully heroic or fully villainous. With the inclusion of a few clowns, like the clerk, Yepikhodov, who keeps tripping over his own feet, Chekhov creates a dramatic genre that is neither fully comic nor fully tragic. In his plays, nonsense coexists with philosophy, and conversations about the weather follow climactic moments that decide characters' fates.

---

15. Mark Lay, Freshman Seminar: Checking Out Chekhov, University of Southern California, Fall 2008.
16. Chekhov to Al. P. Chekhov, October 24, 1887, in *Pis'ma* [Letters], vol. 2 (Moscow: Nauka, 1975), 137–8.

Chekhov in Yalta, 1899.

Similar experimentation had rewarded Chekhov lavishly in the realm of fiction, but it was not to be so in drama. In 1889, the selection committee for the Alexandrinsky Theater in St. Petersburg found his play *The Wood Demon* to be "a beautiful dramatization of a novella, but not a play."[17] Alexander Lensky (Moscow's leading actor) told his good friend Chekhov to "write [only] tales. You refer too scornfully to the stage and to dramatic form. You esteem them too little to write a play."[18]

Flaunting all advice, Chekhov wrote his next play, *The Seagull*, by "mercilessly betraying stage conventions."[19] At its 1897 premiere, the play was audibly booed. Selected as a benefit performance for a famous comic actress of the Alexandrinsky Theatre, *The Seagull* opened to an audience of her fans, who expected broad comedy. The subtlety of Chekhov's new play escaped them. Moreover, critics (who had lobbied against Chekhov's plays) further provoked the crowd's guffaws. Chekhov left the theater midway through the performance, walked the streets in despair, and returned to his home,

17. A. P. Chekhov, *Polnoe sobranie sochinenii i pisem: Sochineniia* [The Complete Collected Works and Letters: Works], vol. 11 (Moscow: Izdatel'stvo khudozhestvennoi literatury, 1948), 614.
18. Ibid.
19. Chekhov to A. S. Suvorin, October 21, 1895, in *Pis'ma* [Letters], vol. 6 (Moscow: Nauka, 1978), 85.

vowing never to write for the theater again. He told his younger brother, "The play flopped, collapsed with a thud. In the theatre I felt the burdensome tension of perplexity and shame. [. . .] The moral is: it's not worth writing plays."[20] He immediately stopped the play's publication and told his editor, "It wasn't just my play which failed, it was me. [. . .] I will never forget what happened, just as I could never forget, for example, being slapped in the face."[21]

Even so, admiration for Chekhov's plays lurked behind the pervasive abuse. Despite the Alexandrinsky Theatre's rejection of *The Wood Demon* in 1889, at least one member of the selection committee had been thrilled with Chekhov's novelistic play. The leading St. Petersburg actor, Pavel Svobodin, praised Chekhov's "life-like figures, living speech, and characters, which are beyond the whole Alexandrinsky trash."[22] Similarly, despite the disastrous premiere of *The Seagull*, at least one playwright saw something new and exciting there too. When Vladimir Nemirovich-Danchenko won the coveted Griboyedov Prize for drama in 1897, he said, "I told the judges that [. . .] the prize should be given to *The Seagull*. [. . .] The judges did not agree with me."[23] Already at the turn of the twentieth century, people earnestly argued over the riddle of Chekhov as a terrible, good playwright.

Extremes of opinion soon traveled to the West. For every reviewer who praised the 1914 production of *Uncle Vanya* in London, there was one who reviled it. The play was either "an unforgettably good play," or "desolate" and "dreary."[24]

Similarly, when the Moscow Art Theatre tours brought Chekhov to the United States in 1923 and 1924,[25] the riddle arrived along

---

20. Chekhov to M. P. Chekhov, October 18, 1896, in *Pis'ma* [Letters], vol. 6 (Moscow: Nauka, 1978), 197.

21. Chekhov to A. S. Suvorin, December 14, 1896, in *Pis'ma* [Letters], vol. 6 (Moscow: Nauka, 1978), 251.

22. Cited and translated by Ernest J. Simmons in *Chekhov: A Biography* (Chicago: The University of Chicago Press, 1962), 198.

23. Vladimir Nemirovitch-Dantchenko [sic], *My Life in the Russian Theatre* (Boston: Little, Brown, 1937), 71. (Note the old-fashioned and now uncommon spelling of Nemirovich-Danchenko's name in this publication; I retain the transliteration as published.)

24. Desmond MacCarthy and Egan Mew in *File on Chekhov,* ed. Nick Worall (New York: Methuen, 1986), 48.

25. In 52 weeks, the Moscow Art Theatre gave 380 performances in the United States, half of which were Chekhov's plays. See Sharon Marie Carnicke,

with his plays. On one side sat audiences who wept in sympathy with Chekhov's characters. During a performance of *Three Sisters*, an actor described catching sight of a young woman who held the play's translation in one hand and "in the other a handkerchief. She cried, then quickly, quickly wiped away her tears, so that she would not miss a word in the book, then again more tears."[26] On the other side of the auditorium sat critics who argued that "the plays of Chekhov, the very cornerstone upon which this admirable, this exemplary Moscow Art Theatre was builded, leave English-speaking peoples cold."[27] For those who wept, watching the actors perform in Chekhov's native language did not interfere with their pleasure. As critic Russell McLauchlan wrote, speech is only one of the many "details of behavior" in a performance; "an inability to understand it is no particular bar to comprehension."[28] For the others, Chekhov only widened the cultural gap between Russia and America by displaying "the Slavic temperament [which] feeds upon self-deprecation, upon pessimism."[29]

In the twenty-first century, the riddle of Chekhov's reception as a playwright is still alive. For every one who makes Chekhov into her "new favorite writer,"[30] there is another who turns up his nose. When I first began to study Russian literature, I, too, turned up my nose. My professor told me that Chekhov, like olives, is an acquired taste. And I do now love the taste. Every time I revisit his plays, I find something new that surprises me, that I had missed before, that makes me laugh and makes me cry. Acquiring a taste

---

Stanislavsky in Focus: An Acting Master for the 21st Century, 2nd ed. (New York: Routledge, 2008), chapter 2.

26. O. S. Bokshanskaya, "Iz perepiski s Vl. I. Nemirovichem-Danchenko (Evropa i Amerika 1922–1924)" [Correspondence with Vl. I. Nemirovich-Danchenko (Europe and America 1922–1924)], in *Ezhegodnik Moskovskogo khudozhevstvennogo teatra: 1943* [The 1943 Yearbook of the Moscow Art Theatre] (Moscow: MkhAT, 1945), 539.

27. John Corbin, review of *Three Sisters, New York Times*, January 31, 1923, in *Chekhov: The Critical Heritage*, ed. Victor Emeljanow (Boston: Routledge and Kegan Paul, 1981), 241.

28. Russell McLauchlan, "*The Cherry Orchard* with Two Bright Stars" (*Clippings*, The New York Public Library for the Performing Arts, no date.)

29. Corbin, review of *Three Sisters*, 241.

30. Sarah Boots, Freshman Seminar: Checking Out Chekhov, University of Southern California, Fall 2008.

for Chekhov begins by putting aside all expectations and meeting him on his own terms.

A Brief Life

When asked by Moscow University to provide an autobiography for his class reunion, Chekhov replied: "An autobiography? I have a disease: autobiographobia. To read any details about myself genuinely torments me, and to write them for publication is even worse."[31] Scholars know a lot about Chekhov. He wrote an enormous number of letters, recording his daily life and registering his opinions. Yet, because he developed restraint and tact in his dealings with others, Chekhov the man still manages to elude us.

Biographers sometimes romanticize the facts of his life, creating novelistic stories about his rags-to-riches career, his love for the actress Olga Knipper, and his tragic death from tuberculosis at the age of forty-four. Biographers sometimes tackle, instead, the naked facts, assembling his complicated comings and goings, disentangling his friends from his acquaintances, and reconstructing his diverse activities and interests. Both types of biographies can lose sight of the forest for the trees. In the all-too-cursory account of Chekhov's life that follows, I point out those particular trees that best illuminate his writing of plays: his social background, his career in medicine, and his marriage to both the Moscow Art Theatre and Olga Knipper.

The Blood of a Slave

On one rare occasion, Chekhov sent his editor a brief, yet accurate, autobiography, masked as an idea for a short story:

> What is free for writers born into the aristocracy comes at a high price for those born into the lower classes. The cost is their youth. Write a story about a young man, the son of a serf, a former shopkeeper, singer [in the church choir], school-boy and university student, raised with respect for rank, kissing the hands of priests, bowing to others' ideas, grateful for every piece of bread, beaten many times, going to school without galoshes,

---

31. Chekhov to G. I. Rossiolimo, October 11, 1899, in *Pis'ma* [Letters], vol. 8 (Moscow: Nauka, 1980), 284.

picking fights, tormenting animals, loving dinners with rich relatives, playing the hypocrite with both God and people because he thought himself good for nothing. Write about how this young man presses the slave out of himself drop by drop, and how he awakens one fine morning and feels he no longer has the blood of a slave in his veins, but that of a real human being.[32]

Anton Pavlovich Chekhov was born on January 16, 1860, in Taganrog;[33] he was the third oldest son in a family of five boys and two girls. For the next forty-four years he celebrated his birthday on January 17, the day dedicated to St. Anthony, for whom he was named.[34] His native city, like the one in *Three Sisters*, was a provincial capital in southern Russia near the Ukraine, with a cosmopolitan population because of its port (where Greek merchants traded) and its military base. His family's background reflected Russia's past. Like Lopakhin's father in *The Cherry Orchard*, Anton's father, Pavel, had been born into serfdom, Russia's form of slavery. When Pavel reached age nineteen, his father, Yegor (Anton's grandfather), had somehow amassed enough money to buy his and his family's freedom from their owner, Count Chertkov.[35]

Pavel Chekhov owned a small shop that sold groceries, sundries, and even medicines (most of them quack preparations). He was especially proud of having joined the merchant guild, because it raised his class status, as measured by the Russian government, by two ranks above the free peasants. He was ambitious for his sons, and thus insured that they learn to respect authority, pay strict attention to church doctrine, and get a solid education (grounded in foreign languages, including Latin and Greek). As choir director for the local churches, Pavel also demanded that his children dedicate themselves to liturgical music. They sang in church every morning. Anton would later use this training to create uniquely musical plays.

32. Chekhov to A. S. Suvorin, January 7, 1889, in *Pis'ma* [Letters], vol. 3 (Moscow: Nauka, 1976), 133.
33. All biographical dates are given according to the Julian calendar, which was used in Russia during Chekhov's life; dates are therefore twelve days earlier than in the Gregorian calendar, used elsewhere.
34. Act I of *Three Sisters* depicts a name-day party.
35. Yegor Chekhov had accumulated only enough to buy his sons' freedom; Chertkov took pity on him and included Yegor's daughter for free.

Given Pavel's roots as a serf, he also expected hard work from his children. Anton tended the store whenever he was not in school or with the choir; his day began at five o'clock in the morning in church and ended at midnight in the store. Even the slightest infraction of the rules meant a physical beating from Pavel. As Chekhov once said, "There was no childhood in my childhood."[36]

In 1876, Pavel Chekhov went bankrupt; he lost his store and his membership in the merchant guild. He dropped in status to one rung above the peasants, the same lowly rank of Treplev's father in *The Seagull*. With no income, Pavel escaped from debtors' prison by leaving town in the dead of night with most of his family. At sixteen Anton was left behind to finish school; the rest of his family resettled in the slums of Moscow. Alone in Taganrog, Anton tried but failed to fend off his father's creditors. It was he who watched his family's house and furniture sold to their former tenant, a civil servant with a penchant for gambling. Echoes of this period find their way into his plays. The title of his play *Fatherless* labels his personal situation; *The Cherry Orchard* depicts the loss of a family's home to their former serf; and in *Three Sisters*, Andrey becomes a civil servant addicted to gambling as was the Chekhovs' former tenant.

The Moscow Art Theatre production of *The Seagull*, 1898. Sitting on the floor is Vsevolod Meyerhold as Treplev, to his right is Olga Knipper as Arkadina, and next to her is Konstantin Stanislavsky as Trigorin.

36. As cited and translated by Simmons, in *Chekhov*, 6.

Chekhov's difficult upbringing taught him restraint. "I am short-tempered, etc., etc.," he later told his wife, "but I have gotten used to holding myself back, because letting oneself go doesn't suit a decent person."[37] Moreover, by "pressing the slave out of himself drop by drop," he developed a lifelong dedication to freedom and fairness.

> I am not a liberal, not a conservative, not an evolutionist, not a monk, but neither am I indifferent. I would like to be a free artist, and I only fear that God has not given me the strength to become one. I hate lies and coercion in any form. [. . .] My holy of holies is the human body, health, the mind, talent, inspiration, love, and the most absolute freedom, freedom from coercion and lies, in whatever ways these might be expressed.[38]

A "Medicle" Career

Anton graduated from high school in 1879 with grades that earned him a scholarship to Moscow University, where he studied medicine. He later recalled that "when I applied for entrance, I wrote down 'medicle' school" in error.[39] Perhaps Anton chose medicine as his career because he had seen desperately ill peasants buying quack medicines at his father's store. Perhaps he hoped to cure the many members of his family who were ill with tuberculosis. In reflecting on two family deaths from this widespread disease, Chekhov wrote, "The trouble is that both these deaths (A. and N.) are not an accident, and not an event in human life, but an ordinary thing."[40] Whatever the motivation, Chekhov devoted himself to medicine his whole life, often calling it "my lawful wife." Literature was "my mistress."[41]

37. Chekhov to O. L. Knipper, February 11, 1903, in *Pis'ma* [Letters], vol. 11 (Moscow: Nauka, 1982), 150.
38. Chekhov to A. N. Pleshcheyev, October 4, 1888, in *Pis'ma* [Letters], vol. 3 (Moscow: Nauka, 1976), 10.
39. Chekhov to G. I. Rossiolimo, October 11, 1899, in *Pis'ma* [Letters], vol. 8 (Moscow: Nauka, 1980), 284.
40. An 1891 notebook entry, cited and translated by Rayfield, *Anton Chekhov*, 322.
41. See, for example, letters by Chekhov on January 17, 1887, in *Pis'ma* [Letters], vol. 2 (Moscow: Nauka, 1975), 14; on February 11, 1893, in *Pis'ma* [Letters], vol. 5 (Moscow: Nauka, 1977), 169; and on March 15, 1896, in *Pis'ma* [Letters], vol. 6 (Moscow: Nauka, 1978), 132.

In moving to Moscow for medical school, Anton also became the de facto head of a large, woefully dependent, and largely dysfunctional family. His father had at last found menial work as a clerk, but his two older brothers were in trouble. Alexander (an intelligent writer) had become an alcoholic; Nikolay (a gifted visual artist and illustrator) was suffering from tuberculosis and was addicted to the treatments of morphine.

It was now up to Anton to pay the rent, buy the food, and make sure his younger siblings finished school. There is little doubt that his prodigious writing during the 1880s provided significant and necessary additional income. His hasty writing reflects the fact that he was paid per line; the more lines he could write the more money he could earn for his family. When his level-headed younger sister, Masha, graduated as a school teacher, she became Anton's right hand, managing the household for him whenever medicine and literature called him away. Like Olga in *Three Sisters*, she never married despite her longings.

Upon graduation in 1884, Dr. Chekhov opened his practice in Moscow. He was already showing early symptoms of the family's disease. When Nikolay died on January 17, 1889 (Anton's nameday), the young doctor fell into a deep depression that he handled in an extraordinary way. In April 1890 he undertook a massive scientific study of Russia's most notorious penal colony, Sakhalin, in the far east. He traveled eighty-one days by horse, rail, and steamship through storms and the cold of Siberia to get to the remote island prison; the grueling journey clearly affected his health and may have accelerated his death. Once in Sakhalin, he spent eight months processing questionnaires for 10,000 convicts and their families, all exiled for life. He conducted as many as 160 interviews daily, amassing information and statistics previously unknown to Russia's government. When he returned home, he exposed the reality of Russia's penal system in his book *The Island of Sakhalin* (1891) and began a fund-raising campaign to send books to the convicts' children.

By 1892 Chekhov had earned enough money to buy a tumbledown country estate called Melikhovo, located forty-five miles by train outside Moscow and six more miles by horse on muddy roads from the railroad station. In *Three Sisters*, Vershinin might well be speaking of Melikhovo when he says, "It's good to live here. Only it's strange that the railroad is twenty-five miles away . . . And no one knows why that is." Chekhov lived at his estate from 1892 until 1899, when his deteriorating health made a move to warmer climates essential.

Chekhov may well have wanted to escape the cruelties of human behavior (which he had so starkly confronted at Sakhalin) and find peace in nature. Melikhovo consisted of 600 acres of birch forests, pastures, and farmland. The dilapidated house was large but had no bathroom or insulation. Chekhov planted a cherry orchard and flowers. He and Masha (like Vanya and Sonya in *Uncle Vanya*) tended the forests and tried to make the farm productive. Chekhov also worked as the area's country doctor, becoming solely responsible for the health of twenty-six surrounding villages and seven factories, with duties and difficulties that mirror those of Dr. Astrov in *Uncle Vanya*.

Over the years, Chekhov's civic work included fund-raising for the victims of Russia's famine in 1891, volunteering as a doctor during the cholera epidemic in 1892, and building three schools for peasants in the villages around Melikhovo and a sanatorium for tuberculosis near the city of Yalta on the Black Sea (where he would eventually move). These endeavors earned him a national award, the Stanislaus Medal (third class) in 1899.[42]

Chekhov's knowledge as a doctor must have made facing his own illness especially difficult. He used a lot of ink in letters to explain away the periodic bleeding from his lungs. He strenuously resisted allowing another doctor to examine him. Over the years he made light of his illness in letters to his siblings and to his wife. Yet, he could hardly hold any illusions about his diagnosis. He had suffered recognizable symptoms of tuberculosis throughout medical school, and in 1894 he joked with a friend that he would live only five or ten more years. In 1897 a serious hemorrhage from the lungs hospitalized him; he could no longer deny the truth. He sold Melikhovo and built a new house in the warmer climate of Yalta. There, he felt exiled from Moscow and longed for the city as fervently as do his *Three Sisters*.

In 1904 he risked one last trip to Moscow, appearing on January 17 (his name-day) for the premiere of his last play, *The Cherry Orchard*. He arrived at the Moscow Art Theatre just before the last act and was promptly called to the stage by loud applause. He was emaciated, pale, and hardly able to stand on stage as the company made speeches in his honor.[43] By spring, his condition turned mortal. On the advice of Muscovite doctors, his wife rushed him to the German health spa of Badenweiler. But the trip itself was dangerous

---

42. Rayfield, *Anton Chekhov*, 507.
43. Ibid., 587.

for him. He died in the warmth of the resort on July 2, 1904. He is buried in Moscow's Novodevichy cemetery, where his *Three Sisters* had buried their father.

Chekhov's medical point of view is everywhere visible in his plays. He invites us to diagnose the ills of his characters' souls in precisely the same way that doctors diagnose physical illnesses—by observing the outward symptoms closely. Masha's whistle in *Three Sisters* and Masha's snuff in *The Seagull* betoken their heartaches; in *The Cherry Orchard* Gayev's obsession with playing imaginary games of billiards whenever emotional matters are about to erupt demonstrates his inability to face reality; Andrey's gambling in *Three Sisters*, Dr. Astrov's drinking in *Uncle Vanya*, and Lomov's hypochondria in *The Proposal* all are telling symptoms of their inner lives.

In addition, good doctors treat their patients without judging their morals. So, too, does Chekhov examine his characters' outward symptoms, leaving all moralizing aside. Consider the following letter in which Chekhov defends his primary technique to his editor:

> You upbraid me for my objectivity, calling it an indifference to good and evil [. . .]. You want me, when I depict horse-thieves, to say: stealing horses is evil. But surely, everyone knows that without my saying so. Let a jury judge them; my business is only to show them as they are. [. . . As I write,] I must speak and think in their tones of voice, I must feel as they do [. . .]. When I write, I rely on my readers, I assume that they will fill in the subjective elements in my story.[44]

If we expect a play to illuminate the ills of society or to teach us how to live, then Chekhov's plays do indeed seem wanting. If, however, we understand that our job as audience is to pay attention to the characters and "fill in the subjective elements,"[45] then Chekhov's plays become endlessly fascinating.

---

44. Chekhov to A. S. Suvorin, April 1, 1890, in *Pis'ma* [Letters], vol. 4 (Moscow: Nauka, 1976), 54.
45. Ibid.

Marriage to the Moscow Art Theatre

Beginning in 1898 with a radically innovative production of *The Seagull* directed by Konstantin Stanislavsky, the Moscow Art Theatre[46] turned Chekhov into a world-famous playwright. Not only did Russian theater audiences see Chekhov through the eyes of the Muscovite company, but so did European and American spectators. First in 1906, and then in 1923 to 1924, the Art Theatre took their Chekhov productions on tour. In many cases, their Russian-language performances were Chekhov premieres in the United States. No wonder that Chekhov's name will be forever linked to that of Stanislavsky and the Moscow Art Theatre.

With Chekhov's marriage in 1901 to Olga Knipper, a founding member of the Moscow Art Theatre, he forged more than a professional link with the company. He had first admired Knipper's acting in 1897. She then took note of him during rehearsals for *The Seagull*, in which she played the leading role of Arkadina. In April 1899, mutual interest turned into a serious relationship and then marriage. However, because she performed on the Moscow stage while he remained in Yalta for his health, they were often apart. This fate meant that thousands of letters between them document their love.

While Chekhov did not need the Art Theatre to become a famous writer, he did need them to become an influential dramatist. In return, Chekhov offered precisely what the company's cofounders needed: the financial stability that comes with sold-out houses and innovative writing that could make their theatrical ideals stunningly visible. His colloquial language, sound effects taken from daily life, and tightly knit groups of characters were in close sympathy with the company's goals.

The Moscow Art Theatre was founded on June 22, 1897, when Stanislavsky and Nemirovich-Danchenko met for dinner at the Slavic Bazaar Hotel (where *The Seagull*'s Nina and Trigorin carry on their love affair). In a now-legendary eighteen-hour meeting, Stanislavsky and Nemirovich-Danchenko laid down the principles of their innovative theater. At thirty-three, Konstantin Sergeyevich Alekseyev had been acting for twenty years under the stage name Stanislavsky. His fresh talent had caught Nemirovich-Danchenko's eye. At thirty-nine, Vladimir Ivanovich Nemirovich-Danchenko

---

46. This company, arguably the most important theatrical enterprise in the twentieth century, was the breeding ground for the now globally famous Stanislavsky System of actor training. For more information, see Carnicke, *Stanislavsky in Focus*.

was a theater critic, a member of the Repertory Committee of the Imperial Theatres, and a successful playwright. In 1891 Nemirovich-Danchenko had become director of a professional actor training program in Moscow, the Philharmonic Society's Drama School. Appalled by the artificiality of professional acting, insufficient rehearsal time, poor standards of scenic design, and lack of respect for the playwright, Nemirovich-Danchenko had begun to dream of a way "to reconstruct [theater's] whole life [. . .] to change at the root the whole order of rehearsals and the preparation of plays; to subject the public itself to the regime essential to our purpose."[47] He had invited Stanislavsky to dinner to see whether they might together reform Moscow's theatrical practice. As they laid down a plan for their new theater, Stanislavsky called it nothing less than "revolutionary":

> We protested against the old manner of acting, against theatricality, against false pathos, declamation, against overacting, against the bad conventions of production and design, against the star system which spoils the ensemble, against the whole construct of the spectacle and against the unsubstantial repertoire of past theatres.[48]

Each partner brought a special angle of vision to the enterprise. As a writer, Nemirovich-Danchenko understood that a play's "main idea" can be used to construct the "scaffolding" for a unified production. As an actor, Stanislavsky put "human life into that scaffolding."[49]

One basic attitude links all points in their program for theatrical reform: respect for theater as art, not mere entertainment. On stage, all theatrical elements would support a central conceptual approach to the play. "Poet, actor, designer, tailor, and stage-hand all work toward one goal, set down by the poet in the foundation of the play."[50] In regard to design, sets were no longer assembled from

---

47. Nemirovitch-Dantchenko [sic], *My Life in the Russian Theatre*, 68.
48. K. S. Stanislavsky, *Sobranie sochinenii* [Collected Works], vol. I (Moscow: Iskusstvo, 1988), 254.
49. Michael Chekhov, "Lecture 10: Experience at the Moscow Art Theatre," audio-taped lecture (Hollywood, 1955) in The New York Public Library for the Performing Arts.
50. Stanislavsky, *Sobranie sochinenii* [Collected Works], vol. I, 250.

The Moscow Art Theatre production of *Uncle Vanya,* 1899. Second from the right is Olga Knipper as Yelena and to her right is Konstantin Stanislavsky as Astrov.

furniture in stock, but were built to express the play's overarching idea. Similarly, unmatched clothes provided by actors were replaced with costumes designed to further the production as an integrated whole.[51] Nemirovich-Danchenko and Stanislavsky even dared to reform their audiences. They put chairs in the auditorium that were not very comfortable in order to insure their spectators' lively attention. They also banned disrespectful late arrivals and applause that might inappropriately interrupt the flow of the play.

In regard to acting, the cofounders expected actors to craft characters that served the play, not to show virtuosity for its own sake. Hence, Nemirovich-Danchenko and Stanislavsky banished stars from their company. "Today—Hamlet , tomorrow—an extra, but even as an extra—an artist. [. . .] There are no small roles, only small actors."[52] Stars may have performed in *The Seagull* at the Alexandrinsky Theatre, but artists filled its roles at the Moscow Art. This attitude toward acting meant that actors had to work together as a cooperative ensemble, like musicians in a well-tuned orchestra. Each instrument contributes to the symphony. Such an orchestra of actors admirably suited Chekhov's plays, where all characters are equally vivid.

---

51. In *The Seagull,* the actress Arkadina complains that she cannot afford to buy her son a new suit because she must provide her own costumes. She alludes to one of the many realities in professional theater, which the Moscow Art Theatre successfully reformed.

52. Stanislavsky, *Sobranie sochinenii* [Collected Works], vol. I, 250.

By 1898 the Moscow Art Theatre had opened to critical acclaim, but it was struggling financially. Nemirovich-Danchenko realized that *The Seagull*, with its innovative structure and a leading character who calls for "new forms" in theatrical art, would be perfect for their company. Moreover, Nemirovich-Danchenko realized that Chekhov's apparent failure as a playwright had less to do with the author's ignorance of stage convention and more to do with standard productions that did not support his fresh conception of drama. For example, the first production of *Ivanov* (1889) "left not a trace in the theatre because there was nothing strictly 'Chekhovian' about it. [... For this production,] the favorite actors had scored a success: it was pleasant to see them again in other attire and in other make-up,"[53] and that was all. In short, Chekhov suffered from routine success. As Nemirovich-Danchenko writes of an 1897 production of *Uncle Vanya* in the Ukrainian city of Odessa:

> The public applauded, the actors were called before the curtain, but with the end of the performance came also the end of the play's life; the spectators did not bear away with them any intensely lived experience; the play did not awaken them to a new understanding of things. I repeat: there was nothing of that new reflection of life which a new poet had brought to his play.[54]

In April 1898 Nemirovich-Danchenko began an aggressive campaign to persuade Chekhov to give the Moscow Art Theatre permission to stage *The Seagull*. But Chekhov was unwilling; he was still deeply pained by its St. Petersburg premiere. Nemirovich-Danchenko argued that "a conscientious production" of *The Seagull* "without banalities will thrill the audience." He promised Chekhov just such a production. "Perhaps the play won't get bursts of applause, but a real production with *fresh* talents, *free of routine*, will be a triumph of art, I guarantee that."[55] Chekhov relented in June, and in September Stanislavsky began to direct the play in consultation with his partner.

---

53. Nemirovitch-Dantchenko [sic], *My Life in the Russian Theatre*, 22–3.
54. Ibid., 50.
55. Vladimir Nemirovich-Danchenko, letter to A. P. Chekhov, April 25, 1898, in *Tvorcheskoe nasledie* [Creative Legacy], vol. I (Moscow: Moskovskii khudozhestvennyi teatr, 2003), 165–6; the italics are Nemirovich-Danchenko's.

The Moscow Art Theatre production opened on December 17, 1898, after a record number of twenty-four regular and three dress rehearsals; the company was not yet confident in their work. Nemirovich-Danchenko vividly recalls the tense mood backstage as the first act curtain closed:

> There was a silence, a complete silence both in the theatre and on the stage, it was as though all held their breath, as though no one quite understood [what they had seen . . .]. This mood lasted quite a long time, so long indeed that those on stage decided that the first act had failed, failed so completely that not a single friend in the audience dared applaud. [. . .] Then suddenly, in the auditorium something happened. It was as if a dam had burst, or a bomb had exploded—all at once there was a deafening crash of applause from all: from friends and from enemies.[56]

The performance had made theatrical history, and, to this day, a simple sketch of a seagull brands the Moscow Art Theatre's work.

At the outset, theatrical reform at the Moscow Art Theatre meant bringing the best of European stage realism to Russia. Hence, the company staged Chekhov's plays with great attention to realistic detail. Three-dimensional sets that looked like real rooms with the fourth wall removed gave audiences the sense that they were eavesdropping on the lives of real people. Realistic props and historically accurate costumes further anchored the play to reality. In fact, Stanislavsky insisted that the actors begin using props and costumes as early as two months before the premiere of each play in order to induce their imaginative belief in Chekhov's world.[57] Stanislavsky also added a great number of production effects in lighting and sound to stimulate further the actors' imaginations. In his 1904 production plan for *The Cherry Orchard*, for example, he ends Act I with a plethora of sounds: "A shepherd plays on his pipe, the neighing of horses, the mooing of cows, the bleating of sheep and the lowing of cattle are heard."[58]

---

56. Nemirovitch-Dantchenko [sic], *My Life in the Russian Theatre*, 187–8.
57. Ibid., 100.
58. K. S. Stanislavsky, *Rezhisserskie ekzempliary K. S. Stanislavskogom* [Directorial Plans of K. S. Stanislavsky], vol. III (Moscow: Iskusstvo, 1983), 337.

Stanislavsky exceeded his European models, however, by melding realism in design with extraordinarily credible acting. Initially, he created three-dimensionality in actors through purely physical and technical means.[59] He carefully directed their movements to create an illusion of truth. Actors appeared oblivious of the audience; they spoke to each other, not to spectators. Sometimes they even turned their backs on the auditorium, as they did in *The Seagull* to watch Treplev's play-within-the-play. When the Moscow Art Theatre toured the United States, critics often commented on precisely this aspect of the actors' work in Chekhov's plays. For example, after viewing *The Cherry Orchard*, Edmund Wilson wrote: "[We watch] the family go about its business [. . .] without anything which we recognize as theatrical, but with the brightness of the highest art."[60]

Following the success of *The Seagull*, the Moscow Art Theatre naturally assumed that Chekhov had joined them. But, unbeknownst to the company, Chekhov had submitted *Uncle Vanya* to their competitor, the Maly Theatre. Only when the Maly rejected it did Chekhov decide to place his fate squarely in Stanislavsky's and Nemirovich-Danchenko's hands. He wrote his last two plays, *Three Sisters* and *The Cherry Orchard*, with the Moscow Art Theatre actors specifically in mind.

A close look at Chekhov's plays makes sense of his equivocation. Chekhov does indeed use daily life and colloquial speech to bring his characters to life, but he does not actually write realistic plays. He carefully selects details from life to express more than surface

"How pleasant it is to play the mandolin!" Yepikhodov (played by Ivan Moskvin) in *The Cherry Orchard*, The Moscow Art Theatre, 1904.

59. Only after Chekhov's death would Stanislavsky begin to develop his system of actor training. See Carnicke, *Stanislavsky in Focus*.
60. Edmund Wilson, review of *The Cherry Orchard*, *Dial*, January 1923 in *Chekhov: The Critical Heritage*, ed. Victor Emeljanow (Boston: Routledge and Kegan Paul, 1981), 236.

"You must fall in love!" Lyubov Andreyevna (played by Olga Knipper) to Trofimov (played by Vassily Kachalov) in *The Cherry Orchard*, The Moscow Art Theatre, 1904.

reality. Wilson recognized this aspect of Chekhov's art when he wrote that the actors of the Moscow Art Theatre "bring out a whole set of aesthetic values to which we are not accustomed in the realistic theater: the beauty and poignancy of an atmosphere, of an idea, a person, a moment are caught, and put before us without emphasis."[61] In this selectivity, Chekhov was influenced by symbolists like the Belgian playwright Maurice Maeterlinck (1862–1949).

Read any of Maeterlinck's short plays from the 1890s, such as *The Intruder* (about a family who sits together through the night waiting for the arrival of Death) or *The Seven Princesses* (a nightmarish fairy tale), and you will better understand Chekhov. Maeterlinck repeats sentences to suggest the depths of human experience behind even the simplest of statements. He uses eerie images and sounds to create transcendental atmospheres. Chekhov, too, uses patterns of repeated dialogue, images, and sounds. Instances include: Chebutykin's repeated refrain, "It's all the same," and the taking of a photograph to stop time at Irina's name-day party in *Three Sisters*; the killing of a seagull and Nina's consequent identification with it

---

61. Ibid.

in *The Seagull;* and the mysterious, unexplained sound, something like the snapping of a string, in *The Cherry Orchard.*

Despite Chekhov's attraction to symbolism, he rejected the movement's interest in abstraction. Treplev's play in *The Seagull* is a brilliant parody of a symbolist drama that has lost its moorings in reality. Thus, while Maeterlinck draws his refrains from the abstract world of poetic imagery, Chekhov transforms the details of ordinary life into poetic images.[62]

No wonder Chekhov found the Moscow Art Theatre's love of realism so problematic! Production effects threatened to dilute and thereby hide his careful selection of expressive details. At a rehearsal of *The Seagull,* Chekhov was overheard asking: "'Why all these details?' [. . .] 'But it's realistic!' he heard in reply, to which Chekhov ironically remarked that a living nose taken from the model for a portrait and placed on the spot of the painted one is also realistic."[63] Annoyed, Chekhov threatened to write the following opening line for his next play: "How wonderful, how quiet! Not a bird, a dog, a cuckoo, an owl, a nightingale, or clocks, or jingling bells, not even one cricket to be heard."[64]

The Devil in the Details

Where can the solution to the riddle of Chekhov as a terrible, good playwright be found? Part of the puzzle becomes clear after examining his overarching innovations in drama. But one also needs to examine his plays through a microscope. The devil, they say, is in the details, and so it is with Chekhov.

During rehearsals for *Uncle Vanya,* Chekhov criticized Stanislavsky for assuming that the title character wears boots and work clothes simply because he manages the estate. "'Listen,' [Chekhov] said getting annoyed, 'everything is written down. You haven't read the play.'" Stanislavsky searched through the text, but

---

62. For more on this topic, see Laurence Senelick, "Chekhov's Drama, Maeterlinck, and the Russian Symbolists," in *Chekhov's Great Plays: A Critical Anthology,* ed. Jean-Pierre Barricelli (New York: New York University Press, 1981), 161–80.

63. V. E. Meyerhold, *O Teatre* [About Theatre] (St. Petersburg: Prosveshchenie, 1913), 24.

64. Jean Benedetti, *Stanislavski: A Biography* (New York: Routledge, 1990), 135.

could find nothing more than an apparently off-hand comment about a "stylish tie." When the puzzled director asked the author to explain, Chekhov said, Vanya "has a wonderful tie; he is an elegant, cultured man. It's not true, that all landowners go around in muddy boots. They are educated people, they dress well, they go to Paris. I wrote all that."[65] This anecdote demonstrates how important the smallest item, like a "stylish tie," could be to Chekhov the playwright. It also suggests how closely he expected directors and actors to read his plays.

One of the pleasures in translating Chekhov involves paying close attention to him. The work of rendering Russian into English reveals the threads that make up the fabric of his plays. Only in a close, close reading can one see Chekhov's precision. Nothing, not one word, is irrelevant to the whole. Every stylish tie suggests the character of the person who wears it; every map that hangs on a wall comments on the action that takes place beneath it. This tightly woven fabric is what allows readers and audiences to revisit Chekhov's plays time after time, always finding something new within them.

I invite you to enter more deeply into Chekhov's plays. Focus your eyes and attune your ears to the kinds of devilish details that Chekhov loves. Discussion of some of these follows.

1. Apparent Non Sequiturs in Conversations and Behavior

Sometimes conversation in a Chekhov play seems comedic because it appears to flow illogically. One famous example of a non sequitur is Charlotta's entrance line, "My dog eats nuts," in *The Cherry Orchard*. While irrelevant to the onstage action, her words presumably make sense in terms of the offstage conversation that is in progress when she enters. Chekhov does nothing new here; Shakespeare used the same technique to make his plays seem as continuous as real life.

But occasionally, Chekhov has a more insidious strategy in mind. He also uses non sequiturs to comment on the wider action of a scene. For example, when Chebutykin, Solyony, and Tuzenbach first enter in *Three Sisters*, they interrupt Olga's reminiscence about her father's military funeral. She has just described how his high status as a general entailed real pomp. Just as she remembers that she "wanted passionately to go back home," the three local military

---

65. Stanislavsky, *Sobranie sochinenii* [Collected Works], 300.

men enter. Not only do their ranks (clearly inferior to her father's) visually point to her family's lowered status since his death, but their first lines also appear to debunk her lofty words: "The devil you say!" and "Of course, it's nonsense." While the men have been arguing offstage and their lines are part of that argument, the audience can hear their exclamations as inadvertent, but appropriate criticisms of Olga. After all, her sister Irina has just expressed annoyance with Olga: "Why remember!"

Another excellent example of Chekhov's strategy occurs in the last act of *The Cherry Orchard*. Anya is comforting her mother: "Mama, you'll come back soon, soon . . . Isn't that true? [. . .] Mama, you'll come back . . ." Lyubov, in turn, reassures her daughter with a hug: "I'll come back, my precious." Next the governess, Charlotta, decides to perform a feat of ventriloquism. She "picks up a bundle and holds it to look like a baby wrapped in a blanket." The baby cries, and Charlotta comforts the imaginary child with "I'm so sorry for you!" Then she abruptly "throws the bundle down." In effect, Charlotta has just debunked Lyubov's motherly reassurance.

2. Apparent Irrelevancies

Details that appear irrelevant can function as creatively as do non sequiturs in Chekhov's world. For every such detail, consider its context within the play. For example, Chekhov draws special attention to a specific prop in his description of the set of *Uncle Vanya* in Act IV: "On the wall there hangs a map of Africa, clearly of no use to anyone here." The only character who pays any attention to this map is Dr. Astrov. Near the play's finale, as he gets ready to leave the estate for the winter, he "goes to the map of Africa and looks at it," saying, "There must be a heat wave in Africa now, terrible thing!" Vanya replies indifferently: "Yes probably." Astrov is preparing to leave reluctantly but dutifully, because he has learned that Vanya's niece, Sonya, is hopelessly in love with him. Is Astrov's irrelevant remark just something to say at an awkward moment? Perhaps so. He had also reverted to a conversation about the weather earlier in the play when caught by Vanya making hot, sexual advances to Sonya's stepmother, Yelena.

But the map of Africa and Astrov's remark may not be as irrelevant as they seem. There is another map in the play, and Chekhov implicitly invites us to compare the two. In contrast to the useless map of Africa, Dr. Astrov has lovingly drawn a detailed chart of the local region in hopes that it will be of use to those who live nearby. In depicting how the flora and fauna are disappearing, he hopes his map will spur civic development. Within the confines of the play, however, he has used it only to seduce Yelena. But for Vanya's interruption, an emotional heat wave might well have hit the estate. Does Astrov look at the map of Africa and think about what might have been? Does Vanya himself do the same? When he inadvertently interrupted Astrov, Vanya had arrived with a bouquet for Yelena, hoping to seduce her himself. His indifferent response to Astrov's remark about Africa's heat wave suggests his own failure with her. Comparing the two maps in *Uncle Vanya* prompts a flood of such associations concerning the play's tight web of relationships. But then again, perhaps the map of Africa merely reminds the audience that there is a world of concerns outside this claustrophobic little estate.

3. Puns, Verbal Tics, Meaningless Phrases, and Eccentric Grammar

Chekhov delights in playing with words, as is obvious in his one-act "jokes." In *The Bear*, Smirnov challenges the young widow Popova to a duel in the standard way: "I demand satisfaction!" These words register as double entendre when he ends by begging for sexual satisfaction instead. In *The Proposal*, Lomov's explicit hypochondria reaches a level of literal absurdity when he asks, "Where's my shoulder?" Instances abound in the full-length plays as well. For example, in *The Seagull*, the school teacher Medvedenko complains of Masha's "indifferentism" to him (not her indifference), a linguistic slip that betrays his comic and anxious longing for her love.

Chekhov's linguistic play includes phrases that fill the air but carry no semantic meaning; these verbal tics often individualize characters. For example, Lomov's would-be father-in-law, Chubukov, blusters through his lines with "etc." and "so forth and so on." In *The Seagull*, Sorin's "and all that" suggests his desire to say more than he can. In *Three Sisters*, Chebutykin's "it's all the same" adds a refrain of absurd futility to the experience of the play.

Chekhov also willfully distorts grammar when it suits him. If something in my translation strikes you as peculiar in English, know that it is also peculiar in Russian. For example, Telegin in *The Seagull* and Yepikhodov in *The Cherry Orchard* speak ungrammatically, getting tangled up in long, convoluted sentences and big, elegant, but incorrectly used, words; their speech alone marks them as Chekhov's clowns.

4. Fractured Foreign Languages

Having studied and often failed at languages in school, Chekhov also delights in peppering his plays with the elegance of French, the educational elitism of Latin, and flourishes from Italian. Shipuchin in *The Anniversary* uses French to demonstrate his appreciation of the finer things in life, but, in so doing, he exposes his pretensions. In *Uncle Vanya*, Maria Vasilyevna uses French to show her aristocratic education, while Astrov's Latin demonstrates his medical training. In *Three Sisters*, Kulygin's overuse of Latin suggests not only his approach to teaching, but also his ability to impress, at least initially, the bright schoolgirl who became his wife. In contrast, his sister-in-law's atrocious French reveals her desire to compete with her husband's over-educated family. When Irina breaks down, she takes her inability to "remember the Italian for window or ceiling" as proof of her despair. As her brother says, "My sisters and I know French, German, and English. And Irina even knows Italian. But what is it worth!"

5. Grandiloquent Speech and Philosophizing

While it is tempting to take the beautiful passages in Chekhov's plays as genuine insights into life, the careful reader may also begin to suspect that sometimes philosophy reveals the underbellies of would-be heroes. Do Vershinin's seductive musings about the future in *Three Sisters* signify wisdom or mask his inability to solve problems caused by his unhappy marriage? Talk, in and of itself, can hide a character's flaws.

For instance, in *The Cherry Orchard,* Trofimov waxes poetic about Russia's genuine need for revolutionary reform. Because history would later prove him right, Trofimov seems prophetic. No wonder interpreters of *The Cherry Orchard* often position him as Chekhov's spokesman![66] But Chekhov undercuts the young revolutionary as much as he applauds him. For example, Trofimov reaches the apex of fine political rhetoric in an inappropriate setting. Consider his only love scene with Anya in Act II. He made his love for her clear to the audience at the end of Act I, but when he finally gets her alone, he launches into a fine political speech that includes his most frequently cited line, "All Russia is our orchard." His eloquence seems no more apropos than does Gayev's earlier pompous salute to a bookcase. Why does Trofimov not speak of his

---

66. See, for example, Maurice Valency, *The Breaking Sting: The Plays of Anton Chekhov* (New York: Schocken Books, 1983).

hangs in the air between them. Tuzenbach clearly finds it hard to leave her. Sensing that something is wrong, she offers to go with him. "No, no . . ." he says in alarm, stopping her. He then "walks away quickly" only to stop short with "Irina!" What does he want to say? His impulse to speak goes nowhere. Chekhov tells us that Tuzenbach stops, "not knowing what to say." When Tuzenbach speaks again, he says only: "I didn't have any coffee today. Ask them to make me some . . ." What remains unspoken seems almost palpable. Then he "exits quickly."

Although one cannot know for certain what happens in such moments of silence, one can infer from the scene's context and the character's situation. Pauses create an illusion that Chekhov's characters are engaged in continuous thinking beyond what they actually say. Although words on a page are two-dimensional, the illusion that something lies underneath them has come to be known as the "subtext."

Such moments challenge actors to decide why their characters stop speaking and to create the unspoken thoughts. The Moscow Art Theatre actors went on a "quest" to find the meanings behind each Chekhovian pause; they used "persistent and involved research, not merely external but also psychological."[69] This struggle led Stanislavsky to redefine the notion of a play. No longer could he view a dramatic text as a finished work of literary art; it became for him (and is for actors today) a blueprint from which to construct a finished performance by filling in the gaps with the artistry of acting.

7. The Music of Everyday Life

Quotations from songs of all sorts, including operatic arias, abound among Chekhov's characters. In *The Bear,* Smirnov quotes lines from a gypsy ballad as he challenges Popova to a duel. In *The Anniversary,* Tatyana tells of being serenaded from the opera *Eugene Onegin,* whose heroine is her namesake. In *The Seagull,* Dorn hums romantic ballads, and Treplev plays soulful waltzes. In *Three Sisters,* Masha and Vershinin communicate their adulterous secrets by singing a duet, and Chebutykin's final refrain from the British music hall adds a flippant counterpoint to an otherwise tragic ending. At times, Chekhov even makes the *absence* of music significant. Yelena in *Uncle Vanya* and Masha in *Three Sisters* are trained pianists whose marriages deny them their music.

69. Ibid., 153.

Introduction   xxxix

love? Anya responds with, "How well you speak!" Her words may be filled with awe, but they also draw attention to his speechifying. In Act III, Anya's mother accuses Trofimov of not yet understanding love. "You must become a man," she tells him, "at your age, you should understand those who love. And you yourself must love...." She seems correct in her appraisal, as her accusation throws him literally off-balance. He exits, only to fall down the stairs, and this literal fall seems to be exactly what he needs. In Act IV, Trofimov says relatively little; instead, he forgives the teasing of others, looks for his galoshes, silently helps Anya pack, and finally ushers her into the future as they exit together. It seems that he has learned sympathy and the ability to express love through the ordinary actions of life.[67]

6. The Pause

Chekhov often calls for moments of silence in his plays by directing his characters to *pause* or by adding ellipses to their lines. In my translations I have scrupulously retained every devilish "..." that Chekhov uses in his Russian texts. Pauses and ellipses can suggest many different things: a thought that remains unspoken, the interruption of one character by another, a momentary lapse, confusion, embarrassment, or a willful refusal to speak. But whatever the function, during every pause or ellipsis something unspoken happens. As Nemirovich-Danchenko explains, "A pause is not something that is dead, but is an active intensification of experience."[68]

Consider the last scene between Irina and Baron Tuzenbach in *Three Sisters*. While she has accepted his proposal of marriage, she has also frankly admitted that she cannot return his deep love. In this scene, he tells her that "I have to go into the city for . . . to say goodbye to my friends." In fact, he is going to fight a duel over her. His pause marks his desire to protect her from the truth. Yet, even though he withholds information about the duel, he still tries to prepare her for the possibility of his death: "Look there, that tree has dried up, but it's still waving in the breeze with the others. So I think that if I die, I too will still participate in life in some way or other. Goodbye my darling . . ." His comforting words are expressed in full and complete sentences, but his broken farewell

---

67. See Bernard Beckerman, "Dramatic Analysis and Literary Interpretation: *The Cherry Orchard* as Exemplum," *New Literary History: A Journal of Thought and Interpretation* 2:3(Spring 1971), 391–406.

68. Nemirovitch-Dantchenko [sic], *My Life in the Russian Theatre*, 163.

—— Three Jokes ——

The sound of her refrain, "We'll rest!" sounds like an exhalation in Russian: *otdókhnem!*

* * *

These seven items are intended only to whet your appetite for more. In my translations, I have been careful to reflect Chekhov (his semantics, repetitions, rhythms, grammar, ellipses, and so on) as closely as I could, so that you can find his devilish details on your own. Taste Chekhov's plays, and as you do, pay attention. The effort, I am certain, will pay rich rewards.

In *The Cherry Orchard,* Chekhov ironically uses music in the same way that melodrama does, even as he subverts the genre's conventions. As Lyubov confesses her sins in Act II, a distant orchestra underscores her words. Do violins match or mock her sentimental story? In Act III, she hires the same orchestra for her inappropriately timed party. As the orchestra merrily plays, the estate is being sold at auction.

Inspired by symbolism, Chekhov also makes his own music from the sounds of dialogue and daily life. His compositions are unique and startlingly beautiful, but easily missed in a quick read. For example, during Act II of *Three Sisters,* Chebutykin quotes an entirely irrelevant fact from the newspaper he is reading: "Balzac was married in Berdichev." Irina sits next to him, playing a game of solitaire; she "sings softly." Chebutykin continues: "I'll make a note of that in my notebook." He writes, "Balzac was married in Berdichev." Irina, "lost in thought," picks up his phrase and repeats, "Balzac was married in Berdichev." The rhythmic repetition of the sentence with its alliteration functions as a meditative duet between the two. Clever actors might use the rustling of the newspaper, the scratching of Chebutykin's pen as he takes a note, and Irina's shuffling of the cards to orchestrate the dialogue. The effect creates a stunning moment of intimate quietude between them.

An extended instance of Chekhov's music occurs at the end of *Uncle Vanya.* From the moment when harness bells signal that the professor and his wife have left the estate, Chekhov begins to write operatically. Read aloud from this point in the play to the end; as you go, make the sounds described in the stage directions. Chekhov's extraordinary musicality will become clear. The word "left" echoes with each new voice. This repetition plays against the sounds of the nurse's knitting needles and Vanya's shuffling of papers and clicking of the beads on the abacus as he calculates the estate's accounts. Sonya's pen on paper also plays its part in the orchestra. It is "quiet," Astrov says. "The pens scratch, the cricket chirps. It's warm, cozy." When the harness bells sound again, they serve as Astrov's cue to leave. At his departure, the word "left" echoes again, repeated by the various voices in the scene. Vanya now adds a percussive beat to the music as he recites numbers from the estate's accounts: "The total is . . . fifteen . . . twenty-five." At this point, the nurse introduces a new melody: "Oh, forgive us our sins." Sonia picks up this melody and embellishes it with a fantasy of future forgiveness and grace. Her final monologue ends the play.

The Bear

A Joke in One Act

[Written in 1888, *The Bear* premiered on October 28, 1888, at the Korsh Theatre in Moscow and quickly became a favorite in Russia's provincial theaters. It had its English language premiere in London in 1911. The United States first saw it in New York four years later. I directed the translation that follows in 1995 for an evening of Chekhov one-acts, *Thirty-Three Faintings,* produced by A/ACT in Los Angeles. —SMC]

The Characters
Yeléna Ivánovna Popóva, a widow with little dimples in her cheeks, a landowner.
Grigóry Stepánovich Smirnóv, a landowner who is not old. [His last name ironically derives from "serene."]
Luká, Popova's servant, an old man.

The living room of Popova's estate.

I

Popova (in deep mourning, unable to take her
eyes off a small photograph) and Luka.

LUKA: It's no good, ma'am . . . You'll only destroy yourself . . . The maid and the cook went out to pick berries. They're enjoying a breath of fresh air. Even the kitty understands she needs some fun, and goes out roaming and catches little birds. But you sit all day long in your room, as if you were in a convent, and that's no fun. Yes, it's true! Count the days. It's been a year since you've been outside! . . .

POPOVA: And I will never go out again . . . Why? My life is now over. He lies in his grave, and I have buried myself within these four walls . . . We both died.

LUKA: Well, there you have it! I can't listen to you. Nikoláy Mikhaílovich died, and so it goes, God's will, may he rest in peace . . . You have grieved—and now, if I can be honest, you've grieved enough. You can't sit out the rest of the century wearing black and crying. My old woman died too . . . What of it? I grieved, I cried for a month, and that was enough. But to wail for a whole century? That won't raise the old woman from the dead! (*Sighs.*) You've forgotten all your neighbors . . . You won't visit them or invite them to visit you. Forgive me for saying so, but we live here like spiders—never seeing the light of day. The mice have eaten away at the coachman's livery . . . That would be fine if there weren't any nice people around, but the place is full of gentlemen . . . There's a regiment stationed nearby, and the officers look as good as candy! And in the camp, a Friday doesn't go by without a ball. And every day the military band plays . . . Akh, Mother of God! You're young, you're beautiful, the picture of health—if only you would live, have some fun . . . Your beauty won't last forever! Ten years will pass, and if you want to strut like a peacock in front of the officers then, it will be too late.

POPOVA: (*Decisively.*) Please, never speak to me about this again! You know, that since Nikolay Mikhailovich died, life means nothing to me. You think I'm alive, but it only seems so! I vowed, that until I am laid in my grave, I will wear black and shun the light of day . . . Are you listening? Let his ghost know how much I love him . . . Yes, I know, it's no secret to you, he was often unfair to me, cruel, and . . . and even unfaithful. But I will be faithful unto the grave, and prove to him, that I know how to love. There, in the afterworld, he will see me just as I was before his death . . .

LUKA: You'd do better to take a walk in the garden than make such vows. Or better yet, have them harness up Toby or Giant and go visit your neighbors . . .

POPOVA: Ahhh! . . . (*Cries.*)

LUKA: Ma'am! . . . Dear lady! . . . What's wrong? God be with you!

POPOVA: He loved Toby! He always rode him to the Korchágins and the Vlásovs. How wonderfully he rode! He had such grace of form, when he pulled back with all his might on the reins! Do you remember? Toby, Toby! Make sure they give him extra oats today.

LUKA: I will!

There is a loud ring at the door.

POPOVA: (*Shudders.*) Who is it? Tell them I won't see anyone!

LUKA: I will, ma'am. (*Exits.*)

II

Popova (alone).

POPOVA: (*Looking at the photograph.*) You will see, *Nicolas*,[1] how I can love and forgive . . . My love will die with me, when my poor heart stops beating. (*Laughs, through tears.*) And won't you be ashamed! I have locked myself up, like a good girl, a faithful little wife, and I will be faithful until the grave, not like you . . . And aren't you ashamed, you naughty boy? You cheated on me, you made scenes, left me alone for whole weeks at a time . . .

III

Popova and Luka.

LUKA: (*Enters, alarmed.*) Ma'am, there's someone out there asking for you. He wants to see . . .

POPOVA: But surely you told him that since my husband died, I will see no one?

LUKA: I told him, but he won't listen. He said he's here on a very important matter.

POPOVA: I—will—not—see—him!

LUKA: I told him, but . . . he's some kind of devil . . . swears and barges in . . . He's already in the dining room . . .

---

1. Using her husband's name in French shows her refinement.

POPOVA: (*Irritated.*) All right, ask him in . . . What a lout! (*Luka exits.*) What trouble these people are! What could he want of me? Why should he disturb my peace and quiet? (*Sighs.*) No, I see now that I should have joined a convent . . . (*Thinks about it.*) Yes, a convent . . .

IV

Popova, Luka, Smirnov.

SMIRNOV: (*Entering, to Luka.*) Blockhead, you like to talk too much . . . Ass! (*Seeing Popova, with dignity.*) Madam, I am honored to introduce myself: Retired Artillery Lieutenant and landowner, Grigory Stepanovich Smirnov! I must disturb you on a most important matter . . .

POPOVA: (*Not offering her hand.*) What do you want?

SMIRNOV: Your late husband, whom I was honored to know, owes me two unpaid promissory notes worth one thousand two hundred rubles.[2] Since I must pay the interest on my mortgage tomorrow, I ask you, madam, to pay me the money you owe me today.

POPOVA: One thousand two hundred . . . Why was my husband was in debt to you?

SMIRNOV: He bought oats from me.

POPOVA: (*Sighing, to Luka.*) Luka, don't forget to see that Toby gets extra oats. (*Luka exits. To Smirnov.*) If Nikolay Mikhailovich owed you money, then I will of course pay it. But, pardon me, please, I do not have any cash on hand. My steward will be back the day after tomorrow, and I will order him to pay you what I owe, but until then I can not satisfy you . . . Besides, today is exactly seven months since my husband's death, and I am in no mood to deal with financial matters.

SMIRNOV: But I am in the mood, because if I don't pay the interest on my loan tomorrow, then everything will blow up in my face. They'll seize my property!

POPOVA: The day after tomorrow you will receive your money.

---

2. An enormous sum in pre-Revolutionary Russia.

SMIRNOV: I do not need the money the day after tomorrow, I need it today.

POPOVA: Excuse me, I can not pay you today.

SMIRNOV: And I cannot wait until the day after tomorrow.

POPOVA: What can I do if I do not have it now?

SMIRNOV: Then, you can't pay up?

POPOVA: I can't . . .

SMIRNOV: Hmmm! . . . Is that your final word?

POPOVA: Yes, it's final.

SMIRNOV: Your final word? Absolutely?

POPOVA: Absolutely.

SMIRNOV: I humbly thank you. I'll take note of this. (*Shrugs his shoulders.*) And they want me to stay cool and calm! I ran into the bank collector on my way here, and he asked, "Why are you so angry, Grigory Stepanovich?" Oh please, how can I not be angry? I need money urgently . . . I've been out since yesterday morning at dawn, driving around to everyone who owes me money, and not one can pay his debt! I chased my tail like a dog, slept in a godforsaken tavern near the vodka barrel . . . Finally, I get here, more than forty miles from home, counting on getting paid, and you treat me to a "mood"! Why shouldn't I be angry?

POPOVA: I have told you quite clearly: my steward will return from town the day after tomorrow and then you will be paid.

SMIRNOV: I came to you, not to your steward! What the hell—pardon my language—do I want with your steward?

POPOVA: Excuse me, kind sir, I am not used to such expressions, to such a tone of voice. I can no longer listen to you. (*Exits quickly.*)

V

SMIRNOV: (*Alone.*) Oh please! A mood! . . . Seven months since her husband's death! But do I have to pay the interest on my mortgage, or don't I? I ask you, do I have to pay the interest or not? Well, your husband died, but I think you're up to some trick... Your steward took off, so to hell with him. What do you expect me to do about it? Fly away from my creditors in a hot-air balloon, is that it? Or run and bash my head against a wall? I go to Grúzdev—no one's home; Yaroshévich hides; I swear at Kúritsin until I'm hoarse and nearly throw him out the window; Mazútov[3] has cholera; and now this one's in no mood. Not one scoundrel will pay up! And it's all because I've coddled them, acted like a cry-baby, a milksop, an old woman! I've been too tactful with them! Well, just you wait! You'll see me as I really am! I will not allow myself be made a fool of! To hell with you! I will stay here, underfoot, until she pays up! Brr!... I feel mean today, mean! My knees are shaking, I'm out of breath, all because I'm mean... Ooh, my God, it's making me sick! (*Yells.*) Hey you!

VI

Smirnov and Luka.

LUKA: (*Enters.*) What do you want?

SMIRNOV: Get me some kvas[4] or some water! (*Luka exits.*) No, it's not logical! A person urgently needs money, enough to hang himself for it, and she won't pay, because, you see, she is not inclined to concern herself with financial matters today!... It's twisted, female logic! This is why I have never liked, why I still don't like to talk to women. It's easier for me to sit on a powder keg, than talk to a woman. Brr!... I've got the shivers—that's how mean that woman in her dress has made me feel! As soon as I see one of these poetic creatures standing in front of me, even if she's off in the distance, I get cramps in my legs, due to my feeling mean. I want to call in the reserves.

---

3. The surnames of Smirnov's creditors sound like "mushroom," a refined Polish gentleman, "chicken," and "fuel oil."
4. A dark, nonalcoholic beer made from black bread.

VII

Smirnov and Luka.

LUKA: (*Enters and hands him water.*) The lady of the house is ill and will not see you.

SMIRNOV: Get out! (*Luka exits.*) Ill and will not see me! No matter. Don't see me then . . . I'll stay, I'll sit right here until you give me my money. If you're ill for a week, I'll sit here a week . . . If you're ill for a year, I'll sit here for a year . . . I'll get my own, little lady! Your black dress, the dimples in your cheeks, they won't affect me . . . I understand those dimples! (*Yells out the window.*) Semyón, unharness the horses! We won't be leaving anytime soon! I'm staying here! Tell them in the stables to give the horses some oats! You idiot, you've got the left tracehorse[5] tangled up in the reins again! (*Mimics Semyon.*) "S'nuthin" . . . I'll give you "s'nuthin"! (*Walks away from the window.*) I don't feel well . . . The heat in here is intolerable, no one will pay me my money, I didn't sleep well last night, and now there's this "mood" who wears a black dress . . . My head aches . . . I'd like some vodka. I need a drink. (*Yells.*) Hey you!

LUKA: (*Enters.*) What do you want?

SMIRNOV: A glass of vodka. (*Luka exits.*) Oof! (*Sits and takes a look at himself.*) I have to say, I'm a sorry sight! Covered in dust, dirty boots, unwashed, uncombed, straw on my jacket . . . The little lady must have thought I was a thief. (*Yawns.*) It was probably not polite to show up in the living room in such a state, but what of it? . . . I'm not a guest, but a creditor, and there's no special outfit for creditors . . .

LUKA: (*Enters and gives him the vodka.*) I see you're making yourself comfortable, sir . . .

SMIRNOV: (*Angry.*) What?

LUKA: I . . . nothing . . . I only . . .

SMIRNOV: Who are you talking to?! Shut up!

LUKA: (*Aside.*) Jumps right into our laps, the devil . . . Trouble's walked in the door . . . (*Luka exits.*)

---

5. One of the two horses harnessed on the outside of a team of three horses.

SMIRNOV: Ah, I feel mean! So mean, that I could grind the whole world into powder . . . It's making me sick! (*Yells.*) Hey you!

VIII

Popova and Smirnov.

POPOVA: (*Enters, lowering her eyes.*) Dear sir, in my solitude I have grown unaccustomed to the human voice and I cannot abide yelling. I beg you not to disturb my peace!

SMIRNOV: Pay me my money and I'll go.

POPOVA: I told you plainly, I do not have any cash on hand, that you will be paid the day after tomorrow.

SMIRNOV: And I told you plainly and respectfully, I do not need the money the day after tomorrow, I need it today. If you do not pay me today, I must hang myself tomorrow.

POPOVA: But what can I do, if I do not have the money? How strange!

SMIRNOV: So you won't pay me now? No?

POPOVA: I can't . . .

SMIRNOV: In that case, I will sit here until I get . . . (*Sits.*) You'll pay me the day after tomorrow? Fine! I'll sit here until the day after tomorrow. I'll sit here like this . . . (*Jumps up.*) I ask you, do I have to pay the interest tomorrow or not? . . . Do you think I'm joking?

POPOVA: Dear sir, I beg you not to yell! This is not a stable!

SMIRNOV: I'm not asking you about stables, but about whether or not I have to pay the interest on my mortgage tomorrow! . . .

POPOVA: You do not know how to conduct yourself in the company of women!

SMIRNOV: No, ma'am, I know exactly how to conduct myself in the company of women!

POPOVA: No, you don't! You are an ill-bred, rude person! Proper people do not speak with ladies as you do!

SMIRNOV: Ah, that's a surprise! How do you expect me to speak with you? In French? (*Gets mean and lisps.*) Madame, je vous *pris* . . . How happy I would be if you would deign to pay me my money . . . Oh, *pardon*[6] that I have disturbed you. What delightful weather we're having today! And that black dress becomes you so! (*Bows to her.*)

POPOVA: You're not witty, just rude.

SMIRNOV: (*Mimics her.*) "You're not witty, just rude." I do not know how to conduct myself in the company of women! Madame, in my time I've seen more women than you've seen sparrows! I dueled over women three times, I gave the brush to a dozen women, and another nine women gave me the brush! Yes, ma'am! There was a time when I played the fool, cooed, spoke words of honey, showered them with pearls, polished my shoes for them . . . I loved, I suffered, I sighed at the moon, felt weak in the knees, felt hot, felt cold . . . I loved passionately, desperately, in all sorts of ways, God help me. I chatted like a magpie about women's liberation, spent half of what I had on the tender passion, but now—I'm no submissive servant! You won't catch me kow-towing now! I've had enough! "Dark eyes, passionate eyes,"[7] scarlet lips, little dimples, moonlight, whispers, a shy sigh—I wouldn't give a kopeck for any of it now! Present company excepted, of course, but all women, short or tall, strike poses, are affected, gossip, hold grudges, lie about everything. They're vain, petty, merciless, they do not think logically, and what's up here (*Strikes his forehead.*) is such a joke, that, forgive my frankness, a sparrow could out-think any philosopher who wears a skirt! Just take a look at any one of these poetic creatures. You see delicate muslins, an ethereal goddess, a million delights. But then look into her soul and you see an ordinary crocodile! (*Grabs the back of a chair; the chair trembles and breaks.*) And what's even more amazing is that this crocodile for some reason or other imagines that her crowning achievement, her privilege, her monopoly is the tender passion! To hell with her! You can hang me from a nail by my heels if she knows how to love anyone other than her pet dog . . . A woman in love only knows how to whimper and snivel! Whereas a man suffers and sacrifices, a woman only swirls her skirts and leads him around by the nose. It's your misfortune to be a woman, so

---

6. "Madam, I beg you . . ." and "pardon" (French).
7. He quotes the first words of a well-known gypsy song of love.

you must know what a woman's nature is like. Tell me truthfully: have you ever known a woman to be sincere, faithful, and constant? You haven't! Only old or ugly women are faithful and constant! You'll find a unicorn before you'll find a constant woman!

POPOVA: Excuse me, who, in your opinion is faithful and constant in love? Surely not the man?

SMIRNOV: Yes, ma'am, the man!

POPOVA: The man! (*A mean laugh.*) The man is faithful and constant in love! Now that's news! (*Heatedly.*) What right do you have to say that? Men are faithful and constant! As far as men go, my late husband, I'll tell you, was as good as they get . . . I loved him passionately, with all my being, as only a young, intelligent woman can love. I gave him my youth, my happiness, my life, my fortune, I breathed with his breath, I worshipped him like a pagan, and . . . and what happened? This man, as good as they get, deceived me without any sense of guilt! After his death I found a whole chest of love letters in his desk. While he was alive—it's terrible to remember—he used to leave me alone for whole weeks at a time, he flirted with other women right under my nose and betrayed me, he spent my money, laughed when I cried . . . But, despite it all, I loved him and remained faithful to him. And even though he's dead, I am still faithful to him and constant. I have buried myself forever within these four walls, and I will wear black until the day I die . . .

SMIRNOV: (*A disdainful laugh.*) Black! . . . Who do you think I am? As if I didn't know why you wear black and have buried yourself within these four walls! I know! Because it's so mysterious and poetic! So that some young officer or maybe a namby-pamby poet will pass your house, look up at your window, and think: "This is where the mysterious Tamara[8] lives, who buried herself behind those four walls because of love." Why play these tricks with me?

POPOVA: (*Getting angry.*) What? How dare you speak to me like that?

SMIRNOV: You may have buried yourself alive, but you haven't forgotten to powder your nose!

---

8. A common name for exotic heroines in Russian romantic novels.

POPOVA: How dare you speak to me like that?

SMIRNOV: Don't yell, please, I am not your steward! Allow me to call a spade a spade. I am not a woman and I am accustomed to speaking my mind! Please stop yelling!

POPOVA: It's not me who's yelling, it's you! Please leave me in peace!

SMIRNOV: Pay me my money and I'll leave.

POPOVA: I won't give you your money!

SMIRNOV: You won't!

POPOVA: Not a kopeck, so there! Just leave me in peace!

SMIRNOV: I do not have the pleasure of being your husband, or your fiancé, so don't bother making a scene for my sake! (*Sits.*) I don't like it.

POPOVA: (*Choking with anger.*) You sat down?

SMIRNOV: Yes.

POPOVA: I beg you to go!

SMIRNOV: Give me my money . . . (*Aside.*) Ah, how mean I feel! How mean!

POPOVA: I do not wish to converse with louts like you! Please get out of here! (*Pause.*) You're not going? No?

SMIRNOV: No.

POPOVA: No?

SMIRNOV: No.

POPOVA: Very well. (*She rings.*)

IX

The same and Luka.

POPOVA: Luka, show this gentleman out!

LUKA: (*Goes to Smirnov.*) Sir, please leave, as you're told! There's nothing here for you . . .

SMIRNOV: Shut up! Who do you think you're talking to? I'll make a salad out of you.

LUKA: (*Clutches at his heart.*) God in heaven! . . . Saints in heaven! . . . (*Falls into a chair.*) Oh, I'll faint, faint! I can't breathe!

POPOVA: Where's Dásha? Dasha! (*Yells.*) Dasha! Pelagéya![9] Dasha! (*Rings.*)

LUKA: Oh! They're all out picking berries . . . No one's home . . . I'll faint! Water!

POPOVA: (*To Smirnov.*) Please get out of here!

SMIRNOV: Couldn't you be a little more respectful?

POPOVA: (*Making a fist and stamping her feet.*) You peasant! You rude bear! You lout! You monster!

SMIRNOV: What? What did you say?

POPOVA: I said that you are a bear, a monster!

SMIRNOV: (*Advancing on her.*) Excuse me, but what right do you have to insult me?

POPOVA: Yes, I'll insult you . . . Well what of it? Do you think I'm afraid of you?

SMIRNOV: And do you think that just because you're a poetic creature that you have the right to insult me without being punished for it? Do you? I demand satisfaction![10]

LUKA: God in heaven! . . . Saints in heaven! . . . Water!

SMIRNOV: Let's shoot it out!

POPOVA: Do you think I'm afraid of you because you've got strong fists and can bellow like a bull? Huh? You are such a lout!

SMIRNOV: I demand satisfaction! I do not allow anyone to insult me, not even a woman, not even the weaker sex!

POPOVA: (*Trying to out-shout him.*) Bear! Bear! Bear!

SMIRNOV: It's time to stop this prejudice, this thinking that only men should have to pay for their insults! Equality means equality, the devil knows! I demand satisfaction.

POPOVA: You want to shoot it out? Fine.

SMIRNOV: Right now!

---

9. An old-fashioned, peasant name.
10. The standard formula for challenging someone to a duel.

POPOVA: Fine! I inherited my husband's pistols . . . I'll bring them here . . . (*Hurries toward the door, and turns back.*) With what pleasure I will put a bullet through your forehead! The devil can take you then! (*Exits.*)

SMIRNOV: I'll shoot her, like a chicken! I'm no schoolboy, no sentimental pup. Women are no weaker than we!

LUKA: Dear, kind sir! . . . (*Gets down on his knees.*) Do me a favor, oh Lord, have mercy on me, an old man, and get out of here! You've frightened me to death, and now you're going to shoot it out!

SMIRNOV: (*Not listening.*) To shoot it out—now that's equality, that's women's liberation! Both sexes equal! I'll shoot her on principle! But what kind of woman is she? (*Mimics her.*) "The Devil can take you then . . . I will put a bullet through your forehead . . ." What kind of woman? She blushed, her eyes blazed . . . She accepted my challenge! Word of honor, this is the first time in my life I've ever seen such a woman! . . .

LUKA: Sir, go away! For the love of God!

SMIRNOV: This is a woman! Now I understand! This is a real woman! Not a sniveler, not a whiner, but fire, gunpowder, a rocket! I'll be sorry to kill her!

LUKA: (*Cries.*) Sir . . . Dearie, get out of here!

SMIRNOV: I positively like her! Positively! Even her dimples, I like them! I could even forget about the debt . . . I don't feel mean any more . . . A remarkable woman!

X

The same and Popova.

POPOVA: (*Enters with the pistols.*) Here they are, the pistols . . . But, before we duel, would you please show me how to shoot . . . I have never before held a pistol in my hand.

LUKA: Save us, oh Lord, have mercy on us . . . I'll go call the gardener and find the coachman . . . What have we done to deserve this plague . . . (*Exits.*)

SMIRNOV: (*Looking at the pistols.*) You see, there are several different kinds of pistols . . . The Mortimer precision-locked pistols are especially designed for dueling. But these are made by Smith and Wesson,[11] triple action with extractor, central fire . . . Excellent pistols! . . . These cost at least ninety rubles a pair . . . You hold the revolver like this . . . (*Aside.*) Her eyes, her eyes! A fiery woman!

POPOVA: Like this?

SMIRNOV: Yes, like that . . . Now cock it . . . Now take aim . . . Head back a bit! Extend your arm properly . . . Like that . . . Now press your finger on this little thing here—and that's all there is to it . . . The main rule is: don't get excited, and don't rush when you take aim . . . And try to keep your arm steady.

POPOVA: Fine . . . But it's not right to shoot inside. Let's go out into the garden.

SMIRNOV: Let's go. Only I warn you, I intend to shoot into the air.

POPOVA: That's the limit! Why?

SMIRNOV: Because . . . Because . . . Because it's my business!

POPOVA: Are you a coward? Is that it? Aaah! No, sir, you won't get out of it! Please follow me! I won't be satisfied until I've put a bullet through your forehead . . . that very forehead, which I hate! Are you a coward?

SMIRNOV: Yes, I am.

POPOVA: You lie! Why don't you want to fight?

SMIRNOV: Because . . . Because . . . I like you.

POPOVA: (*A mean laugh.*) He likes me! He dares say that he likes me! (*Shows him the door.*) This way!

SMIRNOV: (*Quietly lays the revolver down, picks up his hat, and begins to leave; near the door he stops, they silently look at each other for a moment; then he speaks, as he uncertainly approaches her.*) Listen . . . Are you still angry with me? . . . I know the devil has gotten into me, but can you understand . . . How can I express it . . . The thing is that, you see, I've never, honestly never had such a thing happen to me . . . (*Yells.*) Well is it my fault that I like you? (*Seizes the back of a chair; the*

---

11. This type of revolver was standard Russian army issue.

chair trembles and breaks.) Such delicate furniture you have, the devil knows! I like you! Do you understand? I . . . I'm even almost in love!

POPOVA: Get away from me—I hate you!

SMIRNOV: Oh God, what a woman! I have never in my life seen such a one! I've fallen! I'm finished! Caught like a mouse in a trap!

POPOVA: Get away, or I'll shoot!

SMIRNOV: Shoot! You can not imagine how happy I would be to die under the gaze of your wonderful eyes, to die from a revolver that is held in your small, velvet hand . . . I'm going mad! Think about it, and make up your mind right now, because if I'm gone, we'll never see each other again! Make up your mind . . . I'm a landowner, a decent man, I have an income of ten thousand a year . . . I have excellent horses . . . Would you like to be my wife?

POPOVA: (*Indignant, brandishing the revolver.*) Shoot! I demand satisfaction!

SMIRNOV: I've lost my mind . . . I don't understand. (*Yells.*) Hey you, water!

POPOVA: (*Yells.*) Satisfaction!

SMIRNOV: I've lost my mind, fallen in love, like a schoolboy, like a fool! (*He takes her by the hand; she cries out in pain.*) I love you! (*He gets down on his knees.*) I love you, as I have never loved anyone! I gave the brush to a dozen women, another nine women gave me the brush, but I did not love any of them as I do you . . . I've turned to jelly, I'm syrupy sweet, down on the floor . . . standing on my knees, like a fool, and I'm asking for your hand . . . I'm ashamed of myself! Shame on me! I haven't been in love for five years, vowed that I never would again, and suddenly I'm like a square peg in a round hole! I am proposing to you. Yes or no? Do you want to? Never mind! (*Gets up and goes quickly to the door.*)

POPOVA: Wait . . .

SMIRNOV: (*Stops.*) Well?

POPOVA: Nothing, just go . . . But wait . . . No, go, go! I hate you! Or no . . . Don't go! Ah, if only you knew, how mean I feel, how mean! (*Throws the revolver on the table.*) My fingers hurt from that awful thing . . . (*Tears at her handkerchief in rage.*) Why are you standing there? Get out!

SMIRNOV: Forgive me.

POPOVA: Yes, yes, go! . . . (*Yells.*) Where are you going? Wait . . . No, go on. Ah, how mean I feel! Don't come near me, don't come near me!

SMIRNOV: (*Going to her.*) How angry I am with myself! I fell in love, like a schoolboy, got down on my knees . . . Felt hot, felt cold . . . (*Crudely.*) I love you! The last thing I need is to love you! Tomorrow I need to pay the interest on my mortgage, I need to start the harvest, but here you are . . . (*Takes her by the waist.*) I will never forgive myself . . .

POPOVA: Get away! Let me go! I, you . . . I hate you! I demand satisfaction!

A prolonged kiss.

XI

The same, Luka with an axe, the gardener with a rake, the coachman with a pitchfork, and various workmen with staves.

LUKA: (*Seeing the two kissing.*) Saints in Heaven! (*Pause.*)

POPOVA: (*Lowering her eyes.*) Luka, go to the stable and tell them not to give Toby any oats today.

Curtain.

The Proposal

A Joke in One Act

[Written in 1888, *The Proposal* premiered on April 12, 1889, at the Artists' Club in St. Petersburg, Russia. It became one of Chekhov's most popular one-acts. It was staged for the first time in English in 1931 in London, but not in the United States until 1945. I created the translation that follows in 1978 for The Potato Players in Rhinebeck, New York; I played Natalya Stepanovna in that production. I also directed this translation in 1995 for an evening of Chekhov one-acts, *Thirty-Three Faintings,* produced by A/ACT in Los Angeles. —SMC]

The Characters

Stepán Stepánovich Chubukóv, a landowner. [The family name sounds like "the stem" of a pipe and "grape vine."]

Natálya Stepánovna, his daughter, twenty-five years old. [Her nickname is Natásha.]

Iván Vasílyevich Lómov, a neighbor of Chubukov, plump and healthy, but an extreme hypochondriac, a landowner. [In Russian, *lom* is a crowbar and *lomovoi* is a farm horse used for carting.]

The action takes place on Chubukov's estate. The living room in Chubukov's house.

I

Chubukov and Lomov (who enters in a frock coat[12] and white gloves).

CHUBUKOV: (*Going to meet Lomov.*) Who do I see! My dearest, dearest, dearest friend! Ivan Vasilyevich! Always glad to see you! (*Shakes his hand.*) Mother in Heaven, this is in fact a surprise . . . How are you?

---

12. A close-fitting suit coat that flares from the waist to knees, worn on special occasions.

Lomov: Fine, thank you. But please tell me, how are you?

Chubukov: Living from day to day, my angel, thanks to your prayers, etc. Sit down, I humbly beg you . . . Mother in Heaven, it is in fact not good to forget your neighbors. But my dearest, dearest, dearest friend, why are you dressed so officially? A frock coat, and gloves, etc. Surely you must be going somewhere, my treasure?

Lomov: No, I'm only coming to see you, dear Stepan Stepanovich.

Chubukov: Then why the frock coat, you charmer? It looks like you're ready for New Year's!

Lomov: You see, the point is this. (*Takes Chubukov by the arm.*) I came to you respectfully, dear Stepan Stepanovich, to trouble you with a request. I've had the privilege of turning to you for help more than once, and you have always, so to speak . . . But excuse me, I'm nervous. I'll just drink a little water, dear Stepan Stepanovich. (*Drinks some water.*)

Chubukov: (*Aside.*) He's come for money! I won't give him any! (*To him.*) What's the matter, you handsome devil?

Lomov: You see, Respected Stepanovich . . . Sorry, Stepan Respectovich . . . Please, I'm awfully nervous, as you can see . . . In a word, you alone can help me, since, of course, I don't deserve anything and . . . and I don't have the right to count on your help . . .

Chubukov: Ah yes, Mother in Heaven, don't spread it on so thick! Just say what you want! Well?

Lomov: Right away . . . In a minute . . . The point is that I came to ask for your daughter's, Natalya Stepanovna's, hand in marriage.

Chubukov: (*Joyfully.*) My God! Ivan Vasilyevich! Say that again— I'm not sure I heard you right!

Lomov: I have the honor to ask . . .

Chubukov: My dearest, dearest, dearest friend . . . I'm so happy, etc. . . . And, in fact, so forth and so on. (*Embraces Lomov and kisses him.*) It's what I've always wanted . . . This has been one of my fondest wishes for a long time now. (*Wipes a tear away.*) And I always loved you like a son, my angel. May

God give you both some good advice and love, etc. It's what I always wanted . . . But what am I doing standing here like a blockhead? I'm stunned by the joy, completely stunned! Oh, from the bottom of my heart, I . . . Well, I'll go call Natasha and so on.

LOMOV: (*Deeply touched.*) Dear Stepan Stepanovich, what do you think? Can I count on her consent?

CHUBUKOV: You are in fact such a handsome devil—why . . . why sure she'll consent! She's probably head over heels in love with you, like a kitten, etc. . . . Wait just a minute! (*Exits.*)

II

Lomov (alone).

LOMOV: It's cold . . . I'm shaking all over, like I was about to take a test in school. The most important thing is you have to decide. If you think about it too long, if you hesitate, if you talk too much and keep waiting for an ideal, a true love, then you'll never get married . . . Brrr! . . . It's cold! Natalya Stepanovna is a wonderful housekeeper, not bad looking, educated . . . What more do I need? But that ringing in my ears has started up again. It must be nerves . . . (*Drinks some water.*) I can't not get married . . . In the first place, I'm thirty-five years old—an age that's critical, so to speak. In the second place, I need a proper, regular life . . . I have a heart condition, constant palpitations, and I'm quick-tempered and always get so nervous . . . Now look, my lips are trembling, and my right eyelid is jumping around . . . But the worst thing is going to sleep. I hardly lie down and begin to doze off, when suddenly, a spasm shoots through my left side! And then it moves directly to my shoulder and my head . . . I jump up, like a madman, walk around a little and then lie down again, but just as I start to doze off another spasm shoots through my side. And this happens about twenty times . . .

III

Natalya Stepanovna and Lomov.

NATALYA STEPANOVNA: (*Enters.*) Well now! It's you. Papa told me, "Go inside, a merchant's come for his goods!" Hello, Ivan Vasilyevich!

LOMOV: Hello, dear Natalya Stepanovna!

NATALYA STEPANOVNA: Excuse my housedress and apron . . . We're shelling peas to dry them. Why haven't you been to see us for so long? Sit down . . . (*They sit down.*) Do you want some breakfast?

LOMOV: No thank you, I just ate.

NATALYA STEPANOVNA: Would you like to smoke . . . Here are some matches . . . Wonderful weather we're having, but yesterday it rained so hard that none of the men did any work. How many shocks of hay have you mown? Imagine, I was greedy and mowed a whole meadow, and now I'm not happy at all. I'm afraid the hay will rot in the field. It would have been better to wait. But what's this? You're dressed in a frock coat! Well, that's news! Are you on your way to a ball? By the way, it suits you . . . But why are you such a dandy today?

LOMOV: (*Getting nervous.*) You see, dear Natalya Stepanovna . . . The thing is that I decided to ask you to listen to me . . . Of course you'll be surprised and maybe even get angry, but I . . . (*Aside.*) It's so cold!

NATALYA STEPANOVNA: What's the matter? (*Pause.*) Well?

LOMOV: I will try to be brief. You, dear Natalya Stepanovna, know that I have had for a long time, in fact since childhood, the privilege of knowing your family. My late aunt and her husband, from whom I, as I'm sure you know, inherited my land, always treated your father and late mother with deep respect. The Lomov family line and the Chubukov family line have always been on the most friendly terms, you might even say, familial terms. Furthermore, as you probably know, my land comes in close contact with yours. If I may remind you, my Ox Field borders your birches.

NATALYA STEPANOVNA: Excuse me for interrupting you. You said "my Ox Field" . . . Surely it's not yours?

LOMOV: It's mine, ma'am . . .

NATALYA STEPANOVNA: Well, is that so? The Ox Field is ours, not yours!

LOMOV: No, ma'am, it's mine, dear Natalya Stepanovna.

NATALYA STEPANOVNA: That's news to me. Where did you get it from?

LOMOV: Where from? I'm talking about that wedge-shaped Ox Field that runs between your birches and the Burned Swamp.

NATALYA STEPANOVNA: Yes, yes . . . That's ours . . .

LOMOV: No, you're mistaken, dear Natalya Stepanovna—it's mine.

NATALYA STEPANOVNA: Come to your senses, Ivan Vasilyevich! Since when did it become yours?

LOMOV: Since when? As long as I can remember, it's always been ours.

NATALYA STEPANOVNA: Well, excuse me!

LOMOV: It says so in black and white on the papers, dear Natalya Stepanovna. The Ox Field was at one time in dispute, it's true. But now everyone knows that it's mine. And there's nothing to argue about! Allow me to explain that my aunt's grandmother gave the field to your father's grandfather's peasants for limitless, *gratis*[13] use in return for their making bricks for her. Your father's grandfather's peasants used the field *gratis* for about forty years and got used to thinking of it as theirs, then, when circumstances changed[14] . . .

NATALYA STEPANOVNA: But it's not at all as you say! My grandfather and my great-grandfather both said that their land went as far as the Burned Swamp—that means that the Ox Field is ours. What's there to argue about? I don't understand. In fact, this is annoying.

LOMOV: I can show you the papers, Natalya Stepanovna!

NATALYA STEPANOVNA: No, you must be joking, or maybe you're teasing me . . . Or trying to surprise me? We've owned that piece of land for almost three hundred years and suddenly

---

13. "For free" (Latin).
14. Lomov euphemistically refers to the emancipation of the serfs.

you're telling us that the land is yours! Ivan Vasilyevich, excuse me, but I don't believe my ears . . . I'm not particularly attached to the field. It's only about twelve acres in all, and it's worth only about three hundred rubles, but the injustice of it bothers me. Say what you like, but I can't stand injustice.

LOMOV: Listen to me, I beg you! Your father's grandfather's peasants, as I have already had the honor of telling you, made bricks for my aunt's grandmother. So, my aunt's grandmother, wanting to do something nice for them . . .

NATALYA STEPANOVNA: Grandfather, grandmother, aunt . . . I don't understand anything about it! The Ox Field is ours and that's that!

LOMOV: It's mine, ma'am!

NATALYA STEPANOVNA: Ours! Even if you spend two days trying to prove it, even if you put on fifteen frock coats, it's ours, ours, ours! . . . I don't want your property, and I don't want to lose my own either . . . How do you like that?

LOMOV: I don't need the Ox Field, Natalya Stepanovna, but it's the principle of the thing. If you'd like, I'll give it to you.

NATALYA STEPANOVNA: But I could give it to you, because it's mine! . . . If nothing else, this is all very strange, Ivan Vasilyevich! Until now we considered you a good neighbor, a friend. Last year we lent you our thresher, and because of that we couldn't thresh our own wheat until November, but now you treat us like gypsies. Give me my own land! Excuse me, but this is not neighborly! In my opinion, it's impudent, if you ask me . . .

LOMOV: So, that means that in your opinion I'm a usurper? Madam, I have never taken land that was not mine, and I will not allow anyone to accuse me of it . . . (*Quickly walks to the pitcher and drinks some water.*) The Ox Field is mine!

NATALYA STEPANOVNA: Not true, it's ours!

LOMOV: Mine.

NATALYA STEPANOVNA: Not true! And I'll prove it to you! Today I'll send my mowers into that field!

LOMOV: What?

NATALYA STEPANOVNA: My mowers will be in that field today!

Lomov: And I'll throw them out!

Natalya Stepanovna: You won't dare!

Lomov: (*Clutching at his heart.*) The Ox Field is mine. Do you hear? Mine!

Natalya Stepanovna: Please don't yell! You can yell until you're hoarse back at home, but I'll ask you to control yourself while you're here!

Lomov: Madam, if I didn't have these frightening, tormenting palpitations and if the veins in my head weren't throbbing, then I'd talk to you differently. (*Yells.*) The Ox Field is Mine!

Natalya Stepanovna: Ours!

Lomov: Mine!

Natalya Stepanovna: Ours!

Lomov: Mine!

IV

The same and Chubukov.

Chubukov: (*Enters.*) What's this? What are you yelling about?

Natalya Stepanovna: Papa, please tell this gentleman who owns the Ox Field, us or him?

Chubukov: (*To him.*) My little chicken, the field is ours!

Lomov: Have mercy on me, Stepan Stepanovich, how could it be yours? Be a reasonable man! My aunt's grandmother gave the field to your grandfather's peasants for their temporary, *gratis* use. The peasants used it for forty years and got used to thinking of it as theirs, and when circumstances changed . . .

Chubukov: Allow me, my treasure . . . You are forgetting that the peasants in fact did not pay your aunt's grandmother and so forth, because the field was then in dispute, etc. . . . But now every dog in the province knows, in fact, that it is ours. You must not have seen the map!

Lomov: But I'll prove to you that it is mine!

Chubukov: You can't prove it, my pet.

LOMOV: Yes, I can prove it!

CHUBUKOV: Mother in Heaven, why yell like that? You can't, in fact, prove anything by yelling. I don't want what's yours, and I have no intention of letting what's mine go. What for? But, my darling, if it turns out that you want to fight over the field, I'd rather give it to the peasants than to you. So there!

LOMOV: I don't understand! What right do you have to give away someone else's property?

CHUBUKOV: Allow me to know if I have the right or not. In fact, young man, I am not used to anyone talking to me in such a tone of voice, etc. I'm twice as old as you, young man, and I'll ask you to talk to me without such agitation, and so forth.

LOMOV: No, you must think I'm a fool, you must be laughing at me! You call my land yours, and still want me to stay cool and talk to you like a human being! Is that how good neighbors behave, Stepan Stepanovich? You're not a neighbor but a usurper!

CHUBUKOV: What sir? What did you say?

NATALYA STEPANOVNA: Papa, send our mowers into the field right now!

CHUBUKOV: (*To Lomov.*) What did you say, your excellency?

NATALYA STEPANOVNA: The Ox Field is ours, and I won't let him have it, I won't, I won't!

LOMOV: We shall see! I'll prove to you it's mine in court.

CHUBUKOV: In court? You'll take me to court, and so forth, your excellency! You will! I know you, in fact, you're always just itching for a chance to go to court, etc. . . . You have a litigious nature! Your whole family were malicious litigators! The whole family!

LOMOV: I'll ask you not to insult my family line! In the Lomov line, everyone has been honest, not one of us found himself on trial for embezzlement like your uncle!

CHUBUKOV: All the Lomovs were madmen!

NATALYA STEPANOVNA: All of them, all of them, all of them!

CHUBUKOV: Your grandfather drank like a fish, and, in fact, your youngest aunt, Nastásya Mikhaílovna, ran away with an architect, etc. . . .

LOMOV: And your mother was a hunchback. (*Clutches at his heart.*) A spasm in my side . . . The pounding in my head . . . Saints in Heaven! . . . Water!

CHUBUKOV: And your father was a gambler and a glutton.

NATALYA STEPANOVNA: And your aunt was a gossip to say the least!

LOMOV: My left leg's gone to sleep . . . You're an intriguer . . . Oh my heart! . . . And it's no secret that before the elections you . . . I see stars . . . Where's my hat?

NATALYA STEPANOVNA: It's low! It's dishonorable! It's vile!

CHUBUKOV: And, in fact, you yourself are a malicious, two-faced trickster. Yes sir!

LOMOV: Here it is, my hat . . . My heart . . . Where am I going? Where's the door? Oh! . . . I'm dying, I think . . . My foot's dragging behind me . . . (*Goes to the door.*)

CHUHUKOV: (*Following him.*) Don't bother setting those feet in my house again!

NATALYA STEPANOVNA: Take us to court! We'll see! (*Lomov exits, staggering.*)

V

Chubukov and Natalya Stepanovna.

CHUBUKOV: Go to hell! (*Walks around excitedly.*)

NATALYA STEPANOVNA: What a scoundrel! That's a good neighbor for you!

CHUBUKOV: He's a villain! A stuffed scarecrow!

NATALYA STEPANOVNA: A monster! Takes your land and then has the nerve to swear at you.

CHUBUKOV: And this gremlin, in fact this . . . blind dolt . . . dares to make a proposal, etc. Humph! A proposal!

NATALYA STEPANOVNA: What kind of proposal?

CHUBUKOV: What kind! He came here to propose to you.

NATALYA STEPANOVNA: To propose? To me? Why didn't you tell me that before?

CHUBUKOV: That's why he put on a frock coat! The stuffed sausage! The shrimp!

NATALYA STEPANOVNA: To me? To propose? Ah! (*Falls into a chair and moans.*) Bring him back! Bring him back! Ah! Bring him back!

CHUBUKOV: Bring who back?

NATALYA STEPANOVNA: Quick, quick! I feel sick. Bring him back! (*Hysterics.*)

CHUBUKOV: What's that? What's wrong with you? (*Puts his head in his hands.*) I'm so unlucky! I'll shoot myself! I'll hang myself. Everyone's torturing me!

NATALYA STEPANOVNA: I'm dying! Bring him back!

CHUBUKOV: Phuh! Right away! Don't howl! (*Runs out.*)

NATALYA STEPANOVNA: (*Alone, moaning.*) What did we do! Bring him back! Bring him back!

CHUBUKOV: (*Runs in.*) He's coming right back, etc. To hell with him! Oof! Talk to him yourself! I, in fact, don't want to.

NATALYA STEPANOVNA: (*Moans.*) Bring him back!

CHUBUKOV: (*Yells.*) He's coming I tell you. "Oh, my Maker, what kind of task is this, being a grown-up daughter's father?"[15] I'll cut my throat. I'll definitely cut my throat! We've sworn at the man, insulted him and threw him out, and it's all your fault . . . your fault!

NATALYA STEPANOVNA: No, it's your fault!

CHUBUKOV: I'm not guilty, in fact! (*Lomov appears at the door.*) Well, talk to him yourself! (*Chubukov exits.*)

---

15. The final line from the Russian classic play, *Woe from Wit* (1824) by Alexander Sergeyevich Griboyedov.

VI

Natalya Stepanovna and Lomov.

Lomov: (*Enters exhausted.*) Such frightening palpitations . . . My foot's asleep . . . That spasm in my side . . .

Natalya Stepanovna: Forgive me, we got worked up, Ivan Vasilyevich . . . I now recall that the Ox Field is actually yours.

Lomov: My heart's beating frighteningly . . . My field . . . Both my eyelids are jumping around . . .

Natalya Stepanovna: It's yours, your field . . . Sit down . . . (*They sit down.*) We were wrong.

Lomov: It's the principle of the thing . . . I'm not particularly attached to the land, but I am attached to the principle of the . . .

Natalya Stepanovna: Exactly, the principle . . . Let's talk about something else.

Lomov: All the more so too, since I have proof. My aunt's grandmother gave your father's grandfather's peasants . . .

Natalya Stepanovna: Enough, enough of that . . . (*Aside.*) I don't know how to get this going . . . (*To him.*) Will you be going hunting soon?

Lomov: For woodchucks, dear Natalya Stepanovna. I think after the harvest begins. Oh, did you hear? Imagine my bad luck! My Diviner—you remember my dog, don't you? Well, he's gone lame.

Natalya Stepanovna: What a shame! How did it happen?

Lomov: Don't know . . . He must have twisted his ankle or maybe the other dogs bit him. (*Sighs.*) The best dog money can buy! You know I paid Mirónov one hundred and twenty-five rubles for him.

Natalya Stepanovna: You paid too much, Ivan Vasilyevich!

Lomov: In my opinion it was a bargain. He's a miraculous dog.

Natalya Stepanovna: Papa paid eighty-five rubles for his Rover, and Rover's a better dog than your Diviner!

LOMOV: Rover better than Diviner? What's wrong with you! (*Laughs.*) Rover better than Diviner!

NATALYA STEPANOVNA: Of course he's better! It's true that Rover's young, still not full grown, but there's none better for form and for pointing, even in the Volchanyétsky[16] Kennel.

LOMOV: Excuse me, Natalya Stepanovna, but you're forgetting that he's weak-jawed, and a dog with a weak jaw can never really sink his teeth in!

NATALYA STEPANOVNA: Weak-jawed? First I've heard!

LOMOV: I assure you, the lower part of the maxilla is shorter than the upper.

NATALYA STEPANOVNA: Did you measure it?

LOMOV: I measured it. He's good for the chase, of course, but when it comes to retrieving, then he hardly . . .

NATALYA STEPANOVNA: In the first place, our Rover has a pedigree and a good thick coat. He's the son of Sprinter and Chisel, but you'll never know where that muddy skewbald of yours comes from. Besides that, he's old and ugly as a jade.

LOMOV: Old, yes, but I wouldn't trade him for five of your Rovers . . . How could I? Diviner is a dog, but Rover . . . It's stupid even to argue about it. There are animals like your Rover in every kennel, like pigs in a poke. Twenty-five rubles would be too much for him.

NATALYA STEPANOVNA: The devil of contradiction has gotten into you today, Ivan Vasilyevich. First you say the field is yours, then that Diviner's a better dog than Rover. I don't like it when a man says what he doesn't think. You know perfectly well that Rover is one hundred times better than your . . . that stupid Diviner. So why say the opposite?

LOMOV: I can see, Natalya Stepanovna, that you must take me for a blind man or a fool. Try to understand that your Rover is weak-jawed!

NATALYA STEPANOVNA: Not true!

LOMOV: Weak-jawed!

NATALYA STEPANOVNA: (*Yells.*) Not true!

---

16. A famous breeder of pedigree dogs; the surname derives from "wolf."

LOMOV: Why are you yelling, madam?

NATALYA STEPANOVNA: Why are you talking nonsense? This is infuriating! Even though it's about time to put your Diviner out of his misery, you insist on comparing him to Rover!

LOMOV: Excuse me but I can't continue this argument. I have palpitations.

NATALYA STEPANOVNA: I've noticed that those hunters who argue more than anybody else usually understand less than anybody else.

LOMOV: Madam, I beg you, shut up . . . My heart's about to burst . . . (*Yells.*) Shut up!

NATALYA STEPANOVNA: I will not shut up, until you admit that Rover is one hundred times better than your Diviner.

LOMOV: One hundred times worse! I hope he drops dead, your Rover! My head . . . my eye . . . my shoulder . . .

NATALYA STEPANOVNA: Your stupid Diviner doesn't need to drop dead, because he looks dead already!

LOMOV: (*Cries.*) Shut up! I'm having a heart attack!

NATALYA STEPANOVNA: I will not shut up!

VII

The same and Chubukov.

CHUBUKOV: (*Enters.*) What now?

NATALYA STEPANOVNA: Papa, tell us frankly, on your honor. Which dog is better, our Rover or his Diviner?

LOMOV: Stepan Stepanovich, I beg you, just tell us one thing. Is your Rover weak-jawed or not? Yes or no?

CHUBUKOV: So what if he is? Is it so important? He's still the best dog in the province, etc.

LOMOV: But isn't my Diviner better? On your honor!

CHUBUKOV: Don't get so upset, my treasure . . . Allow me . . . Your Diviner, in fact, has his good points . . . He's got a pedigree, stands firmly on his own four legs, has good haunches, etc.

But since you ask, you handsome devil you, your dog has two faults. He's old and pug-nosed.

LOMOV: Excuse me, I have palpitations . . . Let's look at the facts . . . Allow me to remind you that on the Marúskin Green, my Diviner ran neck and neck with the Count's Wagger, but your Rover was a whole half mile behind.

CHUBUKOV: He was behind because the Count's huntsman struck him with his whip.

LOMOV: For a reason. All the dogs were running after the fox, but Rover took off after a sheep!

CHUBUKOV: That's not true, sir! . . . My dearest, dearest, dearest friend, remember I'm quick-tempered and so, in fact, let's stop this argument right now. He was whipped because everyone is jealous of another man's dog . . . Yes sir! Everyone likes to hate! And you, sir, are not without your faults! When you notice whose dog is in fact better than your Diviner, you start arguing about this and that . . . about your own . . . etc. . . . But I remember everything!

LOMOV: And I remember too!

CHUBUKOV: (*Mocks him.*) And I remember too . . . But what do you remember?

LOMOV: My palpitations . . . My foot's asleep . . . I can't!

NATALYA STEPANOVNA: (*Mocks him.*) My palpitations . . . What kind of hunter are you anyway? You should be lying on the stove[17] crunching cockroaches, not out chasing foxes! My palpitations . . .

CHUBUKOV: It's true, what kind of a hunter are you? You should, in fact, be sitting at home with your palpitations, not bobbing around in a saddle. I'd have nothing against your hunting if you didn't do it just to argue and interfere with other people's dogs, etc. I'm quick-tempered, so let's drop this conversation. You are, in fact, not a hunter at all!

---

17. Stoves that heated peasant homes were built into corners, were tall, and had wide shelves on top. Natalya Stepanovna suggests that Lomov is no better than a peasant.

LOMOV: And you call yourself a hunter? You only do it to rub shoulders with the Count and set up intrigues . . . My heart! . . . You are an intriguer!

CHUBUKOV: What sir? I'm an intriguer? (*Yells.*) Shut up!

LOMOV: Intriguer!

CHUBUKOV: You little brat! You whelp!

LOMOV: You old rat! You heretic!

CHUBUKOV: Shut up, or I'll shoot you down like a partridge, and with a dirty gun too! You windbag!

LOMOV: Everyone knows, that—oh, my heart!—that your late wife beat you . . . My foot . . . my head . . . stars . . . I'm falling, falling! . . .

CHUBUKOV: And your housekeeper had you under her thumb!

LOMOV: Look, look, look . . . My heart's burst! My shoulder's torn off . . . Where's my shoulder? . . . I'm dying! (*Falls into a chair.*) A doctor! (*Faints.*)

CHUBUKOV: You little brat! You milk drinker! You windbag! I feel sick! (*Drinks some water.*) Sick!

NATALYA STEPANOVNA: What kind of hunter are you anyway? You don't even know how to sit on a horse! (*To her father.*) Papa, what's wrong with him? Papa! Look, papa! (*Screams.*) Ivan Vasilyevich! He's dead!

CHUBUKOV: I feel sick! . . . Can't catch my breath! . . . Air!

NATALYA STEPANOVNA: He's dead! (*Tugs at Lomov's sleeve.*) Ivan Vasilyevich! Ivan Vasilyevich! What did we do! He's dead! (*Falls into a chair.*) A doctor, a doctor!

(*Hysterics.*)

CHUBUKOV: Oh! . . . What now? What's wrong with you?

NATALYA STEPANOVNA: (*Moans.*) He's dead . . . dead!

CHUBUKOV: Who's dead? (*Looks at Lomov.*) He really is dead! Saints in Heaven! Water! A doctor! (*Puts a glass of water to Lomov's lips.*) Drink it up! . . . No, he's not drinking . . . That means, he's dead and so forth . . . I am the most unlucky man! Why haven't I put a bullet through my head already? Why haven't I cut my throat yet? What am I waiting for? Give me a knife! Give me a pistol! (*Lomov moves.*) It looks like he's coming back to life . . . Drink the water! . . . That's it . . .

LOMOV: Stars . . . fog . . . Where am I?

CHUBUKOV: You better get married quick, and—well, what the hell! She's agreed! (*Joins Lomov's and his daughter's hands.*) She's agreed, and so forth. I congratulate you, etc. Just leave me in peace!

LOMOV: Huh? What? (*Getting up.*) Who?

CHUBUKOV: She's agreed! Well? Kiss each other and . . . and to hell with you both!

NATALYA STEPANOVNA: (*Moans.*) He's alive . . . Yes, yes, I accept . . .

CHUBUKOV: Kiss each other!

LOMOV: Huh? Who? (*Kisses Natalya Stepanovna.*) Very nice . . . Allow me to ask, what's happening? Oh yes, I understand . . . My heart . . . Stars . . . I'm happy, Natalya Stepanovna . . . (*Kisses her hand.*) My foot's asleep . . .

NATALYA STEPANOVNA: I . . . I'm happy too . . .

CHUBUKOV: Oof! The weight of a mountain has been lifted from my shoulders . . .

NATALYA STEPANOVNA: But . . . Still, you ought to agree that Diviner is worse than Rover.

LOMOV: Better.

NATALYA STEPANOVNA: Worse.

CHUBUKOV: Well, the familial happiness has now begun! Champagne!

LOMOV: Better.

NATALYA STEPANOVNA: Worse! Worse! Worse!

CHUBUKOV: (*Trying to out yell them.*) Champagne! Champagne!

Curtain.

The Anniversary

A Joke in One Act

[Written in 1891, *The Anniversary* premiered at the Society of Art and Literature in Moscow on November 20, 1900. The first English-language production took place in London in 1931 and the first American staging in New York thirty years later. Theatre Uptown in New York City produced the translation that follows in 1978. —SMC]

The Characters

Shipúchin, Andréy Andréyevich, Chairman of the Board for the N____[18] Mutual Credit Society, a man who is not old and wears a monocle. [His last name sounds like "hiss."]

Tatyána Alekséyevna, his wife, twenty-five years old. [A very sweet nickname for her is Tanyúsha.]

Hírin, Kuzmá Nikoláyevich, the bank's bookkeeper, an old man. [His last name means "to decay."]

Merchútkina, Nastásya Fyódorovna, an old woman in a coat.

Members of the bank's board

Bank clerks

The action takes place in the N____ Mutual Credit Society, a bank. The office of the Chairman of the Board. There is a door to the left, leading to the bank's business office. Two writing desks. The furnishings display a pretentious desire for grandiosity: velvet-covered furniture, flowers, statues, rugs, a telephone. It is midday. Hirin is alone, wearing slippers.

HIRIN: (*Yells out the door.*) Send out to the drugstore for valerian drops,[19] fifteen kopecks worth, and order them to bring some fresh water into the chairman's office! If I told you once, I told you a hundred times! (*Goes to his desk.*) I'm completely worn out. I've been writing for four days straight without a wink of sleep. I write here from morning to night, and I write at home from night to morning. (*Coughs.*) And now my whole body is

---

18. Used to denote anonymity.
19. A mild herbal sedative.

inflamed. Fever, I'm hot, coughing, my legs ache, and before my eyes I see . . . exclamation marks! (*Sits down.*) This phony of ours, this scoundrel, this chairman of the board will read my report today at the general meeting: *Our Bank, Its Present and Future.* Some orator he is . . . (*Writes.*) Two . . . one . . . one . . . six . . . zero . . . seven. Then six . . . zero . . . one . . . six . . . He wants to set the dust flying, but it's me sitting here, working for him like a convict . . . And yet he'll fill the speech with poetry, nothing else, even though I've been working out these figures on the abacus[20] day after day. Damn him! . . . (*Clicks the abacus.*) I can't stand it! (*Writes.*) So it's one . . . three . . . seven . . . two . . . one . . . zero . . . He promised to reward me for my pains. If everything goes well today, and he succeeds in ingratiating himself with the public, then he promised me a gold medallion and three hundred rubles as a bonus . . . We'll see. (*Writes.*) Well, if all my toil goes for naught, then, brother, watch out . . . I'm a hot-tempered man . . . In the heat of the moment I could even commit a crime . . . Yes sir!

Offstage there is noise and applause. The voice of Shipuchin: "I thank you! I thank you! I'm touched!" Enter Shipuchin. He wears a frock coat and a white tie; in his hands he carries the album that has just been given to him.

SHIPUCHIN: (*Standing at the door and addressing himself to the business office.*) I will treasure this gift of yours, my dear colleagues, until my very death, as a reminder of the happiest days of my life! Yes, my most gracious gentlemen! Once more I thank you! (*Blows a kiss to them, and then goes to Hirin.*) My dear, my most respected Kuzma Nikolayevich!

From time to time, while Shipuchin is on stage, clerks enter and exit with papers for him to sign.

HIRIN: (*Rising*) I am honored to congratulate you, Andrey Andreyevich, on the fifteenth anniversary of our bank, and to wish you . . .

---

20. A calculating machine consisting of beads that slide along wires, mounted on a wooden frame. One moves the beads up and down the wires to keep count.

SHIPUCHIN: (*Shakes his hand firmly.*) I thank you, my dear friend! I thank you! On this momentous day, because it's our anniversary, I propose that we might even kiss! . . . (*They kiss each other on the cheeks.*[21]) I'm very, very glad! Thank you for your service . . . For everything, for everything thank you! If I, as chairman of this bank, am being honored today for getting something useful done, then I am obliged, above all, to my dear colleagues. (*Sighs.*) Yes, old chap, fifteen years! Fifteen years, or I'm not Shipuchin! (*In a lively manner.*) Well, what about my speech? Is it coming along?

HIRIN: Yes. There's only about five pages left.

SHIPUCHIN: Wonderful. Does that mean it will be ready by three o'clock?

HIRIN: If no one disturbs me, I'll finish it. Only some nonsense is left.

SHIPUCHIN: Excellent. Excellent, or I'm not Shipuchin! The general meeting is at four. Please, my chuck, give me the first half and I'll study it over . . . Give it to me quick . . . (*Takes the report.*) I've got high hopes for this speech . . . This is my *profession de foi*,[22] or better yet, my fireworks . . . Fireworks, or I'm not Shipuchin! (*Sits down and silently reads the report.*) But I'm tired as hell . . . Last night I had an attack of gout,[23] I spent the whole morning bustling about, and with all the excitement, ovations, agitation . . . I'm tired!

HIRIN: (*Writes.*) Two . . . zero . . . zero . . . three . . . nine . . . two . . . zero . . . Looking at these figures makes me nauseous . . . Three . . . one . . . six . . . four . . . one . . . five . . . (*Clicks the abacus.*)

SHIPUCHIN: And another unpleasant thing . . . This morning your wife came to me and complained about you again. She said that yesterday evening you took off after her and your sister-in-law with a knife. Kuzma Nikolayevich, now how does that look? Ay-yai-yai!

---

21. In Russian culture, men kiss each other's cheeks as a sign of friendship.
22. "Creed," "belief" (French).
23. A genetic disease characterized by painful swelling of the joints in the legs and feet.

HIRIN: (*Sternly.*) Because it's the anniversary, I will dare to ask a favor of you, Andrey Andreyevich. I beg you, if only out of respect for my being sentenced by you to hard labor, do not interfere in my family life. I beg you!

SHIPUCHIN: (*Sighs.*) You have an impossible character, Kuzma Nikolayevich! You are a fine man, venerable, but with women, you act like some kind of Jack the Ripper.[24] It's true. I don't understand why you hate them so much?

HIRIN: And I don't understand why you love them so much?

Pause.

SHIPUCHIN: The clerks just gave me an album, and the members of the bank's board want to make a speech, so I've heard, and present me with a silver cup . . . (*Playing with his monocle.*) That's good, or I'm not Shipuchin! And it's not excessive . . . For the reputation of the bank it's necessary to have some pomp, the devil knows! But then you're no stranger here, you know it all . . . I wrote their speech myself, I also bought the silver cup myself . . . And I spent forty rubles to have the speech bound, but you can't get around that. They never would have thought of it by themselves. (*Looks around.*) Such furnishings! What furniture! They say I'm petty, because I need the locks on the doors shined, the clerks wearing fashionable ties, and a portly doorman standing at the front door. But no, my dear sirs. The locks on the doors, and the portly doorman are not petty details. At home I can be as *bourgeois*[25] as I like, eat and sleep like a pig, drink myself into a stupor . . .

HIRIN: Please, I beg you, no implications!

SHIPUCHIN: Ah, no one's implying anything! You have an impossible character . . . Here's what I'm saying: at home I can be *bourgeois,* a *parvenu,*[26] indulge my every whim, but here, everything must be done *en grand.*[27] This is a bank. Here, every detail must command respect, so to speak, must look

---

24. The London serial rapist of 1888, who killed and mutilated the women he attacked.
25. "Middle class" (French).
26. "An upstart" (French).
27. "On a grand scale" (French).

triumphant. (*Picks up a piece of paper and throws it into the fireplace.*) In fact, my service lies in my having significantly raised the reputation of the bank! . . . It's important business—setting the right tone! It's important, or I'm not Shipuchin! (*Glances at Hirin.*) My dear friend, any minute now the deputation of the members of the bank's board could appear, and you're wearing slippers, and that scarf . . . and that savagely colored jacket. You might put on a frock coat or at least a black suit . . .

HIRIN: My health is more important to me than the members of your bank. My whole body is inflamed.

SHIPUCHIN: (*Getting excited.*) At least admit that you are out of order! You're ruining the *ensemble!*[28]

HIRIN: If the deputation comes, I can hide. It's no great loss . . . (*Writes.*) Seven . . . one . . . seven . . . two . . . one . . . five . . . zero . . . I don't like disorder either . . . Seven . . . two . . . nine . . . (*Clicks the abacus.*) I can't stand disorder! It would have been better if you hadn't invited ladies to the anniversary dinner today . . .

SHIPUCHIN: What nonsense . . .

HIRIN: I know you want them to fill the hall with their *chic*,[29] but watch out, they'll ruin the whole thing for you. They'll only bring trouble and disorder.

SHIPUCHIN: On the contrary, female society raises the tone.

HIRIN: Yes . . . Your wife may appear well-bred, but a week ago on Monday, she blurted something out that left me wringing my hands for two days afterwards. Out of the blue, in front of strangers she asks, "Is it true my husband bought stocks in the Dryázhky-Pryázhky bank, the one that just bottomed out on the stock market? Ah, my poor husband is so worried!" That in front of strangers! And I don't understand why you're so open about it either! Do you want to be charged with criminal misconduct?

SHIPUCHIN: Well, that's enough! Enough! All that's too gloomy for an anniversary. By the way, you reminded me. (*Looks at his watch.*) My wife is supposed to arrive any minute now. In

---

28. "The general effect" (French).
29. "Stylish elegance" (French).

fact, I should have gone to the station to get her, poor baby, but there wasn't time, and . . . and I'm tired. To be frank, I won't be glad to see her. That is, I'll be glad, but it would have been nicer if she'd stayed a day or two longer at her mother's. She'll want to spend the whole evening with me tonight, and there was supposed to be a little after-dinner excursion, if you catch my drift, that the men were planning for me. (*Winces.*) My twitching has started up again. My nerves are so taut that the most nonsensical thing could bring tears to my eyes! No, I must be strong, or I'm not Shipuchin!

Enter Tatyana Alekseyevna in a raincoat and with a traveling bag slung across her shoulder.

SHIPUCHIN: Well! Speak of the devil!

TATYANA ALEKSEYEVNA: Darling! (*Runs to her husband; a prolonged kiss.*)

SHIPUCHIN: We were just talking about you! (*Looks at his watch.*)

TATYANA ALEKSEYEVNA: (*Panting.*) Did you miss me? Are you well? I haven't even been home yet. I came right here from the station. I have so much, so much to tell you . . . I can't wait . . . I won't even take off my coat, I'll be only a minute. (*To Hirin.*) Hello, Kuzma Nikolayevich! (*To her husband.*) Is everything all right at home?

SHIPUCHIN: Everything. And I see you've gotten plumper, and prettier in the last week . . . Well, how was the trip?

TATYANA ALEKSEYEVNA: Marvelous. Mama and Kátya send their regards. Vasíly Andréyevich sends you a kiss. (*Kisses him.*) My aunt sent you some homemade jam, and everyone's angry with you because you don't write. Zína sends you a kiss. (*Kisses him.*) Ah, if only you knew what happened! What happened! It's awful just to talk about it! Oh, what happened! But I can tell by your face, you're not glad to see me!

SHIPUCHIN: On the contrary . . . Darling . . . (*Kisses her.*)

Hirin angrily coughs.

TATYANA ALEKSEYEVNA: (*Sighs.*) Oh, poor Katya! Poor Katya! I'm so sorry for her, so sorry!

SHIPUCHIN: We're having an anniversary here today, darling, and any minute now a deputation from the bank's board could appear and you're not dressed appropriately.

TATYANA ALEKSEYEVNA: That's right, the anniversary! I congratulate you, gentlemen . . . I wish you . . . Does that mean today's the meeting, the dinner? . . . Oh, I love it. And remember that beautiful speech you wrote for the deputation? Will they read it today?

Hirin angrily coughs.

SHIPUCHIN: (*Embarrassed.*) Darling, you mustn't talk about that . . . Really, you should go home.

TATYANA ALEKSEYEVNA: Right away, right away. I can tell you what happened in a minute, and then I'll leave. I'll tell you everything from the very beginning. Well . . . When you left me off at the station, I sat next to a stout lady, remember? And I started to read. I don't like to talk on trains. For three stops I read the whole time and didn't say a word to anyone . . . Well, then evening came and with it, you know, came all sorts of gloomy thoughts! But just then, sitting across from me was a young man, not bad looking either, brown hair . . . Well, we started talking . . . Then a sailor joined us, and then some sort of student . . . (*Laughs.*) I told them I wasn't married . . . How they flirted with me! We chattered until midnight; the brown-haired young man told some really funny jokes, and the sailor sang the whole way. My sides ached from laughing so much. And when the sailor—ah, these sailors!—when the sailor accidentally found out my name is Tatyana, do you know what he sang? (*Sings in a bass voice.*) "Onégin, I cannot lie, I'll love Tatyana till I die."[30] (*Giggles.*)

Hirin angrily coughs.

SHIPUCHIN: But, Tanyusha, we're disturbing Kuzma Nikolayevich. Go home, darling . . . Later . . .

---

30. From an aria in Pyotr Ilyich Tchaikovsky's 1879 opera, *Eugene Onegin*, based upon Alexander Sergeyevich Pushkin's 1833 novel in verse, whose heroine is named Tatyana.

TATYANA ALEKSEYEVNA: No, no, let him listen, it's very interesting. I'll finish in a minute. At the station Seryózha came to meet me. There was also another young man there, a tax collector, I think . . . not bad, rather good looking, especially his eyes . . . Seryózha introduced us, and we all three rode home together . . . The weather was extraordinary . . .

> *Offstage voices: "You can't go in! You can't! What do you want?" Enter Merchutkina.*

MERCHUTKINA: (*At the door, brushing someone aside.*) What is that you think you're grabbing? What will you go for next! I need to go in there myself! . . . (*Enters; to Shipuchin.*) I'm honored, your excellency . . . I'm Nastasya Fyodorovna Merchutkina, the wife of the provincial secretary, sir.

SHIPUCHIN: What do you want?

MERCHUTKINA: You see, your excellency, my husband, the provincial secretary, Merchútkin, was sick for five months, and while he lay at home getting himself cured, they fired him for no reason, your excellency, and when I went to get his pay, you see, they took twenty-four rubles, thirty-six kopecks out of it. "What for?" I asked. They said: "He borrowed from the company fund, and the loan was guaranteed by the others." How's that? He couldn't borrow anything without my consent, could he? That's not allowed, your excellency! I'm a poor woman, and take in lodgers to feed myself . . . I'm weak, defenseless . . . I endure insults from everyone, and never hear a kind word from anyone . . .

SHIPUCHIN: If you please . . . (*Takes her application and reads it standing up.*)

TATYANA ALEKSEYEVNA: (*To Hirin.*) But I should really start from the beginning . . . Last week I received a letter from Mama out of the blue. She wrote that some Grendilyévsky[31] proposed to my sister Katya. A wonderful, modest young man, but without any means whatsoever, not even a job of any kind. And to make it worse, just imagine, Katya was attracted to him. What could be done? Mama wrote that I should come immediately, and use my influence over Katya . . .

---

31. Sounds like the name of a Polish nobleman.

HIRIN: (*Sternly.*) If you please, you're making me lose count! You, Mama, and Katya! I've lost count and still I don't understand what you're saying!

TATYANA ALEKSEYEVNA: How pompous! You should listen, when a lady is talking to you! Why are you so angry today? Are you in love? (*Laughs.*)

SHIPUCHIN: (*To Merchutkina.*) Excuse me, but what exactly is this? I don't understand what you're saying . . .

TATYANA ALEKSEYEVNA: In love? Aha! He's blushing!

SHIPUCHIN: (*To his wife.*) Tanyusha, darling, go into the business office for a minute. I'll be right there.

TATYANA ALEKSEYEVNA: Very well. (*Exits.*)

SHIPUCHIN: I don't understand. Apparently, madam, you are not in the right place. Your request does not substantively concern us at all. You must take the trouble to address yourself to that agency for which your husband worked.

MERCHUTKINA: Gracious sir, I've already been to five places, and they didn't take my application anywhere. I was losing my head, and then, thanks to my son-in-law, Borís Matvéyich, I thought to come see you. He said: "Mama dear, you go to Mr. Shipuchin; he's a big man, he'll throw his weight around . . ." Help me, your excellency.

SHIPUCHIN: Madam Merchutkina, we can do nothing for you. Try to understand; your husband, as far as I can gather, worked in the Agency for Military Medicine, but our enterprise is absolutely private and commercial. This is a bank. Why can't you understand that?!

MERCHUTKINA: But your excellency, I can show you that my husband was really sick. I have a doctor's certificate. Here it is, please have a look . . .

SHIPUCHIN: (*Annoyed.*) Wonderful, I believe you, but I repeat, this does not concern us.

Offstage Tatyana Alekseyevna's laughter can be heard, then a man's laugh.

SHIPUCHIN: (*Looks at the door.*) She's disturbing the clerks in there. (*To Merchutkina.*) It's strange and even funny! Surely your husband must know where to go?

MERCHUTKINA: Your excellency, as far as I can tell, he doesn't know a thing. All he ever says is, "It's none of your business! Scram!" And that's all.

SHIPUCHIN: I repeat, madam, your husband worked in the Agency for Military Medicine, but this is a bank, a private and commercial enterprise . . .

MERCHUTKINA: Well, well, well . . . I understand, gracious sir. In that case, your excellency, order them to give me just fifteen rubles now. I'll take the rest in installments.

SHIPUCHIN: (*Sighs.*) Ough!

HIRIN: Andrey Andreyevich, with all this noise I'll never finish the report!

SHIPUCHIN: Just a minute. (*To Merchutkina.*) I'm not getting through to you. Try to understand that to come to us with such a request is as strange as taking an application for a divorce to a drugstore, for example, or the Assay Office.[32]

A knock at the door. The voice of Tatyana Alekseyevna: "Andrey, can I come in?"

SHIPUCHIN: (*Yells.*) Wait a minute, darling, just a minute! (*To Merchutkina.*) You weren't paid in full, but why come to us? And besides, madam, today is our anniversary, and we're busy . . . Someone could come in at any moment . . . Excuse me.

MERCHUTKINA: Your excellency, pity me, a poor orphan! I'm a weak, defenseless woman . . . Tormented to death . . . I have to sue the lodgers, take care of my husband's troubles, run around with the housework, and now even my son-in-law's lost his job.

SHIPUCHIN: Madam Merchutkina, I . . . No, excuse me, I can't talk to you! My head is spinning . . . You're disturbing us, and taking up our time for nothing . . . (*Sighs; aside.*) She's trouble, or I'm not Shipuchin! (*To Hirin.*) Kuzma Nikolayevich, you

---

32. A governmental agency that tested gold and silver for purity.

explain it, please, to Madam Merchutkina . . . (*Waves his hand and exits to the business office.*)

HIRIN: (*Approaches Merchutkina, sternly.*) What do you want?

MERCHUTKINA: I'm a weak, defenseless woman . . . Maybe I look strong, but if you'd examine me, you'd see I don't have one healthy vein in my whole body. I'm hardly standing on my feet and I've even lost my appetite. I drank some coffee this morning, without any satisfaction.

HIRIN: I'm asking you, what do you want?

MERCHUTKINA: Gracious sir, order them to give me fifteen rubles now, and I'll get the rest in a month.

HIRIN: But surely, it seems, you've been told already, in plain Russian: This is a bank!?

MERCHUTKINA: Yes, yes . . . But if you need it, I can show you the medical certificate.

HIRIN: Is that a head on your shoulders, or what?

MERCHUTKINA: Dearie, I'm only asking for what's legally mine. I don't need somebody else's money.

HIRIN: I'm asking you, lady: Is that a head on your shoulders, or what? Damn you, I don't have time to talk to you! I'm busy. (*Shows her the door.*) I beg you!

MERCHUTKINA: (*Surprised.*) What about my money? . . .

HIRIN: In one word, you don't have a head on your shoulders. You've got . . . (*Thumps a finger on the desk, then on his forehead.*)

MERCHUTKINA: (*Insulted.*) What? Well, I never . . . Go thump at your wife like that . . . But my husband's the provincial secretary . . . You can't do that to me!

HIRIN: (*Blowing up; in a low voice.*) Get out of here!

MERCHUTKINA: But, but, but . . . You can't!

HIRIN: (*In a low voice.*) If you don't leave this minute, I'll send for the janitor! Get out! (*Stamps his feet.*)

MERCHUTKINA: I never, never! I'm not afraid! I've seen the likes of you before . . . Your head is as empty as a keyhole!

HIRIN: I don't think I've ever seen anyone more repulsive, not in my whole life . . . Ough! My head's pounding . . . (*Breathes heavily.*) I'll tell you just once more . . . Do you hear? If you, you old witch, don't get out of here, I'll pulverize you! I have such a temper that I could cripple you for life. I could commit a crime!

MERCHUTKINA: You bark, but you don't bite. You don't scare me! I've seen the likes of you.

HIRIN: (*In desperation.*) I can't even look at her! I'm sick to my stomach! I can't bear it! (*Goes to his desk and sits.*) They've filled the bank with hens, and I can't write my report! I can't!

MERCHUTKINA: I'm not asking for someone else's money, but what's legally mine. You should be ashamed! You sit in an office in slippers . . . You peasant . . .

Enter Shipuchin and Tatyana Alekseyevna.

TATYANA ALEKSEYEVNA: (*Entering behind her husband.*) In the evening we went to the Berezhnítskys.[33] Katya wore a baby blue silk dress with very delicate lace, and open at the neck . . . Her hair was piled up high on her head and so becoming. I did her hairstyle myself . . . With the way she was dressed and her hair, she was simply bewitching!

SHIPUCHIN: (*Already with a migraine.*) Yes, yes . . . Bewitching . . . They might come in any minute now.

MERCHUTKINA: Your excellency! . . .

SHIPUCHIN: (*Dejected.*) What now? What do you want?

MERCHUTKINA: Your excellency . . . (*Points to Hirin.*) That man, that one there . . . He thumps his finger at me on his forehead and then on the table . . . You ordered him to look into my case, and he made fun of every word I said. I'm a weak, defenseless woman.

SHIPUCHIN: Very well, madam. I'll look into it . . . I'll take the necessary measures . . . later. Just leave now! (*Aside.*) My gout is acting up again!

HIRIN: (*Approaches Shipuchin, quietly.*) Andrey Andreyevich, send for the doorman and kick her out on her ass. What's the matter?

---

33. From the word for "shore."

SHIPUCHIN: (*Scared.*) No, no! She'll squeal like a pig, and don't forget there are apartments in this building.

MERCHUTKINA: Your excellency! . . .

HIRIN: (*In a tearful voice.*) But I have to write the report, don't I? I won't finish in time . . . (*Returns to the desk.*) I can't do it!

MERCHUTKINA: Your excellency, when will I get my money? I need it today.

SHIPUCHIN: (*Aside, with annoyance.*) A remarkably low woman! (*To her, gently.*) Madam, I already told you, this is a bank, a private, commercial enterprise . . .

MERCHUTKINA: Be kind, your excellency, pretend you're my own father . . . If the medical certificate isn't enough, I can show you a certificate from the district inspector too. Tell them to give me my money!

SHIPUCHIN: (*Sighing heavily.*) Ough!

TATYANA ALEKSEYEVNA: (*To Merchutkina.*) Granny, they have told you that you are disturbing them. Who do you think you are!

MERCHUTKINA: Pretty lady, I have no mother, no one to look out for me. I know my place. It's to eat and drink, but these days I drink my coffee without any satisfaction.

SHIPUCHIN: (*At his wit's end; to Merchutkina.*) How much do you want?

MERCHUTKINA: Twenty-four rubles, thirty-six kopecks.

SHIPUCHIN: Very well! . . . (*Takes twenty five rubles from his wallet and gives them to her.*) Here are twenty-five rubles. Take them . . . and get out!

Hirin angrily coughs.

MERCHUTKINA: Most humbly do I thank you, your excellency. (*Hides the money.*)

TATYANA ALEKSEYEVNA: (*Sitting down near her husband.*) It's about time for me to go home . . . (*Looking at her watch.*) But I didn't finish yet . . . I'll finish in half a minute and then go . . . What happened! Ah, what happened! So, we went to the Berezhnitskys for the evening . . . It wasn't bad, it was fun, but nothing special . . . Of course, Katya's Grendilyevsky was there, pining away for her . . . Well, I had a talk with Katya, I cried a little, used my influence over her, and so that very evening she had it out with Grendilyevsky and turned him down. Well, I thought everything was working out all for the best. Mama calmed down, Katya was saved, and even I felt calmer . . . Then what do you know! Just before dinner, Katya and I were walking down the garden path when suddenly . . . (*Gets excited.*) When suddenly we hear a shot . . . No, I can't talk about it coldly! (*Waves her handkerchief.*) No, I can't!

SHIPUCHIN: (*Sighs.*) Ough!

TATYANA ALEKSEYEVNA: (*Cries.*) We run to the garden house, and there . . . there lay poor Grendilyevsky . . . with a pistol in his hand . . .

SHIPUCHIN: No, I can't stand it! I can't stand it. (*To Merchutkina.*) What else do you want?

MERCHUTKINA: Your excellency, couldn't you give my husband his job back?

TATYANA ALEKSEYEVNA: (*Crying.*) He had shot himself right through the heart . . . right here . . . Katya fainted dead away, poor thing . . . He was scared too. He lay there begging us to send for a doctor. The doctor soon arrived . . . and saved the unlucky boy . . .

MERCHUTKINA: Your excellency, couldn't you get my husband's job back?

SHIPUCHIN: No, I can't stand it! (*Cries.*) Can't stand it! (*Stretches out his arms to Hirin in despair.*) Throw her out! Throw her out, I beseech you!

HIRIN: (*Approaching Tatyana Alekseyevna.*) Get out!

SHIPUCHIN: Not her, that one . . . that awful one . . . (*Points to Merchutkina.*) That one!

HIRIN: (*Not understanding him; to Tatyana Alekseyevna.*) Get out of here! (*Stamps his feet.*) Get out of here!

TATYANA ALEKSEYEVNA: What! What did you say? Have you lost your mind?

SHIPUCHIN: This is awful! I am so unlucky! Chase her out! Chase her out of here!

HIRIN: *(To Tatyana Alekseyevna.)* Out! I'll cripple you for life! I'll mutilate you! I'll commit a crime!

TATYANA ALEKSEYEVNA: *(Runs away from him; he follows her.)* How dare you! You lout! *(She yells.)* Andrey! Save me! Andrey! *(Trembles.)*

SHIPUCHIN: *(Runs after them.)* Stop it! I beg you! Quiet! Have mercy on me.

HIRIN: *(Chases Merchutkina.)* Get out of here! Catch her! Beat her. Cut her up into little pieces!

SHIPUCHIN: *(Yells.)* Stop it! I beg you! I beseech you!

MERCHUTKINA: Saints in Heaven . . . Saints in Heaven . . . *(Trembles.)* Saints in Heaven . . .

TATYANA ALEKSEYEVNA: *(Yells.)* Save me! Save me! . . . Ah, ah . . . I'll faint! I'll faint! *(Jumps on the desk, then falls onto the couch, moaning as in a faint.)*

HIRIN: *(Chases Merchutkina.)* Beat her! Skin her alive! Cut her to pieces!

MERCHUTKINA: Ah, ah . . . Saints in Heaven, everything's going black! Ah! *(Falls senseless into the arms of Shipuchin.)*

A knock at the door and a voice offstage: "The Deputation!"

SHIPUCHIN: Deputation . . . reputation . . . occupation . . .

HIRIN: *(Stamps his feet.)* Get out, go to the devil! *(Wringing his sleeves.)* Let me at her! I could commit a crime!

Enter the deputation of five men; all in frock coats. One carries the speech, bound in velvet, another carries the silver cup. The clerks look in from the outer office. Tatyana Alekseyevna is on the sofa; Merchutkina is in the arms of Shipuchin; both women are quietly moaning.

A MEMBER OF THE BANK'S BOARD: *(Reads loudly.)* "Our most respected and dear Andrey Andreyevich! In casting a retrospective glance over the past of our financial establishment and in reviewing intellectually the history of its continual development, we receive a most gratifying impression. It's true, in the initial stages of its existence only small increases in the basic capital, an absence of serious endeavor, and also vague goals led us to ask Hamlet's question: 'To be or not to be?'[34] And, at one time, helpful voices resoundingly answered: 'Close the bank.' But now we have you as the head of our establishment. Your knowledge, energy, and constant tact are the reasons for our unusual success and rare blossoming. The reputation of the bank . . . (*Coughs.*) The reputation of the bank . . ."

MERCHUTKINA: (*Moans.*) Oh! Oh!

TATYANA ALEKSEYEVNA: (*Moans.*) Water! Water!

THE MEMBER OF THE BANK'S BOARD: (*Continues.*) "The reputation . . . (*Coughs.*) The reputation of the bank was raised by you to such heights that our establishment can now compete with the best foreign establishments . . ."

SHIPUCHIN: Deputation . . . reputation . . . occupation . . . "Two friends one night went walking. About their affairs were talking." "Oh, tell me not your young life's ruined. Forget, forget your jealousy of me . . ."[35]

THE MEMBER OF THE BANK'S BOARD: (*Continues in embarrassment.*) "Thus, in casting an objective look at the present, most respected and dear Andrey Andreyevich, we . . ." (*Lowering his voice.*) Under the circumstances, we'd better come back later . . . Later, I think would be better . . .

The deputation leaves in embarrassment.

Curtain.

---

34. A reference to the famous soliloquy in Shakespeare's *Hamlet*, in which the title character contemplates suicide.

35. The first quotation is from a fable in verse about a dog by Ivan Andreyevich Krylov (1769–1844); the second is from a poem, "Gypsy Song," by Nikolay Alekseyevich Nekrasov (1821–1878).

The Major Plays

The Seagull

A Comedy in Four Acts

[Written in 1896, *The Seagull* premiered on October 17, 1896, in St. Petersburg, Russia. The play's most famous production opened at the Moscow Art Theatre on October 17, 1898, under the direction of Konstantin Stanislavsky, who also played Trigorin. Olga Knipper took the role of Arkadina. Playing the role of Treplev was Vsevolod Meyerhold, whose innovative approach to directing would soon launch the "new forms" that his character (Treplev) calls for in the play. Chekhov described his play as "a comedy [with] three women's roles, six men, four acts, a landscape (a view of a lake), many conversations about literature, little action, and a ton of love."[1] Two Russian émigrés, Pavel Orlenov and Alla Nazimova, first staged *The Seagull* in the United States in 1905 in Russian. The first English language staging of the play in the United States was in 1916. I created the translation that follows for John David Lutz, whose production at the University of Evansville, Indiana, won a 1997 Kennedy Center Achievement Award for Translation from the American College Theatre Festival.[2] —SMC]

The Characters
Irína Nikoláyevna Arkádina, her married name Trépleva, an actress.
Konstantín Gavrílovich Tréplev, her son, a young man. [His nickname is Kóstya; his surname sounds like "to speak drivel" or "to blather."]
Pyótr Nikoláyevich Sórin, her brother. [His nickname, Petrúshka, is also the name of a Russian puppet character.]
Nína Mikhaílovna Zaréchnaya, a young girl, the daughter of a rich landowner. [Her last name means "from across the river."]
Ilyá Afanásyevich Shamráyev, a retired lieutenant, Sorin's steward.
Polína Andréyevna, his wife.
Másha, his daughter. [Her formal name is María Ilínichna; her nicknames are Másha and the even sweeter Máshenka.]

---

1. Chekhov to A. S. Suvorin, October 21, 1895, in *Pis'ma* [Letters], vol. 6 (Moscow: Nauka, 1978), 85.
2. One reviewer wrote of this production: "The last time I reviewed a production of *The Seagull*, it broke my heart. This time, I understood why Chekhov called it 'a comedy in four acts.' Sharon Carnicke's translation highlights Chekhov's bitter humor." Sandra Knipe, review of John Lutz's production of *The Seagull*, *The Evansville Press*, September 25, 1996.

Borís Alekséyevich Trigórin, a writer. [His last name means "three mountains."]

Yevgény Sergéyevich Dorn, a doctor. [His last name sounds German; many doctors in Russia were educated in Germany.]

Semyón Semyónovich Medvedénko, a teacher. [His last name comes from the Russian word for "bear."]

Yákov, a workman.

A cook

A maid

The action takes place on Sorin's estate. Two years pass between Acts III and IV.

Act I

A section of the park on Sorin's estate. A wide pathway leading from the auditorium into the depths of the park toward a lake, which is completely obstructed from view by a stage. The stage has been put together hastily in preparation for an amateur play. To the left and right of the stage are bushes. There are several chairs and a table. The sun has just set. Yakov and other workmen are on the stage behind the closed curtain; their coughing and banging around can be heard.

Masha and Medvedenko, who are returning from a walk, enter from the left.

MEDVEDENKO: Why do you always wear black?

MASHA: I'm in mourning for my life. I'm unhappy.

MEDVEDENKO: Why? (*Thoughtfully.*) I don't understand... You're healthy. Your father is not rich, but he's well off. My life is much harder than yours. I make all of twenty-three rubles a month, and most of it goes toward a pension, but I don't wear black. (*Sits down.*)

MASHA: It's not the money. Even a beggar can be happy.

MEDVEDENKO: In theory, yes, but in practice, no. There's me, my mother, my two sisters, my little brother, and a salary of only twenty-three rubles. We have to eat and drink, don't we? We need tea and sugar, don't we? We need tobacco, don't we? We have to make ends meet.

MASHA: (*Glancing at the stage.*) The play will begin soon.

MEDVEDENKO: Yes. Zarechnaya will be acting, and Konstantin Gavrilovich wrote the play. They are in love with one another, and today their souls will merge in one artistic vision. But your soul and mine have no points of common contact. I love you. I can't sit at home yearning for you, so every day I walk six miles here and six miles back again, and all I get is indifferentism from you. I understand. I have no means, and yet I have a big family . . . Who would want to marry a man who can't put food on the table?

MASHA: Nonsense. (*Takes snuff.*[3]) Your love touches me, but I can't return it, that's all. (*Offers him snuff.*) Have some.

MEDVEDENKO: I don't feel like it.

Pause.

MASHA: It's humid. There'll probably be a storm tonight. You're always philosophizing, or talking about money. According to you, poverty is the only source of unhappiness, but according to me, it's a thousand times easier to wear rags and to beg, than to . . . But you wouldn't understand . . .

Sorin and Treplev enter from the right.

SORIN: (*Leaning on a cane.*) Somehow, my boy, I just don't feel like myself in the country, I'll never get used to being here. Last night I went to bed at ten, and today I woke up at nine feeling like my brain was stuck to my skull from too much sleep, and all that. (*Laughs.*) And after dinner, I accidentally dozed off again, and now I'm a wreck. It's a nightmare, when all is said and done . . .

TREPLEV: It's true, you should live in town. (*Seeing Masha and Medvedenko.*) Sir, madam, when the play begins, we'll call you, but you can't stay here now. Please leave.

SORIN: (*To Masha.*) Maria Ilinichna, please ask your papa to untie the dog at night so she won't howl. My sister couldn't sleep again last night.

---

3. A powdered and fermented form of tobacco, usually inhaled through the nostril.

MASHA: Speak to my father yourself, I won't take sides. Spare me, please. (*To Medvedenko.*) Let's go!

MEDVEDENKO: (*To Treplev.*) So you will call us before it starts.

They both exit.

SORIN: That means the dog will howl all night again. The same old story. I've never gotten what I wanted in the country. When I'd get a month off, I'd come out here to relax, and all that, but as soon as I'd arrive, or even when I started thinking about coming here, there would be all kinds of fuss and bother. (*Laughs.*) Well, I always looked forward to coming out here . . . But now that I'm retired, I have nowhere else to go, when all is said and done. Like it or not, you have to live somewhere . . .

YAKOV: (*To Treplev.*) Konstantin Gavrilovich, we're going to take a swim.

TREPLEV: Fine, but be back in ten minutes. (*Looks at his watch.*) We'll be starting soon.

YAKOV: All right. (*Exits.*)

TREPLEV: (*Glancing at the stage.*) There's a theater for you! A curtain, the first set of wings, the second, and then an empty space. No set. Just a direct view of the lake and the horizon. We'll raise the curtain at exactly half past eight, when the moon rises.

SORIN: Magnificent.

TREPLEV: If Zarechnaya is late, then, of course, the whole effect will be spoiled. She should have been here by now. Her father and stepmother keep watch, so it's hard for her to get out of the house. It's like a prison. (*Straightens his uncle's tie.*) Your hair and beard need combing. You need a haircut . . .

SORIN: (*Combing his beard.*) It's the tragedy of my life. Even in my youth I always looked like I'd been out drinking, and all that. Women never fell in love with me. (*Sitting down.*) Why is my sister in such a bad mood?

TREPLEV: Why? She's bored. (*Sits down next to his uncle.*) She's jealous. Of me, of my production, of my play, because Zarechnaya, not she, is acting in it. She hasn't even read my play, but she already hates it.

SORIN: (*Laughs.*) It's just your imagination, that's all . . .

TREPLEV: She's actually annoyed that here on this little stage Zarechnaya will be the star, not her. (*Looking at his watch.*) A psychological curiosity—my mother. She's unquestionably talented, intelligent, able to sob over a book. She knows all of Nekrásov[4] by heart, cares for the sick as if she were an angel. But praise Duse[5] in her presence. Oh no! You can only praise her, only write about her, applaud her, go into ecstasies about her exceptional performance in *La dame aux camélias,* or in *The Fumes of Life.*[6] But here in the country she can't get these drugs. She misses them, and has temper tantrums, and we all become her enemies, all of us are to blame. Then too she's superstitious. She's afraid of three candles[7] and the number thirteen. She's also stingy. She has seven hundred thousand rubles in a bank in Odessa,[8] I know that for a fact. But ask for a loan and she starts to cry.

SORIN: You imagine that your mother won't like your play, and so you worry about it, and all that. Calm down, your mother adores you.

TREPLEV: (*Pulling the petals off a flower.*) She loves me, she loves me not, she loves me, she loves me not, she loves me, she loves me not. (*Laughs.*) You see, my mother does not love me. Of course not! She wants to live, to love, to wear beautiful clothes, and I'm twenty-five years old. I constantly remind her that she is no longer young. When I'm not around, she's only thirty-two years old, but when I'm nearby, she's forty-three, and for that she hates me. She also knows that I do not acknowledge the

---

4. Nikolay Alekseyevich Nekrasov (1821–1878), a Russian poet, known for his democratic and socially radical poems about the downtrodden poor.

5. Eleonora Duse (1858–1924), Italian actress of worldwide fame, who defined natural acting in contrast to her more histrionic contemporary Sarah Bernhardt (1844–1923).

6. *La dame aux camélias* (1852, known in English as *Camille*) is a play based upon a novel by the French writer Alexandre Dumas, *fils;* it tells the story of a prostitute who leaves her lover to save his reputation. As she lies dying of tuberculosis, he returns to her. Both Duse and Bernhardt toured Russia, playing the title role. *The Fumes of Life* (1884) is a Russian melodrama about a fallen woman.

7. Three candles surround the corpse at Russian funerals.

8. A large city in the Ukraine (near Kiev, where Treplev's father lived).

theater. She loves the theater, she thinks that she's serving humanity and art, but in my opinion, today's theater offers nothing but hackneyed characters and formulaic plots. When the curtain rises, there's a room with three walls, illuminated by artificial light, and then the actors—who consider themselves high priests of art—show us how people eat, drink, love, walk around, and wear their jackets. And when you try to find a point to their petty words and banal scenes, the moral turns out to be insignificant and comfortably domestic. And when they serve up the same thing over and over again in thousands of variations, I want to run away, like Maupassant ran from the Eiffel tower,[9] because its banality gave him a headache.

SORIN: We can't do without the theater.

TREPLEV: We need new forms. New forms. And if we can't get them, then we'd do better with nothing at all. (*Looks at his watch.*) I love my mother, love her deeply, but she leads a senseless life, always fussing over that author, with her name always in the papers. I'm tired of it. Sometimes I think I'm being selfish. I regret that my mother is a famous actress and I think that if she were just an ordinary woman I'd be happier. Uncle, can you imagine anything more awful or more absurd than my usual position in the house? Surrounded by all her famous guests—actors and writers—I am the only nobody. They tolerate me because I am her son, and that's all. Who am I? What am I? I left the university after my third year due to circumstances, as they say, over which I had no control.[10] I have no particular talents, no money, not even a kopeck, and on my passport I'm described as lower middle-class from Kiev.[11] My father really is lower middle-class from Kiev, even though he was also a famous actor. So, whenever I sit in her drawing room, I feel that all those actors and writers, who deign to

---

9. The French writer Guy de Maupassant (1850–1893) became well-known in Russia. He considered the technological design of the Eiffel Tower (constructed in 1889) ugly.

10. Treplev implies that he was expelled, perhaps for poor grades or, more likely, for liberal political activity.

11. Tsarist Russia defined economic classes as discrete "ranks," which were printed in people's passports as part of their identity. Treplev's rank is one up from the bottom rank of free peasants. Kiev is the capital of the Ukraine.

treat me so kindly, are also measuring my insignificance. I know what they're thinking and I feel humiliated . . .

SORIN: Speaking of her guests, please, tell me about this author. I can't make him out. He's so quiet.

TREPLEV: He's an intelligent man, simple, a little, you know, melancholic. He's very decent. He's not yet forty, but he's already famous and very well off . . . As for his writing, well . . . What can I say? It's nice, rather talented . . . but . . . after reading Tolstóy or Zóla,[12] you don't want Trigorin.

SORIN: I love authors, my boy. I once passionately wanted two things: I wanted to get married and I wanted to become a writer, but I didn't succeed at either one. Yes, it would have been pleasant to be even a second-rate writer, when all is said and done.

TREPLEV: (*Listening.*) I hear footsteps . . . (*Hugs his uncle.*) I can't live without her . . . Even the sound of her footsteps is beautiful . . . I'm insanely happy. (*Quickly goes to meet Nina Zarechnaya, who enters.*) My enchantress, my dream . . .

NINA: (*Excited.*) I'm not late . . . I can't possibly be late . . .

TREPLEV: (*Kissing her hands.*) No, no, no . . .

NINA: I was worried all day, so frightened! I was afraid that my father wouldn't let me out . . . But he and my stepmother just left. I saw the sky getting red, and the moon about to rise, so I whipped the horse, I kept whipping him. (*Laughs.*) I'm so glad. (*Warmly shakes Sorin's hand.*)

SORIN: (*Laughs.*) Your little eyes are full of tears . . . Now, now! That's not good!

NINA: So they are . . . Look how hard I'm breathing. I have to leave in half an hour, let's hurry. I can't stay, I can't, so please God, don't try to keep me. My father doesn't know I'm here.

TREPLEV: It's time to begin anyway. I'll call everybody.

SORIN: I'll go for them, and all that. I'll go right now. (*Walks to the right, singing.*) "In France there were two gen-er-als . . ."[13]

---

12. Lev Nikolaevich Tolstoy (1828–1910) is usually considered Russia's greatest novelist. The French novelist Emile Zola (1840–1902) promoted "naturalism" as an innovative literary style.

13. Robert Schumann's song, "Two Grenadiers" (1827).

(*Looks back.*) Once I began singing like that, and the Assistant Prosecutor told me, "You have a strong voice, sir . . ." Then he thought better of it, and added, "But . . . not a good one." (*Laughs and exits.*)

NINA: My father and his wife won't let me come here. They say it's bohemian . . . They're afraid that I will want to become an actress . . . But I am drawn here to this lake, like a seagull . . . My heart is full of you. (*Looks around.*)

TREPLEV: We're alone.

NINA: Someone's over there, I think . . .

TREPLEV: No one.

A kiss.

NINA: What kind of tree is that?

TREPLEV: An elm.

NINA: Why is the elm so dark?

TREPLEV: It's evening, and everything looks dark. Don't leave so soon, I beg you.

NINA: I can't.

TREPLEV: And what if I go with you, Nina? I'll stand in the garden all night and look at your window.

NINA: You can't. The watchman will notice you. Trésor[14] is not used to you and will bark.

TREPLEV: I love you.

NINA: Shhh . . .

TREPLEV: (*Hearing foot steps.*) Who's there? Is it you, Yakov?

YAKOV: (*Behind the stage.*) It's me.

TREPLEV: Take your places. It's time. Has the moon risen?

YAKOV: It has.

TREPLEV: Do you have the methane? And the sulphur? When the red eyes appear, there has to be a smell of sulphur. (*To Nina.*) Go on, everything is ready. Are you nervous? . . .

---

14. "Treasure" (French). Chekhov's editor, A. S. Suvorin, had a dog named Trésor.

NINA: Yes, very. Your mama—that's nothing, I'm not afraid of her, but Trigorin is here . . . Acting in front of him frightens me, I feel embarrassed . . . A famous writer . . . Is he young?

TREPLEV: Yes.

NINA: What wonderful stories he writes!

TREPLEV: (*Coldly.*) I don't know. I haven't read them.

NINA: It's hard to act in your play. There are no living characters in it.

TREPLEV: Living characters! You have to portray life not as it is, and not as it should be, but as we see it in our dreams.

NINA: There's no action in your play, it's only a staged reading. And in my opinion, a play should definitely have love in it . . .

They both exit behind the stage. Polina Andreyevna and Dorn enter.

POLINA ANDREYEVNA: It's getting damp. Go back and put on your galoshes.

DORN: I'm hot.

POLINA ANDREYEVNA: You don't take care of yourself. You're stubborn. You're a doctor and you know perfectly well that damp air is bad for you. You don't take care of yourself in order to make me suffer. Yesterday you sat out on the terrace all evening as if on purpose . . .

DORN: (*Sings softly.*) "Never say that youth is wasted . . ."[15]

POLINA ANDREYEVNA: You were so engrossed in your conversation with Irina Nikolayevna . . . you didn't notice the cold. Admit it, you find her attractive . . .

DORN: I'm fifty-five years old.

POLINA ANDREYEVNA: Nonsense, that's not old for a man. You are very well preserved, and women still find you attractive.

DORN: What of it?

---

15. Dorn sings snatches from popular romantic ballads and operatic songs throughout the play. This one sets to music a poem by the poet Nikolay Alekseyevich Nekrasov.

POLINA ANDREYEVNA: All you men fall down on your knees before an actress. All of you!

DORN: (*Sings softly.*) "Once again, I kneel before you, my beloved . . ."[16] If society loves actors and treats them differently than, for example, merchants, that's just as it should be. That's idealism.

POLINA ANDREYEVNA: Women have always fallen in love with you and clung to you. Is that also idealism?

DORN: (*Shrugging his shoulders.*) What of it? My relations with women have always been good. They saw in me an excellent doctor. Ten, fifteen years ago, you'll remember, I was the only decent obstetrician in the whole province. Then too, I have always been an honest man.

POLINA ANDREYEVNA: (*Takes his arm.*) My darling!

DORN: Quiet. They're coming.

Enter Arkadina on Sorin's arm, Trigorin, Shamrayev, Medvedenko, and Masha,

SHAMRAYEV: In 1873, in Poltáva, at the fair, she gave an amazing performance.[17] Sheer ecstasy! A miraculous performance! Madam, would you by any chance know what ever happened to Pável Semyónovich Chádin, the comic actor? His Rasplyúev was inimitable, better than Sadóvsky's.[18] Where is he now?

ARKADINA: You are always asking about antediluvians. How should I know? (*Sits down.*)

SHAMRAYEV: (*Sighing.*) Páshka Chadin! Nobody like him now. The theater's gone downhill, Irina Nikolayevna! Before there were mighty oaks, but now we see only stumps.

---

16. A popular Russian serenade.
17. Poltava is a large manufacturing town in the Ukraine. Annual fairs in Russia featured entertainment like puppet shows, dancing bears, and theatrical presentations.
18. Rasplyuev is a well-known comic role for older actors in *Krechinsky's Wedding* (1855), a satirical play by Alexander Vasilyevich Sukhovo-Kobylin. Prov Mikhailovich Sadovsky (1818–1872) was a leading comic actor in Moscow who originated the role of Rasplyuev. The fictional name "Chadin" means "fumes" as in *The Fumes of Life* mentioned earlier.

DORN: It may be true that there are fewer stars now, but the average actor has gotten much better.

SHAMRAYEV: I can't agree with you. But then, it's a matter of taste. *De gustibus aut bene, aut nihil.*[19]

Treplev comes out from behind the stage.

ARKADINA: (*To her son.*) My dear son, when will it begin?

TREPLEV: In a minute. Patience please.

ARKADINA: (*Recites from Shakespeare's Hamlet.*[20]) "My son! Thou turnst my eyes into my very soul, and there I see such black and grainèd spots, as will not leave their tinct!"

TREPLEV: (*Paraphrases from Hamlet.*) Why did you then surrender to vice, and seek love in the depths of crime?

A horn sounds from behind the stage.

TREPLEV: Ladies and Gentlemen, we begin! Attention please!

Pause.

TREPLEV: I begin. (*Knocks with a stick and speaks loudly.*) O ye esteemed, old shades, who haunt this lake at night, put us to sleep, and let us dream of what will be in two hundred thousand years!

SORIN: Nothing will be in two hundred thousand years.

TREPLEV: So then, let us view that nothing.

ARKADINA: Let us. We are asleep.

The curtain rises revealing a view of the lake; the moon is on the horizon, reflected in the water; Nina Zarechnaya sits on a large rock, dressed all in white.

NINA: People, lions, eagles and partridges, horned deer, geese, spiders, silent fishes that dwell under water, starfish, and those

---

19. "About taste—it's either good, or not" (Latin).
20. Act III, scene 2, when Hamlet confronts his mother about his father's murder.

creatures invisible to the naked eye—in short, all life, all life, having completed its sad cycle, has died out . . . For millennia the earth has born no living being, and this poor moon lights her lamp in vain. In meadows, no longer do cranes call, and no May beetles are heard in linden groves. Cold, cold, cold. Empty, empty, empty. Terrible, terrible, terrible. (*Pause.*) The bodies of all living beings have returned to dust. And this eternal matter has become stones, water, clouds, while all their spirits have merged into one. A common world soul—this is who I am . . . who I am . . . In me are the spirits of Alexander the Great, and Caesar, and Shakespeare, and Napoleon, and the lowliest worm. In me, human consciousness merges with animal instinct, and I remember everything, everything, everything, and I experience every life anew.

Marsh fires appear.

ARKADINA: (*Softly.*) This is decadent stuff.[21]

TREPLEV: (*Imploring and reproaching her.*) Mama!

NINA: I am alone. Once every hundred years I open my lips to speak, and my voice echoes despondently in this void, and no one hears . . . And ye, Pale Fires, do not hear . . . Before dawn the putrid marsh begets you, and you wander until dusk, without thought, without will, without the heartbeat of life. Fearing that life might spring from you, the Devil—the father of eternal matter—conducts a constant interchange of atoms in you, as in stones, as in water. You are constantly changing. In the universe, spirit alone remains constant and unchanging. (*Pause.*) Like a prisoner thrown into a deep and empty well, I know not where I am, nor what awaits me. All is hidden from me, but this: that eventually I am fated to win my persistent, ruthless battle with the Devil, who is the principle of material forces. And after that, matter and spirit will merge in beautiful harmony, and Soul will reign. But this will only gradually come to pass, only after a long, long succession of millennia,

---

21. Symbolism—called "decadent" by its critics—spurred dramatic reform at the turn of the twentieth century by creating a body of nonrealistic, metaphysical plays. Treplev's play parodies the abstract and static qualities of symbolist plays.

when the moon, the bright star Sirius, and the earth itself will have returned to dust . . . Until that time, horror, horror . . .

Pause; two red points appear against the background of the lake.

NINA: My powerful opponent, the Devil, approaches. I see his terrible, blood red eyes . . .

ARKADINA: I smell sulphur. Is that necessary?

TREPLEV: Yes.

ARKADINA: (*Laughs.*) Yes, it's an effect.

TREPLEV: Mama!

NINA: He misses human beings . . .

POLINA ANDREYEVNA: (*To Dorn.*) You took off your hat. Put it on or you'll catch cold.

ARKADINA: The doctor took off his hat to the Devil, the father of eternal matter!

TREPLEV: (*Exploding, loudly.*) The play's over! Enough! Curtain!

ARKADINA: Why are you angry?

TREPLEV: Enough! Curtain! Lower the curtain! (*Stomping his foot.*) Curtain!

The curtain closes.

TREPLEV: I'm guilty! I forgot that only the chosen few can write plays and act. I infringed on the monopoly! I'm . . . I . . . (*Wants to say something more, but merely waves his hand and exits left.*)

ARKADINA: What's the matter with him?

SORIN: Mother in Heaven, Irina, you shouldn't treat a young man's pride like that.

ARKADINA: What did I do?

SORIN: You offended him.

ARKADINA: He told us himself that his play was a joke, and so I treated it like a joke.

SORIN: All the same . . .

ARKADINA: Now, it seems, he has written a masterpiece! If you please! And arranged this spectacle and fumigated us with sulphur not as a joke, but as a demonstration . . . He wanted to teach us how we must write and what we must act. This is becoming a bore. These constant gibes against me, these barbs, if you will, are tiring! He's a capricious, conceited boy.

SORIN: He wanted to please you.

ARKADINA: Oh yes? Then why not choose an ordinary play, instead of making us listen to this decadent raving? I'd be happy to listen to raving for the sake of a joke, but instead we get these pretensions to new forms, to a new era in art. And in my opinion, there are no new forms here, only bad temper.

TRIGORIN: Everyone writes as he likes, and as he can.

ARKADINA: Let him write as he likes, and as he can. Only leave me in peace.

DORN: Jupiter,[22] you are angry . . .

ARKADINA: I am not Jupiter, I am a woman. (*Lights a cigarette.*) And I'm not angry, just annoyed, that a young man could spend his time in such a boring fashion. I didn't mean to offend him.

MEDVEDENKO: No one can actually separate spirit from matter, since spirit itself, I think, is the sum total of material atoms. (*Eagerly, to Trigorin.*) Come to think of it, why doesn't someone write a play describing how we ordinary teachers live, and then act it out on stage? It's a hard, hard life!

ARKADINA: That's right, but let's not talk about plays or atoms. It's such a wonderful evening! Do you hear singing? (*Listens.*) How nice!

POLINA ANDREYEVNA: It's from the opposite shore.

Pause.

ARKADINA: (*To Trigorin.*) Sit next to me. Ten years, fifteen years ago, here on the lake, you could hear music and singing almost every night. There are six estates on these shores. I remember laughter, noise, shooting, and always romance, romance . . .

---

22. The chief god of the ancient Romans who controls lightning.

The *jeune première*[23] and the idol of all six houses was always this man here, let me introduce you. (*Nodding toward Dorn.*) Doctor Yevgeny Sergeyevich. Now he's charming, but then he was irresistible. But my conscience is bothering me. Why did I hurt my poor boy's feelings? I'm uneasy. (*Loudly.*) Kostya! Son! Kostya!

MASHA: I'll go look for him.

ARKADINA: Please do, dear.

MASHA: (*Going toward the left.*) Ooo-hoo! Konstantin Gavrilovich! . . . Ooo-hoo! (*Exits.*)

NINA: (*Coming out from behind the stage.*) Evidently, we won't be continuing, so I might as well come out. Good evening! (*Kisses Arkadina and Polina Andreyevna.*)

SORIN: Brava! Brava!

ARKADINA: Brava! Brava! We loved your performance. With your looks, with your marvelous voice, you shouldn't wither away here in the country. It would be a sin. You have talent. Do you hear? You must go on the stage!

NINA: Oh, it is my dream! (*Sighing.*) But it will never happen.

ARKADINA: Who knows? Allow me to introduce you. Boris Alekseyevich Trigorin.

NINA: Ah, I am so glad . . . (*Shyly.*) I always read your . . .

ARKADINA: (*Sitting her down next to them.*) Don't be shy, dear. He's famous, but he's a simple soul. You see, he's shy too.

DORN: I suggest that we raise the curtain; it won't be so eerie.

SHAMRAYEV: (*Loudly.*) Yakov, my boy, raise the curtain!

The curtain is raised.

NINA: (*To Trigorin.*) It's a strange play, isn't it?

TRIGORIN: I didn't understand anything. But I watched you with pleasure. You acted so sincerely. And the set was beautiful. (*Pause.*) I bet there are a lot of fish in that lake.

NINA: Yes.

---

23. French term for the romantic leading man in a play.

TRIGORIN: I love to fish. For me, there is no greater pleasure than sitting on the bank until evening, watching a float.

NINA: But I would think that once you'd experienced the pleasure of creativity, all other pleasures would disappear.

ARKADINA: (*Laughing.*) Don't talk like that. When people say nice things to him, he just goes to pieces.

SHAMRAYEV: I remember, once in Moscow, at the opera, the famous Silva[24] sang a low C. And, as if on purpose, one of the basses from our church choir happened to be sitting in the balcony. You can imagine our surprise, when suddenly from the balcony we hear, "Bravo, Silva," one full octave lower . . . Like this: (*In a low bass voice.*) "Bravo, Silva . . ." The whole theater froze.

Pause.

DORN: An angel of silence has flown by.[25]

NINA: It's time for me to go. Goodbye.

ARKADINA: Where? Where are you going so early? We won't let you go.

NINA: Papa is waiting for me.

ARKADINA: What a man, really . . . (*They kiss.*) Well, what can be done. It's a pity, a pity to let you go.

NINA: If only you knew how difficult it is for me to leave!

ARKADINA: Someone should see you off, little one.

NINA: (*Frightened.*) Oh no, no!

SORIN: (*Imploring her.*) Please stay!

NINA: I can't, Pyotr Nikolayevich!

SORIN: Stay for one more hour, that's all. Come on . . .

NINA: (*Thinking it over, through tears.*) I can't! (*Shaking his hand and quickly exiting.*)

ARKADINA: She's such an unfortunate girl. They say that when her mother died, her father inherited the entire estate, every

---

24. A tenor from Belgium who toured Russia as an opera star in the nineteenth century.
25. A common saying when a conversation falls silent.

single kopeck, and now the girl has nothing, especially since her father has already written a will leaving everything to his second wife. It's shocking.

DORN: Yes, if truth be told, her dear papa is a real swine.

SORIN: (*Rubbing his cold hands.*) Let's go in, friends, it's getting damp out here. And my legs are aching.

ARKADINA: Your legs are as stiff as boards, you can hardly walk. Well, let's go, you poor old man.

SHAMRAYEV: (*Offering his arm to his wife.*) Madam?

SORIN: I heard the dog howling again last night. (*To Shamrayev.*) Ilya Afanasyevich, would you please untie her?

SHAMRAYEV: I can't, Pyotr Nikolayevich, I'm afraid that thieves will break into the barn. I store the grain in there. (*Walking next to Medvedenko.*) Yes, a whole octave lower, "Bravo, Silva!" And he wasn't a real singer, only a member of the church choir.

MEDVEDENKO: How much does a member of the church choir make?

All exit, except for Dorn.

DORN: (*Alone.*) I don't know. Perhaps I don't understand anything or I've lost my mind, but I liked the play. There's something in it. When the girl spoke of being alone and then, when the red eyes of the Devil appeared, my hands trembled with excitement. It's fresh, it's naïve . . . I think he's coming this way. I want to encourage him.

TREPLEV: (*Enters.*) No one's here.

DORN: I am.

TREPLEV: Mashenka's been searching for me all through the park. Intolerable creature.

DORN: Konstantin Gavrilovich, I very much liked your play. It's rather strange, and of course, I didn't see how it ends, but it has left a strong impression on me. You are a talented person, and you must continue.

Treplev warmly shakes his hand and then impulsively hugs him.

DORN: Whew, how skittish you are! There are tears in your eyes . . . Now what was it I wanted to say? You have chosen a subject from the realm of abstract ideas. That's as it should be, since it is a work of art, and art must absolutely express some kind of great thought. It must be about something serious and beautiful. How pale you are!

TREPLEV: So, you're saying, that I should continue?

DORN: Yes . . . But continue to write only about what is important and eternal. You know, I've lived my life with variety and gusto, and I've been content. But if I had been once able to experience the spiritual exaltation which artists must feel when they create, I would have despised this material shell and everything that belongs to it. I would have soared above the earthly realm.

TREPLEV: I'm sorry, where's Zarechnaya?

DORN: And there's something else too. A work of art must have a clear and definite point. You must know why you write. Otherwise, if you travel down the road of art without a definite aim, you will lose your way, and your talent will destroy you.

TREPLEV: (*Impatiently.*) Where's Zarechnaya?

DORN: She went home.

TREPLEV: (*In despair.*) What should I do? I want to see her . . . I have to see her . . . I'll go there . . .

Masha enters.

DORN: (*To Treplev.*) Calm down, my friend.

TREPLEV: But I have to go. I must go there.

MASHA: Go home, Konstantin Gavrilovich. Your mother is waiting for you. She's uneasy.

TREPLEV: Tell her that I've gone. I beg you all, leave me in peace. Leave me alone! Don't follow me!

DORN: But, but, but, dear . . . don't be so . . . It's not good.

TREPLEV: (*Through tears.*) Goodbye, Doctor. Thank you . . . (*Exits.*)

DORN: (*Sighing.*) Youth, youth!

MASHA: Whenever there's nothing to say, they say, "Youth, youth . . ." (*Takes snuff.*)

DORN: (*Takes the snuff box away from her and throws it into the bushes.*) That's disgusting!

Pause.

DORN: They seem to be playing a game inside. We should go in.

MASHA: Wait a minute.

DORN: What is it?

MASHA: I want to talk to you again. I feel like telling you . . . (*Getting upset.*) I don't love my father . . . But I am fond of you. For some reason, with all my heart, I feel close to you . . . Help me. Help me, or I'll do something stupid, I'll make a mockery of my life, I'll ruin it . . . I can't take it any longer . . .

DORN: How? How can I help you?

MASHA: I'm suffering. No one, no one knows how I'm suffering! (*Places her head on his chest, softly.*) I love Konstantin.

DORN: How skittish you all are! How skittish! And how much love you have . . . Oh, it must be that enchanted lake! (*Tenderly.*) But what can I do, my child? What? What?

Curtain.

Act II

A croquet lawn. In the distance to the right, a house with a large terrace. To the left, the lake, glimmering in the sun. Flowerbeds. It is midday. It is hot. Beside the lawn, in the shade of an old linden tree, Arkadina, Dorn, and Masha sit on a bench. Dorn has an open book in his lap.

ARKADINA: (*To Masha.*) Let's stand up!

They both stand.

ARKADINA: Let's stand side by side. You are twenty-two years old, and I am almost twice that. Yevgeny Sergeyevich, which of us looks younger?

DORN: You, of course.

ARKADINA: Well, well . . . And why is that? Because I work, I experience emotions and sensations, I am in constant motion. But you always sit in one spot, you don't live . . . I have a rule: don't anticipate the future. I never think about old age, or death. What will be, will be.

MASHA: But I feel like I was born a long, long time ago. I drag my life after me like the endless train of a dress . . . And often I feel that I haven't the will to go on living. (*Sits.*) Of course, it's all nonsense. I should shake myself out of this mood.

DORN: (*Sings softly.*) "Speak to her of me, and pretty flowers . . ."[26]

ARKADINA: Then too, I am as correct as an Englishwoman, my dear. I keep myself in check, as they say, and always dress and have my hair done *comme il faut*.[27] Would I ever allow myself to leave the house, even if only to go into the garden, dressed casually or with my hair a mess? Never. That's how I keep myself so young, why I've never become dowdy, or let myself go the way some do . . . (*Walks about the lawn, hands on her hips.*) You see—light as a feather. I can still play a girl of fifteen.

DORN: Well, madam, I will continue reading.[28] (*Takes up the book.*) We stopped at the corn merchants and the rats . . .

ARKADINA: And the rats. Yes, read on. (*Sits.*) But no, why not give it to me? I'll read. It's my turn. (*Takes the book and looks at it.*) And the rats . . . Here it is . . . (*Reads.*) "And, of course, it is as dangerous for the social elite to pamper novelists and entice them into their midst, as it is for corn merchants to breed rats in their barns. And yet novelists are much admired. When a woman chooses a writer, whom she wishes to seduce, she lays siege to him with compliments, courtesies, and favors . . ." Well, that may be true among the French perhaps, but we don't behave like that, we make no such plans. Here, a woman usu-

---

26. From the French opera *Faust* (1859) by Charles Gounod.
27. "As it should be" (French).
28. They are reading aloud to each other from French writer Guy de Maupassant's diary of his Mediterranean cruise, *Sur l'eau* (*On the Water*, 1888). Arkadina stops reading just before Maupassant's detailed description of the specific machinations that a woman used to seduce him.

ally falls madly in love, before she sets out to seduce a writer. You need look no further than myself and Trigorin . . .

Sorin enters, leaning on a cane, and next to him is Nina; Medvedenko follows along after them, pushing an empty wheelchair.

SORIN: (*In the tone of voice one uses to comfort a child.*) Yes? Are we glad? Are we happy today, when all is said and done? (*To his sister.*) We are so glad! Our father and stepmother have gone to Tver,[29] and we are free for three whole days.

NINA: (*Sits next to Arkadina and hugs her.*) I am happy! I now belong to you.

SORIN: (*Sits in his wheelchair.*) She is so pretty today.

ARKADINA: What a fetching outfit . . . What a clever girl! (*Kisses Nina.*) But we mustn't praise you too much, or it will bring bad luck. Where is Boris Alekseyevich?

NINA: He's gone fishing, down near the bathhouse.

ARKADINA: He never gets tired of it! (*Returns to the reading.*)

NINA: What's that?

ARKADINA: Maupassant, *On the Water*, my dear. (*Reads a few lines to herself.*) Well, the rest is uninteresting and untrue. (*Closes the book.*) I feel uneasy. Tell me, what is the matter with my son? Why is he so bored and stern? He spends whole days on the lake, and I hardly see him.

MASHA: He is sick at heart. (*To Nina, shyly.*) I beg you, recite something from his play!

NINA: (*Shrugging her shoulders.*) Would you like me to? It's so uninteresting!

MASHA: (*Restraining her enthusiasm.*) When he recites it, his eyes glow and his face gets pale. He has a beautiful, sad voice, and the manners of a poet.

Sorin snores.

---

29. A city on the Volga River, not far from Moscow, known for manufacturing textiles and growing flax.

DORN: Good night!

ARKADINA: Petrushka!

SORIN: Huh?

ARKADINA: Are you asleep?

SORIN: Of course not.

Pause.

ARKADINA: You need to take your medicine, brother. This is not good.

SORIN: I would be glad to take my medicine, but the doctor here won't prescribe anything.

DORN: Medicine at age sixty!

SORIN: And passion for life at age sixty!

DORN: (*Annoyed.*) Eh! Well, take some valerian[30] drops then.

ARKADINA: The hot springs might do him good.

DORN: The hot springs? It might, and it might not.

ARKADINA: I don't understand.

DORN: There's nothing to understand. It's obvious.

Pause.

MEDVEDENKO: Pyotr Nikolayevich should give up smoking.

SORIN: Nonsense.

DORN: No, that's not nonsense. Under the influence of wine and tobacco we are not ourselves. After a cigar or a glass of vodka, you are not Pyotr Nikolayevich, but Pyotr Nikolayevich plus someone else. You lose your "self," and you begin to see yourself in the third person—"he."

SORIN: (*Laughs.*) Go ahead, talk. You've lived your life. But me? I worked for the Justice Department for twenty-eight years, and I still haven't lived, haven't experienced anything, when all is

---

30. Valerian is a natural sedative made from herbs. In Chekhov's era, it was used as commonly as aspirin is today. The next line refers to mineral springs that were also considered curative. People would commonly "take the waters" at posh health spas built near natural springs.

said and done. It's no mystery, I want to live. You've had your fill, so you don't care. That's why you like to philosophize. But I want to live and that's why I drink sherry at dinner and smoke cigars, and all that. So there, and all that.

DORN: You have to take life seriously. And wanting medicine at age sixty, just because you regret not having enjoyed yourself when you were young, if you'll excuse me, that's a frivolous idea.

MASHA: (*Stands.*) It's time for lunch, it must be. (*Walks with a lazy, lagging gait.*) My foot's asleep . . . (*Exits.*)

DORN: Now she'll go and have a couple of shots of vodka before lunch.

SORIN: The poor girl's not happy.

DORN: Nonsense, sir!

SORIN: You talk like a man who has had his fill.

ARKADINA: Ah, what could be more boring than this sweet country boredom! It's hot, it's quiet, no one does anything, everyone philosophizes . . . It's nice being here with you, my friends. It's pleasant listening to you, but . . . to sit in a hotel room, learning lines—that's much better!

NINA: (*Ecstatic.*) Yes, it must be wonderful! I completely understand.

SORIN: Of course it's better in the city. You sit in your office, the lackey won't let anyone in without an appointment, there's the telephone . . . There are cab drivers in the street, and all . . .

DORN: (*Sings.*) "Speak to her of me, and pretty flowers . . ."

Shamrayev enters with Polina Andreyevna following him.

SHAMRAYEV: Here are our friends. Good day! (*Kisses Arkadina's hand, then Nina's.*) Very glad to see you in such good health. (*To Arkadina.*) My wife tells me that you plan to go with her into town today. Is that true?

ARKADINA: Yes, we do.

SHAMRAYEV: Hmm . . . Very nice, but how do you plan to get there, madam? Today we're carting the rye, and all the workmen are busy. So which horses were you planning to use, if I may ask?

ARKADINA: Which horses? How should I know which horses!

SORIN: Well we have carriage horses.

SHAMRAYEV: (*Getting excited.*) Carriage horses? And where am I to get harnesses for them? Where am I to get harnesses? Amazing! Unbelievable! With all due respect, madam! I revere your talent, I am ready to give you ten years of my life, but I can not give you any horses!

ARKADINA: But what if I had to leave? How strange this is!

SHAMRAYEV: With all due respect, madam, you do not understand farming.

ARKADINA: (*Exploding.*) The same old story! In that case, I'll leave for Moscow today. Hire me some horses from town, or I will go to the train station on foot!

SHAMRAYEV: (*Exploding.*) In that case, I quit! Find yourself another steward! (*Exits.*)

ARKADINA: Every summer it's the same, every summer he insults me! I will never set foot on this estate again!

Exits left in the direction of the bathhouse; after a minute, she is seen approaching the house; Trigorin follows her with fishing rods and a pail.

SORIN: (*Exploding.*) What impudence! The devil knows! I'm tired of it, when all is said and done. Bring all the horses here immediately!

NINA: (*To Polina Andreyevna.*) To refuse Irina Nikolayevna, a famous actress! Surely anything she wants, any caprice at all, is more important than farming. I can't believe it.

POLINA ANDREYEVNA: (*In despair.*) What can I do? Put yourself in my place. What can I do?

SORIN: (*To Nina.*) Let's go to my sister . . . Let's all beg her not to go. Shall we? (*Looking in the direction of Shamrayev's exit.*) Insufferable man! Tyrant!

NINA: (*Preventing him from standing.*) Sit down, sit down . . . We'll push you . . .

She and Medvedenko push the wheelchair.

NINA: Oh, how awful!

SORIN: Yes, yes, it's awful . . . But he won't really quit, I'll have a talk with him as soon as I can.

They exit; only Dorn and Polina Andreyevna remain.

DORN: People are predictable. By rights, they really should kick your husband out, but that old coward and his sister will apologize to him instead. You'll see!

POLINA ANDREYEVNA: My husband sent even the carriage horses out into the field. Every day there are these misunderstandings. If only you knew how it upsets me! It's making me sick. Look how I'm trembling . . . I can't stand his rudeness. (*Imploring.*) Yevgeny, my dear, my beloved, take me home with you . . . Time is passing, we are no longer young, if only we could stop hiding and lying, at least now at the end of our lives . . .

Pause.

DORN: I'm fifty-five years old. It's too late for me to change my life.

POLINA ANDREYEVNA: I know why you refuse me. Because, besides me, there are other women who care for you. You can't take all of us home. I understand. Forgive me, you must be tired of me.

Nina appears near the house; she picks some flowers.

DORN: No, not at all.

POLINA ANDREYEVNA: I suffer from jealousy. I know you're a doctor, you can't avoid women. I understand . . .

DORN: (*To Nina, who approaches.*) How are things inside?

NINA: Irina Nikolayevna is crying, and Pyotr Nikolayevich is having an asthma attack.

DORN: (*Stands.*) I'll go give them both some valerian drops . . .

NINA: (*Gives him the flowers.*) For you!

DORN: Merci bien.[31] (*Goes toward the house.*)

---

31. "Thank you very much" (French).

POLINA ANDREYEVNA: (*Following him.*) What lovely flowers! (*Near the house, in a hollow voice.*) Give me those flowers! Give me those flowers! (*Takes the flowers, tears them up, and throws them aside.*)

Both go into the house.

NINA: (*Alone.*) How strange to see a well-known actress crying, and over something so stupid! And a famous writer—the darling of the public, with his name in all the papers, and his portrait being sold everywhere, and his works being translated into foreign languages—how strange that he goes fishing all day, and is happy when he catches two chub! I thought that celebrities were proud and unapproachable, that they disdained the crowd, and that they somehow used the luster of their names to get back at the world for putting aristocratic families and inherited wealth above their talents. But here they are—crying, catching fish, playing cards, laughing, getting angry—like everybody else . . .

TREPLEV: (*Enters without a hat, with a gun, and a dead seagull.*) Are you here alone?

NINA: I'm alone.

Treplev lays the seagull at her feet.

NINA: What does this mean?

TREPLEV: I committed the ugly crime of killing this seagull today. I'm laying it at your feet.

NINA: What is wrong with you? (*Picks up the seagull and looks at it.*)

TREPLEV: (*After a pause.*) Soon, in the same way, I will kill myself.

NINA: I don't know who you are anymore.

TREPLEV: And I don't know who you are. You have changed toward me, you look at me coldly, my presence embarrasses you.

NINA: You've become irritable lately. You talk in symbols, and they're incomprehensible. And, apparently, this seagull is also a symbol. But forgive me, I don't understand . . . (*Lays the seagull on the bench.*) I am too simple to understand you.

TREPLEV: It all started the evening that my play failed so stupidly. Women do not forgive failure. I've burned it, every last scrap. If only you knew how unhappy I am! Your coldness frightens me, I can't believe how cold you are, as if I had woken up to find that this lake had suddenly dried up or sunk into the earth. You just said that you are too simple to understand me. What is there to understand? You didn't like my play, you show disdain for what inspires me, you already consider me mediocre, insignificant, no different than many others . . . (*Stamps his foot.*) How well I understand, how I understand! It's like having a nail stuck in my head—damn it and damn my self-esteem too—it's sucking my blood, sucking, like a snake . . . (*Seeing Trigorin, who is walking and reading a little book.*) Here comes the true talent, walking around with a book, like Hamlet. (*Mocks.*) "Words, words, words . . ."[32] His sun beams have not yet reached you, but you're already smiling, and the cold look on your face is already melting in his warmth. (*Exits abruptly.*)

TRIGORIN: (*Making a note in the little book.*) Takes snuff and drinks vodka . . . Always wears black. The teacher loves her . . .

NINA: Hello, Boris Alekseyevich!

TRIGORIN: Hello. It seems that we are leaving today due to unanticipated circumstances. I doubt that we will see each other ever again. It's a pity. I don't often get the chance to meet young girls, young and interesting girls. I've forgotten, I can't even imagine, what it feels like to be eighteen, or nineteen years old. No wonder the young girls in my stories and novels usually ring false! I would like to put myself in your place, if only for one hour, to learn how you think, and, generally, what you're made of.

NINA: And I would like to put myself in your place.

TRIGORIN: Why?

NINA: To learn how a famous, talented writer feels. How does being famous feel? What does it mean to experience fame?

TRIGORIN: How? What? No how, nothing. I never thought about it. (*Thinking it over.*) Either you exaggerate my fame, or it really doesn't mean anything.

---

32. In Act II, scene 2, Shakespeare's Polonius asks, "What do you read, my lord?" Hamlet answers, "Words, words, words."

NINA: And when you read about yourself in the papers?

TRIGORIN: When they praise me, it's pleasant, when they damn me, I'm in a bad mood for a couple of days.

NINA: Oh brave world that has such people in it! How I envy you, if only you knew! People's lots are different. Some can barely make it through their boring, unremarkable lives. They're all alike, unlucky. Others, like you for example—but you're one in a million—you get to have an interesting, brilliant life, full of meaning . . . You are lucky . . .

TRIGORIN: Me? (*Shrugging his shoulders.*) Hmm . . . Here you are talking about fame, about luck, about brilliant, interesting lives, but to me these are only pretty words. Forgive me, but it's like a marmalade that I've never tasted. You are very young and very kind.

NINA: Your life is beautiful!

TRIGORIN: What is so good about it? (*Looks at his watch.*) I have to go and write. Excuse me, I have no time . . . (*Laughs.*) You have just found my pet peeve, as they say, and it's getting me upset, even a little angry. So, let's talk. Let's talk about my beautiful and brilliant life . . . Well, where shall we begin? (*Thinking for a moment.*) There is such a thing as a fixed idea when a person can think of nothing else, day and night, except, say, the moon. I have my "moon." Day and night, one nagging idea obsesses me: I must write, I must write, I must . . . As soon as I finish one story, I have to write another, then a third, after the third, a fourth . . . I write constantly, as if I'm riding relay horses, and I can't do it any differently. What's so beautiful and brilliant about that, I ask you? Oh, it's a savage life! Here I am with you, and the whole time I'm worrying. In fact, I am reminding myself right now that an unfinished story is waiting for me. I see that cloud; it looks like a piano. I tell myself I should remember to put a cloud that looks like a piano in a short story. The heliotrope tickles my nose. I quickly make a mental note: remember that cloying scent and widow's weeds when you next describe a summer evening. I catch every phrase we utter, and every word, and put them into my literary storeroom. They may be useful some day! When I finish something, I run off to the theater or I go fishing; surely there I will relax and forget. But no, a new, heavy, iron ball starts rolling around in my head—a new subject. My desk begins to call to me, and I have to hurry home and write and then write some more. It's always like that. I give myself no peace. I use my personal life. I may be offering honey to strangers, but in the process I rob the pollen from my own best flowers, I tear the blossoms, and trample the roots. Surely I must be crazy? But my relatives and friends treat me as if I were sane, don't they? "What are you writing? What will you give us?" It's always the same, always the same, and it seems to me that all this attention from relatives, all the praise, all the excitement—it's all delusion. They're humoring me, like a sick man. And sometimes I'm afraid that at any moment they'll sneak up from behind, grab me, and send me off to the insane asylum, like Poprískhin.[33] In those early years, in the best years, when I first began to write, one thing kept tormenting me. A second-rate writer, especially when he's down on his luck, feels awkward, clumsy, superfluous. He's skittish, overanxious. But he can't keep from hanging around people with literary and artistic ambitions, who won't accept him and don't even notice him. And he's afraid to look them straight in the eye, like a gambler who has no money. I never met my readers, but somehow I imagined them as unfriendly and suspicious. I was afraid of my public. They frightened me. And whenever I had one of my plays produced, it seemed to me, that the brunettes in the audience were hostile and the blondes could care less. Oh, how awful! What a torment!

NINA: But, the inspiration and the very process of creation must give you moments of exaltation and happiness, don't they?

TRIGORIN: Yes. When I'm writing, it's pleasant. And editing what I've written is pleasant. But . . . as soon as it's in print, I can't abide it, I see what a mistake it was to have written at all, and I'm annoyed, I feel worthless . . . (*Laughing.*) The public reads it: "Yes, it's lovely, shows talent . . . lovely, but not up to Tolstoy." Or: "A beautiful piece, but Turgénev's *Fathers and Sons*[34] is better." And this will continue until it's carved on my gravestone—lovely, shows talent, lovely, shows

---

33. In *The Memoirs of a Madman* (1835) by Nikolay Vasilyevich Gogol, the narrator thinks that he is sane and that everyone around him is mad.

34. In this novel from 1862, Ivan Sergeyevich Turgenev portrays the generational gap that occurred when politically active young people began to agitate for an overthrow of the tsar.

talent—nothing more. And when I die, my friends will walk around my grave saying: "Here lies Trigorin. A good writer, but not as good as Turgenev."

NINA: Forgive me, but I refuse to believe you. You are spoiled by success.

TRIGORIN: What success? I have never pleased myself. I don't like myself as a writer. Worst of all, I often feel dazed and don't understand what I've written . . . I love this water, these trees, the sky, I feel in touch with nature, it induces passion in me, an irresistible desire to write. But then, painting landscapes isn't enough, is it? I am a citizen, I love my country and the people. So I feel that, as a writer, I am duty bound to speak about the people, about their sufferings, about their future, to speak about science, and human rights, and so forth and so on. And so I write about everything. I rush to get it all down, as if I were pursued by angry people. I run back and forth like a fox, cornered by dogs. And yet life and science escape me, and I fall further and further behind, like a peasant who misses his train. And in the end, I feel that I can only describe the landscape well, all the rest rings false. I'm false right down to the marrow of my bones.

NINA: You work too hard, and you don't take the time to appreciate your own importance. You may be unsatisfied with yourself, but to others you are great and beautiful! If only I were a writer like you, I would give my whole life to others, but I would also recognize that their happiness lay in rising to my level and in hitching themselves to my chariot.

TRIGORIN: Well, my chariot . . . Am I Agamemnon,[35] now?

Both smile.

NINA: For the joy of being a writer or an actress, I would gladly endure the rejection of my closest friends, poverty, and disillusionment. I would live under the eaves and eat stale bread. I would gladly suffer personal dissatisfaction, the knowledge of my own imperfections. But in return I would demand fame . . .

---

35. A king and commander of the ancient Greek forces that conquered Troy. Upon his return from the Trojan War, Agamemnon's wife killed him in revenge for his betrayal of her.

real, noisy fame . . . (*Covers her face with her hands.*) My head is spinning . . . Ahhh . . .

Arkadina's voice from inside the house: "Boris Alekseyevich!"

TRIGORIN: I'm being called . . . I have to pack. But I don't feel like leaving. (*Looks at the lake.*) Such heavenly grace! . . . It's so good!

NINA: Do you see the house and garden on the other shore?

TRIGORIN: Yes.

NINA: That's my late mother's estate. I was born there. I've lived my whole life near this lake, and I know every little island on it.

TRIGORIN: You have it good here! (*Notices the seagull.*) What's this?

NINA: A seagull. Konstantin Gavrilovich killed it.

TRIGORIN: A beautiful bird. True, I don't want to leave. Why don't you talk to Irina Nikolayevna, and beg her to stay? (*Writes in the little book.*)

NINA: What are you writing?

TRIGORIN: Just making a note . . . I had an idea . . . (*Puts away the book.*) A subject for a short story: a young girl has lived on the shores of a lake since she was a child, just like you. She loves the lake, like a seagull. She's happy and free, like a seagull. But suddenly, a man comes along, notices her, and, because he has nothing better to do, destroys her, like this seagull.

Pause. Arkadina appears at a window.

ARKADINA: Boris Alekseyevich, where are you?

TRIGORIN: Coming! (*Begins to walk and glances back at Nina; to Arkadina, who is still at the window.*) What is it?

ARKADINA: We're staying.

Trigorin exits into the house.

NINA: (*Comes downstage, and after thinking for a moment.*) It's a dream!

Curtain.

Act III

The dining room in Sorin's house. Doors to the right and left. A sideboard. A cabinet with medicines in it. A table in the middle of the room. A suitcase and boxes; obviously a departure is planned. Trigorin is having lunch. Masha stands at the table.

MASHA: I tell you all this because you're a writer. Perhaps you can use it. I swear to you: if he had seriously wounded himself, I couldn't have gone on living for another minute. But still I am brave. So I've decided once and for all to tear this love out of my heart by the roots.

TRIGORIN: How will you do it?

MASHA: I'll get married. To Medvedenko.

TRIGORIN: To the teacher?

MASHA: Yes.

TRIGORIN: I don't understand why that's necessary.

MASHA: To love hopelessly, to wait years for something to happen . . . When I'm married, I won't have time for love. New worries will strangle the old one. And at least it will be a change. Shall we have another?

TRIGORIN: Haven't you had quite a lot?

MASHA: Oh please! (*Pours a shot.*) Don't look at me like that. Women drink more often than you think. A few drink in public, like me; most drink in secret. Yes. Always vodka or cognac. (*Clinks glasses with him.*) To your health! You are a simple soul, I'll be sorry to see you go.

They drink.

TRIGORIN: I don't want to go.

MASHA: Then ask her to stay.

TRIGORIN: No, she won't stay now. Her son has behaved most tactlessly. First he shoots himself, and now, they say, he intends to challenge me to a duel. And for what? He sulks, grumbles, preaches about new forms . . . But surely there's enough room for both old and new forms. Why push and shove?

MASHA: Well, there's the jealousy. But then, it's not my business.

*Pause. Yakov crosses from left to right with a suitcase;
Nina enters and stands near the window.*

MASHA: My teacher is not very bright, but he's a kind man. He's a poor man, but he loves me dearly. I'm sorry for him. And sorry for his dear old mama too. Well, sir, let me wish you all the best. Remember me kindly. (*Warmly shakes his hand.*) I am very grateful for your sympathy. Send me your books, and don't forget to autograph them. Only don't write "with great esteem." Just write: "To Maria, who doesn't remember being born and doesn't know why she's living." Goodbye! (*Exits.*)

NINA: (*Making a fist, she holds her hand out to Trigorin.*) Even or odd?

TRIGORIN: Even.

NINA: (*Sighs.*) No. I have only one pea in my hand. I'm trying to tell my fortune: whether to become an actress or not. If only someone would give me advice.

TRIGORIN: It's better not to give advice in such matters.

Pause.

NINA: We are parting, and . . . perhaps we'll never see each other again. Please accept this little medallion as a remembrance of me. I had it engraved with your initials . . . And on this side is the title of your book, *Days and Nights*.[36]

TRIGORIN: How very gracious! (*Kisses the medallion.*) A lovely gift!

NINA: Remember me sometimes.

TRIGORIN: I'll remember you. I'll remember you as you were on that clear day—do you remember? A week ago, when you were wearing a light dress . . . We were talking . . . A white seagull lay on the bench.

NINA: (*Pensively.*) Yes, the seagull . . .

Pause.

---

36. In 1895 one of Chekhov's admirers, Lidia Avilova, gave him just such a medallion, referencing his story *Neighbors*.

NINA: We can't talk any more, someone's coming . . . Before you leave, give me two more minutes, please . . .

She exits to the left as Arkadina and Sorin enter from the right. Sorin wears a frock coat decorated with a brass star.[37] *Yakov follows, busy with the luggage.*

ARKADINA: Please stay home, old man. You shouldn't go out gallivanting with your rheumatism bothering you. (*To Trigorin.*) Who just left? Nina?

TRIGORIN: Yes.

ARKADINA: Pardon,[38] we've disturbed you . . . (*Sits.*) I've finished packing. I'm worn out.

TRIGORIN: (*Reads from the medallion.*) *Days and Nights,* page 121, lines 11 and 12.

YAKOV: (*Clearing the table.*) Would you like me to pack the fishing rods too?

TRIGORIN: Yes, I'll be needing them again. But you can give the books away.

YAKOV: Yes, sir.

TRIGORIN: (*To himself.*) Page 121, lines 11 and 12. What's in those lines? (*To Arkadina.*) Do we have my books here in the house?

ARKADINA: In my brother's study, on the corner shelf.

TRIGORIN: Page 121 . . . (*Exits.*)

ARKADINA: Really, Petrushka, you should stay home . . .

SORIN: You're leaving, and it will be hard for me here at home without you.

ARKADINA: And what is there for you to do in town?

SORIN: Nothing special, but all the same. (*Laughs.*) They'll be laying the cornerstone for the new town hall, and all that sort of thing . . . I feel like jumping out of this guppy tank for an hour or two. I've been lying around here like an old cigarette

---

37. The frock coat is a long fitted men's dress coat; the military-like decoration on it signifies Sorin's civil service rank in the Justice Department.
38. "Pardon me" (French).

holder for too long. I've ordered the horses for one o'clock, so we'll be leaving at the same time.

ARKADINA: (*After a pause.*) Well, live if you must, but do it here, and don't get bored, and don't catch cold. Look after my son. Watch out for him. Straighten him out. (*Pause.*) I'm going away, and so I won't be able to find out why Konstantin tried to shoot himself. I think that the main reason is jealousy, and the sooner I take Trigorin away from here, the better.

SORIN: How can I put it? There are other reasons too. It's no mystery—a young, intelligent man, who lives in the country, in the backwoods, without money, without a position, without a future. There's nothing to occupy him. He's embarrassed and afraid of his own idleness. I love him deeply, and he's fond of me, but all the same, when all is said and done, he feels superfluous at home, like he's a parasite, a hanger-on. It's no mystery, that his self-esteem . . .

ARKADINA: Oh woe is me! (*Thinking it over.*) I should set him up in some kind of work, don't you think? . . .

SORIN: (*Whistles, then hesitantly.*) I think, that it would be better, if you would . . . give him a little money. First of all, he needs to dress like a human being, and all that. Look at him, he's been wearing the same tattered jacket for three years, and he doesn't even have an overcoat . . . (*Laughs.*) And yes, it would not hurt him to get out a bit . . . Maybe go abroad . . . Surely all this can't be too expensive.

ARKADINA: All the same . . . Perhaps I could manage a suit, but as for going abroad . . . No, at this time I can't even manage a suit. (*Decisively.*) I have no money!

Sorin laughs.

ARKADINA: No!

SORIN: (*Whistles.*) I see. Forgive me, my dear, don't get angry. I believe you . . . You're a generous, gracious lady.

ARKADINA: (*Through tears.*) I have no money!

SORIN: If I had money, I would give him some, you know, but it's no mystery, I have nothing, not a kopeck. (*Laughs.*) The steward takes my whole pension for farming, cattle herding, beekeeping, and all my money goes for nothing. The bees die, the cows die, and I don't even get to use the horses . . .

ARKADINA: Yes, I have some money, but I am an actress; my costumes alone ruin me.[39]

SORIN: You are kind, my dear . . . I respect you . . . Yes . . . But something's wrong with me again . . . (*Staggering.*) My head is spinning. (*Holds onto the table.*) I don't feel well, and all that.

ARKADINA: (*Alarmed.*) Petrushka! (*Trying to support him.*) Petrushka, my dear . . . (*Yells.*) Help me! Help! . . .

Treplev enters, his head bandaged, with Medvedenko.

ARKADINA: He's not feeling well!

SORIN: It's nothing, nothing . . . (*Smiles and drinks some water.*) It has already passed . . . and all that . . .

TREPLEV: (*To his mother.*) Don't be frightened, Mama, it's not dangerous. This often happens to uncle. (*To his uncle.*) Uncle, you'd better lie down.

SORIN: For a while, yes . . . But I'm still going into town . . . I'll lie down for a while, and then I'll go . . . It's no mystery . . . (*Walks, leaning on his cane.*)

MEDVEDENKO: (*Leads Sorin by the arm.*) There's a riddle: what walks on all fours in the morning, on two legs at noon, and on three in the evening? . . .[40]

SORIN: (*Laughs.*) Exactly. And flat on his back at night. Thank you, I can walk by myself . . .

MEDVEDENKO: Now, now, don't stand on ceremony! . . .

He and Sorin exit.

ARKADINA: How he frightened me!

---

39. At the time when Chekhov wrote this play, actors were expected to supply all their own costumes, which could be costly.
40. This is the riddle of the Sphinx in Sophocles' *Oedipus the King;* the answer is "a human being."

TREPLEV: It's not healthy for him to live in the country. He gets depressed. But, Mama, if you were suddenly to become generous, and give him, say a thousand and a half or two thousand rubles, he could live in town for a whole year.

ARKADINA: I have no money. I am an actress, not a banker.

Pause.

TREPLEV: Mama, change my bandage. You do it so well.

ARKADINA: (*Takes iodine and fresh bandages from the medicine cabinet.*) The doctor is late.

TREPLEV: He promised to come at ten, and it's already noon.

ARKADINA: Sit down. (*Takes the bandage from his head.*) You look like you're wearing a turban. Yesterday, a passer-by asked the cook what nation you come from. It's almost healed. There's only a small spot left. (*Kisses him on the head.*) Now you won't do any more bang-bang while I'm away, will you?

TREPLEV: No, Mama. It was a moment of insane despair, when I couldn't control myself. I won't ever do it again. (*Kisses her hand.*) You have golden hands. I remember, a very long time ago, when you were still acting in the state theater[41]—I was little then—there was a fight in our courtyard, and one of the tenants, a washerwoman, was badly beaten. Do you remember? They found her unconscious . . . You looked after her, gave her medicine, washed her children in the trough. Do you remember?

ARKADINA: No. (*Puts a new bandage in place.*)

TREPLEV: At that time, two ballerinas lived in the same building, where we did . . . They would come and drink coffee with you . . .

ARKADINA: I remember that.

TREPLEV: They were so religious. (*Pause.*) Lately, these last few days, I find I love you as tenderly and wholeheartedly as I did when I was a child. I have no one but you. Only why, why do you allow that man to influence you?

---

41. The state-subsidized theaters of Russia were located only in St. Petersburg and Moscow, so Treplev describes an urban scene.

ARKADINA: You don't understand him, Konstantin. He is the noblest of men . . .

TREPLEV: And yet his nobility didn't stop him from acting like a coward when he heard that I was planning to challenge him to a duel. He's leaving. An ignoble flight!

ARKADINA: What nonsense! I begged him to leave.

TREPLEV: The noblest of men! Look, you and I are nearly quarrelling over him, and he is sitting somewhere in the drawing room or in the garden laughing at us, at this very minute . . . He's educating Nina, trying to convince her that he is most definitely a genius.

ARKADINA: You enjoy saying mean things to me. I respect that man, and I beg you not to speak ill of him.

TREPLEV: But I do not respect him. You want me to consider him a genius, but forgive me, I cannot lie. His writing makes me sick.

ARKADINA: That's envy. Pretentious untalented people have no other recourse than to malign true talent. Small comfort, I'd say!

TREPLEV: (*Ironically.*) True talent! (*Angrily.*) I am more talented than all of you, when it comes right down to it! (*Rips the bandage from his head.*) You are hacks, who have elbowed your way into the first ranks of art, and you think that only what you yourself produce is legitimate and real. You stifle and suppress everything else! I do not acknowledge you. I do not acknowledge you or him!

ARKADINA: You are decadent! . . .

TREPLEV: Go back to your dear little theater and act in your pitiful, inane plays.

ARKADINA: I have never acted in such plays. Leave me out of this! You're not even in a position to write a pitiful vaudevillian farce. You're lower middle-class from Kiev! A hanger-on!

TREPLEV: You're a skinflint!

ARKADINA: You're a ragamuffin!

Treplev sits and quietly cries.

ARKADINA: A nonentity! (*Walking around agitatedly.*) Don't cry. There's no need to cry . . . (*Cries.*) There's no need . . . (*Kisses his forehead, his cheeks, his head.*) My dear child, forgive me . . . Forgive your sinful mother . . . Forgive me, unfortunate me.

TREPLEV: (*Hugs her.*) If only you knew! I have lost everything. She doesn't love me. I can no longer write . . . I've lost all my hopes . . .

ARKADINA: Don't despair . . . It will pass. He's leaving soon. She will fall in love with you again. (*Wipes away his tears.*) Let it be. Let's make up.

TREPLEV: (*Kisses her hand.*) Yes, Mama.

ARKADINA: (*Tenderly.*) And make up with him, too. There's no need for a duel . . . There's no need, is there?

TREPLEV: All right . . . Just don't let me see him again, Mama. It's hard for me . . . It's beyond my strength . . .

Trigorin enters.

TREPLEV: Well . . . I'm going . . . (*Hurriedly puts the medicine cabinet in order.*) The doctor will re-do my bandage later . . .

TRIGORIN: (*Looks in a book.*) Page 121 . . . Lines 11 and 12 . . . Here it is . . . (*Reads.*) "If you ever need my life, then come and take it."

Treplev picks up the bandage from the floor and walks out.

ARKADINA: (*Looking at her watch.*) They'll bring the horses soon.

TRIGORIN: (*To himself.*) "If you ever need my life, then come and take it."

ARKADINA: I hope you have finished packing?

TRIGORIN: (*Impatiently.*) Yes, yes . . . (*Pensively.*) Why does this appeal, that comes from such a pure soul, make me sad, and wring my heart? . . . "If you ever need my life, then come and take it." (*To Arkadina.*) Let's stay one more day! (*Arkadina shakes her head no.*) Let's stay!

ARKADINA: My darling, I know what's keeping you here. But take control of yourself. You're a little intoxicated. You need to sober up.

TRIGORIN: You should sober up too. Be smart, be reasonable, I beg you. Look at this as if you were a true friend . . . (*Presses her hand.*) You are capable of sacrifice . . . Be my friend, and let me go.

ARKADINA: (*Highly upset.*) Are you that attracted to her?

TRIGORIN: I am infatuated. Perhaps, it's just what I need.

ARKADINA: The love of a provincial girl? Oh, how little you know yourself!

TRIGORIN: Sometimes people sleepwalk, and that's how I'm talking to you now, as if I were asleep and dreaming about her . . . Sweet, miraculous dreams possess me . . . Let me go . . .

ARKADINA: (*Trembling.*) No, no . . . I am an ordinary woman, you can't talk to me this way . . . Don't torment me, Boris . . . I'm frightened . . .

TRIGORIN: If you want, you could be an extraordinary woman. A young, lovely, poetic love, that carries you off into a reverie—only a love like this can offer true joy on earth! I have never experienced such a love . . . I had no time for it when I was young. I spent my time in editorial offices, fighting off poverty . . . Now, here it is, this love, and I am infatuated at last . . . Why should I run away from her?

ARKADINA: (*Angrily.*) You've gone mad!

TRIGORIN: So be it.

ARKADINA: You are all conspiring to torment me today! (*Cries.*)

TRIGORIN: (*Holding his head in his hands.*) She doesn't understand! She doesn't want to understand!

ARKADINA: Am I really so old and ugly, that you can talk to me about other women without feeling embarrassed? (*Hugs him and cries.*) Oh you've lost your senses! My excellent, marvelous . . . You are the last page of my life! (*Kneels.*) My happiness, my pride, my bliss . . . (*Hugs his knees.*) If you throw me over, even for one hour, I will not survive, I will go mad. My remarkable, exceptional man, my lord and master . . .

TRIGORIN: Someone may come in. (*Helps her up.*)

ARKADINA: Let them. I'm not ashamed of my love for you. (*Kisses his hand.*) My treasure, you may be in despair, you may want this madness, but I don't want it for you, I won't let you . . . (*Laughs.*) You are mine . . . You are mine . . . This is my forehead, my eyes, and this beautiful silky hair is mine . . . You are all mine. You are talented, smart, better than any other living writer, Russia's best hope . . . You have sincerity, simplicity, freshness, good humor . . . In a single line you convey what's most important about a person or a landscape, you create living characters. It's impossible to read you without going into ecstasies! You think I'm exaggerating? That I'm flattering you? Well, look me in the eyes . . . Come on, look . . . Do I look like a flatterer? You see, I'm the only one who really knows your worth. I'm telling you the truth, darling, sweetheart . . . Will you come with me? Yes? Will you throw me over? . . .

TRIGORIN: I have no will of my own . . . I have never had a will of my own . . . I'm flaccid, soft, submissive—do women really find this attractive? Take me with you, carry me away, but don't ever let me out of your sight . . .

ARKADINA: (*To herself.*) Now he's mine. (*Casually, as if nothing had occurred.*) By the way, if you'd like, you can stay. I'll go by myself, and you can join me later, after a week or so. Why should you have to rush?

TRIGORIN: No, let's go together.

ARKADINA: As you like. Together then, together . . .

Pause. Trigorin jots something in his little book.

ARKADINA: What's that?

TRIGORIN: I heard a good expression this morning, "Virginal forest . . ." It might be of use. (*Stretches.*) So then, we're going? Once again the trains, the stations, the buffets and their repulsive cutlets, the conversations . . .

SHAMRAYEV: (*Enters.*) I have the sad honor to inform you that they've brought the horses. It's time to go to the station, dear madam; the train pulls in at five past two. Please, Irina Nikolayevna, find out where the actor Súzdaltsev is now? Whether he's still alive? Whether he's in good health? Please don't forget! We used to go out drinking together . . . His performance in *The Great Mail Robbery* was unmatchable . . . At that time, in the town of Elizabeth, I also recall that the tragedian Izmaílov—a remarkable character—acted with him . . .[42] Don't rush, dear madam, you still have five minutes. Once they were playing conspirators in a melodrama, and when they were suddenly caught, he was supposed to say, "We've fallen into a trap." But instead he said, "We've fallen into a cap." (*Giggles.*) A cap! . . .

As he speaks, Yakov fusses with the suitcases, a maid brings Arkadina's hat, mantle, umbrella, and gloves; all help her put her things on. A cook peeps out at the door on the left, and then enters hesitantly. Polina Andreyevna enters, followed by Sorin and Medvedenko.

POLINA ANDREYEVNA: (*Carrying a basket.*) Here are some plums for the journey . . . They're very sweet. You may want something to eat on the way . . .

ARKADINA: You're very kind, Polina Andreyevna.

POLINA ANDREYEVNA: Goodbye, my dear! If anything was amiss, I'm sorry. (*Cries.*)

ARKADINA: (*Hugs her.*) Everything was fine, everything was fine. And there's no need to cry.

POLINA ANDREYEVNA: Time is passing!

ARKADINA: What can we do!

SORIN: (*Enters from the left door in an overcoat with a cape, a hat, and carrying a cane; crosses through the room.*) Sister, it's time. Let's not be late, when all is said and done. I'll go take my seat in the carriage. (*Exits.*)

MEDVEDENKO: And I'll walk to the station on foot . . . to see you off. I'll make it in good time . . . (*Exits.*)

ARKADINA: Goodbye, my dear ones . . . If you're still alive and well come summer, I'll see you all again . . .

The maid, Yakov, and the cook kiss her hand.

---

42. *The Great Mail Robbery* was a Russian adaptation of a popular French melodrama from the mid-nineteenth century.

ARKADINA: Don't forget me. (*Gives the cook a ruble.*) Here is a ruble to split among the three of you.

THE COOK: Thank you very much, madam. Have a good trip! We wish you all the best!

YAKOV: God speed you!

SHAMRAYEV: A letter would make us happy! Goodbye, Boris Alekseyevich!

ARKADINA: Where's Konstantin? Tell him that I'm leaving. We have to say goodbye. Well, remember me kindly. (*To Yakov.*) I gave a ruble to the cook. It's for the three of you.

All exit to the right. The stage is empty. The noise of people being seen off can be heard. The maid returns to get the basket of plums from the table, and exits again.

TRIGORIN: (*Returning.*) I forgot my walking stick. I think it's on the terrace. (*Goes to the door on the left where he meets Nina, who enters.*) It's you? We're leaving . . .

NINA: I knew we would see each other again. (*Excited.*) Boris Alekseyevich, I have decided, irrevocably, the die is cast, I will go on the stage. Tomorrow, I will no longer be here. I will leave my father, give up everything here, and begin a new life . . . I'm leaving, just like you . . . Going to Moscow. We will see each other there.

TRIGORIN: (*Glancing around.*) Stay at the hotel called "The Slavic Bazaar"[43] . . . Let me know as soon as you've arrived . . . I live on Molchánov Street, the Grokhólsky building . . . I'll hurry over to see you . . .

Pause.

NINA: One more minute . . .

TRIGORIN: (*In a whisper.*) You are so lovely . . . Oh, what happiness to think that we will see each other again! (*She leans on his*

---

43. A popular hotel and restaurant in the center of Moscow, famous as the place where Stanislavsky and Nemirovich-Danchenko began their legendary eighteen-hour meeting during which they laid the foundations of the future Moscow Art Theatre. Molchanov Street is nearby.

chest.) I will see these miraculous eyes again, this inexpressibly lovely, tender smile . . . these gentle features, this expression of angelic purity . . . My darling . . .

A prolonged kiss.

Curtain.

Act IV

Two years pass between the Third and Fourth Acts.

A drawing room in Sorin's house, which Treplev has turned into a study. To the right and left, doors leading to other interior rooms. A glass door opening out onto the terrace. Aside from the usual drawing-room furniture, there is a desk in the right corner, a Turkish divan and a cupboard stand near the left door. There are books on the shelves of the cupboard and on the chairs. Evening. One lamp with a shade is lit. The leaves of the trees and the howling of the wind in the chimney can be heard. The watchman is tapping.[44]

Medvedenko and Masha enter.

MASHA: (*Calls out.*) Konstantin Gavrilovich! Konstantin Gavrilovich! (*Looks around.*) No one's here. The old man is always asking, where's Kostya, where's Kostya . . . Can't live without him . . .

MEDVEDENKO: He's afraid of loneliness. (*Listens.*) What awful weather! Two full days of this.

MASHA: (*Turns up the lamp.*) There are waves on the lake. Huge waves.

MEDVEDENKO: It's dark in the garden. We should tell them to tear down that theater out there. It looks naked, ugly, like a skeleton, and the curtain flaps in the wind. Last night I walked by it, and I thought I heard someone crying . . .

MASHA: Yes, well . . .

Pause.

---

44. Watchmen took care of security on Russian estates by walking the property and tapping on a wooden board to scare away any intruders.

MEDVEDENKO: Let's go home, Masha!

MASHA: (*Shakes her head no.*) I'm staying the night.

MEDVEDENKO: (*Imploringly.*) Masha, let's go! Our baby will get hungry.

MASHA: Nonsense. The nurse will feed him.

Pause.

MEDVEDENKO: It's a pity. Three nights in a row and he hasn't seen his mother.

MASHA: You're becoming a bore. You used to philosophize, and now all you talk about is baby and home, baby and home—I never hear anything else from you.

MEDVEDENKO: Let's go, Masha!

MASHA: Go yourself.

MEDVEDENKO: Your father won't give me any horses.

MASHA: Yes he will. Ask him and he'll give you some.

MEDVEDENKO: Please, please. Will you come home tomorrow?

MASHA: (*Takes snuff.*) Tomorrow's another day. Let me be . . .

Treplev and Polina Andreyevna enter; Treplev carries a pillow and a blanket; Polina Andreyevna has bed linens; they put these things on the Turkish divan, then Treplev goes to his desk and sits down.

MASHA: What's that for, Mama?

POLINA ANDREYEVNA: Pyotr Nikolayevich has asked to sleep here in Kostya's room.

MASHA: Let me . . . (*Helps make the bed.*)

POLINA ANDREYEVNA: (*Sighing.*) An old man's just like a baby . . . (*Goes to the desk, leans on her elbows, and looks at a manuscript.*)

Pause.

MEDVEDENKO: So then, I'm leaving. Goodbye, Masha. (*Kisses his wife's hand.*) Goodbye, Mama. (*Wants to kiss the hand of his mother-in-law.*)

POLINA ANDREYEVNA: (*Annoyed.*) Well! God be with you!

MEDVEDENKO: Goodbye, Konstantin Gavrilovich.

Treplev silently shakes his hand; Medvedenko exits.

POLINA ANDREYEVNA: (*Looking at the manuscript.*) No one thought, no one could have guessed, that you, Kostya, would turn out to be a real writer. But, here you are, thank God. The journals send you money now. (*Passes her hand over his hair.*) And you've become handsome . . . Dear Kostya, be a good boy, and be a little nicer to my Mashenka! . . .

MASHA: (*Making the bed.*) Let him be, Mama.

POLINA ANDREYEVNA: (*To Treplev.*) She's a wonderful girl. (*Pause.*) Women don't need much, Kostya, only a tender glance now and again. I know from my own experience.

Treplev stands up and exits without a saying a word.

MASHA: You've made him angry. You must stop!

POLINA ANDREYEVNA: I'm sorry for you, Mashenka.

MASHA: Don't be!

POLINA ANDREYEVNA: It makes my heart sick to see you. I see everything, and I understand.

MASHA: It's all so stupid. Hopeless love—that's only for novels. It's all nonsense. The main thing is not to allow yourself to expect anything, not to expect the tide to turn . . . When love takes root in your heart, you should tear it out. They've promised to transfer my husband to another district. As soon as we move, I'll forget everything . . . I'll tear it from my heart by the roots.

A melancholy waltz is being played two rooms away.

POLINA ANDREYEVNA: Kostya is playing. He's sick at heart.

MASHA: (*Without making any noise, she dances a few steps of the waltz.*) The most important thing, Mama, is for me not to see him. As soon as they give Semyon the transfer, believe me, after one month I'll forget everything. It's all nonsense.

The left door opens. Dorn and Medvedenko wheel in Sorin.

MEDVEDENKO: I support six people in my house now. And flour costs two kopecks a pound.

DORN: It's so crowded there, I bet you can barely turn around.

MEDVEDENKO: Go ahead, laugh at me. You have money to burn.

DORN: Money? After thirty years of practice, my friend, thirty tireless years, when my life was not my own, day or night, I managed to squirrel away only two thousand rubles, and then, I went and spent it all on a trip abroad. I have nothing.

MASHA: (*To her husband.*) You haven't left?

MEDVEDENKO: (*Guiltily.*) What can I do? They won't give me horses!

MASHA: (*With bitter vexation, in a whisper.*) I wish I'd never set eyes on you!

They stop the wheelchair on the left side of the room; Polina Andreyevna, Masha, and Dorn sit down near it; Medvedenko, sadly, walks off to the side.

DORN: How many changes you've made! You've turned the drawing room into a study.

MASHA: It's more comfortable for Konstantin Gavrilovich to work here. He can go into the garden to think whenever he likes.

The watchman taps.

SORIN: Where's my sister?

DORN: She went to the station to meet Trigorin. She'll be right back.

SORIN: If you sent for my sister, I must be dangerously ill. (*Falls silent.*) The same old story! I am dangerously ill, but all the same, he won't give me any medicine.

DORN: And what do you want? Valerian drops? Bicarbonate of soda? Quinine?

SORIN: Go on, start philosophizing. Oh, what a torture! (*Nodding toward the divan.*) Have you made that bed for me?

POLINA ANDREYEVNA: For you, Pyotr Nikolayevich.

SORIN: Thank you.

DORN: (*Sings.*) "The moon sails on high, in the midnight sky . . ."[45]

SORIN: I'd like to suggest a subject for Kostya's next story. The title will be: "The Man Who Wanted." Or, if you prefer it in French, "*L'homme qui a voulu.*" In my youth, once upon a time, I wanted to become a literary man, but it didn't happen. I also wanted to speak eloquently, but I speak disgustingly. (*Imitates himself.*) "And all that, when all is said and done, and all that . . ." Whenever I tried to get directly to the point, as I would get to the point I'd break out in a sweat. I wanted to get married, but I didn't. I always wanted to live in the city, and here I am, at the end of my life, in the country, and that's all.

DORN: You wanted to become a civil servant, and you became one.

SORIN: (*Laughs.*) I didn't try to become that. It just happened.

DORN: To say you're dissatisfied with life at sixty-two years of age is not very magnanimous of you, wouldn't you agree?

SORIN: How stubborn you are! Try to understand, that I want to live!

DORN: That's a frivolous idea. According to the laws of nature, all life must come to an end.

SORIN: You say that, because you've had your fill. You've had your fill, and so you are indifferent to life, it's all the same to you. But even you must be frightened of death.

DORN: The fear of death is an animal fear . . . We must overcome it. To consciously fear death while believing in eternal life makes sense only for those who have sins they regret. But for you, in the first place, you don't believe in God, and in the second place, what sins could you possibly have committed? You served in the Department of Justice for twenty-five years—and that's all.

SORIN: (*Laughs.*) Twenty-eight . . .

---

45. A popular nineteenth-century serenade.

Treplev enters and sits on a stool at Sorin's feet. Masha does not take her eyes off him the whole time.

DORN: We're keeping Konstantin Gavrilovich from working.

TREPLEV: No, not at all.

Pause.

MEDVEDENKO: Allow me to ask, Doctor, when you went abroad, what city did you like the most?

DORN: Genoa, Italy.

TREPLEV: Why Genoa?

DORN: There are wonderful crowds in the street. When you leave the hotel in the evening, the whole flow of the street is dammed up with people. You can only move here and there, zigzagging along, without any particular aim, and you feel alive, you psychologically merge with the throng, and you begin to believe, that there really is a world soul, like the kind in your play, that Nina Zarechnaya played. By the way, where is Zarechnaya now? Where is she and how is she?

TREPLEV: She must be all right.

DORN: I heard that she was leading a peculiar life. What could that mean?

TREPLEV: It's a long story, Doctor.

DORN: But you can make it short.

Pause.

TREPLEV: She ran away from home and got together with Trigorin. Did you know that?

DORN: Yes.

TREPLEV: She had a baby. The baby died. Trigorin fell out of love with her and returned to his former attachments, as was expected. By the way, he had never actually given up his former attachments. He lacks character, so he had simply connived to be here and there. As far as I can understand, as far as I know, Nina's personal life is a complete failure.

DORN: And the stage?

TREPLEV: That's even worse, it seems. She made her debut in a summer theater outside Moscow, then she went off to the provinces. For a while, I didn't let her out of my sight, I went wherever she did. She always chose the big roles, but played them crudely, tastelessly, stridently, and with abrupt gestures. There were moments, when she cried out with talent, or died with talent, but they were only momentary sparks of talent.

DORN: Then at least she has talent.

TREPLEV: It's hard to tell. Yes she must. I wanted to see her, but she didn't want to meet me, and the maid wouldn't let me into her hotel room. I understood what she must be feeling, and I didn't insist. (*Pause.*) What more can I tell you? Later, when I returned home, I received letters from her. Smart, warm, interesting letters. She didn't complain, but I felt that she was deeply unhappy. Every line betrayed sick, strained nerves. And her imagination was somehow out of tune. She signed them "The Seagull." In *The Water Sprite*,[46] the miller says he is a crow. That's the way she would keep repeating that she was a seagull in her letters. She's here now.

DORN: What do you mean, she's here?

TREPLEV: She's in town, at the inn. She's been there for five days. I would go to see her. Maria Ilinichna went, but she won't see anyone. Semyon Semyonovich swears he saw her last night, after dinner, in a field about two miles from here.

MEDVEDENKO: Yes, I saw her. She was walking in that direction, towards town. I bowed and asked her why she didn't come to visit us. She said she would.

TREPLEV: She won't. (*Pause.*) Her father and stepmother disowned her. They've put watchmen everywhere, so that she can't get near the estate. (*Walks to the desk with the doctor.*) How easy it is to be a philosopher on paper, Doctor, and how hard in practice!

SORIN: She was a lovely girl.

---

46. A poetic fragment (c. 1826) by the father of Russian poetry, Alexander Sergeyevich Pushkin (1799–1837). It describes a young girl who is loved by the local miller. Despite his love, she gives in to the seductions of a prince, who then betrays her. In despair, she throws herself into the river, near the mill where the water is a whirling maelstrom. Instead of death, she finds herself transformed into a water sprite.

DORN: What, sir?

SORIN: I said she was a lovely girl. A civil servant named Sorin once fell in love with her.

DORN: You old Lovelace![47]

Shamrayev's laughter is heard.

POLINA ANDREYEVNA: I think they're back from the station . . .

TREPLEV: Yes, I hear Mama.

Arkadina and Trigorin enter, followed by Shamrayev.

SHAMRAYEV: (*Entering.*) We all get older and weather-beaten by the storms in our lives, but you, dear madam, always get younger . . . A slip of a girl. So full of life . . . Graceful . . .

ARKADINA: You're going to bring me bad luck by saying so, you bore!

TRIGORIN: (*To Sorin.*) Hello, Pyotr Nikolayevich! Are you still ailing? That's not good! (*Sees Masha, happily.*) Maria Ilinichna!

MASHA: You recognize me? (*Presses his hand.*)

TRIGORIN: Married?

MASHA: For a long time now.

TRIGORIN: Happy? (*Bows to Dorn and Medvedenko, and then hesitantly approaches Treplev.*) Irina Nikolayevna told me that you have buried the hatchet and have stopped being angry with me.

Treplev offers Trigorin his hand.

ARKADINA: (*To her son.*) Boris Alekseyevich brought the journal with your latest short story in it.

TREPLEV: (*Taking the journal, to Trigorin.*) Thank you. You are very kind.

---

47. A name commonly used to describe a man who is easily infatuated with women; Lovelace is a character in Samuel Richardson's novel *Clarissa* (1748).

They sit.

TRIGORIN: Your fans send their regards . . . In Petersburg and Moscow, everyone is very interested in you. They all ask me about you. They ask, what is he like, how old is he, is he blond or brunette. For some reason they all think that you're old. And no one knows your real name, since you write under a pseudonym. You are mysterious, a real Iron Mask.[48]

TREPLEV: Will you be staying long?

TRIGORIN: No, I'm thinking about leaving for Moscow tomorrow. I must. I'm rushing to finish a story, and then I promised to get something ready for an anthology. In short, the same old story.

As they converse, Arkadina and Polina Andreyevna set up a card table in the middle of the room; Shamrayev lights candles and sets up chairs. They get a lotto set[49] *from the cupboard.*

TRIGORIN: The weather has not been good. A cruel wind. Tomorrow morning, if it dies down, I'll go fishing on the lake. By the way, I must have a look in the garden, at that place,—do you remember?—where your play was acted. I have a theme ready, but I have to refresh my memory of the spot where it takes place.

MASHA: (*To her father.*) Papa, please give my husband a horse! He needs to go home.

SHAMRAYEV: (*Teases.*) A horse . . . Home . . . (*Sternly.*) You know the horses just got back from the station. We can't send them out again tonight.

MASHA: But surely there must be other horses . . . (*Seeing that her father is silent, she waves her hand.*) Why try . . .

MEDVEDENKO: Masha, I'll walk home. Really . . .

POLINA ANDREYEVNA: (*Sighing.*) Walk, in this weather . . . (*Sits at the card table.*) Please, ladies and gentlemen.

---

48. A famous political agitator, imprisoned by Louis XIV, who kept his face and hence his identity hidden behind an iron mask.

49. The earliest name (1778) for a game of chance commonly called "bingo" in the United States.

MEDVEDENKO: It's only six miles . . . Goodbye . . . (*Kisses his wife's hand.*) Goodbye, Mama. (*His mother-in-law reluctantly offers him her hand for a kiss.*) I don't want to be a bother, but the baby . . . (*Bows to everyone.*) Goodbye . . . (*Exits with a guilty gait.*)

SHAMRAYEV: Don't worry, he can walk. He's no general.

POLINA ANDREYEVNA: (*Taps on the table.*) Please, ladies and gentlemen. Let's not waste time. They'll be ready with dinner soon.

Shamrayev, Masha, and Dorn sit at the table.

ARKADINA: (*To Trigorin.*) When the long autumn evenings begin, we play lotto. Look. It's the old lotto set, the same one that we used when we played with our late mother, when we were children. Don't you want to play with us before dinner? (*She and Trigorin sit at the table.*) It's a boring game, but once you get used to it, it's not bad. (*Deals each person three cards.*)

TREPLEV: (*Leafing through the journal.*) He read his own story, but he didn't even cut the pages of mine.[50] (*Lays the journal on the desk, then goes toward the door on the left; crossing in front of his mother he kisses her on the head.*)

ARKADINA: And you, Kostya?

TREPLEV: Forgive me, I don't feel like it . . . I'm going for a walk. (*Exits.*)

ARKADINA: The stake is ten kopecks. Put it down for me, Doctor.

DORN: I obey, madam.

MASHA: Has everybody made their bets? I'll begin . . . Twenty-two!

ARKADINA: Got it.

MASHA: Three! . . .

DORN: Right here, madam.

---

50. In the past, the pages of books were manufactured on folded sheets of paper (folios). Readers used paper knives to cut along the folds and reveal the printing on the inner pages of the folio. In the journal given to him by Trigorin, Treplev notices that Trigorin has only cut the pages on his own story, proving that he has read only his own work, not Treplev's.

MASHA: Did you bet three? Eight! Eighty-one! Ten!

SHAMRAYEV: Not so fast.

ARKADINA: What a reception I got in Kharkov,[51] gentlemen! My head is still spinning.

MASHA: Thirty-four!

A melancholy waltz is heard off stage.

ARKADINA: The students gave me a standing ovation . . . Three baskets, and two wreaths, and this . . . (*Takes a brooch from her breast and throws it on the table.*)

SHAMRAYEV: Yes, quite something . . .

MASHA: Fifty! . . .

DORN: Fifty even?

ARKADINA: I was wearing a remarkable outfit . . . But then, I always dress well.

POLINA ANDREYEVNA: Kostya is playing. The poor boy's sick at heart.

SHAMRAYEV: They've been abusing him in the papers lately.

MASHA: Seventy-seven!

ARKADINA: He shouldn't pay attention!

TRIGORIN: He's unlucky. He can't seem to find his own style. It's a little strange, a little vague, sometimes it even reads like a kind of delirium. And not a single living character.

MASHA: Eleven!

ARKADINA: (*Glancing toward Sorin.*) Petrushka, are you bored? (*Pause.*) He's asleep.

DORN: Our civil servant is asleep.

MASHA: Seven! Ninety!

TRIGORIN: If I lived on an estate like this, near a lake like this, do you think I would write? I would have overcome this passion of mine and spent my time fishing.

MASHA: Twenty-eight!

---

51. An important cultural and mercantile city in the Ukraine.

TRIGORIN: Catching a perch or a bass—that's bliss!

DORN: I believe in Konstantin Gavrilovich. He has something! He thinks in images, his stories are beautiful, vivid, and they always move me deeply. The only pity is that he doesn't have a definite aim. He makes an impression, and that's all, and you can't go far on impressions alone. Irina Nikolayevna, are you happy that your son is a writer?

ARKADINA: Imagine, I haven't read him yet. There's never any time.

MASHA: Twenty-six!

Treplev quietly enters and sits at his desk.

SHAMRAYEV: (*To Trigorin.*) You left one of your things here, Boris Alekseyevich.

TRIGORIN: Which one?

SHAMRAYEV: When Konstantin Gavrilovich shot the seagull, you asked me to get it stuffed for you.

TRIGORIN: I don't remember. (*Thinking it over.*) Don't remember!

MASHA: Sixty-six! One!

TREPLEV: (*Throws open the window and listens.*) How dark it is! I don't understand why I feel so uneasy.

ARKADINA: Kostya, close the window. It's blowing in.

Treplev closes the window.

MASHA: Eighty-eight!

TRIGORIN: This game is mine, ladies and gentlemen!

ARKADINA: (*Happily.*) Bravo! Bravo!

SHAMRAYEV: Bravo!

ARKADINA: This man is always so lucky. (*Stands.*) And now let's go have something to eat. Our celebrity did not have any lunch today. We'll play some more after dinner. (*To her son.*) Kostya, leave your manuscript, and come eat.

TREPLEV: I don't want to, Mama, I'm full.

ARKADINA: As you like. (*Wakes Sorin.*) Petrushka, it's dinner time! I will tell you all about my reception in Kharkov . . .

Polina Andreyevna extinguishes the candles on the table, then she and Dorn push the wheelchair. All exit through the door on the left; only Treplev remains on stage, at the desk.

TREPLEV: (*Getting back to his writing; looking over what he has already written.*) I talked so much about new forms, but now little by little I've gotten myself into a rut. (*Reads.*) "The poster on the fence proclaimed . . . A pale face framed by dark hair . . ." Proclaimed, framed . . . It's talentless. (*Crosses it out.*) I'll start from where the hero is woken up by the sound of the rain, and I'll throw out everything else. My description of the moonlit evening is long and forced. Trigorin's got his devices all worked out. It's easy for him . . . He makes a broken bottleneck glitter on the dam, and the shadow cast by a windmill grows darker, and there it is—a moonlit night. I've got a flickering light, and the quiet sparkle of the stars, and the far-away strains of a piano, dying away in the quiet aromatic air . . . It's tormenting . . . (*Pause.*) More and more I'm convinced that the point is not old forms or new forms, but that a person writes, not thinking about forms, writes because it pours out of the soul.

Someone knocks on the window closest to the desk.

TREPLEV: What's that? (*Looks at the window.*) Can't see anything . . . (*Opens the glass door and looks out into the garden.*) Someone's running down the steps. (*Calls out.*) Who's there?

Exits; he is heard running along the terrace; after half a minute he returns with Nina Zarechnaya.

TREPLEV: Nina! Nina!

Nina places her head on his chest and although she tries not to, sobs.

TREPLEV: (*Moved.*) Nina! Nina! It's you . . . you . . . I had a premonition it was you. All day I felt sick at heart. (*Takes off her hat and cloak.*) Oh, my darling, my beloved, she's come back! Let's not cry, let's not!

NINA: Someone is here.

TREPLEV: No one.

NINA: Lock the doors, so they won't come in.

TREPLEV: No one will come in.

NINA: I know Irina Nikolayevna is here. Lock the doors . . .

TREPLEV: (*Locks the right door with a key and goes to the left one.*) There's no lock here. I'll put a chair against it. (*Places a chair against the door.*) Don't be afraid; no one will come in.

NINA: (*Looks intently into his eyes.*) Let me look at you. (*Looking around.*) It's warm here, good . . . This used to be the drawing room. Have I changed much?

TREPLEV: Yes . . . You've gotten thinner, and your eyes look bigger. Nina, it's so strange to be seeing you. Why didn't you let me see you earlier? Why didn't you come sooner? I know you've been in town for almost a week . . . I went to see you, several times a day, every day. I stood under your window like a beggar.

NINA: I was afraid you'd hate me. Every night I dream that you look at me, and you don't recognize me. If you only knew! As soon as I arrived I came here . . . to the lake. I was near your house many times, but I couldn't come in. Let's sit down. (*They sit.*) We'll sit and talk, talk . . . It's good here, warm, cosy. Listen, it's the wind! Turgenev wrote: "He, who sits with a roof over his head, in a corner all his own, on nights such as these, is a lucky man." I'm the seagull . . . No, that's not so. (*Rubs her forehead.*) What was I talking about? Oh, yes . . . Turgenev . . . "And may the Lord help all homeless wanderers . . ."[52] It's nothing. (*Sobs.*)

TREPLEV: Nina, you're crying again . . . Nina!

NINA: It's nothing. It makes it easier for me . . . I haven't cried for two years. Yesterday, late at night, I went into the garden to see if our theater was still there. And it's still standing. I started to cry, for the first time in two years, and I felt better, things became clearer. You see, I'm not crying now. (*Takes his hand.*) So, you've become a writer . . . You—a writer, and I—an actress . . . You and I have both fallen into the whirling maelstrom[53] . . . I used to live happily, like a child. I'd get up

---

52. A paraphrase from Ivan Sergeyevich Turgenev's novel *Rudin* (1856).
53. A reference to Pushkin's *The Water Sprite*. See note 46.

in the morning and start singing. I loved you, I dreamed of glory, but now? Early tomorrow morning I travel to Yéletz[54] by train, third class . . . Riding with the peasants. And in Yeletz the merchants will pester me with their attentions. It's a coarse life!

TREPLEV: Why Yeletz?

NINA: I took an engagement there for the whole winter. It's time to go.

TREPLEV: Nina, I cursed you, hated you, tore up your letters and photographs, but every minute I knew that my heart was tied to yours, forever. I don't have the strength to fall out of love with you, Nina. Since I lost you, and my work started to be published, life has become unbearable for me. I'm suffering . . . It's as if my youth had been suddenly torn out of me, I feel as if I've lived ninety years. I call to you, I kiss the ground you walk on. Wherever I look, everywhere I see your face, this affectionate smile, which lit the best years of my life . . .

NINA: (*Upset.*) Why talk like this? Why talk like this?

TREPLEV: I'm alone, no one warms my heart. I'm cold, as if I were in a cellar. And whatever I write, it's all dry, stale, and dull. Stay here Nina! I beg you. Or let me go with you!

Nina quickly puts on her hat and cloak.

TREPLEV: Nina, why? For God's sake, Nina . . . (*Watches while she gets dressed. Pause.*)

NINA: My horses are waiting at the gate. Don't see me off, I'll go myself . . . (*Through tears.*) Give me some water . . .

TREPLEV: (*Gives her something to drink.*) Where are you going now?

NINA: To town. (*Pause.*) Is Irina Nikolayevna here?

TREPLEV: Yes . . . On Thursday my uncle was ill, and we telegraphed her to come.

NINA: Why do you say you kiss the ground I walk on? You should have killed me. (*Leans on the table.*) I'm so tired! I'd like to rest . . . to rest! (*Raises her head.*) I am the seagull . . . Not so.

---

54. An industrial city in western Russia.

I am an actress. Yes! (*Having heard the laughter of Arkadina and Trigorin, she listens, then runs to the left door and looks through the keyhole.*) He's here too . . . (*Returning to Treplev.*) Yes . . . It's nothing . . . Yes, well . . . He didn't believe in the theater, he always laughed at my dreams, and little by little I also stopped believing and lost heart . . . And then love's anxieties, jealousy, constant fear for the baby . . . I became petty, insignificant, I played senselessly . . . I didn't know what to do with my hands, didn't know how to stand on stage, couldn't control my voice. You don't understand how it feels when you're playing badly. I am the seagull. No, not so . . . You remember, you shot a seagull? By chance a man comes along, sees it, and because he has nothing better to do, kills it . . . A subject for a short story . . . That's not so . . . (*Rubs her forehead.*) What was I talking about? . . . I was talking about the stage. Now, it's not like that . . . I'm a real actress, I act with pleasure, with ecstasy, I'm drunk on stage, and I feel beautiful. And now, since I've been staying here, I've been walking, walking and thinking, thinking and feeling that with every day, I'm getting my inner strength back . . . I know now, I understand, Kostya, that in our business—whether we act or write—the important thing is not fame, not glitter, not what I dreamed of, but the ability to persist, to endure. To know how to bear your cross and have faith. When I have faith, it's not so painful. And when I think of my calling, I'm not afraid of life.

TREPLEV: (*Sadly.*) You've found your way, you know where you're going. But I still haven't found my way through this chaos of fantasies and images. I don't know what it's for, or who needs it. I don't have faith in anything, and I don't know what my calling is.

NINA: (*Listening.*) Shhh . . . I'm going. Goodbye. When I become a great actress, come see me. Promise? But now, (*Pressing his hand.*) it's late. I can barely stand up . . . I'm exhausted, and I want to get something to eat . . .

TREPLEV: Stay. I'll get you some supper . . .

NINA: No, no . . . Don't see me off, I'll go myself . . . My horses are close by . . . She's brought him with her, then? So what? It's all the same. When you see Trigorin, don't tell him anything . . . I do love him. I love him even more than before. A subject for a short story . . . I love him, I love him passionately, I love him desperately. It was good before, Kostya! You remember? What a clear, warm, happy, clean life, and feelings like tender, elegant little flowers . . . Do you remember? (*Recites.*) "People, lions, eagles and partridges, horned deer, geese, spiders, silent fishes that dwell under water, starfish, and those creatures invisible to the naked eye—in short, all life, all life, having completed its sad cycle, has died out . . . For millennia the earth has born no living being, and this poor moon lights her lamp in vain. In meadows, no longer do cranes call, and no May beetles are heard in linden groves . . ." (*Embraces Treplev impulsively and runs out through the glass door.*)

TREPLEV: (*After a pause.*) I hope no one meets her in the garden and tells mama. That would upset Mama . . .

In the next two minutes, he silently tears up his manuscripts and throws them under the table, then opens the right door, and exits.

DORN: (*Trying to open the left door.*) Strange. The door seems to be locked . . . (*Enters and puts the chair back in its place.*) An obstacle race.

Arkadina and Polina Andreyevna enter, followed by Masha and Yakov with some bottles, then Shamrayev and Trigorin.

ARKADINA: Put the red wine and beer for Boris Alekseyevich here, on the table. We'll drink while we play. Let's sit down, ladies and gentlemen.

POLINA ANDREYEVNA: (*To Yakov.*) Please bring some tea. (*Lights the candles, sits at the card table.*)

SHAMRAYEV: (*Approaches Trigorin who stands near the cupboard.*) Here's that thing I was telling you about . . . (*Takes a stuffed seagull from the cupboard.*) You ordered it.

TRIGORIN: (*Looking at the seagull.*) I don't remember! (*Thinking it over.*) Don't remember!

From the right of the stage, there is a shot, startling everyone.

ARKADINA: (*Frightened.*) What's that?

DORN: Nothing. Maybe something in my medicine case exploded. Don't worry... (*Exits through the right door, and returns in half a minute.*) So it was. A bottle of ether exploded. (*Sings.*) "Once again, I kneel before you, my beloved..."

ARKADINA: (*Sitting down at the table.*) Uhf, I was frightened. It reminded me of that time when Kostya... (*Covers her face with her hands.*) Everything suddenly went black...

DORN: (*Paging through the journal, to Trigorin.*) There was an article published two months ago... a letter from America, and I've been meaning to ask you about it... (*Takes Trigorin by the waist and leads him downstage.*) Since I'm very interested in matters of this kind... (*In a low tone of voice, whispering.*) Get Irina Nikolayevna out of here. The thing is—Konstantin Gavrilovich has killed himself...

Curtain.

Uncle Vanya

Scenes of Country Life in Four Acts

[In 1889, Chekhov wrote *The Wood Demon*, a sprawling romantic comedy that opened to mixed reviews. In 1897, he radically cut, reshaped, and transformed it into a new play, *Uncle Vanya*, which premiered in Odessa, Kiev. During 1897, more provincial productions in Saratov and Tblisi followed. The Moscow Art Theatre production opened on October 26, 1899. Konstantin Stanislavsky directed and played Astrov; Olga Knipper played Yelena. In discussing the two principal male roles, Chekhov told Stanislavsky: "Uncle Vanya cries, but Astrov whistles."[1] Staged in 1914 in English in London, America first saw it performed in Russian in 1924 by the Moscow Art Theatre during the company's tour. It was not until 1929 that an English language version was performed in the United States. The translation that follows was created for this volume. —SMC]

The Characters

Serebryakóv, Alexánder Vladímirovich, a retired professor.[2] [His last name derives from the Russian word for "silver;" his first name recalls both the ancient conqueror and Paris (often called Alexander in ancient literature), who abducted Helen and thus began the Trojan War. His mother-in-law calls him by the French *Alexandre*.[3]]

Yeléna Andréyevna, his wife, twenty-seven years old. [Her first name is the Russian form of Helen, thus recalling the beautiful Helen of Troy. Her nickname is Lénochka; her name in French is *Hélène*.]

Sofía Aleksándrovna, Serebryakov's daughter from his first marriage. [Her first name means "wisdom" in Greek, a fact generally known to Russians, whose orthodox faith came from Byzantium. Her nicknames are Sónya, Sónyushka, and Sónyechka. Her mother was named Véra, the Russian word for "faith."]

---

1. K. S. Stanislavsky, *Sobranie sochinenii* [Collected Works], vol. I (Moscow: Iskusstvo, 1988), 410–11.

2. In pre-Revolutionary Russia, professors held the same civil rank as generals. Consequently, contemporary censors objected to this play because they saw Chekhov's portrayal of Serebryakov as offensive.

3. The use of French names suggests aristocratic roots or aspirations, because Russian aristocracy spoke French fluently.

Voinítskaya, María Vasílyevna, the widow of a privy councilor[4] and mother of Serebryakov's first wife. [She is often called *Maman,* French for "mother."]

Voinítsky, Iván Petróvich, her son. [The family name of Voinítsky (male)/Voinítskaya (female) derives from the Russian word for "warrior." His nickname is Ványa; *Jean* is the French form of his first name.]

Ástrov, Mikhaíl Lvóvich, a doctor. [His last name derives from "aster," a colorful flower that has no scent; a secondary derivation is "astral."]

Telégin, Ilyá Ilyích, an impoverished landowner. [His last name means "wagon" in Russian, a simple form of transportation used by peasants. He is called "Waffles" because his face is pock-marked.]

Marína, the old nanny. [Her formal name is Marína Timoféyevna.]

A workman

The action takes place on Serebryakov's estate.

Act I

An orchard. Part of the orchard and a porch can be seen. There is a table for serving tea set up under an old poplar in an alley of trees. Benches, chairs; a guitar lies on one of the benches. Not far from the table is a swing. It is past two o'clock in the afternoon. It is cloudy. Marina, a fat, slow-moving old woman, sits near the sámovar,[5] knitting socks. Astrov is walking around nearby.

MARINA: (*Pours a glass of tea.*) Have something to eat, sir.

ASTROV: (*Takes the glass reluctantly.*) I don't much feel like it.

MARINA: Maybe some vodka?

ASTROV: No. I don't drink vodka every day. Besides, it's too muggy. (*Pause.*) Nanny, how many years have we known each other?

---

4. A fairly high-ranking government official, something like a senator.

5. A samovar (literally a "self-boiler") is a large metal urn that boils water. In the nineteenth century, samovars used charcoal as fuel, and therefore they could be taken outside. A pot with strong tea is placed on top of the samovar's lid so that the tea can be kept warm. One serves tea by pouring a small amount of tea into a glass and then adding water from the samovar's spigot to taste.

MARINA: *(Thinking.)* How many? God, let me remember . . . You came here, to these parts . . . When was it? . . . Véra Petróvna, Sonyechka's mother, was still alive. You visited us for two winters during her lifetime . . . Well, that means about eleven years have passed. *(Thinking again.)* But maybe even more . . .

ASTROV: Have I changed a lot since then?

MARINA: A lot. You were young then, and handsome, but now you've gotten old. Your looks aren't what they were. And I have to say it, you've taken to drinking vodka now.

ASTROV: Yes . . . In ten years I've become a different man. And what's the reason? Overwork, Nanny. I'm on my feet from morning until night, don't get any rest, and at night I hide under the covers, afraid they'll come and drag me off to a patient. The whole time we've known each other, I haven't had one day off. How could I not get old? And then too, life itself is boring, stupid, dirty . . . Life drags you down. Eccentric people surround you, everywhere nothing but eccentrics. You live with them for two or three years, and little by little, without even noticing, you become eccentric too. An inescapable fate! *(Twirls the ends of his large mustaches.)* Look at these enormous mustaches . . . Stupid mustaches. I've become an eccentric, Nanny . . . But at least I haven't become stupid. Thank God, my brain still works. But my feelings have gotten dull. I don't want anything, I don't need anything, I don't love anyone . . . Except you. *(Kisses her on the head.)* In my childhood, I had a nanny just like you.

MARINA: Maybe you'd like something to eat?

ASTROV: No. During the third week of Lent,[6] I went to the village of Málitskoye[7] to an epidemic . . . typhoid fever . . . People lay side by side in the huts . . . There was dirt, stench, smoke, calves on the floor next to the sick people . . . Even piglets . . . I didn't stop moving the whole day, didn't sit down once, didn't have a crumb to eat. Then I got home and still couldn't get any rest. They brought in a railroad worker. I put him

---

6. The forty-day period of fasting and repentance that, according to Christian tradition, precedes the anniversary of the resurrection of Jesus Christ on Easter Sunday.

7. The town's name derives from "small."

on the table to operate, and he died under the chloroform. And then, the last thing I need, my feelings woke up. I felt conscience-stricken, as if I'd killed him on purpose . . . I sat down, closed my eyes—like this, and thought: Will those who live one hundred, or two hundred years from now, those for whom we are preparing the way, will they remember us with a kind word? Nanny, they won't remember!

MARINA: People won't remember, but God will remember.

ASTROV: Thanks for that. You said that well.

Enter Voinitsky.

VOINITSKY: (*Exits from the house; he fell asleep after lunch and looks tousled; sits on a bench, and straightens his stylish tie.*) Yes . . . (*Pause.*) Yes . . .

ASTROV: Had enough sleep?

VOINITSKY: Yes . . . Slept very well. (*Yawns.*) Ever since the professor and his wife arrived, life has jumped the tracks . . . I don't sleep when it's time, I eat all sorts of spicy food at lunch and dinner, drink wine . . . It's not healthy! Before this, I never had a free minute. Sonya and I both worked. But now, I admit with all due respect, Sonya works alone. I sleep, eat, drink . . . It's not good!

MARINA: (*Shaking her head.*) There's no order in the house! The professor gets up at twelve o'clock, and the samovar's been boiling all morning long, waiting for him. Without the two of them, we always ate by one o'clock like everybody else, but with them, we eat around seven. At night, the professor reads and writes, and then, just before two in the morning, the bell suddenly goes off . . . What is it, sir? Tea! Wake everybody up, put on the samovar . . . No order!

ASTROV: Will they be here much longer?

VOINITSKY: (*Whistles.*) For a hundred years. The professor has decided to move in.

MARINA: Take now for instance. The samovar's been boiling on this table for two hours, but they've gone out for a stroll.

VOINITSKY: They're coming, they're coming . . . Don't worry.

Voices are heard; Serebryakov, Yelena Andreyevna, Sonya, and Telegin are seen in the orchard, returning from their stroll.

SEREBRYAKOV: Wonderful, wonderful . . . Wonderful views.

TELEGIN: Remarkable, your excellency.

SONYA: We'll go to the forestry tomorrow, Papa. Would you like to?

VOINITSKY: Ladies and gentlemen, there's tea to drink!

SEREBRYAKOV: My friends, send my tea to my office, please! I still have things to do today.

SONYA: And you'll really like the forestry . . .

Yelena Andreyevna, Serebryakov, and Sonya exit into the house; Telegin goes to the table and sits next to Marina.

VOINITSKY: It's hot, it's muggy, and yet our great scholar wears a coat and galoshes, and his gloves, and takes an umbrella with him.

ASTROV: It shows he takes good care of himself.

VOINITSKY: How good looking she is! How good looking! In my whole life, I've never seen a more beautiful woman.

TELEGIN: Whether I ride through the open field, Marina Timofeyevna, or stroll through the shady orchard, or look at this table here, I experience inexpressible bliss! The weather is charming, the birds are singing, we live together in peace and harmony. What more could we want? (*Takes a glass of tea.*) I feel deeply grateful to you!

VOINITSKY: (*Dreamily.*) Her eyes . . . A marvelous woman!

ASTROV: Tell me something, Ivan Petrovich.

VOINITSKY: (*Listlessly.*) What should I tell you?

ASTROV: Something new?

VOINITSKY: There's nothing new. Everything's old. I'm the same as I was. If anything, I'm worse because I've gotten lazy, don't do anything. I only grumble like an old fogy. The old crow, my *maman*, still babbles about women's emancipation. She's got one eye on the grave, and with the other eye she looks forward to the dawn of a new life, one that she finds on the pages of her smart little books.[8]

ASTROV: And the professor?

VOINITSKY: And the professor does as he always did. He sits in his office and writes from morning until deep into the night. "With sharpened mind and furrowed brow, all our odes we write, we write. And never a hint of praise hear we."[9] The poor paper! He'd do better to write his autobiography. What an excellent subject that would be! A retired professor, you understand, a dry corncob, an educated fish, pulled from the Caspian Sea. Gout, rheumatism, migraine, a liver swollen with jealousy and envy . . . And this fish lives on his first wife's estate, lives there not because he wants to, but because he can't afford to live in the city. He complains endlessly about being unhappy, even though he is unusually fortunate. (*Nervously.*) Just consider how fortunate he is! A seminary student, the son of a simple deacon, attains a doctorate and a professorship, becomes "his excellency," the son-in-law of a privy councilor, and so forth and so on. But none of that matters. Consider this instead. For a full twenty-five years, he lectures and writes about art, while fully understanding nothing about art. For twenty-five years, he regurgitates other people's ideas about realism, naturalism, and every other kind of nonsense. For twenty-five years he reads and writes about things that intelligent people already know, and that stupid people find uninteresting. That means, that for twenty-five years he has churned out empty nonsense. And yet, what a high opinion he has of himself! What pretension! When he retired, not one living soul knew who he was. He's completely unknown. That means, that for twenty-five years, he's had the wrong job. And look at him, he struts around like a demi-god!

ASTROV: Well, it seems you're jealous of him.

VOINITSKY: Yes, I'm jealous! What success he has had with women! No other Don Juan has known such complete success! His

---

8. Pamphlets from the Russian socialist utopian movement of the 1860s, an ideological and populist movement that favored doing good works for the peasantry and emancipating women. Central to this movement was Nikolay Gavrilovich Chernyshevsky's novel *What Is to Be Done?* (1863), a title that is echoed in many lines throughout this play.

9. From a satirical poem by Ivan Ivanovich Dmitriyev (1760–1837).

first wife was my sister, a wonderful, gentle creature, as pure as the cloudless blue sky, noble, with more admirers than he had students. She loved him as only pure angels can love those who are as pure and as wonderful as they. My mother, his mother-in-law, worships him to this day, and to this day he inspires her with reverent awe. His second wife, that intelligent beauty you just saw, married him when he was already old. She gave him her youth, beauty, freedom, her brilliance. For what? Why?

ASTROV: Is she faithful to the professor?

VOINITSKY: Unfortunately yes.

ASTROV: Why unfortunately?

VOINITSKY: Because her faithfulness is false from beginning to end. It's rhetorical, not logical. Betraying your old husband, whom you can't stand, is morally wrong, but smothering your own poor youth and your most vital feelings—that's not morally wrong.

TELEGIN: (*In a tearful voice.*) Vanya, I don't like it when you talk like that. Well now, really . . . Anyone who betrays a husband or wife, you see, is an unfaithful person, and might even betray his country!

VOINITSKY: (*Annoyed.*) Turn off the fountain, Waffles!

TELEGIN: Please, Vanya. My wife ran off with the man she loved the day after our wedding because of my unattractive appearance. After that I never broke my vows to her. I love her to this day, I help her however I can. I gave her my property, so that she could raise the progeny she bore for the man she loved. Happiness may be denied me, but I still retain my pride. And she? Her youth is gone, her beauty has dimmed in accord with the laws of nature, the man she loved has died . . . What does she have left?

Enter Sonya and Yelena Andreyevna; a little later Maria Vasilyevna enters with a book; she sits down and reads; she is served tea and she drinks it without looking up.

SONYA: (*Hurriedly, to the nurse.*) Nanny, some peasants have come. Go speak to them, and I'll take care of the tea . . . (*Pours tea.*)

*Marina exits. Yelena Andreyevna takes her
tea, sits on the swing, and drinks.*

ASTROV: (*To Yelena Andreyevna.*) I came for your husband. You wrote that he was very ill, rheumatism and more, but it turns out he's perfectly healthy.

YELENA ANDREYEVNA: Last night he was laid low and complained about the pain in his legs, but today, nothing . . .

ASTROV: But I galloped forty-five miles at breakneck speed to get here. Well, if it's nothing, it's not the first time. So I'll make the best of it, and stay until morning. At least, I'll get a good night's sleep *quantum satis.*[10]

SONYA: That's wonderful. It's so rare that you spend the night. I don't suppose you've already eaten?

ASTROV: No, ma'am, I haven't.

SONYA: Well then, you'll have dinner with us. These days, we don't have dinner until seven. (*Drinks.*) The tea is cold!

TELEGIN: The temperature of the samovar has significantly dropped.

YELENA ANDREYEVNA: It's nothing, Iván Ivánich. We'll drink it cold.

TELEGIN: Excuse me, madam . . . It's not Ivan Ivanich, but Ilya Ilyich, madam . . . Ilya Ilyich Telegin. But some people call me "Waffles" because of my pitted face. I'm Sonyechka's godfather, and your esteemed husband knows me very well. I live with you, madam, here on this estate . . . If you'll notice, I eat dinner with you every day.

SONYA: Ilya Ilyich is our steward, our right-hand man. (*Tenderly.*) Let me give you some more tea, godfather.

MARIA VASILYEVNA: Aahh!

SONYA: What's wrong, Grandmother?

MARIA VASILYEVNA: I forgot to tell *Alexandre* . . . I'm losing my mind . . . Today I received a letter from Khárkov,[11] from Pável Alekséyevich . . . He sent his new pamphlet . . .

---

10. "As much as is needed" (Latin). The phrase is commonly used in medical prescriptions.
11. A major city in the Ukraine with a famous university.

ASTROV: Is it interesting?

MARIA VASILYEVNA: Interesting, but somewhat strange. He disproves what he himself proved seven years ago. It's awful!

VOINITSKY: There's nothing awful in that. Drink your tea, *Maman*.

MARIA VASILYEVNA: But I want to talk!

VOINITSKY: But we've been talking and talking, and reading pamphlets for fifty years. It's time to stop.

MARIA VASILYEVNA: For some reason you find it unpleasant to listen to me talk. Pardon me, *Jean*, but in the last year you have changed so much that I no longer recognize you . . . You used to be a man of conviction, an enlightened individual . . .

VOINITSKY: Oh yes! An enlightened individual, who shed no light on anyone . . . (*Pause.*) An enlightened individual . . . You shouldn't make such poisonous jokes! I'm forty-seven years old now. Until last year, I was just like you, deliberately trying to cloud my vision with this scholasticism of yours, so that I wouldn't have to see life as it really is. And I could think that everything was just fine. But now, if you only knew! I don't sleep nights, annoyed and resentful, knowing that I spent my time stupidly, when I could have had everything that my old age now denies me!

SONYA: Uncle Vanya, that's boring!

MARIA VASILYEVNA: (*To her son.*) It's as if you were blaming your former convictions . . . But they aren't to blame, you are. You've forgotten that convictions by themselves are nothing but an alphabet for life . . . You should have done something.

VOINITSKY: Done something? Everyone can't write like a *perpetuum mobile* like your *Herr* Professor.[12]

MARIA VASILYEVNA: What do you mean by that?

SONYA: (*Pleading.*) Grandmother! Uncle Vanya! I beg you!

VOINITSKY: I'll shut up. I'll shut up and apologize. (*Pause.*)

YELENA ANDREYEVNA: It's good weather today . . . Not too hot . . . (*Pause.*)

---

12. *Perpetuum mobile:* "perpetual motion machine" (Latin). *Herr:* "mister" (German).

VOINITSKY: Good weather to hang yourself . . .

> *Telegin tunes his guitar; Marina enters near the house and calls the chickens.*

MARINA: Cheep, cheep, cheep . . .

SONYA: Nanny, what did the peasants want?

MARINA: Always the same thing, about the empty field. Cheep, cheep, cheep . . .

SONYA: Who are you calling?

MARINA: The speckled hen went off with her chicks . . . The crows could attack them . . . (*Exits.*)

> *Telegin plays a polka; everyone listens silently; a workman enters.*

WORKMAN: Is the doctor here? (*To Astrov.*) Please, Mikhail Lvovich, they've sent for you.

ASTROV: From where?

WORKMAN: From the factory.

ASTROV: (*Irritated.*) I humbly thank you. Well, got to go . . . (*Glances around for his hat.*) It's annoying, damn it . . .

SONYA: How unpleasant, honestly . . . Come back from the factory for dinner.

ASTROV: No, it'll be too late. Where is . . . Now where is . . . (*To the workman.*) Look, be nice and bring me a glass of vodka.

> *Workman exits.*

ASTROV: (*Continuing.*) Where is . . . Now where is . . . (*Finds hat.*) In some play or other by Ostróvsky,[13] there's a man with large mustaches and small abilities . . . Just like me. Well ladies and gentlemen, I bid you . . . (*To Yelena Andreyevna.*) I would be sincerely pleased if you would stop by my place sometime, perhaps with Sofia Aleksandrovna. I have a little estate of

---

13. Alexander Nikolayevich Ostrovsky (1823–1886) was the first Russian writer to write plays exclusively. Astrov references a character from *The Dowerless Girl* (1879).

about eighty acres, and, if you're interested, there's a model garden and nursery, such as you won't find for a thousand miles around. Next to my estate is the state forestry . . . The forester there is old, and always sick, so, in fact, I take care of everything myself.

YELENA ANDREYEVNA: I've been told that you like forests very much. Of course forestry can be very useful, but surely it must interfere with your true calling? After all, you're a doctor.

ASTROV: Only God knows what our true calling is.

YELENA ANDREYEVNA: And is it interesting?

ASTROV: Yes, the work's interesting.

VOINITSKY: (*Ironically.*) Very!

YELENA ANDREYEVNA: (*To Astrov.*) You're still a young man, you look . . . well, thirty-six, thirty-seven years old . . . and it can't be as interesting as you say. Forests and more forests. It sounds monotonous.

SONYA: No, it's extraordinarily interesting. Mikhail Lvovich plants new forests every year, and has already been awarded a bronze medal and a certificate. He makes sure that the old forests are not exhausted. If you listened to him you would agree completely. He says that forests adorn the earth, that they teach humanity to understand beauty, that they inspire lofty thoughts. Forests temper severe climates. In countries where there's a temperate climate, humanity spends less energy on the battle with nature, and so people are gentler and more loving. The people there are beautiful, lithe, easily aroused, their speech is elegant, their movements gracious. Science and art blossom among them. They are not pessimistic. Men's relations with women are refined and noble . . .

VOINITSKY: (*Laughing.*) Bravo, bravo! . . . All this is nice, but not convincing, so (*To Astrov.*) allow me, my friend, to continue burning wood in my stove, and making my barns from lumber.

ASTROV: You can burn peat in your stove, and build your barns from stone. Well, I admit, you can cut wood when necessary, but why exhaust the supply? Russian forests tremble under the axe, millions of trees are perishing, the habitats of wild animals and birds are being ravaged, streams are drying up, magnificent views are disappearing forever, and all because the human being is too lazy to see any sense in bending down and picking fuel up from the ground. (*To Yelena Andreyevna.*) Aren't I right, Yelena Andreyevna? You'd have to be a barbarian, bereft of reason, to burn such beauty in your stove, to destroy that which you cannot create. Humanity has been endowed with reason and creative energy in order to increase what was given to us, but up to now we have done nothing but destroy. There are fewer and fewer forests, the rivers are drying up, game birds are becoming extinct, the climate is being damaged, and with each day the earth becomes more and more barren and hideous. (*To Voinitsky.*) There you are, looking at me ironically and not taking anything I say seriously, and . . . and maybe I am just eccentric, but when I walk through the peasants' forests that I saved from being cut down, or when I hear the rustling of leaves in my young forest, planted with my own hands, then I know I have some control over the climate, and that, if after a thousand years humanity is happy, I will have been somewhat to blame. When I plant a birch, and then see how green it gets and how it sways in the wind, I am filled with pride and I . . . (*Seeing the workman, who enters carrying a glass of vodka on a tray.*) However . . . (*Drinks.*) It's time to go. It's probably only eccentricity after all . . . I bid you farewell. (*Goes toward the house.*)

SONYA: (*Takes him by the arm and goes with him.*) When will you come back to see us again?

ASTROV: I don't know . . .

SONYA: After another month? . . .

Astrov and Sonya exit into the house; Maria Vasilyevna and Telegin remain near the table; Yelena Andreyevna and Voinitsky walk toward the porch.

YELENA ANDREYEVNA: And you, Ivan Petrovich, behaved badly again. You had to irritate Maria Vasilyevna by talking about a *perpetuum mobile*! And today at lunch you fought with Alexander again! How petty!

VOINITSKY: But what if I hate him!

YELENA ANDREYEVNA: There's no reason to hate Alexander, he's like everybody else. No worse than you.

VOINITSKY: If only you could see your face, the way you move . . . How lazily you live! Ah, how lazy!

YELENA ANDREYEVNA: Ah, lazy and bored! Everyone curses my husband, and everyone looks at me sympathetically. How unfortunate she is to have such an old husband! Your concern for me—oh how I understand it! It's like Astrov just said: you cut down the forests without thinking, and soon there'll be nothing left on earth. You cut down people like that too, without thinking, and soon, thanks to you, there'll be no faithfulness, no purity, no capacity for sacrifice left on earth. Why can't you look at another man's woman indifferently? The doctor is right—it's because there's a devil of destruction in all of you. You don't pity forests, birds, women, or each other.

VOINITSKY: I don't like this philosophy! (*Pause.*)

YELENA ANDREYEVNA: That doctor has a tired, nervous face. An interesting face. It's obvious that Sonya likes him, she's in love with him, and I understand her. I've seen him here three times now, and still I feel timid in front of him. I haven't once spoken with him properly, haven't treated him kindly. He must think I'm mean-spirited. Probably that's why you and I, Ivan Petrovich, are such good friends, because we're both tedious, boring people! Tedious! Don't look at me like that, I don't like it.

VOINITSKY: How else can I look at you, if I love you? You are my happiness, life, my youth! I know that my chances with you are negligible, roughly zero, but I don't need anything much. Just allow me to look at you, listen to your voice . . .

YELENA ANDREYEVNA: Be quiet, they can hear you! (*Goes toward the house.*)

VOINITSKY: (*Following her.*) Allow me to speak about my love, don't drive me away, that alone will give me great happiness . . .

YELENA ANDREYEVNA: This is tormenting . . .

Both exit into the house. Telegin plucks the strings of the guitar and plays a polka; Maria Vasilyevna makes a note in the margins of her pamphlet.

Curtain.

Act II

The dining room in Serebryakov's house. Night. The watchman can be heard tapping in the garden.[14] Serebryakov sits dozing in an armchair before an open window and Yelena Andreyevna sits beside him, also dozing.

SEREBRYAKOV: (*Wakes up.*) Who's here? Sonya, is it you?

YELENA ANDREYEVNA: It's me.

SEREBRYAKOV: You, Lenochka . . . What unbearable pain!

YELENA ANDREYEVNA: Your lap robe has fallen on the floor. (*Wraps his legs.*) I'll close the window, Alexander.

SEREBRYAKOV: No, I'm suffocating . . . I just dozed off and dreamed that my left leg was not my own. I woke up from the tormenting pain. No, this is not gout,[15] it's probably rheumatism. What time is it?

YELENA ANDREYEVNA: Twenty minutes past twelve.

Pause.

SEREBRYAKOV: In the morning, go look for a copy of Bátyushkov[16] in the library. I think we have him there.

YELENA ANDREYEVNA: Huh?

SEREBRYAKOV: Go look for Batyushkov in the morning. I remember that we had him. But why is it so hard for me to breathe?

YELENA ANDREYEVNA: You're tired. You haven't slept for two nights.

SEREBRYAKOV: They say that Turgénev developed *angina pectoris*[17] from gout. I'm afraid that I might too. Damnable, disgusting old age! To hell with it! When I got old, I became repellent to

---

14. To scare off intruders, watchmen on Russian estates tapped on wooden boards.

15. A genetically inherited disease in which the joints swell due to an accumulation of uric acid.

16. Konstantin Nikolayevich Batyushkov (1781–1855), a Russian Romantic poet.

17. Ivan Sergeyvich Turgenev (1818–1883) set many of his novels and his play *A Month in the Country* (1872) on country estates like the one in this play. *Angina pectoris* is the medical term for severe chest pain.

myself. Yes, and all of you too must find it repellent to look at me.

YELENA ANDREYEVNA: You speak of your old age as if we were all to blame for it.

SEREBRYAKOV: You were the first to find me repellent. (*Yelena Andreyeva walks away and sits down further from him.*) Of course, you're right. I'm not stupid, I understand. You're young, healthy, beautiful, you want to live, but I'm an old man, almost a corpse. Isn't that it? Don't I understand? And of course it's stupid of me to go on living. But just wait, I'll soon set you all free. I won't drag it out much longer.

YELENA ANDREYEVNA: I'm exhausted . . . For God's sake, be quiet.

SEREBRYAKOV: So, as it happens, because of me, everyone is exhausted, bored, wasting their youth, and I'm the only one who's enjoying life and feeling content. Well yes, of course!

YELENA ANDREYEVNA: Be quiet! You're tormenting me!

SEREBRYAKOV: I've tormented all of you. Of course.

YELENA ANDREYEVNA: (*Through tears.*) It's unbearable! Tell me what you want from me?

SEREBRYAKOV: Nothing.

YELENA ANDREYEVNA: Well then, be quiet. I beg you.

SEREBRYAKOV: It's strange, that when Ivan Petrovich starts talking, or that old idiot Maria Vasilyevna, then nothing's wrong, everyone listens. But whenever I say just one word, everyone begins to feel unhappy. Even my voice is repellent. Well, let's suppose that I am repellent, that I am an egotist, that I am a despot. Don't I have some right to egotism in my old age? Haven't I earned it? Don't I have the right, I ask you, to a peaceful old age, to some attention from people?

YELENA ANDREYEVNA: No one is disputing your rights. (*The window bangs from the wind.*) The wind is picking up, I'll close the window. (*Closes it.*) Now there'll be rain. No one is disputing your rights.

Pause. In the garden, the watchman is tapping and singing a song.

SEREBRYAKOV: To have worked all my life on behalf of scholarship, to have gotten used to my office, to lecture halls, to having respectful colleagues—and suddenly, for no rhyme or reason, to find myself in this crypt, seeing stupid people here every day, listening to their trivial conversations . . . I want to live, I love success, love fame, excitement, but here—it's like being in exile. Every minute longing for the past, following the success of others, fearing death . . . I can't stand it! I don't have the strength! And here they won't even forgive me my old age!

YELENA ANDREYEVNA: Give it time, have some patience, and in five or six years I'll be old too.

Sonya enters.

SONYA: Papa, you ordered us to send for Doctor Astrov, but when he came, you refused to see him. It's impolite. We've disturbed the man for no reason . . .

SEREBRYAKOV: What's your Astrov to me? He knows medicine as well as I know astronomy.

SONYA: We can't send for the whole medical faculty for your gout.

SEREBRYAKOV: I won't even talk to that dunce.

SONYA: As you wish. (*Sits down.*) It's all the same to me.

SEREBRYAKOV: What time is it now?

YELENA ANDREYEVNA: Nearly one.

SEREBRYAKOV: I'm suffocating . . . Sonya, give me the drops that are on the table!

SONYA: Right away. (*Gives him a bottle of drops.*)

SEREBRYAKOV: (*Annoyed.*) Ah, not these! I can't ask for anything!

SONYA: Please, don't act like a child. Some people might find it endearing, but spare me, do me that kindness! I don't like it. And I don't have the time for it, I have to get up early to deal with the hay.

Voinitsky enters in a dressing gown and with a candle.

VOINITSKY: There's a storm brewing outside. (*Lightning.*) There it is! *Hélène,* Sonya, go to sleep, I've come to relieve you both.

SEREBRYAKOV: (*Frightened.*) No, no! Don't leave me with him! No. He'll talk me to death!

VOINITSKY: But you need to let them rest! They haven't slept for two nights in a row.

SEREBRYAKOV: Let them go to sleep, but you go too. Thank you. I beg you. For the sake of our former friendship, don't protest. We'll talk later.

VOINITSKY: (*With a smile.*) Our former friendship . . . Former . . .

SONYA: Be quiet, Uncle Vanya.

SEREBRYAKOV: (*To his wife.*) My dear, don't leave me with him! He'll talk me to death.

VOINITSKY: That makes me laugh.

Marina enters with a candle.

SONYA: You should be in bed, Nanny dear. It's late.

MARINA: The samovar's still on the table. Going to bed isn't so much-of-a-much.

SEREBRYAKOV: No one's asleep, they're exhausted, only I am in bliss.

MARINA: (*Goes to Serebryakov, gently.*) What is it, dear father? Are you in pain? My own legs ache me sometimes, they ache so much. (*Straightens his lap robe.*) You've had this sickness a long time. Vera Petrovna, now deceased, Sonyechka's mother, lost many nights of sleep for you, killing herself . . . She loved you so very much . . . (*Pause.*) Old people, just like babies, just want someone to feel sorry for them, but no one feels sorry for the old. (*Kisses Serebryakov's shoulder.*) Let's go, dear father, to bed . . . Let's go, my starlight . . . I'll brew you some lime tea, and warm your feet . . . I'll pray for you . . .

SEREBRYAKOV: (*Moved.*) Let's go, Marina.

MARINA: My own legs ache me sometimes, they ache so much! (*Leads him with Sonya's help.*) Vera Petrovna was always killing herself, always crying . . . You, Sonyushka, were little then, still stupid . . . Come on, come on, dear father . . .

Serebryakov, Sonya, and Marina exit.

YELENA ANDREYEVNA: I've tormented myself with him. I'm hardly standing on my legs.

VOINITSKY: You with him and I with myself. It's been three nights since I slept.

YELENA ANDREYEVNA: It's unhappy in this house. Your mother hates everyone except her brochures and the professor. The professor is annoyed, doesn't trust me, and fears you. Sonya is mean to her father, mean to me, and hasn't spoken with me for two whole weeks. You hate my husband and openly disdain your mother. I'm annoyed and today I started crying nearly twenty times . . . It's unhappy in this house.

VOINITSKY: Let's drop the philosophy!

YELENA ANDREYEVNA: You, Ivan Petrovich, are educated and smart. So, it seems to me, that you should understand that it's not thieves, not fires that destroy world peace, but hatred, enmity, these petty fights . . . You should make it your business not to growl, but to make peace with everyone.

VOINITSKY: First let's you and I make peace! My dear . . . (*Grasps her hand.*)

YELENA ANDREYEVNA: Let me go! (*Takes her hand away from him.*) Go away!

VOINITSKY: The rain will soon be over, and everything in nature will feel refreshed and breathe easily. Only I will not be refreshed by the storm. Day and night, the thought that my life has been irrevocably lost suffocates me, as if a demon were robbing me of my breath. I have no past, it was squandered stupidly on petty things. And the present is awful in its absurdity. That's my life for you, and my love. What have I done with them, what should I do with them? My feelings have perished in vain, like rays of sun that have fallen into a pit, and I myself am perishing.

YELENA ANDREYEVNA: When you talk to me about your love, I feel somehow dull, and I don't know what to say. Forgive me, I cannot say anything to you. (*Starts to leave.*) Good night.

VOINITSKY: (*Blocking her way.*) And if you knew how I suffer from the thought, that beside me in this very house another life is perishing—yours! What are you waiting for? What kind of damned philosophy is getting in your way? Try to understand, understand . . .

YELENA ANDREYEVNA: (*Staring at him.*) Ivan Petrovich, you're drunk!

VOINITSKY: Maybe, maybe . . .

YELENA ANDREYEVNA: Where's the doctor?

VOINITSKY: He's there . . . Spending the night with me. Maybe, maybe . . . Anything may be!

YELENA ANDREYEVNA: And drinking today? What for?

VOINITSKY: At least it passes for some sort of life . . . Don't get in my way, *Hélène!*

YELENA ANDREYEVNA: You never used to drink before, and you never used to talk so much . . . Go to sleep! You're boring me.

VOINITSKY: (*Grabbing her hand.*) My dear . . . You're miraculous!

YELENA ANDREYEVNA: (*Annoyed.*) Let go of me. This has finally become repellent. (*She leaves.*)

VOINITSKY: (*Alone.*) She left . . . (*Pause.*) Ten years ago I met her at my late sister's home. She was seventeen then, and I was thirty-seven. Why didn't I fall in love with her then and propose to her? Surely it would have been possible then! And now she would have been my wife . . . Yes . . . Now we both would have been awakened by the storm. She would have been frightened by the thunder, and I would have held her tight in my arms and whispered: "Don't be afraid, I'm here." Oh, what miraculous thoughts, how good, it even makes me laugh . . . But, my God, the thoughts in my head are tangled up . . . Why am I old? Why doesn't she understand me? Her rhetoric, her lazy morality, her nonsensical, lazy thoughts about destroying world peace—that's all deeply hateful to me. (*Pause.*) Oh, how I have been deceived! I worshiped this professor, this pitiful sufferer of gout, I worked for him like an ox! Sonya and I squeezed every last drop of juice out of this estate for him. We sold vegetable oil, peas, cottage cheese, just like the peasants. And we never once ate our fill, so that we could scrimp and save kopecks by the thousands and send them off to him. I was proud of him and his scholarship, I lived and breathed for him! Everything that he wrote or uttered seemed like genius to me . . . God, and now? Here he is retired, and now the sum total of his life can be seen for what it is. Not one page of his work will remain after him, he is completely unknown, he is nothing! A soap bubble! And I have been deceived . . . Now I see it, deeply deceived . . .

Astrov enters wearing a frock coat[18] but without a waistcoat or necktie; he is tipsy; following him is Telegin with a guitar.

ASTROV: Play!

TELEGIN: Everyone's asleep, sir!

ASTROV: Play!

Telegin plays softly.

ASTROV: (*To Voinitsky.*) You're here alone? No ladies? (*Waves his arms and sings.*) "Gone the hut, gone the hearth, gone the master's comfy cot . . ."[19] Storm woke me up. A hard rain. What time is it?

VOINITSKY: The devil knows.

ASTROV: I thought I heard Yelena Andreyevna's voice.

VOINITSKY: She was just here.

ASTROV: A luxurious woman. (*Examines the medicine bottles on the table.*) Medications. What a lot of prescriptions here! From Kharkov, and Moscow, and Túla[20] . . . Every city must be tired of his gout. Is he sick or pretending?

VOINITSKY: Sick.

Pause.

ASTROV: Why are you so sad today? Sorry for the professor, is that it?

VOINITSKY: Let me be.

ASTROV: But maybe you are in love with the professor-ess?

VOINITSKY: She's my friend.

ASTROV: Already?

---

18. A man's suit coat, fitted at the waist and knee-length.
19. From a Russian folk song.
20. Tula is a large industrial city about two hundred miles from Moscow.

VOINITSKY: What do you mean by "already"?

ASTROV: A woman can become a man's friend only in this sequence: first an acquaintance, then a lover, and after that a friend.

VOINITSKY: A crass philosophy.

ASTROV: What? Yes . . . I must confess, I've become crass. You see, I'm drunk. Usually I get drunk like this once a month. When I'm in this state, I become insolent and impudent in the extreme. Then everything's nothing to me! I can take on the most difficult operations and do them beautifully. I can draw up the biggest plans for the future. At these times, I don't even seem eccentric to myself any more, and I believe that I can be of great use to humanity . . . Great use! And at these times, I have my own philosophical system, and all of you, my brothers, appear to me to be like little insects . . . Microbes. (*To Telegin.*) Waffles, play!

TELEGIN: Dear sweet friend, I would be happy to play for you with all my heart, but try to understand—people are sleeping in this house!

ASTROV: Play! (*Telegin plays softly.*) Must drink our fill! Let's go, in there, I think some cognac's left in there. And when it gets light, let's go to my place. Shall we "vacuate" this place? I have a military medical assistant who always says "vacuate" instead of "evacuate." A real swindler! So shall we "vacuate"? (*Seeing Sonya, who enters.*) Excuse me, I don't have my necktie on. (*Quickly exits, with Telegin following him.*)

SONYA: So, Uncle Vanya, you've been drinking with the doctor again! What a pair of paragons! He's always been like that, but you? At your age, it doesn't suit you at all.

VOINITSKY: Age has nothing to do with it. When you have no real life, you look for mirages. They're better than nothing.

SONYA: All our hay has been mown, it's out there rotting in the rain, and you spend your time on mirages. You've completely neglected the farming . . . I'm working alone, and I've worn myself out . . . (*Frightened.*) Uncle, you have tears in your eyes!

VOINITSKY: What tears? It's nothing . . . Nonsense . . . Just now you looked at me like your late mother used to. My dear . . . (*Intensely kissing her hands and her face.*) My sister . . . My dear sister . . . Where is she now? If only she knew! Ah, if only she knew!

SONYA: What? Uncle, knew what?

VOINITSKY: What a burden . . . It's not good . . . It's nothing . . . Later . . . It's nothing . . . I'll go . . . (*Exits.*)

SONYA: (*Knocks on the door.*) Mikhail Lvovich! You're not sleeping, are you? Come out for a minute!

ASTROV: (*Behind the door.*) Right away! (*After a moment's wait he enters, now dressed in his tie and jacket.*) Your wish is my command.

SONYA: Go ahead and drink if you don't find it repellent, but I beg you, don't let my uncle drink. It's bad for him.

ASTROV: Fine. We won't drink any more. (*Pause.*) I'll go home right away. Our agreement's signed and sealed. By the time the horses are harnessed, it will be dawn.

SONYA: It's still raining. Wait until morning.

ASTROV: The storm is passing, we're in the tail end of it. I'll go. And, please, don't ever ask me to come here for your father again. I tell him it's gout, he says it's rheumatism. I ask him to lie down, he sits up. And today, he wouldn't speak to me at all.

SONYA: He's spoiled. (*Looks in the sideboard.*) Do you want something to eat?

ASTROV: Yes, please.

SONYA: I love to eat at night. It looks like there's something left in the sideboard. Throughout his life he's had great success with women, they say, and the ladies have spoiled him. Here, take some cheese.

Both stand at the sideboard and eat.

ASTROV: I didn't eat anything today, only drank. Your father's character makes him a burden. (*Takes a bottle from the sideboard.*) May I? (*Downs a glass full.*[21]) There's no one here, so I can speak openly. You know, I think I couldn't endure living in your house for even a month. I'd suffocate in this

---

21. Russians usually drink vodka by emptying the glass in a single long gulp.

atmosphere . . . Your father, who's always going on about his gout and his books, your Uncle Vanya with his depression, your grandmother, and finally your stepmother . . .

SONYA: What about my stepmother?

ASTROV: Everything about a person should be beautiful: face, clothes, soul, thoughts. She's beautiful, there's no argument there, but . . . All she does is eat, sleep, go for a stroll, charm us all with her beauty, and nothing more. She doesn't have any responsibilities. Others do the work for her . . . Isn't that so? But an idle life can not be pure. (*Pause.*) But then, maybe I'm being too hard on her. I'm not satisfied with life, just like your Uncle Vanya, and so we both grumble.

SONYA: You're not with satisfied life?

ASTROV: Generally I love life, but I can't endure our life, this provincial, Russian, narrow-minded life. I despise it with all the strength of my soul. And as for my own personal life, well, dear God, there's absolutely nothing good there. You know, when you're walking through a forest at night, if you can see a light shining in the distance, then you don't notice how tired you are, how dark it is, or how the thorny branches hit you in the face . . . I work like no one else in the district, you know this. Fate beats me up, without stopping, and sometimes I suffer unbearably, but there is no light in the distance for me. I no longer expect anything for myself, I don't love people. . . . It's been a long time since I've loved anyone.

SONYA: No one?

ASTROV: No one. I do feel some affection for your nanny, for old times' sake. All the peasants are very much alike, backward, living a dirty life. And I don't get on much with the intelligentsia either. They're tiresome. All of them, all our dear acquaintances, think small, have small feelings, they don't see further than their own noses. Simply put, they're stupid. And those who are a bit smarter, a bit more serious, they suffer from hysteria, and are consumed by analysis and introspection . . . They drink, hate, gossip obsessively. They walk up to a person, look at him sideways, and decide, "Oh, this one's a psychopath!" or "That one's a windbag!" Or when they don't know what label to stick on a person's forehead, they say, "That one's strange, strange!" I love forests—that's strange. I don't eat meat—that's strange too. There are no more direct, pure, free exchanges with nature or with people . . . No, no more! (*Goes for a drink.*)

SONYA: (*Stopping him.*) No, I beg you, please, don't drink any more.

ASTROV: Why?

SONYA: It doesn't suit you! You're elegant, you have such a gentle voice . . . What's more, you are like no one else that I know. You're a beautiful person. Why would you want to act like ordinary people who drink and play cards? Oh, don't do this, I beg you! You always say, that people don't create anything, just destroy what's given to them from above. So why, why do you destroy yourself? There's no need, no need, I beg you, I entreat you.

ASTROV: (*Taking her hand.*) I will drink no more.

SONYA: Give me your word.

ASTROV: My word of honor.

SONYA: (*Strongly shaking his hand.*) Thank you!

ASTROV: *Basta!*[22] I've sobered up. You see, I'm completely sober now, and I will stay like this until the end of my days. (*Looks at his watch.*) Well then, let's continue talking. As I was saying, my time has already passed, it's too late for me . . . I've gotten old, worn myself out with work, gotten crass, dulled all my feelings, and, it seems, I can no longer attach myself to anyone. I don't love anyone, and . . . I won't fall in love anymore. But what still attracts me is beauty. I'm not indifferent to that. It seems to me, that if Yelena Andreyevna wanted to, she could turn my head in a day . . . (*Covers his eyes with his hand and shudders.*)

SONYA: What's wrong?

ASTROV: It's just . . . During Lent, one of my patients died under chloroform.

SONYA: It's time to forget that. (*Pause.*) Tell me, Mikhail Lvovich . . . If I had a friend, or a younger sister, and if you knew that she . . . Well, let's suppose, that she loved you, then what would you think about that?

---

22. "Enough" (Italian).

ASTROV: (*Shrugging his shoulders.*) Don't know. Probably not much. I would let her understand that I couldn't love her . . . Yes, that my head is full of other things. But there's not much time if I'm going. (*Shakes her hand.*) I'll go out through the living room, if you don't mind. Otherwise I'm afraid your uncle will stop me. (*Exits.*)

SONYA: (*Alone.*) He didn't say anything to me . . . His heart and soul are still hidden from me, but why do I feel so happy? (*Laughs from happiness.*) I said to him: you're elegant, noble, you have such a gentle voice . . . Maybe it didn't come out right? His voice trembles, caresses . . . I still feel it in the air. But when I spoke about a younger sister, he didn't understand . . . (*Wringing her hands.*) Oh, how terrible it is that I'm not beautiful! How terrible! And I know that I'm not beautiful, I know, I know . . . Last Sunday, when we were coming out of church, I heard them talking about me and one woman said, "She is good, generous, but it's a pity she's not very beautiful." Not beautiful . . .

Yelena Andreyevna enters.

YELENA ANDREYEVNA: (*Opens the windows.*) The storm is over. What fresh air! (*Pause.*) Where's the doctor?

SONYA: He left.

YELENA ANDREYEVNA: Sofia!

SONYA: What?

YELENA ANDREYEVNA: How long are you going to be cross with me? We haven't wronged each other. Why should we be enemies? Enough of this . . .

SONYA: I myself want to . . . (*Embraces her.*) There's been enough anger.

YELENA ANDREYEVNA: Excellent.

Both are agitated.

SONYA: Did papa go to bed?

YELENA ANDREYEVNA: No, he's sitting in the living room . . . We don't talk to each other for weeks at a time, and God knows why . . . (*Sees the sideboard open.*) What's this?

SONYA: Mikhail Lvovich had supper.

YELENA ANDREYEVNA: There's some wine . . . Let's drink to our friendship.

SONYA: Let's.

YELENA ANDREYEVNA: Out of one glass . . . (*Pours.*) It's better that way. Well, this means—friends?[23]

SONYA: Friends. (*They drink and kiss each other.*) I've wanted to make peace for a long time, and it's been on my conscience . . . (*Cries.*)

YELENA ANDREYEVNA: What's this, you're crying?

SONYA: It's nothing, just the way I am.

YELENA ANDREYEVNA: Well, let it be, let it be . . . (*Cries.*) Such an eccentric girl, I've started crying too . . . (*Pause.*) You're angry with me because it looks like I married your father for money . . . If you believe in oaths, I'll swear to you, I married him for love. I was attracted to him as an educated and famous man. My love wasn't real, it was artificial, but it seemed real to me then. I'm not guilty. But since our marriage, you have not stopped accusing me with your intelligent, suspicious eyes.

SONYA: Well, peace, peace! Let's forget it.

YELENA ANDREYEVNA: You shouldn't look like that—it doesn't suit you. You have to believe in people, otherwise it's impossible to live.

Pause.

SONYA: Tell me honestly, as a friend . . . Are you happy?

YELENA ANDREYEVNA: No.

SONYA: I knew it. One more question. Tell me frankly, wouldn't you rather have a young husband?

YELENA ANDREYEVNA: You're still such a little girl! Of course I would . . . (*She laughs.*) Well, go on ask me something else. Ask . . .

---

23. They drink *bruderschaft* (German for "fellowship") by linking arms and drinking from one glass. They also switch from the formal Russian pronoun for "you" (*vy*) to the more intimate form (*ty*).

SONYA: Do you like the doctor?

YELENA ANDREYEVNA: Yes, very much.

SONYA: (*Laughs.*) I have a stupid face . . . Yes? He left, but I keep hearing his voice and his steps, and when I look at the dark window, I imagine that I see his face there. Let me tell you everything . . . But I can't talk so loudly, I'm embarrassed. Let's go to my room, we'll talk there. Do I seem stupid to you? Admit it . . . Tell me something about him.

YELENA ANDREYEVNA: What?

SONYA: He's intelligent . . . He knows how to do everything, and he can do everything . . . He cures people and plants forests . . .

YELENA ANDREYEVNA: Forests and medicine, that's not the point . . . My dear, you must understand, he has talent! Do you know what talent means? Boldness, a free mind, a wide scope . . . He plants a sapling and already he sees what will become of it in a thousand years, already he imagines the happiness of humanity. Such people are rare, one must love them . . . He drinks, he can be crude, but what of it? A talented man in Russia cannot remain pure. Just think what sort of life this doctor has! Thick mud on the roads, frosts, snowstorms, enormous distances to cover, crude savage people, all around him poverty, sickness. Under such circumstances, it's hard for someone who works and struggles from day to day to keep himself pure and sober into his forties . . . (*Kisses her.*) I wish you, from the bottom of my heart . . . you deserve happiness . . . (*Gets up.*) But I am a boring, secondary character . . . In my music, in my husband's house, in all my affairs, in short, everywhere I have been only a secondary character. Frankly speaking, Sonya, when you think about it, I'm very, very unhappy! (*Walks agitatedly around the stage.*) There is no happiness for me in this world. No! Why are you laughing?

SONYA: (*Laughs, covering her face.*) I'm so happy . . . Happy!

YELENA ANDREYEVNA: I feel like playing the piano . . . I'd like to play something.

SONYA: Play! (*Embraces her.*) I can't sleep . . . Play!

YELENA ANDREYEVNA: Right away. Your father's not asleep. When he's sick, music irritates him. Go ask him . . . If he doesn't mind, then I'll play. Go on.

SONYA: I'll be right back. (*Exits.*)

> *The watchman is heard tapping in the garden.*

YELENA ANDREYEVNA: I haven't played for a long time. I'll play and cry, cry like a fool. (*At the window.*) Is that you tapping, Yefím?

THE WATCHMAN'S VOICE: It's me.

YELENA ANDREYEVNA: Don't tap. The master's not feeling well.

THE WATCHMAN'S VOICE: I'll leave right now. (*Whistles to his dog.*) Hey, Fido! Come here, boy! Come here, Fido!

> *Pause.*

SONYA: (*Returning.*) You can't.

> *Curtain.*

Act III

> The living room in the Serebryakov house. There are three doors: right, left, and center. It is day. Voinitsky and Sonya are seated and Yelena Andreyevna is walking around the stage, thinking about something.

VOINITSKY: *Herr* professor has kindly requested that we all meet today, here in this room at one o'clock in the afternoon. (*Looks at his watch.*) It's quarter to one. He wants to inform the world about something.

YELENA ANDREYEVNA: It's probably business of some kind.

VOINITSKY: He doesn't have any kind of business. He writes nonsense, grumbles and gets jealous, nothing more.

SONYA: (*In a reproachful tone.*) Uncle!

VOINITSKY: Yes yes, sorry. (*Points toward Yelena Andreyevna.*) Take a look at her. She sways as she walks, from laziness. Very nice! Very!

YELENA ANDREYEVNA: All day long you drone on and on, always droning. How it must tire you out! (*With melancholy.*) I'm dying of boredom, I don't know what to do with myself.

SONYA: (*Shrugging her shoulders.*) Is there really so little to do? If only you wanted, there'd be something to do!

YELENA ANDREYEVNA: Like what?

SONYA: There's farming to do, teaching, nursing the sick. Is that so little? When you and papa weren't here, Uncle Vanya and I used to go to market ourselves to sell the flour.

YELENA ANDREYEVNA: I don't know how to do such things. And then too, it's not interesting. People teach and nurse peasants only in ideological novels,[24] and besides, how could I, for no rhyme or reason, suddenly take up nursing or teaching?

SONYA: But I don't understand why you don't go and teach. Give it time, and you'll get used to it. (*Embraces her.*) Don't be bored, my dear kith and kin. (*Laughs.*) You're bored, you don't feel comfortable, but boredom and idleness are infectious. Look, Uncle Vanya does nothing, only follows you around, like a shadow. And I have set aside my business to come and talk things over with you. I've gotten lazy too, I can't help it! The doctor, Mikhail Lvovich, used to come to see us only rarely, once a month, and persuading him to visit was not easy, but now he travels here every day, and abandons both his forests and medicine. You're a sorceress, you must be!

VOINITSKY: Why pine away? (*In a lively manner.*) Well, my darling, my luxurious one, be smart! A nymph's blood flows through your veins, so act like a nymph! Give in, for once in your life, fall madly in love with a sprite, fall head over heels, plunge headlong into the maelstrom,[25] so that *Herr* professor and the rest of us can do nothing but throw up our hands helplessly!

YELENA ANDREYEVNA: (*Angrily.*) Let me be! How cruel this is! (*Begins to leave.*)

VOINITSKY: (*Does not allow her to leave.*) Now, now, my joy, forgive me . . . I apologize. (*Kisses her hand.*) Peace.

---

24. Such as Nikolay Gavrilovich Chernyshevsky's novel *What Is to Be Done?* (1863).

25. An implicit reference to *The Water Sprite* (1826) by Alexander Sergeyevich Pushkin, about a woman betrayed in love who tries to commit suicide by jumping into a river's maelstrom and is transformed, instead, into a sprite (a kind of nymph).

YELENA ANDREYEVNA: Admit that you would try the patience of an angel.

VOINITSKY: As a token of peace and of my admission I will bring you the bouquet of roses that I picked for you this morning . . . Autumn roses, charming, sad roses . . . (*Exits.*)

SONYA: Autumn roses, charming, sad roses . . .

Both look out the window.

YELENA ANDREYEVNA: It's only September. How shall we endure the winter here! (*Pause.*) Where's the doctor?

SONYA: In Uncle Vanya's room. He's writing something. I'm happy that Uncle Vanya left, I have to talk with you.

YELENA ANDREYEVNA: About what?

SONYA: About what? (*Lays her head on Yelena Andreyevna's breast.*)

YELENA ANDREYEVNA: Well, enough, enough . . . (*Smoothes Sonya's hair.*) That's enough.

SONYA: I'm not beautiful.

YELENA ANDREYEVNA: You have wonderful hair.

SONYA: No! (*Glances back to look at herself in the mirror.*) No! When a woman is not beautiful, then they tell her, "You have wonderful eyes, you have wonderful hair . . ." I have loved him for six years, I love him more than my own mother. I seem to hear his voice all the time, feel the touch of his hands, and I watch the door and wait because I think that he could enter at any moment. And look, you see, I keep coming to you to talk about him. Now he's here every day, but he doesn't look at me, doesn't see me . . . It's so painful! I have no hope at all, none, none! (*In despair.*) Oh God, give me strength . . . I prayed all night . . . I often approach him, start talking with him, look him in the eyes . . . I have no more pride, no strength left to control myself . . . Yesterday I couldn't keep myself from admitting to Uncle Vanya, that I love . . . And all the servants know that I love him. Everyone knows.

YELENA ANDREYEVNA: And him?

SONYA: No. He doesn't notice me.

YELENA ANDREYEVNA: (*Thoughtfully.*) He's a strange person . . . You know what? Allow me to speak with him . . . I'll do it carefully, with hints . . . (*Pause.*) Honestly, to remain uncertain after so much time . . . Allow me! (*Sonya nods her head affirmatively.*) Wonderful. Whether he loves you or not—that shouldn't be so hard to find out. Don't be embarrassed, dear friend, don't worry, I'll conduct my interrogation carefully, he won't even notice. All we need to know is if it's yes or no. (*Pause.*) If it's no, then he can stop coming here. Isn't that so? (*Sonya nods her head affirmatively.*) It will be easier when you don't see him. Let's not put it off for long, let's question him right now. He was planning to show me some drawings . . . Go tell him I want to see him.

SONYA: (*Strongly shaken.*) Will you tell me the whole truth?

YELENA ANDREYEVNA: Yes, of course. It seems to me that the truth, whatever it might be, is less terrible than uncertainty. Rely on me, dear friend.

SONYA: Yes . . . Yes . . . I'll tell him you want to see his drawings . . . (*Goes and then stops near the door.*) No, uncertainty is better . . . At least there's hope . . .

YELENA ANDREYEVNA: What's that?

SONYA: Nothing. (*Exits.*)

YELENA ANDREYEVNA: (*Alone.*) No, there's nothing worse than knowing someone else's secret and not being able to help. (*Thinking.*) He's not in love with her, that's clear. But why shouldn't he get married to her? She's not beautiful, but for a country doctor, of his age, she would make a wonderful wife. She's smart, so kind, pure . . . No, that's not it, not it . . . (*Pause.*) I understand the poor girl. In the midst of desperate boredom, when grey splotches, instead of people, wander around the house, when everything you hear is crass, when everything anyone knows how to do is eat, drink, sleep—he arrives and he's unlike all the others, handsome, interesting, attractive—it's like seeing a clear moon rise in the darkness . . . To yield to the charms of such a man, to forget oneself . . . It seems that even I am attracted to him a little. Yes, I'd miss him. Look, I'm smiling now because I'm thinking about him . . . This Uncle Vanya here says that nymph's blood runs through my veins. "Give in, for once in your life . . ." What if I did? Maybe that's what I need . . . To fly as freely as a bird away from all of you, away from your sleepy faces, your conversations, to forget that all of you even exist . . . But I'm a coward, timid . . . My conscience would torment me . . . He's here every day, and I can guess why he's here. I already sense that I'm to blame. I'm ready to fall on my knees before Sonya, and confess to her, to cry . . .

ASTROV: (*Enters with a hand drawn map.*) Good day! (*Shakes her hand.*) You wanted to see my artwork?

YELENA ANDREYEVNA: Yesterday you promised to show me your work . . . Are you free now?

ASTROV: Oh, of course. (*Unrolls the hand-drawn map on the card table and tacks it down.*) Where were you born?

YELENA ANDREYEVNA: (*Helping him.*) In St. Petersburg.[26]

ASTROV: And where were you educated?

YELENA ANDREYEVNA: At the Music Conservatory there.

ASTROV: Then perhaps this won't interest you.

YELENA ANDREYEVNA: Why not? True, I don't know country life, but I read a lot.

ASTROV: Here in this house I have my own desk . . . In Ivan Petrovich's room. When I am completely exhausted, to the point of stupefaction, I drop everything and run over here, and amuse myself with this thing for an hour or two . . . Ivan Petrovich and Sofia Aleksandrovna click away on the abacus,[27] while I sit near them at my own desk, daubing with my paints, and I feel warm, peaceful, and the cricket chirps. But I don't allow myself this pleasure very often, about once a month . . . (*Shows her the map.*) Now look. This is a picture of our district as it was fifty years ago. The dark and light green colors mark the forests. Half of the area was covered by forests. Where the green is cross-hatched with red, there lived elk, goats . . . You see I mark both the flora and fauna. On this lake there were swans, geese, ducks, and, as the old folk say, there was a powerful crowd of birds, all kinds.

---

26. Russia's capital during Chekhov's lifetime. It was founded by Peter the Great and widely believed to be the country's most cosmopolitan city. The St. Petersburg Conservatory of Music was founded in 1862.

27. A calculating machine that uses beads that slide along wires to keep count. The beads click against each other as they are moved.

When they took flight, it looked like a storm cloud. Besides the little towns and villages, you can see various settlements scattered here and there, little farms, hermitages made by Old Believers,[28] water mills ... There were a lot of horned cattle and horses. That's shown by the sky-blue color. For example, in this section, the blue is very thick. Here there were whole herds, and in every yard three horses. (*Pause.*) Now let's look lower down. This section shows what was here in the district twenty-five years ago. Only one-third of the forests remain. There are no more goats, but there are still some elk. The green and blue colors are paler. And so forth and so on. Let's go to the third section of the map: a picture of the district as it is now. There is some green here and there, in splotches, but it's not solid. The elk, and swans, and grouse have vanished ... There's no longer a trace of the settlements, the farms, hermitages, the mills. In general, the picture shows a gradual and indisputable degeneration, which, obviously, will be complete in about ten or fifteen years. You'll say that this is the influence of culture, that the old life must give way to the new. Yes, I could understand that, if highways and railroads had been laid down to replace the devastated forests, if there were factories, manufacturing, and schools, if the people were healthier, richer, smarter, but there's nothing of the sort! The same swamps and mosquitoes are still here in the district, the same dirt roads, poverty, typhus, diphtheria, fires ... We are dealing here with degeneration caused by a struggle for survival that is beyond us. This degeneration comes from stagnation, from ignorance, from a complete lack of awareness. Degeneration occurs whenever a frostbitten, hungry, sick person tries to save what remains of his life and tries to take care of his children by grabbing instinctively, unconsciously for anything that can stave off hunger or give some warmth. He destroys everything without thinking about tomorrow ... Nearly everything has been destroyed, and nothing has been created to replace it. (*Coldly.*) I can see from your face that this does not interest you.

YELENA ANDREYEVNA: But I understand so little about it ...

---

28. A religious sect which broke from the Orthodox Church during the seventh century, when certain rituals were changed by the patriarch.

ASTROV: There's nothing here to understand, it's simply uninteresting.

YELENA ANDREYEVNA: To speak frankly, my thoughts were elsewhere. Forgive me. I need to conduct a little interrogation of you, and I'm embarrassed. I don't know how to begin.

ASTROV: Interrogation?

YELENA ANDREYEVNA: Yes, an interrogation, but . . . innocent enough. Let's sit down! (*They sit.*) The matter concerns a certain young individual. We'll talk like honest people, like friends, without beating about the bush. Let's talk and then forget what's been said. Yes?

ASTROV: Yes.

YELENA ANDREYEVNA: The matter concerns my stepdaughter, Sonya. Do you like her?

ASTROV: Yes, I respect her.

YELENA ANDREYEVNA: Do you like her as a woman?

ASTROV: (*Not immediately.*) No.

YELENA ANDREYEVNA: Just two or three more words, and that'll be that. Have you noticed nothing?

ASTROV: Nothing.

YELENA ANDREYEVNA: (*Takes him by the hand.*) You do not love her, I can see it in your eyes . . . She's in pain . . . Understand this, and . . . stop coming here.

ASTROV: (*Stands up.*) Time has passed me by . . . Yes, there's no time . . . (*Shrugs his shoulders.*) When could I find time? (*Embarrassed.*)

YELENA ANDREYEVNA: Ough, what an unpleasant conversation! I feel as shaken, as if I were dragging a ton of weight behind me. Well, thank God, we've finished. Let's forget, as if we had never spoken of it, and . . . And go away. You're a smart person, you'll understand . . . (*Pause.*) I'm blushing all over.

ASTROV: If you had said something a month or two ago, then maybe I would have given it some thought, but now . . . (*Shrugs his shoulders.*) But if she's in pain, then of course . . . There's only one thing I don't understand. Why did you need to conduct this interrogation? (*Looks her in the eye and threatens her with his finger.*) You are cunning!

YELENA ANDREYEVNA: What do you mean?

ASTROV: (*Laughing.*) Cunning! Let's suppose that Sonya is in pain. I'll gladly accept that, but then why is this your interrogation? (*Preventing her from speaking, in a lively manner.*) Please, don't put that surprised look on your face. You know perfectly well why I come here every day . . . Why and for whom I come here is something you know perfectly well. My dear predator, don't look at me like that, I'm an old hand . . .

YELENA ANDREYEVNA: (*In confusion.*) Predator? I don't understand.

ASTROV: You beautiful, furry weasel . . . You need prey! Look, I've been here for a whole month, doing nothing, dropping everything, greedily seeking you out, and you like it this way, very much, very . . . Well, what of it? I've been caught, you knew that without an interrogation. (*Crossing his hands and bowing his head.*) I give up. Here, devour me!

YELENA ANDREYEVNA: You've lost your mind!

ASTROV: (*Laughs between his teeth.*) You're timid . . .

YELENA ANDREYEVNA: Oh, I'm better and more high-minded than you think! I swear to you! (*Starts to exit.*)

ASTROV: (*Blocking her path.*) I'll leave today, I won't come here anymore, but . . . (*Takes her by the hand, looks around.*) Where shall we see each other? Tell me quickly, where? Someone could come in at any moment, tell me quickly. (*Passionately.*) What a miraculous, luxurious woman . . . One kiss . . . I'll kiss just your fragrant hair . . .

YELENA ANDREYEVNA: I swear to you . . .

ASTROV: (*Preventing her from speaking.*) Why swear? There's no need to swear. No need for unnecessary words . . . Oh, what a beauty! What hands! (*Kisses her hands.*)

YELENA ANDREYEVNA: That's finally enough . . . Go away . . . (*Pulls away her hands.*) You are forgetting yourself.

ASTROV: Just tell me, tell me where shall we see each other tomorrow? (*Takes her by the waist.*) You see, it's inevitable, we must see each other.

Astrov kisses her; at this moment Voinitsky enters with a bouquet of roses, and stops at the door.

YELENA ANDREYEVNA: (*Not seeing Voinitsky.*) Have mercy on me . . . Let me go . . . (*Astrov lays his head on her chest.*) No! (*Starts to exit.*)

ASTROV: (*Holding her by the waist.*) Come to the forestry tomorrow . . . About two o'clock . . . Yes? Yes? Will you come?

YELENA ANDREYEVNA: (*Seeing Voinitsky.*) Let me go! (*Walks to the window, deeply embarrassed.*) This is awful.

VOINITSKY: (*Places the bouquet on a chair; disturbed, he wipes his face and the inside of his collar with his handkerchief.*) It's nothing . . . Yes . . . Nothing . . .

ASTROV: (*All stirred up.*) Today, my dear respected Ivan Petrovich, the weather's not bad. In the morning it was overcast, as if it were going to rain, but then the sun came out. To be honest, autumn is turning out wonderfully . . . And the winter crops won't be bad either. (*Rolls up his hand-drawn map.*) The only thing is, the days are getting short . . . (*Exits.*)

YELENA ANDREYEVNA: (*Quickly goes to Voinitsky.*) You must try, use all your influence, to make sure that my husband and I leave here today! Do you hear? Today!

VOINITSKY: (*Wiping his face.*) Ah? Well, yes . . . Fine . . . *Hélène*, I saw everything, everything . . .

YELENA ANDREYEVNA: (*Nervously.*) Do you hear? I must leave here today!

Serebryakov, Sonya, Telegin, and Marina enter.

TELEGIN: I too, your excellency, am not in good health. For two days now, I've been ill. There's something with my head . . .

SEREBRYAKOV: Where are the others? I don't like this house. What a labyrinth! Twenty-six enormous rooms, everybody scatters, and you can never find anyone. (*Rings.*) Invite Maria Vasilyevna and Yelena Andreyevna to come here!

YELENA ANDREYEVNA: I'm here.

SEREBRYAKOV: Ladies and gentlemen, please be seated.

SONYA: (*Approaching Yelena Andreyevna, impatiently.*) What did he say?

YELENA ANDREYEVNA: Later.

SONYA: Are you trembling? Are you upset? (*Looks at Yelena Andreyevna's face inquisitively.*) I understand . . . He said he won't be coming here anymore . . . Is that right? (*Pause.*) Tell me, is that right?

Yelena Andreyevna nods her head affirmatively.

SEREBRYAKOV: (*To Telegin.*) You can come to terms with ill health, whatever it is, but I can not swallow the medicine prescribed by this country life. I feel like I have fallen off the face of the earth and landed on another planet. Be seated, ladies and gentlemen, I beg you. Sonya! (*Sonya does not hear; she stands with her head bowed in sadness.*) Sonya! (*Pause.*) She doesn't hear. (*To Marina.*) And you, Nanny, sit down. (*The nurse sits and knits a sock.*) I beg you, ladies and gentlemen, as they say, "lend me your ears."[29] (*Laughs.*)

VOINITSKY: (*Disturbed.*) Maybe you don't need me? Can I go?

SEREBRYAKOV: No, I need you the most.

VOINITSKY: What can I do for you?

SEREBRYAKOV: You . . . Are you angry? (*Pause.*) If I have somehow offended you, then forgive me, please.

VOINITSKY: Drop that tone of voice. Let's get down to business . . . What do you need?

Maria Vasilyevna enters.

SEREBRYAKOV: Now *Maman* is here. Ladies and gentlemen, I will begin. (*Pause.*) "I invited you here, ladies and gentlemen, to announce that the Inspector General is coming."[30] But all jokes aside. This is a serious matter. Ladies and Gentlemen, I have gathered you together in order to ask for your help and advice, and, counting on your customary civility, I hope to receive these from you. I am a scholar, a man of books, and the practicalities of life have always seemed foreign to me. I cannot get by without the guidance of knowledgeable people,

---

29. From Marc Antony's plea for attention in the funeral oration in Shakespeare's *Julius Ceasar*.

30. The mayor's opening line from Nikolay Vasilyevich Gogol's *The Inspector General* (1842).

and I beg you, Ivan Petrovich, and you too, Ilya Ilyich, and you *Maman* . . . The fact of the matter is, *manet omnes una nox*,[31] that we are all mortal in God's eyes. I am old, sick, and thus the time has come to put my worldly affairs in order so far as they concern my family. My life is already finished, I am not thinking about myself, but I have a young wife, a maiden daughter. (*Pause.*) It is impossible for me to remain living in the country. We were not made for country life. Yet it is impossible for us to live in the city on the income that we receive from this estate. If we were to sell, let's say, the forest, it would be an extraordinary measure that we could not repeat every year. We must find those measures that would guarantee us a constant, more or less fixed income. I have thought up one such measure, and I have the honor of proposing it to you for discussion. Omitting the details, I will lay it out in its general outline. Our estate produces on average no more than two percent. I propose to sell it. If we turn the profit into interest-bearing securities, then we shall receive from four to five percent, and I think, that there will even be a surplus of several thousand, with which we could buy a small summer house in Finland.[32]

VOINITSKY: Stop . . . I think my ears are deceiving me. Repeat what you said.

SEREBRYAKOV: Put the money into interest-bearing securities, and on the surplus, whatever is left, buy a summer house in Finland.

VOINITSKY: Not Finland . . . You said something else.

SEREBRYAKOV: I proposed selling the estate.

VOINITSKY: That's the very thing. You will sell the estate, superb, a rich idea . . . And where will you send me, and your old mother, and Sonya here?

SEREBRYAKOV: We'll discuss all that in good time. Not right now.

VOINITSKY: Stop. Apparently, until now I haven't had a drop of common sense. Until now I was stupid enough to think that this estate belonged to Sonya. My late father bought this estate

---

31. "The same night awaits us all" (Latin, from Horace).
32. Once part of the Russian Empire; many aristocrats bought summer houses in Finland because it is close to St. Petersburg.

as a dowry for my sister. Until now I was naïve, I didn't know that we were living under the laws of Turkey, and so I thought that Sonya inherited the estate from my sister.

SEREBRYAKOV: Yes, the estate belongs to Sonya. Who's contesting that? I will not decide to sell it without Sonya's consent. And besides that, I'm proposing to do this for Sonya's good.

VOINITSKY: This is incomprehensible, incomprehensible! Either I have lost my mind, or . . . or . . .

MARIA VASILYEVNA: *Jean,* don't contradict *Alexandre.* Trust that he knows better than we, what's good and what's bad.

VOINITSKY: No, get me some water. (*Drinks the water.*) Say what it is you want, what you want!

SEREBRYAKOV: I don't understand why you're upset. I'm not saying that my plan is ideal. If everyone finds it unsuitable, then I won't insist.

Pause.

TELEGIN: (*Embarrassed.*) Your excellency, I cultivate not only feelings of reverence toward scholarship, but also kinship. My brother's, Grigóry Ilyích's, wife's brother, Konstantín Trofímovich Lackeydémonov, maybe you know him, held a masters degree . . .

VOINITSKY: Stop, Waffles, we're talking business . . . Wait, later . . . (*To Serebryakov, about Telegin.*) Look, just ask him. The estate was bought from his uncle.

SEREBRYAKOV: Ah, why should I ask? What for?

VOINITSKY: The estate was bought at that time for ninety-five thousand. My father paid only seventy, and the debt that remained was twenty-five thousand. Now listen . . . The estate would never have been bought, if I had not given up my inheritance for the sake of my sister, whom I fervently loved. Besides that, I worked for some ten years, like an ox, and paid off the whole debt . . .

SEREBRYAKOV: I am sorry I started this conversation.

VOINITSKY: The estate is debt-free and has not fallen apart thanks to my personal efforts. And now that I'm old, I'm thrown out on my ass!

SEREBRYAKOV: I don't understand what you're aiming at!

VOINITSKY: For twenty-five years I've been running this estate, working, sending you money, like an honest steward, and all that time you didn't once thank me. All that time, when I was young and now too, I got a salary from you of five hundred rubles a year, a beggarly sum! And not once did you even think to add as much as a single ruble!

SEREBRYAKOV: Ivan Petrovich, how was I to know? I'm not a practical man and I don't understand such things. You yourself could have added as much as you wanted.

VOINITSKY: Why didn't I steal? Do you despise me for not stealing? I would have been right to do it, and I wouldn't be a beggar now!

MARIA VASILYEVNA: (*Sternly.*) Jean!

TELEGIN: (*Upset.*) Vanya, dear friend, there's no need . . . No need . . . I'm trembling . . . Why spoil good relationships? (*Kisses him.*) No need.

VOINITSKY: For twenty-five years I've been living here, with my old mother, like a mole, sitting inside these four walls . . . All our thoughts and feelings were of you alone. All day long we talked about you, about your work, we took pride in you, spoke your name with reverence. All night long we pored over journals and books that I now deeply despise!

TELEGIN: There's no need, Vanya, no need . . . I can't . . .

SEREBRYAKOV: (*Angrily.*) I don't understand. What do you want?

VOINITSKY: You were for us a being of a higher order, and we knew your articles by heart . . . But now, my eyes are open! I see clearly! You write about art, but you don't understand anything about art! All your works, which I loved, are not worth a kopeck! You pulled the wool over our eyes!

SEREBRYAKOV: Ladies and gentlemen! Make him, at least, calm down! I'm going!

YELENA ANDREYEVNA: Ivan Petrovich, I demand that you be quiet! Do you hear?

VOINITSKY: I won't be quiet! (*Blocking Serebryakov's path.*) Stop, I'm not finished! You ruined my life! I'm not living, not living! For your sake, I poured out, I destroyed the best years of my life! You are my arch enemy!

TELEGIN: I can't . . . can't . . . I'm going . . . (*Exits deeply disturbed.*)

SEREBRYAKOV: What do you want from me? And what right do you have to speak to me in such a tone? A nobody! If the estate is yours, take it, I don't need it!

YELENA ANDREYEVNA: I am leaving this hell right this minute! (*Screams.*) I can't stand it any longer!

VOINITSKY: My life has collapsed! I'm talented, smart, bold . . . If I had lived a normal life, I might have been another Schopenhauer, a Dostoyevsky[33] . . . I've let my tongue run away from me! I'm losing my mind . . . Mother, I am in despair! Mother!

MARIA VASILYEVNA: (*Sternly.*) Obey *Alexandre!*

SONYA: (*Kneeling in front of the nurse and clinging to her.*) Nanny! Nanny!

VOINITSKY: Mother! What can I do? There's no need to answer! I myself know what to do! (*To Serebryakov.*) You will remember me! (*Exits through the door in the center.*)

Maria Vasilyevna follows him out.

SEREBRYAKOV: Ladies and gentlemen, what's this, the end? Keep that madman away from me! I can't live under the same roof with him! He lives there, (*Pointing to the door in the center.*) right next to me . . . Let him move into the village, or into a separate wing, or I'll move away from here, but I can't stay in the same house with him . . .

YELENA ANDREYEVNA: (*To her husband.*) We'll leave here today! Let's go pack our things right now.

SEREBRYAKOV: A nobody that man!

SONYA: (*Still kneeling, turning to her father, and nervously, through tears.*) You must have mercy, Papa! Uncle Vanya and I are so unhappy! (*Restraining her despair.*) You must have mercy! Remember when you were younger, Uncle Vanya and grandmother used to translate your books at night, and copy

---

33. Arthur Schopenhauer (1788–1860), the German philosopher known for his atheistic pessimism; Fyodor Mikhailovich Dostoyevsky (1821–1881), the Russian novelist known for dark, psychological novels.

your papers ... Every night, every night! Uncle Vanya and I worked without rest, we were afraid to waste even a kopeck on ourselves, we sent it all to you ... The bread we ate was not wasted! I'm not making myself clear, not making it clear, but you must understand us, Papa. You must have mercy!

YELENA ANDREYEVNA: (*Worried, to her husband.*) Alexander, for God's sake, settle it with him ... I beg you.

SEREBRYAKOV: Fine, I'll settle it with him ... I'm not accusing him of anything, I'm not angry, but at least admit that his behavior is strange. Let me go see him. (*Exits through the door in the center.*)

YELENA ANDREYEVNA: Be gentle with him, calm him down ... (*Exits after him.*)

SONYA: (*Clinging to the nurse.*) Nanny! Nanny!

MARINA: It's nothing, child. The geese will cackle, and then they'll stop ... Cackle, then stop ...

SONYA: Nanny!

MARINA: (*Strokes Sonya's head.*) You're trembling, as if it were cold in here! Well, well, little orphan, God is merciful. A little lime tea, or raspberry, and it will all pass ... No more burning tears, little orphan ... (*Looking at the door in the center, crossly.*) Go fly off the handle, you geese, just take it out to the empty fields!

Offstage there is a shot; Yelena Andreyevna is heard screaming; Sonya shutters.

MARINA: Ooo, what are you folk doing in there!

SEREBRYAKOV: (*Runs in, shaking with fear.*) Hold him back! Hold him! He's lost his mind!

Yelena Andreyevna and Voinitsky are fighting in the doorway.

YELENA ANDREYEVNA: (*Trying to take a revolver away from him.*) Give it to me! Give it, I say!

VOINITSKY: Let me go, *Hélène!* Let me go! (*Breaking free of her, he runs in and eyes the room, looking for Serebryakov.*) Where is he? Ah, there he is! (*Shoots at Serebryakov.*) Bah! (*Pause.*)

Did I hit him? Another miss? (*Angrily.*) Ah, damn, damn. . . . Damn him to hell. . . .

Vanya throws the revolver on the floor and sits down on a chair, exhausted. Yelena Andreyevna leans against a wall, feeling nauseous.

YELENA ANDREYEVNA: Take me away from here! Take me, take me away, but . . . I can't stay here, I can't!

VOINITSKY: (*In despair.*) Oh, what am I doing! What am I doing!

SONYA: Nanny! Nanny!

Curtain.

Act IV

Ivan Petrovich's room; his bedroom and also the estate's office. Near the window is a large table, and on it are accounting books and all kinds of papers; a writing desk, bookshelves, and scales. There is also a smaller table for Astrov; on this table are drawing supplies and paints; beside it is a portfolio for documents. A birdcage with a starling. On the wall there hangs a map of Africa, clearly of no use to anyone here. An enormous sofa, upholstered in oilcloth. On the left is a door leading to the sleeping chamber; on the right is a door to the hall, in front of which is a doormat, so that the peasants do not muddy the floor. An autumn evening. It is quiet. Telegin and Marina sit across from each other, winding a ball of woolen yarn.

TELEGIN: Hurry up, Marina Timofeyevna, they could call us at any moment to say goodbye. They've already asked for the horses.

MARINA: (*Trying to wind faster.*) Only a little more to go.

TELEGIN: They're going to Kharkov. They'll live there.

MARINA: And that'll be better.

TELEGIN: They've been scared off . . . Yelena Andreyevna keeps saying, "I don't want to live here, not one more hour. . . . Let's leave here, yes, let's leave. . . . We'll stay in Kharkov," she says. "We'll have a look around and then we'll send for our things. . . ." They're traveling light. That means, Marina Timofeyevna, it's not their fate to live here. Not their fate. . . . Fatal predestination.

MARINA: And that'll be better. Just now they were making such noise, guns going off—a crying shame!

TELEGIN: Yes, it would make a good subject for a painting by Aivazóvsky.[34]

MARINA: I wish I'd never seen it. (*Pause.*) We'll go back to our old ways again. Have tea at eight in the morning, lunch by one, and in the evenings we'll sit down to supper. We'll have order again, just like everybody else . . . like real Christians. (*With a sigh.*) Ah, it's been a while, sinner that I am, since I've eaten noodles.

TELEGIN: Yes, quite a while since they made us noodles. (*Pause.*) Quite a while . . . This morning, Marina Timofeyevna, I go to the village and the shopkeeper yells at me. "Hey, you freeloading sponger!" And that left a bitter taste in my mouth!

MARINA: Don't pay any attention, dear father. We all sponge off God. You, Sonya, Ivan Petrovich—no one sits doing nothing, all of us toil! All of us . . . Where's Sonya?

TELEGIN: In the orchard. She's still walking around with the doctor, looking for Ivan Petrovich. They're afraid he might lay hands on himself.

MARINA: Where's his pistol?

TELEGIN: (*Whispering.*) I hid it in the cellar!

MARINA: (*With a laugh.*) Forgive us our sins!

Voinitsky enters from the yard with Astrov.

VOINITSKY: Leave me alone. (*To Marina and Telegin.*) Get out of here, leave me alone for at least an hour! I can't bear this surveillance.

TELEGIN: Right away, Vanya. (*Tiptoes out.*)

MARINA: The goose's gander goes "honk-honk-honk"! (*Gathers up her yarn and exits.*)

VOINITSKY: Leave me alone!

---

34. Ivan Konstantinovich Aivazovsky (1817–1900), a Russian painter known for his depictions of storms and battles at sea.

ASTROV: With great pleasure. I was supposed to leave quite a while ago, but, I repeat, I will not go until you return what you took from me.

VOINITSKY: I didn't take anything from you.

ASTROV: I'm serious, don't keep me. It's time for me to go.

VOINITSKY: I took nothing from you.

Both sit down.

ASTROV: Is that so? Well, I'll wait a little longer, and then, I'm sorry, but I'll have to use force. We'll tie you down and search you. I am absolutely serious.

VOINITSKY: Whatever you want. (*Pause.*) To have played the role of fool. To shoot twice and not to hit him once! I can never forgive myself for that!

ASTROV: If you felt like shooting, well, you should have shot yourself in the head.

VOINITSKY: (*Shrugging his shoulders.*) It's strange. I attempt murder, and I'm not arrested, not hauled off to court. That means they must consider me crazy. (*A mean laugh.*) I am crazy, but the others are not crazy, even though they mask their talentlessness, dullness, and utter heartlessness with false faces, posing as professors, as learned wizards. And those who marry old men, then betray them in plain sight, they're not crazy either. I saw, I saw how you embraced her!

ASTROV: Yes, sir, I embraced her, sir, and that's that. (*Thumbs his nose at Voinitsky.*)

VOINITSKY: (*Looking at the door.*) And the earth is crazy too, for keeping you on it!

ASTROV: Well, that's stupid.

VOINITSKY: What of it, I'm crazy, irresponsible, I have the right to say stupid things.

ASTROV: That's a stale joke. You're not crazy, only eccentric. A buffoon. I used to think that every eccentric person was sick, abnormal. But now I am of the opinion that being eccentric is part of the normal human condition. You are completely normal.

VOINITSKY: (*Covers his face with his hands.*) I'm ashamed! If only you knew how ashamed! I can't compare this acute feeling of shame with any other kind of pain. (*With anguish.*) It's unbearable! (*Leans on the table.*) What can I do? What can I do?

ASTROV: Nothing.

VOINITSKY: Give me something! Oh my God . . . I'm forty-seven years old. If I live, let's say, until sixty, then I have thirteen more years left. A long time! How can I get through these thirteen years? What will I do, how will I fill them? Oh, try to understand . . . (*Convulsively grasps Astrov's hand.*) Understand, if only I could live these remaining years in a new way. If you could wake up one clear, quiet morning and feel that life was beginning again, that everything past was forgotten, blown away like smoke. (*Cries.*) To start a new life . . . Tell me how to start . . . where to start . . .

ASTROV: (*Annoyed.*) Oh, come on! What kind of new life could there be! Our situation, yours and mine, is hopeless.

VOINITSKY: Is it?

ASTROV: I'm sure of it.

VOINITSKY: Give me something . . . (*Pointing to his heart.*) I'm on fire, here.

ASTROV: (*Shouts angrily.*) Stop it! (*Softening.*) Those who will live one hundred, or two hundred years from now, and who will despise us for living our lives so stupidly and so tastelessly, maybe they can find a way to be happy, but we . . . There's only one hope for you and me. The hope that when we are buried in our graves, apparitions will come and visit us, maybe even pleasant ones. (*Sighing.*) Yes, brother. In the whole district there once were two proper, intelligent people, you and I. But after some ten years or so, this narrow-minded, this contemptible life has pulled us in. It has poisoned our blood with its rotten fumes, and we have become as vulgar as everyone else. (*In a lively manner.*) But, don't distract me with smooth talk. Give me what you took from me.

VOINITSKY: I didn't take anything from you.

ASTROV: You took a vial of morphine from my medical bag. (*Pause.*) Listen, if you really want to kill yourself, then go out into the forest and shoot yourself there. Give me back the morphine, or there'll be talk, surmises, people will think that I gave it to you . . . It's enough that I'll have to do your autopsy . . . Do you think I'll find that interesting?

Sonya enters.

VOINITSKY: Leave me alone!

ASTROV: (*To Sonya.*) Sofia Aleksandrovna, your uncle pulled a vial of morphine out of my medical bag, and won't give it back. Tell him that he . . . that it's not very smart, after all. And besides, I don't have time for this. It's time for me to go.

SONYA: Uncle Vanya, did you take the morphine?

Pause.

ASTROV: He took it. I'm sure of it.

SONYA: Give it back. Why are you frightening us? (*Gently.*) Give it back, Uncle Vanya! I may be as unhappy as you are, but I will not give in to despair. I will bear up, and I will bear up as long as my life goes on . . . You too can bear up. (*Pause.*) Give it back! (*Kisses his hands.*) My dear, honorable uncle, give it back! (*Cries.*) You're a good person, you'll take pity on us and give it back. Bear up, Uncle! Bear up!

VOINITSKY: (*Gets the vial from the table and gives it to Astrov.*) Here, take it! (*To Sonya.*) But we must get to work as soon as possible, do something as soon as possible, or else I won't be able . . . I won't be able . . .

SONYA: Yes, yes, to work. As soon as we see our family off, we'll sit down to work . . . (*Nervously sorts through papers on the table.*) Everything's all mixed up.

ASTROV: (*Puts the vial in his medical bag and tightens the straps.*) Now I can be on my way.

YELENA ANDREYEVNA: (*Enters.*) Ivan Petrovich, are you here? We're about to leave . . . Go to Alexander, he wants to talk to you.

SONYA: Go on, Uncle Vanya. (*Leads Voinitsky by the arm.*) Let's go. Papa and you must make peace. It's necessary.

Sonya and Voinitsky exit.

YELENA ANDREYEVNA: I'm leaving. (*Offers Astrov her hand.*) Goodbye.

ASTROV: Already?

YELENA ANDREYEVNA: The horses are waiting.

ASTROV: Goodbye.

YELENA ANDREYEVNA: Today you promised me that you would leave here too.

ASTROV: I remember. I'm going now. (*Pause.*) Were you frightened? (*Takes her by the hand.*) Surely it wasn't that terrifying, was it?

YELENA ANDREYEVNA: Yes.

ASTROV: But you might stay! But? Then tomorrow at the forestry . . .

YELENA ANDREYEVNA: No . . . It's already decided . . . And that's why I can look at you so bravely, because our departure is set . . . There's one thing I beg of you. Think better of me. I want you to respect me.

ASTROV: Ah! (*A gesture of impatience.*) Stay, I beg you. Admit that, since you do nothing in the world, have no goal in life, pay no attention to anything, that sooner or later you will give in to your feelings. It's inevitable. It would be better to do that here, not in Kharkov, or somewhere in Kursk,[35] but here in the lap of nature . . . At least it's poetic, and autumn is even beautiful . . . The forestry's here, and dilapidated mansions like those in Turgenev's writings . . .

YELENA ANDREYEVNA: How funny you are . . . I'm angry with you, but yet . . . I'll remember you with pleasure. You're an interesting person, an original. We shall never see each other again, so why hide it? I was attracted to you a little. Well, let's shake hands and part as friends. Don't think ill of me.

ASTROV: (*Shakes her hand.*) Yes, leave . . . (*Thoughtfully.*) You seem a good, sincere person, but there also seems to be something strange in your nature. You came here with your husband, and everyone who was working here, and bustling about, and making something, dropped whatever they were doing to take care of your husband's gout and of you for the whole

---

35. A city in central Russia, founded in medieval times.

summer. You both—you and he—infected all of us with your idleness. I got carried away, for a whole month I did nothing. And yet during that time people got sick, and peasants took their livestock into my forests to graze on my young trees . . . It seems that wherever you and your husband go, you bring destruction with you . . . I'm joking, of course, but all the same . . . it's strange. And I'm sure that if you were to stay, the devastation would be enormous. And I would perish, and even you would . . . It wouldn't turn out so well. So leave. *Finita la comedia!*[36]

YELENA ANDREYEVNA: (*Takes a pencil off his table and quickly hides it.*) I'm taking this pencil with me to remember you.

ASTROV: It's strange somehow . . . We knew each other, and then suddenly for some reason . . . we find that we'll never see each other again. That's the way it is with everything on earth . . . While no one's here and before Uncle Vanya comes in with a bouquet, let me . . . kiss you . . . a kiss goodbye . . . Yes? (*Kisses her on the cheek.*) Well, that's it . . . Wonderful.

YELENA ANDREYEVNA: I wish you all the best. (*Looking around.*) For whatever it's worth, for once in my life! (*Embraces him impetuously, then immediately they both quickly walk away from each other.*) We must leave.

ASTROV: Leave as soon as possible. If the horses are waiting, then you must get going.

YELENA ANDREYEVNA: I think they're coming in here.

Both listen.

ASTROV: *Finita!*

Serebryakov, Voinitsky, Maria Vasilyevna with a book, Telegin, and Sonya enter.

SEREBRYAKOV: (*To Voinitsky.*) Let bygones be bygones. After what's happened in the last few hours, I have lived through so much and thought so many thoughts, that, it seems to me, I could write a whole tract about how one must live one's life for the edification of posterity. I gladly accept your apology and I

---

36. "The comedy is ended!" (Italian).

myself apologize to you. Goodbye! (*Kisses Voinitsky three times.*)

VOINITSKY: You will receive exactly what you received before. Everything will go back to the old way.

Yelena Andreyevna embraces Sonya.

SEREBRYAKOV: (*Kisses Maria Vasilyevna's hand.*) Maman . . .

MARIA VASILYEVNA: (*Kissing him.*) Alexandre, have a photograph taken of yourself again, and send it to me. You know how dear you are to me.

TELEGIN: Goodbye, your excellency! Don't forget us!

SEREBRYAKOV: (*Having kissed his daughter.*) Goodbye . . . Goodbye to everyone! (*Extending his hand to Astrov.*) Thank you for your pleasant company . . . Ladies and gentleman, I respect your way of thinking, your passions, your impulses, but allow an old man to make just one observation as a parting piece of advice: one must, ladies and gentlemen, do things! One must do things! (*A general bow to all of them.*) All the best to you! (*Exits; Maria Vasilyevna and Sonya follow him out.*)

VOINITSKY: (*Firmly kisses Yelena Andreyevna's hand.*) Goodbye . . . Forgive me . . . We'll never see each other again.

YELENA ANDREYEVNA: (*Touched.*) Goodbye, dear friend. (*Kisses him on the head and exits.*)

ASTROV: (*To Telegin.*) Waffles, tell them to get my horses ready too.

TELEGIN: Yes sir, my dear dear friend. (*Exits.*)

Only Astrov and Voinitsky remain.

ASTROV: (*Takes his paints off the table and puts them in his suitcase.*) Aren't you going to see them off?

VOINITSKY: Let them leave, but I . . . I can't. It's a burden for me. I have to get busy with something as soon as possible . . . To work, to work! (*Shuffles through the papers on the table.*)

Pause; harness bells are heard.

ASTROV: They left. The professor is no doubt glad. Nothing would induce him to come back here.

MARINA: (*Enters.*) They left. (*Sits down in an easy chair and knits socks.*)

SONYA: (*Enters.*) They left. (*Wipes her eyes.*) God keep them safe. (*To her uncle.*) Well, Uncle Vanya, let's do something.

VOINITSKY: To work, to work . . .

SONYA: It's been a while, a while since we sat together at this table. (*Lights the lamp on the table.*) There's no ink, it seems . . . (*Takes the inkwell and fills it.*) But I'm sad that they've left.

MARIA VASILYEVNA: (*Slowly enters.*) They left. (*Sits down and gets absorbed in her reading.*)

SONYA: (*Sits at the table and pages through a book of accounts.*) Let's write up the bills first, Uncle Vanya. We've neglected them terribly. Again today they asked for the bills. Write. You write one, and I'll do another . . .

VOINITSKY: (*Writes.*) Received by . . . mister . . .

Both write silently.

MARINA: (*Yawns.*) Lullaby and goodnight . . .

ASTROV: The quiet. The pens scratch, the cricket chirps. It's warm, cozy . . . I don't want to leave here. (*Harness bells are heard.*) They've brought the horses . . . The only thing left is to say goodbye to you, my friends, to say goodbye to my table and— be off! (*Puts his diagrams in the portfolio.*)

MARINA: Why the hurry? Sit for a while.

ASTROV: I can't.

VOINITSKY: (*Writes.*) And the balance of the debt is two seventy-five . . .

A workman enters.

WORKMAN: Mikhail Lvovich, the horses are waiting.

ASTROV: I can hear. (*Gives the workman the medical bag, suitcase, and portfolio.*) Here, take these. Look, don't crumple the portfolio.

WORKMAN: Yes sir. (*Exits.*)

ASTROV: Well then . . . (*Starts to say goodbye.*)

SONYA: When shall we see you again?

ASTROV: No sooner than the summer, most likely. Hardly during the winter . . . Of course, if something happens, let me know and I'll come. (*Shakes hands.*) Thank you for the hospitality, and for the kindness . . . in a word, for everything. (*Goes to the nurse and kisses her on the head.*) Goodbye, old woman.

MARINA: Are you leaving without having any tea?

ASTROV: I don't want any, Nanny.

MARINA: Maybe a little vodka?

ASTROV: (*Indecisively.*) Please . . . (*Marina exits; after a pause.*) One of my trace horses has gone lame.[37] I noticed it yesterday when Petrúshka[38] was leading him to the water.

VOINITSKY: You'll need to reshoe him.

ASTROV: I'll have to stop in the village of Rozhdéstvenny[39] for the blacksmith. Can't skip it. (*Goes to the map of Africa and looks at it.*) There must be a heat wave in Africa now, a terrible thing!

VOINITSKY: Yes probably.

MARINA: (*Returning with a tray that has a glass of vodka and piece of bread on it.*) Have a bite. (*Astrov drinks the vodka.*) To your health, dear father. (*Marina bows low.*) You should also eat the bread.

ASTROV: No, I'm fine . . . So then, the best to you! (*To Marina.*) Don't see me out, Nanny. There's no need.

He exits. Sonya exits with him carrying a candle in order to see him off; Marina sits down in her easy chair.

VOINITSKY: (*Writes.*) February second, vegetable oil, twenty pounds . . . February sixteen, vegetable oil, another twenty pounds . . . Buckwheat . . .

---

37. When three horses are harnessed together, the trace horses are those on the outside of the trio.
38. A nickname for Pyotr and also the name of a traditional Russian puppet.
39. The town's name means "Christmas."

Pause; harness bells are heard.

MARINA: He left . . .

Pause.

SONYA: (*Returning, places the candle on the table.*) He left . . .

VOINITSKY: (*Uses the abacus to add the numbers and makes a note.*) The total is . . . fifteen . . . twenty-five . . .

Sonya sits down and writes.

MARINA: (*Yawns.*) Oh, forgive us our sins . . .

Telegin tiptoes in, sits down near the door, and quietly tunes the guitar.

VOINITSKY: (*To Sonya, running his hand through her hair.*) My child, what a burden it is for me! Oh, if only you knew what a burden it is for me!

SONYA: What is there to do but go on living! (*Pause.*) We'll live, Uncle Vanya. We'll live through a long, long series of days, and lengthy evenings. We'll patiently get through whatever tribulations fate sends us. We'll toil for the others, now and in our old age, without knowing any peace. But when our hour comes, we'll die humbly. And then, there beyond the grave, we'll say that we suffered, that we cried, that it left a bitter taste in our mouths, and God will pity us, you and I, Uncle, dear uncle, and then we'll see life as something bright, wonderful, luxurious. We'll rejoice, and we'll look back at our present unhappiness with tenderness, with a smile, and we'll rest. I believe, Uncle, I believe fervently, passionately . . . (*Kneels before him and places her head in his hands; with a tired voice.*) We'll rest! (*Telegin quietly plays the guitar.*) We'll rest! We'll hear the angels, we'll see a sky full of diamonds, we'll see all earthly evil drowned in the mercy that will engulf the whole world. And our life will become quiet, gentle, and as sweet as kindness. I believe, believe . . . (*Wipes his tears away with her shawl.*) Poor, poor Uncle Vanya, you're crying . . . (*Through tears.*) You haven't known joy in your life, but wait a little, Uncle Vanya, wait a little . . . We'll rest . . . (*Embraces him.*) We'll rest!

> *The watchman is heard tapping. Telegin quietly plays; Maria Vasilyevna writes in the margins of a pamphlet; Marina knits socks.*

SONYA: We'll rest!

> *The curtain falls slowly.*

Three Sisters

A Drama in Four Acts

[Chekhov wrote *Three Sisters* in 1900 for the actors of the Moscow Art Theatre, where it premiered on January 31, 1901. Konstantin Stanislavsky directed and played Vershinin. Chekhov's wife, Olga Knipper, appeared as Masha. In advising her on her role, the author wrote, "People who have long carried a grief inside themselves and have gotten used to it, only whistle and often withdraw into themselves."[1] The soon-to-be director Vsevolod Meyerhold played the congenial Baron Tuzenbach; Chekhov gave the role a Germanic last name to match the actor's. First produced in English in 1920 in London, American audiences saw *Three Sisters* for the first time in Russian when the Moscow Art Theatre toured in 1923 and 1924. An English language production followed in 1926, directed by the leading American actress Eve Le Galliene. The translation that follows was created in 1979 for Lion Theatre in New York (cofounded by Gene Nye and Garland Wright); Gene Nye directed.[2] —SMC]

The Characters

Prózorov, Andréy Sergéyevich. [The last name suggests someone "prescient" who can see into the future. His nicknames are Andryúsha and the saccharine sweet Andryushchánchik.]

Natálya Ivánovna, his fiancée, later his wife. [Her nickname is Natásha.]

Ólga Sergéyevna, his sister. [Her nicknames are Ólya, Olyúsha, and Ólechka.]

Másha, his sister. [Masha is a nickname. María Sergéyevna is her formal name; other nicknames are Máshka and Máshenka.]

Irína, his sister. [Her nicknames are Arísha and Arínushka; she is also referred to by her formal name, Irina Sergeyevna]

Kulýgin, Fyódor Ilyích, a high school teacher, Masha's husband. [His nickname is Fédya.]

Vershínin, Alexánder Ignátyevich, lieutenant-colonel, the commander of the battery. [His last name means "pinnacle" or "summit."]

---

1. Chekhov to O. L. Knipper, January 2, 1901, in *Pis'ma* [Letters], vol. 9 (Moscow: Nauka, 1980), 173.

2. About this production, one reviewer wrote: "Carnicke's text is faithful to the spirit underlying each line and entirely avoids the awkwardness that cripples most English versions of Chekhov." Eileen Blumenthal, review of Gene Nye's production of *Three Sisters, The Village Voice,* February 19, 1979.

Tuzenbách, Nikoláy Lvóvich, a baron and lieutenant. [His last name sounds German.]
Solyóny, Vasíly Vasílyevich, second captain. [His last name means "salty."]
Chebutýkin, Iván Románych, a military doctor.
Fedótik, Alekséy Petróvich, second lieutenant.
Rodé, Vladímir Kárlovich, second lieutenant. [His last name sounds neither Russian nor German; it seems vaguely French; his patronymic is from the German "Karl." Circus performers often used unusual stage names of this sort.]
Ferapónt, the watchman for the District Board,[3] an old man. [His name is old-fashioned; his formal name is Ferapónt Spriridónich.]
Anfísa, the nanny, an old woman of eighty.
[Unseen characters: *Protopópov* (whose name means "archpriest") is chairman of the District Board and Natasha's lover; *Bóbik* (a name used in Russia for puppies) and *Sófochka* (the nickname for Sofia, which means "wisdom" in Greek) are Natasha and Andrey's children.]

The action takes place in a provincial capital city.

Act I

In the home of the Prozorovs. A parlor with columns behind which can be seen a large hall. Midday; outside it is sunny, cheerful. In the hall, a table is being set for lunch. Olga, dressed in the blue uniform of a school teacher at the girls' high school, stands and walks about correcting student notebooks the whole time; Masha, in a black dress, with a hat on her knees, sits reading a book; Irina, in a white dress, stands lost in thought.

OLGA: Father died exactly a year ago, this very day, the fifth of May, on your name-day,[4] Irina. It was very cold. It snowed then. I thought I wouldn't live through it. You fainted and lay there like a corpse. But you see, a year has passed, we can think about it easily, you can wear a white dress already, your face is shining . . . (*The clock strikes twelve.*) The clock struck twelve

---

3. A local governmental agency with control over land management in the immediate area.
4. A name-day is the yearly holiday dedicated to the saint after whom a person is named. May 5 is the Feast of St. Irina. Name-days are celebrated like birthdays in Russia.

then too. (*Pause.*) I remember at his funeral, when they carried father out a military band played music, and at the cemetery the honor guard saluted by shooting off their guns. He was a general, commanded a brigade, but even so, few people came. Of course, it was raining then. A hard rain and snow.

IRINA: Why remember!

Baron Tuzenbach, Chebutykin, and Solyony appear behind the columns in the hall near the table.

OLGA: Today it's warm, we can keep the windows open, but the birches still haven't blossomed. Father was put in command of a brigade, and took us from Moscow eleven years ago, and I remember perfectly that it was at the beginning of May. You see, at that time of year Moscow is all in bloom, warm and drenched with sunlight. Eleven years have passed, and I remember everything there as if we had left yesterday. My God! This morning I woke up, saw such a lot of light, saw it was spring, and I felt joy stirring in my heart. I wanted passionately to go back home.

CHEBUTYKIN: The devil you say!

TUZENBACH: Of course, it's nonsense.

Masha, lost in her book, softly whistles a song.

OLGA: Don't whistle Masha. How can you! (*Pause.*) I always have a headache from going to school every day and then giving private lessons until evening. I think the thoughts of someone who's already old. And in the last four years, since I've been working at the high school, I feel that every day I actually do lose some of my strength and youth, drop by drop. And only one dream keeps growing and getting stronger . . .

IRINA: To go to Moscow. To sell the house, finish with everything here, and go to Moscow . . .

OLGA: Yes! To Moscow, as soon as possible.

Chebutykin and Tuzenbach laugh.

IRINA: Our brother will be a professor, of course, so he won't stay here. The only obstacle, you see, is poor Masha.

OLGA: Masha will come to see us in Moscow for the whole summer every year.

Masha softly whistles a song.

IRINA: God willing, everything will work out. (*Looking out the window.*) It's beautiful weather today. I don't know why my heart's so sunny! This morning I remembered that it's my name-day, and I suddenly felt such joy, and I remembered my childhood, when Mama was still alive! And such wondrous thoughts excited me, such thoughts!

OLGA: Today you're shining, you seem extraordinarily beautiful. And Masha is beautiful too. Andrey would be good-looking, but he's gotten very heavy and it doesn't suit him. But I've gotten older, and much thinner. It must be because I get so angry with the girls at school. But today I'm free, I'm home, and I don't have a headache. So I feel younger than yesterday. I'm twenty-eight years old, only . . . Everything's for the best, everything comes from God, but I think that if I had gotten married, and sat home all day long it would have been better. (*Pause.*) I would have loved my husband.

TUZENBACH: (*To Solyony.*) You're talking such nonsense, that I'm getting tired of listening to you. (*Enters the parlor.*) I forgot to tell you. Today you will receive a visit from our new battery commander, Vershinin. (*Sits down at the piano.*)

OLGA: Well what do you know! I'll be pleased.

IRINA: Is he old?

TUZENBACH: No, not at all. At most about forty, forty-five. (*Plays softly.*) Apparently he's a well-meaning sort. Not stupid—that's for certain. Only he talks a lot.

IRINA: Is he an interesting person?

TUZENBACH: Yes, he's not bad, but there's a wife, a mother-in-law, and two little girls. By the way, he's been married twice. Everywhere he visits he says he has a wife and two little girls. And he'll tell you too. His wife is some kind of a half-wit, wears a long braid like a young girl's,[5] and she says only

---

5. A single braid signifies an unmarried girl. The Russian folk wedding includes a ritualistic unbraiding of the single plait and rebraiding of the hair into two braids.

grandiloquent things, philosophizes, and often tries to commit suicide, apparently to annoy her husband. I would have left her long ago, but he's patient, and only complains.

SOLYONY: (*Entering, from the hall into the parlor with Chebutykin.*) With one hand alone I can lift about sixty pounds, and with two hands, two hundred pounds, even two hundred and fifty pounds. From this I can conclude that two men are stronger than one not by twice, but by three times, no, even more . . .

CHEBUTYKIN: (*Reading a newspaper as he walks.*) For hair loss . . . Two measures of naphthalene to half a bottle of alcohol . . . Dissolve and apply daily . . . (*Makes a note in his notebook.*) Let's write it down! (*To Solyony.*) So, as I was saying, put the cork into a little bottle, put a glass tube through it . . . Then you take a pinch of common everyday alum[6] . . .

IRINA: Ivan Romanych, dear Ivan Romanych!

CHEBUTYKIN: What, my little girl, my joy?

IRINA: Tell me, why am I so happy today? It's like I'm sailing on air, with the wide blue sky and big white birds soaring above me. Why is it? Why?

CHEBUTYKIN: (*Kissing both her hands, tenderly.*) My little white bird . . .

IRINA: When I woke up this morning, got out of bed and washed, I suddenly thought that everything on this earth was clear to me, that I knew how one must live. Dear Ivan Romanych, I know everything. A person must labor, work until he sweats, whoever he is, and in that alone can he find the meaning and goal of life, happiness, ecstasy. How good to be a worker who gets up at dawn to break stones in the street, or a shepherd, or a teacher who teaches children, or an engineer for the railroad . . . My God, not even human, it's better to be an ox, better to be a simple horse, if one works, than to be a young woman who gets up at noon, then drinks her coffee in bed, then gets dressed at two o'clock . . . Oh how terrible that is! I want to work, the way you sometimes want to drink a glass of

---

6. Naphthalene, used in mothballs, and alum are common chemical crystals.

water on a hot day. And if I don't get up and go to work then refuse me your friendship, Ivan Romanych.

CHEBUTYKIN: (*Gently.*) I'll refuse it, I'll refuse it . . .

OLGA: Father taught us to get up at seven o'clock. Now Irina wakes up at seven, and lies in bed until at least nine thinking about something or other. And what a serious face she has! (*Laughs.*)

IRINA: You're used to thinking of me as a little girl and so you think it's strange when I'm serious. I'm twenty years old!

TUZENBACH: A longing for work, oh my God, how I understand that! I never worked, not once in my life. I was born in St. Petersburg, a cold and idle city,[7] in a family which never knew work or worry. I remember when I came home from the military academy, a lackey pulled off my boots for me. I acted like a child then, but still my mother watched with devotion in her eyes, and was surprised when others saw me differently. My parents tried to shield me from work. And they succeeded, but just barely, just barely! The time has come, something huge is moving in on us, a healthy powerful storm is brewing, and it will come, it's already close by, and soon it will blow away our society's laziness, its indifference, its bias against work, this awful boredom. I will work and in some twenty-five or thirty years everyone will be working. Everyone!

CHEBUTYKIN: I won't work.

TUZENBACH: You don't count.

SOLYONY: In twenty-five years you won't be around, thank God. In a year, or two or three, you'll die from apoplexy,[8] either that or I'll put a bullet through your head myself, my angel. (*Takes a bottle of eau de cologne out of his pocket and sprinkles some on his chest and hands.*)

---

7. Founded in 1703 by Tsar Peter the Great, St. Petersburg was Russia's capital until the 1917 Soviet Revolution. Located on the Gulf of Finland, it is characterized by French and Italian architecture. In contrast, Moscow was founded in the twelfth century with architecture that is purely Russian. Moscow is now Russia's capital, as it was prior to the eighteenth century and during the Soviet era.

8. Any sudden attack or seizure.

CHEBUTYKIN: (*Laughs.*) As a matter of fact, I too have never done anything. When I finished the university, I didn't lift a finger, didn't read a book, only read newspapers . . . (*Takes another newspaper out of his pocket.*) You see . . . I know from newspapers that there was, let's say, this critic Dobrolyúbov,[9] but what it was he wrote—I don't know . . . God knows who he is . . . (*Someone knocks on the floor from below.*) You see . . . They're calling me downstairs, someone's come to see me. I'll be right back . . . Just a minute . . . (*Hurriedly exits, combing his beard.*)

IRINA: He's up to something.

TUZENBACH: Yes. He left with a triumphant look on his face. It's obvious he's bringing you a present.

IRINA: Oh no!

OLGA: Yes, it's terrible. He's always doing something stupid.

MASHA: "On a curved seashore a green oak stood. A golden chain upon that oak. A golden chain upon that oak . . ."[10] (*Stands and sings softly.*)

OLGA: You're not cheerful today, Masha.

Masha, singing, puts on her hat.

OLGA: Where are you going?

MASHA: Home.

IRINA: That's strange . . .

TUZENBACH: Leaving a name-day party!

MASHA: It's all the same . . . I'll come back in the evening. Goodbye, my pretty one . . . (*Kisses Irina.*) One more time, let me wish you health and happiness . . . Before, when father was alive, every time we had a name-day party thirty or forty officers would come, it was noisy, but today there's only a man and

---

9. Nikolay Alexandrovich Dobrolyubov (1836–1861) was a literary critic and journalist with radical political leanings.

10. The opening lines of Alexander Sergeyevich Pushkin's fairy tale poem "Ruslan and Lyudmilla" (1820), about a hero whose wife is abducted by a wizard on their wedding night. The verse continues: "and to the chain is tied a learned tom cat, who circles round and round, day and night. When he moves to the left, he sings a song; when he moves to the right, he tells a tale."

a half, and it's as quiet as a desert . . . I'm going . . . I'm in the doldrums today, I'm not happy, so don't listen to me. (*Laughing through tears.*) We'll talk later, but for now, goodbye my dear. I'll go off somewhere.

IRINA: (*Not pleased.*) Well, you're so . . .

OLGA: (*Tearfully.*) I understand you, Masha.

SOLYONY: If a man philosophizes, you get philosophy, or maybe sophistry, but if a woman philosophizes, or two women, what you get is . . . flimflam.

MASHA: What do you mean? You're a terrible, frightening man . . .

SOLYONY: Nothing. "He no sooner cried 'Alack,' than the bear was on his back."[11]

MASHA: (*To Olga, angrily.*) Don't howl!

Anfisa and Ferapont enter with a cake.

ANFISA: Come here, Grandpa. Come on in, your feet are clean. (*To Irina.*) From the District Board, from Protopopov, from Mikhail Ivanovich . . . A cake.

IRINA: Thank you. Thank him for me. (*Takes the cake.*)

FERAPONT: What?

IRINA: (*Louder.*) Thank him for me!

OLGA: Nanny, give him some of our meat pie.[12] Ferapont, go on into the kitchen, they'll give you some pie.

FERAPONT: What?

ANFISA: Let's go, Grandpa Ferapont Spiridonich. Let's go. (*Exits with Ferapont.*)

MASHA: I don't like Protopopov, that Mikhaíl Potápich or Ivánich or whatever his name is. You shouldn't have invited him.

IRINA: I didn't invite him.

MASHA: That's good.

---

11. From a Russian fable, "The Peasant and the Free Laborer," by Ivan Andreyevich Krylov (1769–1844).
12. The featured fare at a name-day party is the meat pie, not the cake.

Chebutykin enters followed by a soldier's aide carrying a silver samovar;[13] a murmur of astonishment and displeasure.

OLGA: (*Covers her face with her hands.*) A silver samovar! This is terrible! (*Goes to the table in the hall.*)

IRINA: Darling dear Ivan Romanych, what are you doing!

TUZENBACH: (*Laughs.*) I told you!

MASHA: Ivan Romanych, you have no shame!

CHEBUTYKIN: My dears, my pretty ones, I have only you. You are dearer to me than anything else on earth. I'll soon be sixty, I'm an old man, and lonely, a useless old man . . . There's nothing good in me except my love for you, and if it weren't for you, then I would long ago have stopped living on this earth . . . (*To Irina.*) My dear, my little child, I knew you from the day you were born . . . held you in my arms . . . I loved your late mama . . .

IRINA: But why such expensive gifts!

CHEBUTYKIN: (*Tearfully, angrily.*) Expensive gifts . . . Don't be like that! (*To the aide.*) Take the samovar over there. (*Mimics her.*) Expensive gifts.

The aide carries the samovar into the hall.

ANFISA: (*Crossing through the parlor.*) My dears, a stranger, a colonel! He's already taken off his coat, my children, and he's coming this way. Arinushka, you be nice now, and polite . . . (*Exiting.*) And it's already time for lunch.

TUZENBACH: It must be Vershinin.

Vershinin enters.

TUZENBACH: Lieutenant-Colonel Vershinin!

VERSHININ: (*To Masha and Irina.*) Let me introduce myself: Vershinin. Very, very pleased to visit your home at last. How you've grown! My! My!

---

13. A samovar, used for making tea, is usually made from less expensive metal; this one is an especially extravagant gift. Such samovars are generally given by husbands to their wives for their silver anniversaries.

IRINA: Please sit down. We're very pleased to meet you.

VERSHININ: (*Cheerfully.*) How pleased I am, how pleased I am! But weren't there three sisters? I remember three little girls. I don't remember your faces now, but I remember perfectly well that your father, Colonel Prozorov, had three little girls and I saw them with my own eyes. How time flies! My, my, how time flies!

TUZENBACH: Alexander Ignatyevich is from Moscow.

IRINA: From Moscow? You're from Moscow?

VERSHININ: Yes, from there. Your late father was the battery commander there and I was an officer in the same brigade. (*To Masha.*) I seem to remember your face a little.

MASHA: I don't remember yours!

IRINA: Olya! Olya! (*Yells into the hall.*) Olya, come here!

Olga enters the parlor from the hall.

Irina: It seems that Lieutenant-Colonel Vershinin is from Moscow.

VERSHININ: You must be Olga Sergeyevna, the eldest . . . And you're Maria . . And you're Irina, the youngest.

OLGA: You're from Moscow?

VERSHININ: Yes, I studied in Moscow, started my career in Moscow, and served there for a long time. Finally was put in command of a battery here, as you see. I don't exactly remember you, I only remember that there were three sisters. I remember your father perfectly. I close my eyes and can see him as if he were alive. I used to visit you in Moscow . . .

OLGA: I thought I remembered everyone, but now . . .

VERSHININ: My name is Alexander Ignatyevich . . .

IRINA: Alexander Ignatyevich, you're from Moscow . . . What a surprise!

OLGA: We're planning to move there.

IRINA: We think we'll be there by autumn. It's our native city, we were born there . . . On Old Basmánny Street . . .

Both laugh joyfully.

MASHA: So we've unexpectedly met a fellow countryman. (*Lively.*) Now I remember! Remember Olya, we called him the "lovesick major." You were a lieutenant then, and in love with someone, and we all teased you, for some reason calling you a major . . .

VERSHININ: (*Laughs.*) That's it, that's it . . . The lovesick major, that's right . . .

MASHA: You only had a mustache then . . . Oh how old you've gotten! (*Tearfully.*) How old you've gotten!

VERSHININ: Yes, when you called me the "lovesick major" I was still young, I was in love, but not now.

OLGA: But you don't have one gray hair. You're older, but still not old.

VERSHININ: I am, however, forty-three years old. Did you leave Moscow long ago?

IRINA: Eleven years ago. What's wrong Masha, you're crying, you silly thing . . . (*Tearfully.*) And I'm starting to cry too . . .

MASHA: Nothing's wrong. What street did you live on?

VERSHININ: On Old Basmanny.

OLGA: We lived there too.

VERSHININ: Once I lived on Nemyétsky Street. From Nemyetsky Street I used to walk to the Krásny[14] Barracks. There's a gloomy bridge along the way, and under the bridge you could hear the water running. It makes a lonely man feel sick at heart. (*Pause.*) But here there's such a wide, such a rich river! A wondrous river!

OLGA: Yes but it's cold. It's cold here and there are mosquitoes.

VERSHININ: What's wrong with you! This is a good healthy Slavic climate. A forest, a river . . . And there are birches here too. Sweet modest birches.[15] I love them more than any other tree. It's good to live here. Only it's strange that the railroad is twenty-five miles away . . . And no one knows why that is.

---

14. *Nemyetsky* means "German"; *krasny* means "red" and also "beautiful."
15. The birch tree is a traditional symbol of Russia.

SOLYONY: But I know why. (*Everyone looks at him.*) Because if the station were nearby, then it would not be far away, and if it is far away, that means, it is not nearby.

An uncomfortable silence.

TUZENBACH: You're a joker, Vasily Vasilyevich.

OGLA: Now I remember you too. I remember.

VERSHININ: I knew your mother.

CHEBUTYKIN: A good woman she was, may she rest in peace.

IRINA: Mama was buried in Moscow.

OLGA: In the Novodévichy Cemetery.[16]

MASHA: Imagine, I'm already beginning to forget her face. They'll forget about us too. They'll forget.

VERSHININ: Yes. They'll forget. Such is our fate, nothing to be done. What seems to us to be serious, significant, and very important will be forgotten in time, or at least it will seem unimportant. (*Pause.*) It's interesting that we can't know now what exactly will be considered great and important, and what will be considered pitiful and ridiculous. Didn't Copernicus' experiments, let's say, or Columbus' discovery, seem at first unnecessary and ridiculous, while some empty nonsense, written by cranks, seemed to be true? And maybe, it will turn out that our lives to which we are reconciled, will seem after a while, strange, uncomfortable, unintelligent, not innocent enough, perhaps even sinful . . .

TUZENBACH: Who knows, maybe they'll call our time great and will remember it with respect. There are no more tortures or executions, or invasions after all, but even so there's so much suffering.

SOLYONY: (*In a thin voice.*) Cheep, cheep, cheep . . . Don't feed the Baron crumbs, just let him philosophize.

TUZENBACH: Vasily Vasilyevich, I beg you to leave me in peace. (*Sits in another place.*) This is getting boring.

SOLYONY: (*In a thin voice.*) Cheep, cheep, cheep . . .

---

16. The "New Virgin" Convent in Moscow has a cemetery where many famous people, including Anton Chekhov, are buried.

TUZENBACH: (*To Vershinin.*) All the same, the suffering which you see now—and there is so much of it—shows the moral development of our society.

VERSHININ: Yes, yes of course.

CHEBUTYKIN: You just said, Baron, that our lives may be called great, but people are still rather low . . . (*Stands up.*) Look at how low I am. You must tell me that my life is great and has meaning to comfort me.

Offstage violin music is heard.

MASHA: That's Andrey playing, our brother.

IRINA: He's our scholar. He's going to be a professor. Papa was a military man, but his son has chosen an academic career for himself.

MASHA: It's what Papa wanted.

OLGA: We've been teasing him today. It seems that he's a little bit in love.

IRINA: With a local girl. She'll probably visit us today.

MASHA: Ah, how she dresses! It's not only not pretty and not fashionable, but simply pathetic. Some kind of strange bright, yellowish skirt with an insipid fringe, and a red blouse. And her cheeks are so well-scrubbed, well-scrubbed! Andrey isn't in love. I won't allow it! He has taste, after all. He's just teasing us, playing pranks. Yesterday I heard that she's marrying Protopopov, the chairman of the local District Board. That's fine . . . (*Towards a side door.*) Andrey come here! Darling, just for a minute!

Andrey enters.

OLGA: This is my brother, Andrey Sergeyevich.

VERSHININ: Vershinin.

ANDREY: Prozorov. (*Wipes his sweaty face.*) You've come here as battery commander?

OLGA: Can you imagine, Alexander Ignatyevich is from Moscow.

ANDREY: Yes? Well, I congratulate you. Now my sisters will give you no peace.

VERSHININ: I've already succeeded in boring your sisters.

IRINA: Look at this little portrait frame Andrey gave me today! (*Shows him a little frame.*) He made it himself.

VERSHININ: (*Looking at the frame without knowing what to say.*) Yes . . . Quite a thing . . .

IRINA: And that little frame there, on the piano, he made that too.

Andrey waves his hand and walks away.

OLGA: He's our scholar, plays the violin, and whittles various little things—in short, a jack-of-all-trades. Andrey, don't leave! He has a way of disappearing. Come here!

Masha and Irina take him by the arm and lead him back, laughing.

MASHA: Come on, come on!

ANDREY: Leave me alone, please.

MASHA: How funny you are! We used to call Alexander Ignatyevich the lovesick major, and he didn't get angry, not at all.

VERSHININ: Not at all!

MASHA: And I want to call you the lovesick violinist!

IRINA: Or the lovesick professor! . . .

OLGA: He's in love! Andryusha's in love!

IRINA: (*Applauding.*) Bravo, bravo! Encore! Andryusha's in love!

CHEBUTYKIN: (*Approaches from behind and puts both arms around Andrey's waist.*) "Nature put us on this earth for love alone!"[17] (*Chuckles, all the time still holding his newspaper.*)

ANDREY: Well, that's enough, enough . . . (*Wipes his face.*) I didn't sleep all night and now I'm not quite myself, as they say. I read until four in the morning, then lay down, but nothing came of it. I thought about this and that, and then it was dawn, and the sun was creeping into the bedroom. During the summer, while I'm here, I'd like to translate a pamphlet from the English.

---

17. The opening line from a popular nineteenth-century operetta.

VERSHININ: You read English?

ANDREY: Yes. Father, may he rest in peace, oppressed us with education. It's funny and stupid, but still I must admit, that after his death I started gaining weight. In just one year I put on all this weight as if my body had been freed from the oppression. Thanks to Father, my sisters and I know French, German, and English. And Irina even knows Italian. But what is it worth!

MASHA: In this city, knowing three languages is an unnecessary luxury. Not even a luxury, an unnecessary appendage, like a sixth finger. We know a lot of superfluous things.

VERSHININ: How do you like that! (*Laughs.*) You know a lot of superfluous things! It seems to me, that no city can be so dull and so sad that it does not need an intelligent, educated person. Let's say that among the hundred thousand people of this backwards and coarse city there are only three like you. Of course you will not be able to prevail over the dark masses which surround you. In the course of your lives, little by little you will be forced to yield and get lost in the crowd of a hundred thousand. Life will smother you, but still you will not totally disappear. You will leave behind your influence. Six people like you will appear after you, then twelve, and so on, until finally, people like you will become the majority. In two hundred, three hundred years life on earth will become unimaginably beautiful, astonishing. People need that kind of life, and if it doesn't exist now then they must prophesy it, wait for it, dream and prepare for it. For its sake they must see and know more than their fathers and grandfathers saw and knew. (*Laughs.*) And you complain that you know so much that is superfluous.

MASHA: (*Takes off her hat.*) I'm staying for lunch.

IRINA: (*With a sigh.*) Honestly, you should write that all down . . .

Andrey is gone; he left unnoticed.

TUZENBACH: After many years, you say, life on earth will be beautiful, astonishing. That's true. But, in order to participate in that now, if only from far away, one must prepare for it, one must work . . .

VERSHININ: (*Stands up.*) Yes. But how many flowers you have here! (*Looks around.*) And what wonderful quarters. I envy you!

All my life I moved from one small apartment to the next, with two chairs, one sofa, and a stove that always smoked. What my life lacks are flowers just like these . . . (*Wipes his hands.*) Eh! Well, now how about that!

TUZENBACH: Yes, one must work. You probably think that the German's getting sentimental, but I assure you, on my honor, that I'm Russian, and I don't even speak German. My father was Russian Orthodox . . .

Pause.

VERSHININ: (*Walks around the stage.*) I often wonder, what if a person could live life over again, consciously? What if one life, which has already been lived, were, so to speak, a rough draft, and the next the clean copy! Then I think each of us would try not to repeat ourselves, or at least, would try to arrange our circumstances differently, would get quarters with flowers and with a lot of light . . . I have a wife and two little girls, but my wife is not well and so forth and so on. Well, if I started my life over again, I wouldn't marry . . . No, no!

Kulygin enters, dressed in his school uniform.

KULYGIN: (*Goes to Irina.*) Dear sister, allow me to congratulate you on your saint's day, and let me sincerely wish you, from the bottom of my heart, health and everything that one can wish for a girl of your age. And then accept as a present from me this little book. (*Gives her the book.*) The history of our high school over the last fifty years written by me. A trifling little book, written because I had nothing else to do, but read it anyway. Hello, ladies and gentlemen! (*To Vershinin.*) Kulygin, a teacher in the local high school. Auxiliary Councilor.[18] (*To Irina.*) In this book you will find a list of all the students who graduated from our high school

---

18. By way of introduction, Kuligin gives his rank in the civil service. Significantly, an "auxiliary councilor" is the civil rank that is exactly equivalent to the military rank of lieutenant-colonel, which is Vershinin's rank. That means that in this play Masha loves two men who hold essentially the same position in their respective careers.

over the last fifty years. *Feci, quod potui faciant meliora potentes.*[19] (*Kisses Masha.*)

IRINA: But you gave me the same book for Easter!

KULYGIN: (*Laughs.*) It can't be! In that case, give it back, or better yet, give it to the colonel. Take it, colonel. Read it sometime when you're bored.

VERSHININ: Thank you. (*Gets ready to go.*) I'm most happy that we met . . .

OLGA: You're leaving? No, no!

IRINA: Stay and have lunch with us. Please.

OLGA: I beg you!

VERSHININ: (*Bows.*) It seems that I dropped in on a name-day party. Excuse me, I didn't know. I didn't congratulate you . . . (*Exits with Olga into the hall.*)

KULYGIN: Today, ladies and gentlemen, is Sunday, a day of rest, so let's rest, let's be of good cheer, each according to his age and position. You should take up the rugs for the summer and put them away until winter . . . Use Persian Powder[20] on them, or naphthalene . . . The Romans were healthy because they knew how to work, knew how to rest. They had *mens sana in corpore sano.*[21] Their life flowed on according to well-known forms. Our headmaster says, the most important thing in every life is its form . . . That which loses its form comes to an end. And it's just the same with our prosaic lives. (*Takes Masha by the waist, laughing.*) Masha loves me, my wife loves me. You should take down the curtains too and put them away along with the rugs . . . Today I'm happy, in excellent spirits. Masha, at four o'clock today we have to go to the headmaster's house. He's arranging an outing for the teachers and their families.

MASHA: I'm not going.

KULYGIN: (*Annoyed.*) Masha dear, why?

---

19. "I did what I could, let them who can do better" (Latin, from Cicero).

20. Persian powder, made from flowers in the chrysanthemum family, was used to exterminate insects.

21. "A healthy mind in a healthy body" (Latin).

MASHA: We'll talk about it later . . . (*Angrily.*) All right, I'll go, just leave me alone please . . . (*Walks away.*)

KULYGIN: And afterwards we'll spend the evening at the headmaster's. Despite the fact he's sickly that man still tries to be sociable. An excellent, noble individual! A splendid person. Yesterday after the meeting he said to me, "I'm tired, Fyodor Ilyich! Tired!" (*Looks at the clock, then at his watch.*) Your clock is seven minutes fast. Yes, he said, "tired"!

Offstage violin music is heard.

OLGA: Ladies and gentlemen, please come have lunch! It's a meat pie!

KULYGIN: Ah, my dear Olga, my darling! Yesterday I worked from morning until eleven o'clock at night, and was tired, but today I feel happy. (*Goes to the table in the hall.*) My dear . . .

CHEBUTYKIN: (*Puts the newspaper in his pocket and combs his beard.*) A pie? Splendid!

MASHA: (*Sternly to Chebutykin.*) Just be careful, don't drink anything today. You hear? It's bad for you to drink.

CHEBUTYKIN: Humph! I'm over that. I haven't been on a binge for two years now. (*Impatiently.*) Ah, Mother-in-Heaven, it's all the same anyway!

MASHA: Still, don't you dare drink. Don't you dare. (*Angrily, but not loud enough for her husband to hear.*) Damn it, another boring evening at the headmaster's!

TUZENBACH: If I were you, I wouldn't go . . . It's very simple.

CHEBUTYKIN: Don't go, dear heart.

MASHA: Yes, don't go . . . This damned, unbearable life. (*Goes into the hall.*)

CHEBUTYKIN: (*Goes after her.*) Now, now!

SOLYONY: (*Entering the hall.*) Cheep, cheep, cheep . . .

TUZENBACH: That's enough, Vasily Vasilyevich. Drop it!

SOLYONY: Cheep, cheep, cheep . . .

KULYGIN: (*Cheerfully.*) To your health, colonel! I'm a teacher, and here in this house I'm part of the family. Masha's husband . . . She's a kind woman, very kind . . .

VERSHININ: I'll have some of this dark vodka . . . (*Drinks.*) To your health! (*To Olga.*) I feel so comfortable in your house! . . .

Irina and Tuzenbach remain alone in the parlor.

IRINA: Masha is not in good spirits today. She got married at eighteen, when he seemed to her to be the most intelligent of men. But now it's not so. He's the kindest, but not the most intelligent.

OLGA: (*Impatiently.*) Andrey, come here now!

ANDREY: (*Offstage.*) Right away. (*Enters and goes to the table.*)

TUZENBACH: What are you thinking about?

IRINA: Nothing. I don't like, I'm even afraid of your Solyony. He says only stupid things . . .

TUZENBACH: He's a strange man. I'm sorry for him and annoyed too, but mostly sorry. I think he's shy . . . When we're alone, he's intelligent and friendly, but with other people he's a coarse man, a bully. Don't go until they're all sitting down at the table. Let me stay with you for a little while. What are you thinking about? (*Pause.*) You're twenty years old, I'm not yet thirty. Think of how many years there are ahead for us, a long, long line of days, filled with my love for you . . .

IRINA: Nikolay Lvovich, don't talk to me about love.

TUZENBACH: (*Not obeying.*) I have a passionate thirst for life, struggle, work. And that thirst is mingled in my heart with my love for you, Irina. And today, as if it were planned, you're beautiful and, I think, life is just as beautiful. What are you thinking about?

IRINA: You say that life is beautiful. Yes, but what if it only seems that way! For us three sisters life has not been so beautiful. It's smothered us like the weeds do grass . . . I have tears in my eyes. That's not what's needed . . . (*Quickly wipes her face and smiles.*) To work is what's needed, to work. That's why we're not cheerful and why we look at life so gloomily, because we don't work. We were born among people who disdain work . . .

Natalya Ivanovna enters; she wears a pink dress with a green belt.

NATASHA: They've already sat down to lunch . . . I'm late. (*For a second she looks in the mirror and primps.*) I think my hair's all right . . . (*Seeing Irina.*) Dear Irina Sergeyevna, I congratulate you! (*Gives Irina a firm and prolonged kiss.*) You have so many guests, I really feel awful . . . Hello, Baron!

OLGA: (*Entering the parlor.*) Well, so it's Natalya Ivanovna. Hello my dear! (*They kiss.*)

NATASHA: Congratulations on the name-day. You have so much company. I'm terribly embarrassed . . .

OLGA: Enough now, it's only the family. (*In a shocked whisper.*) You have a green belt on! My dear, that's not right!

NATASHA: It's not an omen is it?

OLGA: No, it just doesn't go . . . and it's somehow a strange . . .

NATASHA: (*In a whining voice.*) Really? But it's not bright green, it's more neutral. (*Follows Olga into the hall.*)

*In the hall they are sitting down to lunch;
there's not a soul in the parlor.*

KULYGIN: Irina, I hope you find a nice fiancé. It's time for you to get married.

CHEBUTYKIN: Natalya Ivanovna, I hope you find a nice beau too.

KULYGIN: Natalya Ivanovna already has a beau.

MASHA: (*Strikes her fork against her plate.*) I'll drink a glass of this darling red wine! Ah yes, life is just as rosy and all too short to waste!

KULYGIN: Your conduct gets a C minus.

VERSHININ: This vodka's tasty. What's in it?

SOLYONY: Cockroaches.

IRINA: (*In a whining voice.*) Ugh! Ugh! How disgusting! . . .

OLGA: For supper there'll be roast turkey and apple pie for dessert. Thank God, all day today I'm home, and all night at home . . . Ladies and gentlemen, come back this evening . . .

VERSHININ: Allow me to come back too!

IRINA: Please do.

NATASHA: They're very informal here.

CHEBUTYKIN: "Nature put us on this earth for love alone!" (*Laughs.*)

ANDREY: (*Angrily.*) Stop it, ladies and gentlemen! I'm getting sick and tired of you.

Fedotik and Rodé enter with a big basket of flowers.

FEDOTIK: They're eating already.

RODÉ: (*Loudly, rolling his r's.*) Are they eating? Yes, they are already eating.

FEDOTIK: Hold still one minute! (*Takes a photograph.*) One! A little longer . . . (*Takes another photograph.*) Two! That's it!

He takes the basket and they go into the hall where they are met noisily.

RODÉ: (*Loudly.*) I congratulate you, I wish you all the best, all the best! The weather today is charming, in fact, it's excellent. All morning long I went strolling with the school boys. I teach physical education at the high school . . .

FEDOTIK: You can move now, Irina Sergeyevna, you can move! (*Takes a photograph.*) You're a remarkably interesting subject today. (*Takes a top out of his pocket,*) By the way, here's a top for you . . . It makes a surprising sound . . .

IRINA: How charming!

MASHA: "On a curved seashore a green oak. A golden chain upon that oak . . ." (*Plaintively.*) Why am I saying that? That phrase has been stuck in my head since morning . . .

KULYGIN: Thirteen at the table!

RODÉ: (*Loudly.*) Ladies and gentlemen, do you attach any significance to superstitions?

Laughter.

KULYGIN: If there are thirteen at the table, that means that someone's in love. It wouldn't be you Ivan Romanych, would it? . . .

CHEBUTYKIN: I'm an old sinner. But look how embarrassed Natalya Ivanovna is. I can't understand why that could be.

*Loud laughter; Natasha runs out of the hall
into the parlor; Andrey follows.*

ANDREY: That's enough, don't pay them any attention! Wait . . . Stay, I beg you . . .

NATASHA: I'm embarrassed . . . I don't know what to do with myself, and they laugh at me. It wasn't proper for me to leave the table like that, but I can't stand it . . . Can't stand it . . . (*Covers her face with her hands.*)

ANDREY: My darling, I beg you, I implore you, don't be upset. I assure you that they're joking, they don't mean any harm. My darling, my pretty one, they're all good people, warm people, and they love me and they love you too. Come over here to the window, they can't see us here . . .

NATASHA: I'm not used to being in society! . . .

ANDREY: Oh youth, wondrous beautiful youth! My darling, my pretty one, don't be so upset! . . . Believe me, believe me . . . I feel so good, my heart is full of love and ecstasy . . . Oh, they can't see us! They can't see! Why, why I fell in love with you, when I fell in love . . . Oh, I don't understand anything. My darling, my pretty one, innocent one, be my wife! I love you, love you . . . like no one else, ever . . .

A kiss.

*Two officers enter and seeing the kissing
couple, leave in embarrassment.*

Curtain.

Act II

*The first act set. Eight o'clock in the evening. Offstage on the
street an accordion can be heard faintly. There is no light. Natalya
Ivanovna enters in a dressing gown, carrying a candle; she comes
in and stops at the door which leads to Andrey's room.*

NATASHA: Andryusha, what are you doing? Reading? Nothing, I only . . . (*Goes over and opens the other door, looks around and then closes it.*) I wonder if there're any candles lit . . .

ANDREY: (*Enters with a book in his hand.*) What is it, Natasha?

NATASHA: I'm looking to see if any candles are burning . . . It's carnival week[22] and the servants aren't themselves, so you have to watch and watch, and make sure that everything's all right. Yesterday at midnight, I walked through the dining room and a candle was burning. Who lit it? I couldn't find out. (*Puts the candle down.*) What time is it?

ANDREY: (*Looking at the clock.*) A quarter after eight.

NATASHA: Yet Olga and Irina still aren't home. They haven't arrived. Always toiling, poor dears, Olga at the teachers' council, Irina at the telegraph office . . . (*Sighs.*) This morning I told your sister, "Take care of yourself," I said, "Irina, my darling." But she doesn't listen. A quarter after eight you say? I'm afraid that our Bobik is not at all well. Why is he so cold? Yesterday he was burning up, and today he's cold all over . . . I'm so afraid!

ANDREY: It's nothing, Natasha. The boy is fine,

NATASHA: But all the same, it would be better to watch his diet. I'm afraid. And today around nine o'clock they say the maskers will be stopping by. It would be better if they didn't come, Andryusha.

ANDREY: Well, I don't know. They were invited after all.

NATASHA: This morning, the dear little boy woke up and looked at me, and suddenly smiled. That means he recognized me. "Bobik," I said, "Hello! Hello, dear!" And he laughed. Children understand, they understand perfectly. So, Andryusha, I'll tell them not to let the maskers in.

ANDREY: (*Indecisively.*) But what about my sisters. They're the mistresses here.

NATASHA: And them too, I'll tell them. They're so kind . . . (*Walks around.*) For supper I ordered curdled milk. The doctor says you must only have curdled milk or you won't lose weight.

---

22. The festival days in late March which precede the Orthodox Church's season of Lent. Because Lent entails forty days of fasting in preparation for Easter Sunday, carnival is celebrated with eating, drinking, and carousing. During this time, maskers visit houses, trading dancing and singing for food. Sweet pancakes, called *blyny,* are a traditional carnival food and are later referenced by Ferapont.

(*Stops.*) Bobik is cold. I'm afraid it may be too cold for him in his room. We should move him to another room, at least until the weather gets warm. Irina's room for example is just right for a child. It's dry and gets the sun all day. We'll have to tell her that she and Olga can share one room for a while . . . It's all the same to her since she's not home all day, only sleeps here. (*Pause.*) Andryuschanschik, why are you so quiet?

ANDREY: Just thinking . . . Yes, there's nothing to say . . .

NATASHA: Yes . . . What did I want to tell you . . . Ah yes, Ferapont's come from the Board asking for you.

ANDREY: (*Yawns.*) Send him in.

Natasha exits; Andrey, bent over her forgotten candle, reads his book. Ferapont enters; he is wearing an old tattered coat, with a turned up collar covering his ears.

ANDREY: Hello, dear friend. What do you say?

FERAPONT: The chairman sent a little book and papers of some kind. Here it is . . . (*Gives Andrey a book and a bundle of papers.*)

ANDREY: Thank you. Good. Why didn't you come earlier? It's already after eight.

FERAPONT: What?

ANDREY: (*Louder.*) I said you've come late. It's already after eight.

FERAPONT: That's just it. I came to see you when it was still light, but they wouldn't let me in. The Master's busy, they said. Well what of it? Busy means busy, and I'm not in a hurry. (*Thinking that Andrey asked him about something.*) What?

ANDREY: Nothing. (*Examining the book.*) Tomorrow is Friday, we don't have any sessions but I'll go in anyway . . . Keeps me busy. It's boring at home . . . (*Pause.*) Well, Grandpa, it's strange how things change, how life cheats you! Today, because I was bored, didn't have anything to do, I took a look at this notebook—my old university lectures—and I thought how funny it's all turned out . . . My God, I'm secretary of the District Board, the same board that Protopopov chairs. I'm the secretary, and the most I can hope for is to become a member of the Board! A member of the local District Board, when every night I dream that I'm a professor of Moscow University, a famous scholar of whom all Russia is proud!

FERAPONT: I don't know . . . I don't hear well . . .

ANDREY: If you heard well perhaps I wouldn't talk to you. I have to talk to somebody and my wife doesn't understand me. I'm afraid of my sisters for some reason, afraid they'll laugh at me, make me ashamed . . . I don't drink, don't like taverns, my friend, but I'd gladly sit at Tyéstov's Restaurant in Moscow now, or at the Bolshóy Moskóvsky Hotel.[23]

FERAPONT: And in Moscow, a while ago now, a contractor told us at the Board how some merchants were eating pancakes, and one of them, who ate forty pancakes, almost died. Maybe it wasn't forty but fifty. I don't remember.

ANDREY: You sit in Moscow in a huge hall of a restaurant and you don't know anyone, and no one knows you, and yet you don't feel like a stranger. But here, you know everyone and everyone knows you, but you're a stranger, a stranger . . . A stranger and lonely.

FERAPONT: What? (*Pause.*) And that same contractor said—maybe he was lying—that a cable is strung across the whole of Moscow.

ANDREY: What for?

FERAPONT: Don't know. The contractor said so.

ANDREY: Nonsense. (*Reads the book.*) Were you ever in Moscow?

FERAPONT: (*After a pause.*) Never was. God didn't ordain it. (*Pause.*) Should I go?

ANDREY: You can go. Farewell.

Ferapont exits.

ANDREY: Farewell. (*Reading.*) Tomorrow morning come and take the papers . . . Go on. (*Pause.*) He left.

A bell.

---

23. Tyestov was the owner of the restaurant; the hotel is the Grand Moscow where Chekhov often stayed.

ANDREY: Well, to business ... (*Stretches and goes slowly to his own room.*)

Offstage the nurse sings, rocking a child to sleep. Masha and Vershinin enter. While they talk the maid lights the lamp and candles.

MASHA: I don't know. (*Pause.*) I don't know. Of course habit means a lot. After the death of my father, for example, we couldn't get used to the fact that there were no longer any of his aides in the house. But aside from habit, it seems to me, that I'm right on this. Maybe in other places it's not so, but in our city the most decent, the most noble, and the best educated people are the military men.

VERSHININ: I'm thirsty. I'd like some tea.

MASHA: (*Glancing at the clock.*) They'll serve it soon. I was married off when I was eighteen, and I was afraid of my husband because he was a teacher, and I had hardly finished school. He seemed terribly learned, intelligent, and important then. But now it's not the same unfortunately.

VERSHININ: That's so ... yes.

MASHA: I'm not talking about my husband. I'm used to him. But among the civilians there are usually so many coarse, impolite, uneducated people. Their coarseness upsets me, offends me, I suffer when I see that a man is not sensitive enough, tender enough, polite. When I happen to be with the teachers, my husband's colleagues, I simply suffer.

VERSHININ: Yes, ma'am ... But it seems to me that it's all the same, civilian and military men are equally uninteresting, at least in this city. It's all the same! If you listen to a local member of the "intelligentsia" either civilian or military, his wife torments him, his house torments him, his horses torment him ... The Russian is possessed by a desire to have exalted thoughts. But tell me, why does he fall so far short of his ideal in his life? Why?

MASHA: Why?

VERSHININ: Why do his children torment him, and his wife torment him? Why does he torment his wife and his children?

MASHA: You're not in a very good mood today.

VERSHININ: Perhaps not. I didn't have lunch, I haven't eaten anything since morning. One of my daughters is not very well, and when my little girls get sick I worry. My conscience torments me because I gave them such a mother. Oh, if only you had seen her today! What a good-for-nothing! We began swearing at each other at seven o'clock in the morning and at nine I slammed the door and left. (*Pause.*) I never talk about this and it's strange, I only complain to you. (*Kisses her hands.*) Don't be angry with me. Except for you I have no one—no one.

Pause.

MASHA: What a noise in the stove! Just before my father died, there was a racket in the chimney. Exactly like that.

VERSHININ: You're superstitious?

MASHA: Yes.

VERSHININ: That's strange. (*Kisses her hands.*) You're a remarkable, a wondrous woman. Remarkable, wondrous! It's dark here, but I see the sparkle in your eyes.

MASHA: (*Sits on another chair.*) It's lighter here . . .

VERSHININ: I love you, love you, love you . . . I love your eyes, your movements, I dream of them. A remarkable, wondrous woman!

MASHA: (*Laughing quietly.*) When you talk to me like this, I laugh for some reason, although it terrifies me. Don't repeat it, I beg you . . . (*Whispering.*) But say it, it's all the same to me. (*Covers her face with her hands.*) It's all the same to me. They're coming. Talk about something else.

Irina and Tuzenbach enter through the hall.

TUZENBACH: I have a triple last name. My name is Baron Tuzenbach-Krone-Altschauer, but I'm Russian, Russian Orthodox like you. There's very little German left in me, only my patience, my stubbornness, which bores you. I've been walking you home every evening.

IRINA: How tired I am!

TUZENBACH: And every evening I will come to the telegraph office and I will walk you home, even if it's ten, twenty years, until you chase me away . . . (*Seeing Masha and Vershinin, joyfully.*) Is it you? Hello.

IRINA: Well, I'm finally home. (*To Masha.*) Just now, a woman came in to send a telegram to her brother in Sarátov[24] that her son had died, but she couldn't remember his address for anything. So she just sent it without an address to Saratov. She was crying. And I was rude to her for no reason at all. "I have no time," I said. It was so stupid. Are the maskers coming tonight?

MASHA: Yes.

IRINA: (*Sits in an easy chair.*) Ah, for some rest. I'm tired.

TUZENBACH: (*With a smile.*) When you come home from work you seem so young, so unhappy . . .

Pause.

IRINA: I'm tired. No, I don't like the telegraph office, I don't like it.

MASHA: You've gotten thinner . . . (*Whistles.*) And younger, your face has started to look like a little boy's . . .

TUZENBACH: That's because of her hair style.

IRINA: I have to look for other work, this isn't right for me. What I wanted so much, what I dreamed of, there's none of that in it. It's labor without poetry, without meaning.

A knock on the floor.

IRINA: The Doctor's knocking. (*To Tuzenbach.*) Dear Baron, knock back for me . . . I can't do it . . . I'm too tired . . . (*Tuzenbach knocks on the floor.*) He's coming right away. We must do something about this. Yesterday the doctor and our Andrey lost at the club again. They say Andrey lost two hundred rubles.

MASHA: (*Indifferently.*) What's to be done now!

IRINA: Two weeks ago he lost, in December he lost. I hope he loses everything as soon as possible and maybe then we'd leave this city. Good Lord, I dream of Moscow every night. I'm like a

---

24. A city on the Volga River.

madwoman. (*Laughs*.) We'll move there in June, and before June there's still . . . February, March, April, May . . . almost half a year!

MASHA: Only we must make sure that Natasha doesn't hear anything about the loss.

IRINA: I don't think she cares.

Chebutykin enters the hall, having just gotten up from bed. He took a nap after dinner. He combs his beard, then sits at the table and takes a newspaper out of his pocket.

MASHA: Here he is . . . Did he pay his rent?

IRINA: (*Laughs*.) No. Not a kopeck in eight months. He's evidently forgotten.

MASHA: (*Laughs*.) How importantly he sits there!

All laugh. A pause.

IRINA: Why are you so quiet, Alexander Ignatyevich?

VERSHININ: Don't know. I'd like some tea. Tea! Half my life for a glass of tea! I haven't eaten since morning . . .

CHEBUTYKIN: Irina Sergeyevna!

IRINA: What do you want?

CHEBUTYKIN: Please come here. *Venez ici.*[25] (*Irina goes and sits at the table.*) I can't do without you.

Irina lays out a game of solitaire on the table.

VERSHININ: Well? If they won't serve tea, let's philosophize a bit.

TUZENBACH: Let's. About what?

VERSHININ: About what? Let's daydream . . . For example, about the life that will come after us, in about two hundred, three hundred years.

TUZENBACH: What about it? After us, people will fly in balloons, change the cut of their jackets, perhaps discover a sixth sense, even develop it, but life will remain essentially the same—hard,

---

25. "Come here" (French).

happy, and full of mysteries. And after a thousand years, people will still sigh and say, "Ah how hard life is!" Besides that, they'll still fear death, and not want to die, just like now.

VERSHININ: (*Thinking about it.*) How shall I put it? I think that everything on earth must change little by little, and people are already changing before our very eyes. After two hundred, three hundred, finally a thousand years—the point is not how long it takes—there will come a new, happy life. We won't participate in that life, of course, but we're living for it now, working and suffering to create it. This alone is the goal of our existence, or, if you like, our happiness.

Masha laughs softly.

TUZENBACH: What's wrong?

MASHA: I don't know. All day today, since morning, I've been laughing.

VERSHININ: I finished the same school as you did, but didn't go to the military academy. I read a lot, but don't know how to choose my books, and so perhaps I read a lot that's unnecessary, but anyway, the more I live, the more I want to know. My hair's turning gray, I'm almost an old man, but I know so little, ah, so little! But all the same, I think that what's most important and real, I do know and know well. But how can I prove to you that we won't have, and don't even need happiness ourselves ... We must only work and work, but happiness—that's fated for our descendants, far in the future. (*Pause.*) Not for me but for the descendants of my descendants.

Fedotik and Rodé appear in the hall; they sit down and sing quietly, playing a guitar.

TUZENBACH: According to you, we shouldn't even dream of happiness! But what if I feel happy!

VERSHININ: You don't.

TUZENBACH: (*Throwing up his hands and laughing.*) Obviously we don't understand each other. Well, how can I convince you?

Masha laughs quietly.

TUZENBACH: (*Gesturing to her with a finger.*) Laugh! (*To Vershinin.*) Not only in two hundred or three hundred, but even in a million years, life will remain exactly the same as it is. It does not change, it stays constant, following its own laws, which you'll never discover, or at least over which you'll never have any control. Migratory birds, cranes for example, fly and fly and whether great thoughts or small ones wander through their minds, they all still fly, not knowing where or why. They fly and will fly, no matter what philosophers may come among them. Let them philosophize as they will, so long as they fly . . .

MASHA: Still where is the meaning?

TUZENBACH: The meaning . . . Look, it's snowing. What meaning does that have?

Pause.

MASHA: I think that one must be a believer, or must search for beliefs, otherwise life is empty, empty . . . To live and not to know why the cranes fly, why children are born, why there are stars in the sky . . . Either you know why you live, or it's all nonsense, just tinsel . . .

Pause.

VERSHININ: Still it's sad that my youth has passed . . .

MASHA: Gogol said, "It's boring to live on this earth, ladies and gentlemen!"[26]

TUZENBACH: And I say, "It's hard to argue with you, lady and gentleman." You're completely . . .

CHEBUTYKIN: (*Reading a newspaper.*) Balzac was married in Berdíchev.[27]

Irina sings softly.

---

26. The last line of a short story by Nikolay Vasilyevich Gogol (1809–1852) entitled "The Tale of How Ivan Ivanovich Quarreled with Ivan Fyodorovich."
27. The French writer Honoré de Balzac (1799–1850) died in the Ukrainian town of Berdichev a few months after marrying a Polish woman.

CHEBUTYKIN: I'll make a note of that in my notebook. (*Makes a note.*) Balzac was married in Berdichev. (*Reads the paper.*)

IRINA: (*Lays out a game of solitaire, lost in thought.*) Balzac was married in Berdichev.

TUZENBACH: The die is cast. You know, Maria Sergeyevna, that I'm retiring?

MASHA: I heard. And I don't see any good in it. I don't like civilians.

TUZENBACH: It's all the same . . . (*Stands up.*) I'm not handsome, what kind of military man do I make anyway? Well, yes, it's all the same, and besides . . . I'll work. If only for once in my life, I'll work so hard that I'll come home, fall into bed exhausted, and fall asleep immediately. (*Going into the hall.*) Workers must sleep soundly!

FEDOTIK: (*To Irina.*) At Pýzhnikov's store on Moskóvsky Street I bought you a box of colored pencils. And here's a little knife . . .

IRINA: You're used to treating me like a little girl, but I'm grown up now . . . (*Takes the pencils and the knife, joyfully.*) How charming!

FEDOTIK: And I bought a knife for myself too . . . Have a look. One blade, and still another blade, and a third one. This is to clean your ears, scissors, to clean your nails . . .

RODÉ: (*Loudly.*) Doctor, how old are you?

CHEBUTYKIN: Me? I'm thirty-two.

Laughter.

FEDOTIK: Now I'll show you another kind of solitaire . . . (*Lays out a game of solitaire.*)

The samovar is brought in; Anfisa stands near the samovar; a little later Natasha enters and also fusses around the samovar; Solyony enters and, after greeting everyone, sits at the table.

VERSHININ: That's quite a wind!

MASHA: Yes. I'm sick and tired of winter. I've already forgotten what summer is like.

IRINA: I can see how the solitaire is turning out. We'll go to Moscow.[28]

FEDOTIK: No, it's not turning out that way. See how the eight is on top of the two of spades. (*Laughs.*) That means you won't go to Moscow.

CHEBUTYKIN: (*Reads the newspaper.*) Tsitsikár.[29] Smallpox is raging there.

ANFISA: (*Approaching Masha.*) Masha, drink some tea, dear one. (*To Vershinin.*) Please, your excellency . . . Please, dear sir, I forgot your name . . .

MASHA: Bring it here, Nanny. I won't go there.

IRINA: Nanny!

ANFISA: Com-ming!

NATASHA: (*To Solyony.*) Little babies understand beautifully. "Hello," I said to Bobik, "Hello, my darling!" He looked at me as if he knew what I said. You think I'm only saying this because I'm his mother, but no, no. I assure you! He is an exceptional child.

SOLYONY: If he were my child, I would fry him in a frying pan and eat him. (*Takes his glass of tea into the parlor and sits in a corner.*)

NATASHA: (*Covering her face with her hands.*) A coarse, uneducated man!

MASHA: Happy is he who does not notice whether it's summer or winter. I think that if I were in Moscow, then I would be completely indifferent to the weather . . .

VERSHININ: The other day I was reading the diary of a certain minister in the French government, written while he was in prison. The minister was found guilty of corruption in the Panama Canal scandal.[30] With what rapture and ecstasy he writes about the birds he saw from his prison window,

---

28. Irina is using the game to tell fortunes; if the cards line up properly her fortune will be good.

29. A city in Manchuria, once part of the Russian Empire.

30. When the Panama Canal Company went bankrupt in the late 1880s, the French Minister of Public Works, Charles Baïhaut, was convicted of bribery and imprisoned for five years. His memoirs were published in 1898.

birds he never noticed before, when he was minister. Now, of course, when he's set free, he won't notice the birds anymore. You wouldn't notice Moscow either if you lived in it. We never have happiness and we won't ever have it, we only long for it.

TUZENBACH: (*Takes a box from the table.*) Where's the candy?

IRINA: Solyony ate it.

TUZENBACH: All of it?

ANFISA: (*Handing out the tea.*) You have a letter here, dear sir.

VERSHININ: For me? (*Takes the letter.*) It's from my daughter. (*Reads.*) Yes of course . . . Excuse me, Maria Sergeyevna, I'll just slip out quietly. I won't have any tea. (*Stands; he is upset.*) Always the same story . . .

MASHA: What is it? It's not a secret, is it?

VERSHININ: (*Quietly.*) My wife's taken poison again. I must go. I'll leave without anyone noticing. All this is terribly unpleasant. (*Kisses Masha's hand.*) My dear, fine, beautiful woman . . . I'll leave here quietly . . . (*Exits.*)

ANFISA: Now where did he go? And I poured tea for him . . . What a man!

MASHA: (*Angrily.*) Stop it. You keep after me, don't give me any peace . . . (*Takes her tea to the table.*) I'm sick and tired of you, old woman!

ANFISA: What's upset you? Darling!

The voice of Andrey: "Anfisa."

ANFISA: (*Mimics him.*) Anfisa! He's sitting out there . . . (*Exits.*)

MASHA: (*At the table in the hall, angrily.*) Let me sit down! (*Mixes up the cards on the table.*) You put your cards down all over the whole table. Drink your tea!

IRINA: Mashka, you're mean.

MASHA: If I'm mean, then don't talk to me. Don't touch me!

CHEBUTYKIN: (*Laughing.*) Don't touch her, don't touch . . .

MASHA: You're sixty years old, but you're just like a little baby, the devil knows what the hell you're always babbling about.

NATASHA: (*Sighs.*) My dear Masha, why use such expressions in your conversation? With such a pretty appearance, I'll tell you quite frankly, you could be charming in proper, well-bred company, if you didn't use those words. *Je vous prie, pardonnez moi, Marie, mais vous avez des mannières un peu grossieres.*[31]

TUZENBACH: (*Holding back his laughter.*) Give me . . . Give me . . . I think there's some cognac there . . .

NATASHA: *Il parait, que mon Bobik déja ne dort pas.*[32] He's woken up. He wasn't well today. I'll go to him, excuse me . . . (*Exits.*)

IRINA: And where did Alexander Ignatyevich go?

MASHA: Home. He had something unusual happen to his wife again.

TUZENBACH: (*Goes to Solyony, a bottle of cognac in his hand.*) You're always sitting alone, thinking about something or other, and I can't figure out what it is. Well, let's make peace. Let's drink some cognac together. (*They drink.*) I'll probably have to play the piano all night tonight. I'll play all kinds of nonsense . . . That's the way it goes!

SOLYONY: Why make peace? I'm not quarrelling with you.

TUZENBACH: You always make me feel like something has happened between us. You have a strange character, you must admit.

SOLYONY: (*Declaiming.*) "I am strange, but who is not strange!" "Be not angry, Aleko!"[33]

TUZENBACH: What does Aleko have to do with it . . .

Pause.

SOLYONY: When I'm alone with someone, then I'm all right, but in company I'm melancholy, shy, and . . . I say all kinds of

---

31. "Please pardon me, Marie, but you have rather coarse manners" (ungrammatical French).
32. "It seems that my Bobik is already not asleep" (ungrammatical French).
33. The first quotation is from Alexander Sergeyevich Griboyedov's satirical play *Woe from Wit* (1823); the second is a paraphrase from Alexander Sergeyevich Pushkin's narrative poem "The Gypsies" (1824), in which the European Aleko, having discovered that his Gypsy wife has taken a lover, kills both wife and lover.

nonsense. But still I'm more honorable and well-bred than many, many others. And I can prove it.

TUZENBACH: I often get angry with you. You're constantly looking for a quarrel with me when we're in company, but still I like you for some reason. In any case, I'll get drunk tonight. Let's drink.

SOLYONY: Let's drink.

They drink.

SOLYONY: I don't have anything against you, Baron, never could have anything against you. But I have the character of Lérmontov.[34] I even look a little like him, I've been told . . . (*Takes a bottle of eau de cologne out of his pocket and pours some on his hands.*)

TUZENBACH: I'm retiring. *Basta!*[35] After thinking about it for five years now, I finally decided. I'll work.

SOLYONY: (*Declaiming.*) "Be not angry Aleko. Forget, forget thy dreams."

While they talk Andrey enters quietly with a book and sits down near a candle.

TUZENBACH: I'll work.

CHEBUTYKIN: (*Going into the parlor with Irina,*) And the food too was genuine Caucasian: onion soup and a roast—*chekhartmá*, a meat dish.

SOLYONY: *Cheremshá* is not a meat dish at all but a vegetable, something like an onion.[36]

---

34. Mikhail Yurevich Lermontov (1814–1841) was Russia's most important Romantic poet. His works are often set in the Caucasus Mountains and full of melancholic introspection. Solyony may be fashioning himself on Lermontov's main character in the novel *A Hero of Our Time* (1839), who dies in a duel. Challenged by a fellow military officer, Lermontov himself was killed in a duel.
35. "Enough!" (Italian.)
36. *Chekhartmá* is a meat soup and *cheremshá* is a type of leek; Chebutykin and Solyony are both incorrect.

CHEBUTYKIN: No, no, my angel, *chekhartma* is not an onion but a roast of lamb.

SOLYONY: And I tell you, *cheremsha* is an onion.

CHEBUTYKIN: And I tell you, *chekhartma* is lamb.

SOLYONY: And I tell you, *cheremsha* is an onion.

CHEBUTYKIN: Why should I argue with you? You were never even in the Caucasus and never ate *chekhartma*.

SOLYONY: I never ate it because I couldn't stand it. *Cheremsha* has the same kind of smell as garlic.

ANDREY: (*Palliating them.*) Enough, gentlemen! I beg you.

TUZENBACH: When are the maskers coming?

IRINA: They promised to come about nine, so that means soon.

TUZENBACH: (*Hugs Andrey.*) "Eh, my porch, my brand new porch . . ."[37]

ANDREY: (*Dances and sings.*) "My porch made strong with maple boughs . . ."

CHEBUTYKIN: (*Dances.*) "Strong the weaving of the boughs, eh! . . ."

Laughter.

TUZENBACH: (*Kisses Andrey.*) To hell with it, let's drink, Andryusha, let's drink to our friendship. And you and I, Andryusha, we'll go to Moscow, to the University.

SOLYONY: To which one? In Moscow there are two universities.[38]

ANDREY: In Moscow there is one university.

SOLYONY: And I tell you, there are two.

ANDREY: So what if there were three. The more the better.

SOLYONY: In Moscow there are two universities!

Murmurs and grumbles.

---

37. A folk song that speeds up as it is sung.

38. There are two campuses of Moscow University, colloquially called the old and the new, but both are under the same administration.

SOLYONY: In Moscow there are two universities, the old one and new one. But if you don't like hearing about it, if my words irritate you, then I won't tell you. I can even leave the room. (*Exits through one of the doors.*)

TUZENBACH: Bravo, Bravo! (*Laughs.*) Ladies and gentlemen, let's start, I will sit down and play! He's a funny one, that Solyony . . . (*Sits down at the piano and begins to play a waltz.*)

MASHA: (*Dances to the waltz by herself.*) The Baron is drunk, is drunk, is drunk!

Natasha enters.

NATASHA: (*To Chebutykin.*) Ivan Romanych! (*Says something to Chebutykin and then quietly exits.*)

Chebutykin puts his hand on Tuzenbach's shoulder and whispers something in his ear.

IRINA: What is it?

CHEBUTYKIN: It's time for us to go. Farewell.

TUZENBACH: Goodnight. It's time to go.

IRINA: Excuse me . . . What about the maskers? . . .

ANDREY: (*Embarrassed.*) There won't be any maskers, You see, my dear, Natasha says that Bobik is not completely well and so . . . In short, I don't know, it's really all the same to me.

IRINA: (*Shrugging her shoulders.*) Bobik's not well!

MASHA: What a waste! If we're being thrown out, then we must go. (*To Irina.*) It's not Bobik who's sick, it's her . . . Right here! (*Touches her finger to her forehead.*) She's so common!

Andrey exits right to his own room; Chebutykin follows him; they say goodbye in the hall.

FEDOTIK: What a pity! I was counting on spending the evening here, but if the little baby is sick then of course . . . I'll bring him a toy tomorrow . . .

RODÉ: (*Loudly.*) I purposely slept after dinner because I thought that I would be dancing all night. It's only nine o'clock, isn't it?

MASHA: Let's go outside and talk. We'll think of something.

"Goodbye, farewell" is heard. Tuzenbach's cheerful laughter is heard; everybody leaves. Anfisa and the maid clear the table; put out the candles. A nurse is heard singing a lullaby. Andrey in a coat and hat followed by Chebutykin quietly enters.

CHEBUTYKIN: I never had the time to get married, because life flashed by like lightning, and because I loved your mother madly and she was already married . . .

ANDREY: It's not necessary to get married. It's not necessary because it's boring.

CHEBUTYKIN: That may be so, but there's loneliness too . . . Philosophize all you want, but loneliness is a terrible thing, my dear . . . Even though essentially . . . Of course, it's really all the same!

ANDREY: Let's go quickly.

CHEBUTYKIN: Why are you rushing? We have time.

ANDREY: I'm afraid my wife will stop us.

CHEBUTYKIN: Ahh!

ANDREY: Today I won't play, I'll just sit and watch. I'm not feeling well . . . What should I do, Ivan Romanych, about shortness of breath?

CHEBUTYKIN: Why ask me? I don't remember, my dear. I don't know.

ANDREY: Let's go through the kitchen.

A bell rings, then rings again; voices are heard, laughter. They exit.

IRINA: (*Enters.*) Who's there?

ANFISA: (*In a whisper.*) The maskers!

The bell rings.

IRINA: Tell them that no one's home, Nanny. Make our excuses.

Anfisa exits. Irina walks about the room in thought; she is upset. Solyony enters.

SOLYONY: (*Puzzled.*) No one's here . . . Where did everyone go?

IRINA: They went home.

SOLYONY: That's strange. You're here alone?

IRINA: Alone. (*Pause.*) Goodbye.

SOLYONY: Recently I've been acting unrestrainedly, tactlessly. But you're not like everyone else, you're fine and innocent, you can see the truth . . . You alone can understand me. I love, deeply, infinitely love you . . .

IRINA: Goodbye. Leave!

SOLYONY: I can't live without you. (*Going to her.*) Oh my bliss! (*Tearfully.*) Oh happiness! Luxurious, wondrous, astonishing eyes, like I've never seen on another woman . . .

IRINA: (*Coldly.*) Stop it, Vasily Vasilyevich!

SOLYONY: This is the first time I've talked to you about love and it's as if I'm not on this earth, but on a different planet. (*Rubs his forehead.*) Well, it's all the same. I can't force you to love me of course . . . But I will not allow any fortunate rivals . . . I will not . . . I swear to you by all that is holy, that I will kill any rival . . . Oh my wondrous one!

Natasha crosses with a candle.

NATASHA: (*Looks in at one door, then at another and crosses in front of the door leading to her husband's room.*) Andrey's there. Let him read. Excuse me, Vasily Vasilyevich, I didn't know you were here, I'm not dressed . . .

SOLYONY: It's all the same to me. Goodbye! (*Exits.*)

NATASHA: You look tired, my darling, my poor little girl! (*Kisses Irina.*) You should go to bed earlier.

IRINA: Is Bobik sleeping?

NATASHA: He's sleeping. But sleeping restlessly. By the way darling, I wanted to tell you, but either you weren't here or I couldn't find the time . . . Bobik's nursery, I think, is cold and damp. And your room is so nice for a child. Darling sister, move in with Olya for a while!

IRINA: (*Not understanding.*) Where?

*One can hear the approach of a troika[39]
with bells on the harness.*

NATASHA: You and Olya will be in one room while Bobik is in your room. He's so sweet. Today I said to him, "Bobik you're mine! Mine!" And he looked right at me with his little bitty eyes. (*A bell.*) That must be Olga. How late she is! (*A maid approaches Natasha and whispers in her ear.*) Protopopov? What an eccentric man! Protopopov's come to ask me for a ride in his troika. (*Laughs.*) How strange these men are . . . (*A bell.*) Someone's ringing . . . It must be Olga . . . (*Exits.*)

The maid runs out. Irina sits lost in thought; Kulygin and Olga enter, and following them Vershinin.

KULYGIN: So there you are! But I was told you were having a party here.

VERSHININ: That's strange, I left not long ago, half an hour ago, and they were all waiting for the maskers . . .

IRINA: They all left.

KULYGIN: Masha left too? Where did she go? And why is Protopopov waiting downstairs in a troika? Who is he waiting for?

IRINA: Don't ask questions . . . I'm tired.

KULYGIN: Well, well, you're peevish . . .

OLGA: The meeting just finished. It tormented me. Our principal is sick and so I'm replacing her. My head, my head aches, my head. (*Sits down.*) Andrey lost at cards again, two hundred rubles . . . The whole city is talking about it . . .

KULYGIN: Yes and I'm tired from the meeting too. (*Sits down.*)

VERSHININ: My wife thought she'd scare me by nearly poisoning herself. It's all over now and I'm glad I can rest . . . But we should leave, shouldn't we? Anyway, allow me to wish you all the best. Fyodor Ilyich, let's go somewhere together! I can't spend the evening at home, I really can't . . . Let's go!

KULYGIN: I'm tired. I'm not going. (*Stands.*) Tired. My wife went home?

---

39. A sleigh pulled by a team of three horses. Troika rides were popular during carnival.

IRINA: She must have.

KULYGIN: (*Kisses Irina's hand.*) Goodbye. Tomorrow and the next day I'll rest all day. All the best! (*Starts to go.*) I'd like some tea. I was counting on spending the evening in pleasant company and—oh, *falicem hoininem spem!*[40] Use the accusative case with an exclamation . . .

VERSHININ: That means I'll have to go alone. (*Exits with Kulygin, whistling.*)

OLGA: My head aches, my head . . . Andrey lost . . . The whole city's talking . . . I'll go lie down. (*Goes.*) Tomorrow I'm free, the day after that I'm free . . . My head aches, my head . . . (*Exits.*)

IRINA: (*Alone.*) They've all left. No one's here.

An accordion is heard outside. The nurse sings a song.

NATASHA: (*In a fur coat and hat goes through the hall; the maid follows her.*) I'll be home in half an hour, I'll only ride around a little. (*Exits.*)

IRINA: (*Remaining alone, she grieves.*) To Moscow! To Moscow! To Moscow!

Curtain.

Act III

Olga and Irina's room. To the left and right, beds with screens around them. It is past two o'clock in the morning. Offstage a fire alarm rings for a fire which began long ago. It is obvious that no one in the house has gone to bed yet. Masha lies on the sofa, dressed as usual in a black dress. Olga and Anfisa enter.

ANFISA: Now they're sitting under the staircase downstairs . . . I said to them, "Please go upstairs; it's all right to go there," but they just keep crying and saying, "We don't know where Papa is. Please God," they said, "he wasn't burned." Can you imagine! And in the yard there are others . . . They're not dressed either.

---

40. "Man's fleeting hope" (Latin, from Cicero).

OLGA: *(Takes a dress out of the wardrobe.)* Take this gray one . . . And this one . . . The blouse too . . . And this skirt, take it, Nanny . . . What does it mean, my God! Apparently Kirsánovsky Road burned down completely. Take this . . . Take this . . . *(Throws a dress to her.)* The Vershinins, poor things, are afraid . . . Their house nearly burned down. Let them stay here tonight . . . We can't let them go home . . . Poor Fedotik lost everything, nothing's left.

ANFISA: Call Ferapont, Olyushka, or I won't be able to carry . . .

OLGA: *(Rings.)* I can't get him . . . *(Through the door.)* Come here, whoever's in there!

Through the open door, a window can be seen, all red from the fire; the fire patrol can be heard passing the house.

OLGA: What a horror! And so tiring!

Ferapont enters.

OLGA: Here take this downstairs . . . The Kolotílin girls are standing under the stairs . . . Give it to them. And give this away.

FERAPONT: Yes madam. In the year 12, Moscow burned too. Lord God Almighty! The French were surprised.[41]

OLGA: Go on, hurry up!

FERAPONT: Yes madam. *(Exits.)*

OLGA: Nanny, darling, give it all away. We don't need anything, give it all away, Nanny . . . I'm tired, hardly standing on my feet . . . We can't let the Vershinins go home. The little girls can sleep in the parlor, and Alexander Ignatyevich can stay downstairs with the Baron. Fedotik can also go with the Baron, or let him stay in the hall . . . The doctor's drunk, as if on purpose, terribly drunk, so we can't put anyone in with him. Vershinin's wife can stay in the parlor too.

ANFISA: *(Exhausted.)* Olyushka, my dear, don't throw me out! Don't throw me out!

---

41. He recalls Napolean's invasion of 1812 and the burning of Moscow that followed the city's capture.

OLGA: What stupid things are you saying now, Nanny. No one will throw you out.

ANFISA: (*Lays her head on Olga's chest.*) My own, my treasure, I serve you, I work . . . But when I get weak, everyone will say, "Get out!" And where can I go? Where? I'm over eighty years old. Eighty-two years old . . .

OLGA: Sit down, Nanny . . . You're tired, you poor dear . . . (*Sits her down.*) Rest, my darling. How pale you look!

Natasha enters.

NATASHA: They say that we should form a committee to help the victims of the fire. What of it? A wonderful idea. It's always necessary to help the poor people. It's the duty of the rich. Bobik and Sofochka are sleeping, sleeping as if nothing had happened. We have so many people here, everywhere you go, the house is full. Now there's influenza in the city too . . . I'm afraid that the children will catch it.

OLGA: (*Not listening to her.*) You can't see the fire from this room; it's peaceful here.

NATASHA: Yes . . . I must be a mess. (*In front of the mirror.*) They say I've gained weight . . . But it's not true! Not a bit! Masha's sleeping too, exhausted, poor thing . . . (*To Anfisa, coldly.*) Don't you dare sit in my presence! Stand up! Get out of here! (*Anfisa exits; pause.*) I don't understand why you keep that old woman!

OLGA: (*Taken aback.*) Excuse me, I don't understand either . . .

NATASHA: She's of no use here. She's a peasant. She should live in the country . . . What pampering she gets! I like order in a house! There shouldn't be any unnecessary people. (*Strokes Olga's cheek.*) Poor dear thing, you're tired! Our principal is tired! When my Sofochka grows up and goes to the high school, I'll be afraid of you.

OLGA: I won't be principal.

NATASHA: They'll elect you Olyechka. That's settled.

OLGA: I'll refuse. I couldn't stand it . . . I don't have the strength . . . (*Drinks some water.*) You treated Nanny so coarsely just now . . . Excuse me, I'm in no condition to endure . . . I feel faint . . .

NATASHA: (*Excitedly.*) Forgive me, Olya, forgive me . . . I didn't want to annoy you.

Masha gets up, takes her pillow, and exits, angrily.

OLGA: Try to understand, dear . . . Maybe we were brought up strangely, but I cannot endure this. Such treatment weighs me down, I get sick . . . I lose heart!

NATASHA: Forgive me, forgive me . . . (*Kisses her.*)

OLGA: Everything, even the slightest vulgar or coarse word, upsets me . . .

NATASHA: I often say too much, it's true, but you'll agree, my darling, that she should live in the country.

OLGA: She's been with us for thirty years.

NATASHA: But she can't work now, can she? Either I don't understand you, or you don't want to understand me! She is not fit to work. All she does is sleep and sit.

OLGA: So let her sit.

NATASHA: (*Surprised.*) What do you mean, let her sit? She's a servant after all. (*Tearfully.*) I don't understand you, Olya. We have a governess, and a wet nurse, a maid, a cook. What do we need that old woman for? What for?

Offstage, a fire alarm.

OLGA: I've aged ten years tonight.

NATASHA: We must come to an agreement, Olya. You are at the high school, I am at home. You have your teaching, I have the housework. So if I tell you something concerning the servants, then I know what I am talking about. I know what I-am-talking-a-bout . . . And tomorrow that old crow, that old hag, will be gone . . . (*Stamps her foot.*) That witch! . . . Don't you dare provoke me! Don't you dare! (*Recovering herself.*) Really, if you don't move downstairs, we'll always be arguing. It's terrible.

Kulygin enters.

KULYGIN: Where is Masha? It's time to go home now. They say the fire's dying out. (*Stretches.*) Only one square block burned completely, but there was a wind, and so at first it seemed that the whole city would burn. (*Sits down.*) I'm exhausted. Olyechka, my dear . . . I often think that if it weren't for Masha, then I would have married you, Olyechka. You're so good . . . I'm worn out. (*Listens.*)

OLGA: What is it?

KULYGIN: As if on purpose the doctor's gone carousing. He's terribly drunk. As if on purpose! (*Stands.*) I think he's coming this way . . . Do you hear? Yes, this way . . . (*Laughs.*) What a fellow, really . . . I'll hide . . . (*Goes to the wardrobe and stands in the corner.*) What a rascal!

OLGA: For two years he didn't drink and now suddenly he goes and gets drunk . . .

She and Natasha go to the back of the room.
Chebutykin enters; without staggering, as if sober,
he crosses the room, stops, looks around, then goes
to the washstand and begins to wash his hands.

CHEBUTYKIN: (*Sullenly.*) To hell with all of them . . . Tell off all of them . . . They think that I'm a doctor, can cure all kinds of sicknesses, but I don't really know anything, forgot everything that I knew, don't remember anything, absolutely nothing.

Olga and Natasha exit unnoticed by him.

CHEBUTYKIN: To hell with them. Last Wednesday, I treated a woman on Zasípin Street. She died, and it was my fault she died. Yes . . . I knew a little something twenty-five years ago, but now I don't remember anything. Nothing. Maybe I'm not even human, just pretending that I have hands, and feet, and a head. Maybe I don't even exist at all, but only think that I do, that I walk, eat, sleep. (*Cries.*) Oh, if only I didn't exist! (*Stops crying, sullenly.*) To hell with them . . . Day before yesterday, there was a conversation at the club. They were talking about Shakespeare, Voltaire . . . I never read, never read them at all, but I tried to look as if I had. And others too did the same! How petty! How low! And that woman that I killed on Wednesday . . . I remembered her . . . It all came back to me, and I felt that my soul had become twisted, disgusting, nasty . . . so I went and got drunk.

Irina, Vershinin, and Tuzenbach enter; Tuzenbach wears a civilian suit of clothes which is new and fashionable.

IRINA: Let's sit here a while. No one will come in here.

VERSHININ: If it weren't for the soldiers, the whole city would have burned. They're excellent men! (*Rubs his hands with pleasure.*) Real heroes! Ah, what excellent men!

KULYGIN: (*Approaching them.*) What time is it, ladies and gentlemen?

TUZENBACH: It's already after three o'clock. It's getting light.

IRINA: Everyone's still sitting in the hall, no one's leaving. And your Solyony is sitting there too . . . (*To Chebutykin.*) You should go to sleep, Doctor.

CHEBUTYKIN: Not at all, madam . . . Thank you, madam. (*Combs his beard.*)

KULYGIN: (*Laughs.*) Drunk yourself tipsy, Ivan Romanych! (*Clasps his shoulder.*) Excellent fellow! *In vino veritas,*[42] as the ancients said.

TUZENBACH: They're all asking me to arrange a benefit concert for the victims of the fire.

IRINA: But who can . . .

TUZENBACH: Maybe we can arrange it, if we want. Maria Sergeyevna, in my opinion, plays the piano beautifully . . .

KULYGIN: She does play beautifully!

IRINA: She's forgotten how. She hasn't played in three years . . . or four . . .

TUZENBACH: In this city, no one really understands music, not one soul, but I, I understand and I give you my word of honor that Maria Sergeyevna plays excellently, with real talent.

KULYGIN: You're right, Baron. I love her very much, my Masha. She's a fine woman.

---

42. "In wine there is truth" (Latin).

TUZENBACH: To know how to play so splendidly and at the same time know that no one, no one understands!

KULYGIN: (*He sighs.*) Yes . . . But would it be proper for her to take part in a concert? (*Pause.*) I certainly don't know, ladies and gentlemen. Maybe it would be good. I must confess, our headmaster is a good man, even a very good, a most intelligent man, but he has certain opinions . . . Of course, it's not his business, but still, if you want, then I could perhaps talk it over with him.

Chebutykin takes a porcelain clock in his hands and examines it.

VERSHININ: I got dirty at the fire. How I must look! (*Pause.*) Yesterday, by chance, I heard that they may want to move our brigade somewhere far away. Some say to Poland, others to Chitá.[43]

TUZENBACH: I heard that too. Well? The city would be completely empty then.

IRINA: And we'll leave too!

CHEBUTYKIN: (*Drops the clock, which shatters.*) Smithereens!

A pause; everyone is annoyed and embarrassed.

KULYGIN: (*Picking up the pieces.*) To break such an expensive thing, ah, Ivan Romanych, Ivan Romanych! F minus for your conduct!

IRINA: That was Mama's clock.

CHEBUTYKIN: Maybe . . . Mama's, so it was Mama's. Maybe I didn't break it, but only think that I did. Maybe we only think that we exist, but in fact we don't. I don't know anything, no one knows anything. (*At the door.*) Can't you see? Natasha is having an affair with Protopopov, but you don't see. Here you sit, seeing nothing at all, while Natasha is having an affair with Protopopov . . . (*Sings.*) "Wouldn't you really like to eat this fig?"[44] (*Exits.*)

---

43. The country of Poland is to the west and the city of Chita in Siberia is to the east, so rumor has them going in two entirely different directions.
44. A refrain from a popular operetta of the day.

VERSHININ: Yes . . . (*Laughs.*) How strange this all is! (*Pause.*) When the fire started I ran home quickly. I got there, saw that our house was in one piece, not in danger, out of harm's way, but my little girls were standing on the doorstep wearing only their underwear. Their mother wasn't to be found. There was a commotion! Horses and dogs were running around, and on the faces of my little girls I saw pleading looks of alarm, terror, I don't know what else. It wrung my heart to see their faces. My God, I thought, what else will these little girls have to endure in their long lives! I grabbed them and ran, thinking all the time about that one thing: what they would have to endure on this earth! (*A fire alarm; pause.*) I came here and their mother was here, yelling, angry. (*Masha enters with her pillow and sits down on the sofa.*) And when my little girls were standing on the doorstep, wearing only their underwear, and the street was red from the flames, with that frightening noise all around, I thought that it must have been something like that, years ago, when an enemy unexpectedly attacked, plundering, setting fires . . . And yet, what a difference there is really between what is and what was! Some more time will pass, some two hundred, three hundred years, and our lives today will be looked upon with fright, and with contempt. Everything today will seem narrow-minded, hard, very uncomfortable, and strange. Oh, what a life that will surely be, what a life! (*Laughs.*) Excuse me, I'm beginning to philosophize again. Please allow me to continue, ladies and gentlemen. I feel so much like philosophizing. The mood has come over me. (*Pause.*) Everyone seems to be asleep. So, as I was saying, what a life that will be! You can only imagine . . . Here, in this city, there are only three people like yourselves, but in generations that follow there will be more, all the time more and more, and a time will come, when everyone will become like you, everyone will live as you do. And later, your ways too will be outgrown. People will be born who are better than you . . . (*Laughs.*) Today I'm in a special mood. I desperately want to live . . . (*Sings.*) "To love at all ages we yield, its trials are bless-ed . . ."[45] (*Laughs.*)

MASHA: Tram-ta-tam.

---

45. From the old general's aria in Pyotr Ilyich Tchaikovsky's 1879 opera, *Eugene Onegin,* based upon Pushkin's novel in verse.

VERSHININ: Ta-tam.

MASHA: Tra-ta-ta?

VERSHININ: Tra-ta-ta. (*Laughs.*)

Fedotik enters.

FEDOTIK: (*Dances.*) It's burned, it's burned! All burned to the ground!

Laughter.

IRINA: Where's the joke? Everything's burned?

FEDOTIK: (*Laughs.*) Down to the ground. Nothing's left. Even my guitar burned, and my photographs burned, and all my letters . . . And I wanted to give you a little notebook, but it burned too.

Solyony enters.

IRINA: No, please, leave, Vasily Vasilyevich. You can't come in here.

SOLYONY: Why can the Baron come in and I can't?

VERSHININ: We must go actually. How is the fire?

SOLYONY: They say it's dying out. No, I think it's positively strange that the Baron can come in and I can't! (*Takes a bottle of eau de cologne out of his pocket and sprinkles himself.*)

VERSHININ: Tram-ta-tam?

MASHA: Tra-tam.

VERSHININ: (*Laughs; to Solyony.*) Let's go into the hall.

SOLYONY: All right, sir, but I'll make a note of this. "This thought could be a lot more clear. But t'would provoke the geese I fear . . ."[46] (*Looking at Tuzenbach.*) Cheep, cheep, cheep . . . (*Exits with Vershinin and Fedotik.*)

IRINA: How that Solyony smells up a room . . . (*Confused.*) The Baron's asleep! Baron! Baron!

---

46. Lines from Ivan Andreyevich Krylov's fable *The Geese* (1811).

TUZENBACH: (*Waking up.*) I'm tired, but . . . A brick factory . . . I'm not talking in my sleep. Soon I'm actually going to the brick factory. I'll start working . . . I've already talked to them about it. (*To Irina, tenderly.*) You are so pale, beautiful, enchanting . . . I think your pallor brightens the dark air like a shaft of light . . . You're sad, you're dissatisfied with life . . . Oh come with me. Let's go work together! . . .

MASHA: Nikolay Lvovich, leave here.

TUZENBACH: (*Laughing.*) Are you here? I didn't see you. (*Kisses Irina's hands.*) Goodbye, I'm going . . . I look at you now, and can remember once long ago, on your name-day, when you were so bold and happy, talking about the joy of work. And how I dreamed then of a happy life! Where is it? (*Kisses her hands.*) There are tears in your eyes. Go to sleep. It's already light . . . Morning's begun. If only I could give my life for you!

MASHA: Nikolay Lvovich, leave! Well, really . . .

TUZENBACH: I'm leaving . . . (*Exits.*)

MASHA: (*Lying down.*) Are you asleep, Fyodor?

KULYGIN: Huh?

MASHA: You should go home.

KULYGIN: My darling, Masha, my dear one, Masha.

IRINA: She's exhausted. Let her rest, Fedya.

KULYGIN: I'm going now . . . My wife is a good, a fine woman . . . I love you, my only one . . .

MASHA: (*Angrily.*) Amo, amas, amat, amamus, amatis, amant.[47]

KULYGIN: (*Laughs.*) No, really, she's always surprising me. I married you seven years ago, and it's like we were married just yesterday. On my word of honor. No, really, you're a surprising woman. I'm content, I'm content, I'm content!

MASHA: I'm bored, bored, bored . . . (*Talks while she sits up.*) I can't get it out of my mind . . . It's simply revolting. It's like a nail stuck in my head. I can't keep quiet about it. I'm talking about Andrey . . . He took a loan on this house from the bank and his wife took all the money, and the house doesn't only

---

47. "I love; you love; he, she, it loves; we love; you love; they love" (Latin).

belong to him, does it? But to all four of us! He must know that, if he's a respectable man.

KULYGIN: Why bother about it, Masha? What is it to you? Andryusha owes money all over the place and so, God be with him.

MASHA: It's still revolting. (*Lies down.*)

KULYGIN: We're not poor. I work. I teach at the school and give private lessons too . . . I'm a respectable man. A simple man. *Omnia mea mecum porto,*[48] as they say.

MASHA: I don't need anything, but what revolts me is the injustice of it. (*Pause.*) Go home, Fyodor!

KULYGIN: (*Kisses her.*) You're tired. Rest for half an hour, and I'll sit outside, and wait for you. Sleep . . . (*Goes.*) I'm content, I'm content, I'm content. (*Exits.*)

IRINA: It's true, our Andrey has gotten petty, he's come to nothing, and gotten older, since he's been around that woman! Once he was studying to be a professor, but yesterday he was bragging that he finally got a chance to be a member of the District Board. He's a member of the Board, but Protopopov is the chairman . . . The whole city's talking, laughing, and he's the only one who doesn't know, who doesn't see . . . And now everyone's running over to the fire, but he's sitting in his room, paying no attention. All he does is play the violin. (*Nervously.*) Oh it's terrible, terrible, terrible! (*Cries.*) I can't, I can't bear it any more! . . . I can't, I can't! . . .

Olga enters, straightens up around her dressing table.

IRINA: (*Sobs loudly.*) Throw me out, throw me out, I can't bear it anymore! . . .

OLGA: (*Getting worried.*) What's the matter, what's the matter? Darling!

IRINA: (*Sobbing.*) Where? Where has it all gone? Where is it? Oh my God, my God! I've forgotten everything, forgotten . . . It's all mixed up in my head . . . I can't remember the Italian for window or ceiling . . . I'm forgetting everything, everyday I forget, and life is running out and it will never come back,

---

48. "I carry all that's mine with me" (Latin, from Cicero).

never, we'll never go to Moscow . . . I can see that we won't go . . .

OLGA: Darling, darling . . .

IRINA: (*Controlling herself.*) Oh, I'm so unhappy . . . I can't work, I can't stand work. Enough of that, enough! I was a telegraph clerk, now I work in the city council, and I hate and despise everything that they give me to do . . . I'm nearly twenty-four, I've been working for a long time, and my brain has dried up, I've gotten thinner, gotten plainer, gotten older, and nothing, nothing, no satisfaction, but time passes and it seems that I get further away from a genuine, a beautiful life, and head into a horrible pit. I'm in despair and I don't understand why I'm alive, why I haven't killed myself.

OLGA: Don't cry, my little one, don't cry . . . I can't bear to see you cry.

IRINA: I'm not crying, not crying . . . Enough . . . Well, see I'm not crying now. Enough . . . Enough!

OLGA: Darling, I'm talking to you as your sister, as a friend, if you want my advice, marry the Baron! (*Irina cries quietly.*) After all, you respect him, don't you? You value him highly . . . True, he's not attractive, but he's such a respectable person, pure . . . People don't really marry because of love, but out of duty. I, at least, think so, and I would marry without love. Whoever courted me, it wouldn't matter who, I'd marry him, as long as he was a respectable man. Even if he was an old man.

IRINA: I was always waiting until we moved to Moscow, to meet my one true love there . . . I dreamed of him, loved him . . . But it's turned out to be all nonsense, nonsense . . .

OLGA: (*Embraces her sister.*) My dear, beautiful sister, I understand everything. When Baron Nikolay Lvovich retired from military service and came to see us in civilian clothes, he seemed so unattractive to me, that I even started to cry . . . He asked, "Why are you crying?" How could I tell him! But if God meant you to marry him, I would be happy. Then surely it would be different. Completely different.

Natasha crosses the stage with a candle from the right door to the left without saying a word.

MASHA: (*Sits up.*) She walks around as if she set the fire.

OLGA: Masha, you are stupid. The most stupid one in our family is you. Pardon me, please.

Pause.

MASHA: I feel like confessing, dear sisters. There's a longing in my soul. I'll confess to you and then to no one else, ever . . . I'll tell you this minute. (*Quietly.*) This is my secret, but you must know . . . I can't keep silent . . . (*Pause.*) I love, love . . . love that man . . . You just saw him . . . Well, that's it. In a word, I love Vershinin . . .

OLGA: (*Goes to her place behind the screen.*) Stop this. Anyway, I'm not listening.

MASHA: What can I do! (*Takes her head in her hands.*) He seemed strange to me at first, then I felt sorry for him . . . Then I fell in love . . . Fell in love with his voice, his words, his unhappiness, his two little girls . . .

OLGA: (*Behind the screen.*) I'm still not listening. Whatever stupid things you're saying, I'm still not listening.

MASHA: Oh you're the stupid one, Olya. I love him, I mean, that's my fate. I mean, that's my lot . . . And he loves me. It's all so frightening. Isn't it? It's not good, is it? (*Reaches a hand out and draws Irina toward herself.*) Oh my dear . . . Somehow we'll get through our lives, whatever happens to us . . . When you read some novel, then it all seems so old hat, and all so easy to understand, but when you fall in love yourself, then you see that no one knows anything, and everyone must decide for herself. My darlings, my sisters . . . I admitted it to you. Now I will be silent . . . I will be like Gogol's madman[49] . . . silence . . . silence . . .

Andrey enters followed by Ferapont.

ANDREY: (*Angrily.*) What do you want? I don't understand.

---

49. The narrator in Gogol's story "Diary of a Madman" (1835) inadvertently reveals the depths of his insanity by telling his own story of unrequited love; the diary ends with his confinement to a mental institution.

FERAPONT: (*At the door, impatiently.*) I've already told you, Andrey Sergeyevich, ten times.

ANDREY: In the first place, I am not Andrey Sergeyevich to you, but "your excellency!"

FERAPONT: The Fire Patrol, your honor, asks permission to cross through your garden to get to the river. Otherwise they have to go around and to go around is a real bother.

ANDREY: All right. Tell them it's all right.

Ferapont exits.

ANDREY: I'm sick and tired of them! Where's Olga?

Olga comes out from behind the screen.

ANDREY: I've come to ask you to give me your key to the cupboard. I've lost my own. You have it, the little one. (*Olga gives him the key without saying a word; Irina goes behind her own screen. Pause.*) What a huge fire! Now it's calming down. The devil knows what made me act so badly with Ferapont. I said such stupid things to him . . . Your excellency . . . (*Pause.*) Why are you so quiet, Olya? (*Pause.*) It's time to stop these stupidities and not be angry with each other, and live peaceably. You are here, Masha's here, Irina's here, and so it's wonderful. We can discuss it all openly, once and for all. What do you have against me? What?

OLGA: Stop it, Andryusha. Let's discuss it tomorrow. (*Upset.*) What a tormenting night!

ANDREY: (*Very confused.*) Don't get upset. I'm just asking you quite calmly. What do you have against me? Tell me frankly.

The voice of Vershinin: "Tram-ta-tam."

MASHA: (*Stands, loudly.*) Tra-ta-ta! (*To Olga.*) Goodbye, Olya. God be with you. (*Goes behind the screen and kisses Irina.*) Sleep soundly . . . Goodbye, Andrey. Leave them, they're exhausted . . . Discuss it tomorrow . . . (*Exits.*)

OLGA: Honestly, let's put it off until tomorrow, Andryusha . . . (*Goes to her place behind the screen.*) It's time to go to sleep.

ANDREY: I'll just have my say and then I'll go. So then . . . In the first place, you have something against Natasha, my wife, and I've noticed it since the first day of our marriage. Natasha is a fine, honorable person, frank and noble. That's my opinion. I love and respect my wife, do you understand? I respect her and demand that you and the others respect her too. I repeat, she is an honorable, noble person, and all your grievances, excuse me for saying so, are just capricious. (*Pause.*) In the second place, you seem angry because I didn't become a professor, and don't do research. But I serve the district, I'm a member of the District Board, and I consider my work just as sacred and as great as research. I'm a member of the local District Board and proud of it, if you want to know . . . (*Pause.*) In the third place . . . I still have more to say . . . I took a loan on the house, and didn't ask your permission . . . For that, I'm at fault, and I beg you to forgive me . . . I was forced to do it because of my debts . . . Three thousand five hundred . . . I'm not gambling now, gave it up long ago, but the main thing I can say to justify myself, is that you girls, you receive Father's pension, but I don't have that . . . income, so to speak.

Pause.

KULYGIN: (*At the door.*) Is Masha here? That's strange. (*Exits.*)

ANDREY: They're not listening. Natasha is an excellent, honorable person. (*Walks about the stage, not saying anything, then stops.*) When I got married, I thought that we would be happy . . . All of us, happy . . . But my God . . . (*Cries.*) My darling sisters, dear sisters, don't trust me, don't trust . . . (*Exits.*)

KULYGIN: (*At the door, worried.*) Where's Masha? Isn't Masha here? That's surprising. (*Exits.*)

A knocking; the stage is empty.

IRINA: (*Behind the screen.*) Olya! Who's knocking on the floor?

OLGA: It's the doctor, Ivan Romanych. He's drunk.

IRINA: What a restless night! (*Pause.*) Olya! (*Looks out from behind the screen.*) Did you hear? The brigade is being taken away from us, transferred somewhere far away.

OLGA: It's only a rumor.

IRINA: We'll be left all alone . . . Olya!

OLGA: Yes?

IRINA: Darling, dear, I respect, I value the Baron, he's a wonderful person. I'll marry him, I accept, only let's go to Moscow! I beg you, let's go! Nothing on earth could be better than going to Moscow. Let's go, Olya! Let's go!

Curtain.

Act IV

The old garden in front of the Prozorov house. A long avenue of firs, at the end of which, a river can be seen. On the other side of the river is a forest. To the right, the porch of the house; here there is a table with bottles and glasses; it is obvious that they have been drinking champagne. It is twelve o'clock in the afternoon. From time to time passersby cross from the street to the river. Five soldiers cross quickly. Chebutykin in an amiable mood which he does not lose during the course of the act, sits in an easy chair in the garden, waiting until he is called; he wears a military cap and carries a walking stick. Irina, Kulygin with a decoration around his neck and without a mustache, and Tuzenbach are standing on the porch, seeing off Fedotik and Rodé, who are descending the steps; both officers are in field uniform.

TUZENBACH: (*He and Fedotik kiss each other on the cheeks.*) You're a good man. We've gotten on very well together. (*Rodé and he kiss.*) One more time . . . Goodbye, my friend!

IRINA: Until we meet again!

FEDOTIK: Not "until we meet again," but "goodbye." We'll never meet again!

KULYGIN: Who knows! (*Wipes his eyes, smiles.*) You see, I've started to cry.

IRINA: We'll meet again someday.

FEDOTIK: In ten years, fifteen years? But then we'll hardly recognize each other. We'll greet each other coldly . . . (*Takes a photograph.*) Stand still . . . Once more, for the last time.

RODÉ: (*Embraces Tuzenbach.*) We won't meet again . . . (*Kisses Irina's hand.*) Thank you for everything, for everything!

FEDOTIK: (*Irritated.*) Hold still a minute!

TUZENBACH: God willing, we'll meet again. Write to us, be sure to write.

RODÉ: (*Glances around the garden.*) Goodbye, trees! (*Shouts.*) Yoo-hoo! (*Pause.*) Goodbye, echo!

KULYGIN: All the best. Get married there in Poland . . . A Polish wife will kiss you and say *Kokhánje*![50] (*Laughs.*)

FEDOTIK: (*Looking at his watch.*) Less than an hour left. In our battery, only Solyony will go on the barge. We'll go with the rank and file. Three divisions will leave today, and three more tomorrow and then peace and quiet will reign in the city.

TUZENBACH: And terrible boredom.

RODÉ: Where is Maria Sergeyevna?

KULYGIN: Masha's in the garden,

FEDOTIK: I'd like to say goodbye to her.

RODÉ: Goodbye, we must leave or I'll start to cry . . . (*Embraces Tuzenbach and Kulygin and quickly kisses Irina's hand.*) We've gotten along splendidly together . . .

FEDOTIK: (*To Kulygin.*) This is for you as a remembrance . . . A notebook with a little pencil . . . We'll go from here to the river . . .

They walk away, glancing back over their shoulders.

RODÉ: (*Shouts.*) Yoo-hoo!

KULYGIN: (*Shouts.*) Goodbye.

Upstage, Fedotik and Rodé meet Masha and say goodbye to her; she exits with them.

IRINA: They've left . . . (*Sits down on a low porch step.*)

CHEBUTYKIN: They forgot to say goodbye to me.

IRINA: Well, what about you?

CHEBUTYKIN: And I somehow forgot them too. Besides, I'll see them again soon. I leave tomorrow. Yes . . . One more day left.

---

50. "Beloved" (Polish).

After a year, I'll retire and then I'll come back again, and I'll live out the rest of my days here with you . . . Only one more short year remains until I get my pension . . . (*Puts his newspaper into his pocket and takes out another one.*) I'll come back here to you and change my life from the roots up . . . I'll become quiet, well . . . well behaved, proper . . .

IRINA: You should change your life, dear. You really should.

CHEBUTYKIN: Yes. I think so. (*Sings softly.*) "Tar-rar-ra boom-dee-ay . . . Sit on the curb dee-ay . . ."[51]

KULYGIN: Incorrigible, Ivan Romanych! Incorrigible.

CHEBUTYKIN: Yes, I should have gone to you for lessons. Then I would have straightened out.

IRINA: Fyodor shaved his mustache off. I can't bear to look at him!

KULYGIN: Why not?

CHEBUTYKIN: I could tell you what your physiognomy looks like, but I won't.

KULYGIN: What of it! It's the accepted thing, the *modus vivendi*.[52] Our headmaster shaved off his mustache, so I did too. When I became a supervisor I shaved. No one likes it, but I don't care. I'm content. With or without a mustache I'm just as content. (*Sits down.*)

> Upstage in the garden, Andrey pushes a
> baby carriage with a sleeping child.

IRINA: Ivan Romanych, dear, my own, I'm terribly worried. You were on the boulevard yesterday, tell me what happened there.

CHEBUTYKIN: What happened? Nothing. Rubbish. (*Reads a newspaper.*) It's all the same.

KULYGIN: They say that Solyony and the Baron met yesterday on the boulevard near the theater . . .

TUZENBACH: Stop it! Now really . . . (*Waves his hand and exits into the house.*)

---

51. A well-known tune from the British music hall.
52. "The way of life" (Latin).

KULYGIN: Near the theater . . . Solyony started to tease the Baron and the Baron couldn't bear it and said something offensive . . .

CHEBUTYKIN: I don't know. It's all nonsense.

KULYGIN: In a certain seminary, a teacher wrote on a composition "nonsense" and the student, thinking it was Latin, read "consensus" . . . (*Laughs.*) Amazingly funny. They say that Solyony's in love with Irina and hates the Baron . . . That's understandable. Irina is a very pretty girl. She even looks like Masha, the same pensiveness. Only you, Irina, have a gentler character. Although Masha too has a very good character. I love her, my Masha.

Offstage in the garden: "Ayy! Yoo-hoo!"

IRINA: (*Trembles.*) Everything frightens me today. (*Pause.*) I have everything all packed. After dinner I'll send my things off. The Baron and I will be married tomorrow, and tomorrow we'll leave for the brick factory. And the day after tomorrow, I'll be at the school. I'll start a new life. God will help me! When I passed the teachers' examination, I cried for joy, for gratitude . . . (*Pause.*) The cart will soon be here for my things.

KULYGIN: That's all fine, but it doesn't sound very serious somehow. Only ideas, and very little seriousness. But anyway, I wish you all the best, from the bottom of my heart.

CHEBUTYKIN: (*Moved.*) My sweet child, my pretty one . . . My treasure . . . You've gone so far beyond us, I can't catch up with you. I'm left behind just like a migratory bird who's gotten old and can't fly anymore. Fly, my dear ones, fly and may God be with you. (*Pause.*) Fyodor Ilyich, you shaved off your mustache for nothing.

KULYGIN: That will do! (*Sighs.*) So, today the soldiers are leaving and everything will go back to the old ways. No matter what anyone says, Masha is a good, honorable woman, I love her very much and thank her for my fate . . . Different people have different fates . . . There's a man who works in the excise office here named Kozýrov.[53] We went to school together and he was thrown out in the last year of high school because he

---

53. From the Russian for "trump card."

couldn't understand *ut consecutivum*[54] for anything. Now he lives in terrible poverty, is sick and when I meet him I say, "Hello, *ut consecutivum!*" "Yes," he says, "that's exactly it, *consecutivum*," and then he coughs . . . And here I am, lucky all my life. I'm happy, now I've received the Order of Stanislav, Second Class,[55] and now I myself teach others this same *ut consecutivum*. Of course, I'm an intelligent person, more intelligent than many others, but that doesn't make for happiness . . .

In the house, someone is playing "The Maiden's Prayer"[56] *on the piano.*

IRINA: Tomorrow evening I will no longer hear "The Maiden's Prayer," and I won't have to see Protopopov. (*Pause.*) Protopopov is sitting in the parlor right now. He came today too.

KULYGIN: Has the principal arrived yet?

IRINA: No. We sent for her. If only you knew how hard it is for me to live here alone, without Olya . . . She lives at the high school. She's the principal and all day long she's busy, and I'm alone, I'm bored, with nothing to do. The room I live in is hateful . . . So I decided. If I'm not fated to be in Moscow, then so be it. That means it's not my fate. Nothing to do about it . . . It's all God's will, that's the truth. Nikolay Lvovich proposed to me. Why not? I thought about it and decided. He's a good person, even surprisingly good . . . And suddenly, I felt that my heart had grown wings. I feel cheerful, and at ease, and I started wanting to work again, to work . . . But yesterday, something happened, some kind of mystery is hanging over me . . .

CHEBUTYKIN: Consensus. Nonsense.

NATASHA: (*At the window.*) The principal's here!

KULYGIN: The principal has arrived. Let's go.

He goes into the house with Irina.

54. A Latin conjunction used to introduce subjunctive clauses.
55. An award given in pre-Revolutionary Russia. Chekhov received one (third class) for his civic work.
56. A sentimental Polish composition, often played by students of the piano.

CHEBUTYKIN: (*Reads his newspaper and sings quietly.*) "Tar-rar-ra boom dee-ay . . . Sit on the curb dee-ay . . ."

Masha approaches; upstage Andrey pushes the baby carriage.

MASHA: There he sits; just sitting . . .

CHEBUTYKIN: What's that?

MASHA: (*Sits down.*) Nothing . . . (*Pause.*) You loved my mother?

CHEBUTYKIN: Very much.

MASHA: And did she love you?

CHEBUTYKIN: (*After a pause.*) That I don't remember.

MASHA: Is "my man" here? That's the way our cook Márfa talks about her policeman, "my man." Is "my man" here?

CHEBUTYKIN: Not yet.

MASHA: When you take your happiness in bits and pieces, and then lose it, like me, little by little you get coarse, and spiteful. (*Gestures to her chest.*) I'm seething in here . . . (*Looking at her brother Andrey, who is pushing the baby carriage.*) There's Andrey, our brother . . . All our hopes lost. It took a thousand people to raise the bell, much money and labor were spent on it, and suddenly it fell and shattered. Suddenly, without rhyme or reason. Just like Andrey . . .

ANDREY: When will it finally calm down in the house? Such noise.

CHEBUTYKIN: Soon. (*Looks at his watch.*) I have an old-fashioned watch that strikes the hour . . . (*Takes out his watch and it strikes the hour.*) The first, second, and fifth batteries leave exactly at one o'clock . . . (*Pause.*) And I go tomorrow.

ANDREY: Forever?

CHEBUTYKIN: I don't know. Maybe I'll return after a year. But the devil knows . . . It's all the same . . .

The music of a harp and violin are heard, somewhere far away.

ANDREY: The city is emptying out. It's getting quiet as if it were being covered by a hood. (*Pause.*) Something happened yesterday near the theater. Everyone's talking about it but I don't know what it was.

CHEBUTYKIN: Nothing. A stupid thing. Solyony began to tease the Baron, the Baron lost his temper and insulted him, and it turned out that Solyony was obliged to challenge him to a duel. (*Looks at his watch.*) I think it's almost time . . . At half past twelve, in the public grove, the one you can see from here, on the other side of the river . . . Bang-bang. (*Laughs.*) Solyony imagines that he's Lermontov, and even writes verse. A joke's a joke, but this is his third duel.

MASHA: Whose?

CHEBUTYKIN: Solyony's.

MASHA: And what about the Baron?

CHEBUTYKIN: What about the Baron?

Pause.

MASHA: My mind's confused . . . Still, I tell you, it shouldn't be allowed. He might wound the Baron or even kill him.

CHEBUTYKIN: The Baron is a good person, but one baron more or less . . . It's all the same, isn't it? So let them! It's all the same! (*Beyond the garden, a yell: "Ayy! Yoo-hoo!"*) Let's wait and see what happens. That's Skvortsóv[57] yelling, one of the seconds. He's in the boat.

Pause.

ANDREY: In my opinion, to participate in a duel or to be present at one, even in the capacity of doctor, is simply immoral.

CHEBUTYKIN: It only seems that way . . . We are not here, nothing is here on this earth, we don't exist but only think we exist . . . And so it's all the same, isn't it!

MASHA: All day long, you talk, talk . . . (*Walks about.*) We live in a climate in which you never know when it's going to snow, and then there are these conversations too. (*Stops.*) I won't go into the house, I can't set foot in there . . . When Vershinin comes, tell me . . . (*Walks along the avenue of trees.*) Already the birds are migrating. (*Looks up.*) Swans or geese . . . My dears, my happy ones . . . (*Exits.*)

---

57. From the Russian word for "starling."

ANDREY: Our house is emptying out. The officers are leaving, you're leaving, my sister's getting married, and I'll be left in the house alone.

CHEBUTYKIN: And your wife?

Ferapont enters with papers.

ANDREY: A wife is a wife. She's honorable, decent, and good, but for all of that there is still something in her that lowers her to the level of a petty, blind, thick-skinned animal. In any case, she's not a person. I'm talking to you as a friend, as the only person to whom I can open my heart. I love Natasha, that's true, but sometimes she seems so surprisingly vulgar to me that I feel lost and don't understand why I love her, or at least, loved . . .

CHEBUTYKIN: (*Stands.*) Brother, I'm leaving tomorrow. Maybe we'll never see each other again, so I'll give you some advice. Put on your hat, take your walking stick in your hand, and leave . . . Leave, and go, go away without a single look back. And the farther you go, the better.

Solyony crosses upstage with two officers; seeing Chebutykin he turns toward him; the officers continue on further.

SOLYONY: Doctor, it's time! It's already half past twelve. (*Greets Andrey.*)

CHEBUTYKIN: Right away. I'm sick and tired of all of you. (*To Andrey.*) If they ask for me, Andryusha, say that I'll be right back . . . (*Sighs.*) Oh-ho-ho!

SOLYONY: "He no sooner cried 'Alack,' than the bear was on his back . . ." (*Goes with him.*) Why are you grunting, old man?

CHEBUTYKIN: Humph!

SOLYONY: How's your health?

CHEBUTYKIN: (*Angrily.*) Feel like a newborn.

SOLYONY: The old man's upset over nothing. I'll allow myself very little amusement. I'll only wing him like a woodcock. (*Takes his eau de cologne out of his pocket and sprinkles his hands.*)

I've used a whole bottle today, and my hands still stink. They stink like a corpse. (*Pause.*) Yes sir . . . Do you remember Lermontov's verse? "And he, the rebellious one, seeks the storm. As if in the storm he could find peace . . ."[58]

CHEBUTYKIN: Yes. "He no sooner cried 'Alack,' than the bear was on his back." (*Follows Solyony out.*)

Shouts are heard: "Yoo-hoo! Ayy!" Andrey and Ferapont enter.

FERAPONT: Sign the papers.

ANDREY: (*Nervously.*) Get away from me! Get away! I beg you! (*Exits with the baby carriage.*)

FERAPONT: But what are papers for if not to be signed. (*Goes upstage.*)

Tuzenbach, wearing a straw hat, and Irina enter. Kulygin crosses the stage, shouting: "Oh Masha! Yoo-hoo!"

TUZENBACH: I think he's the only person in the city who's glad that the military is leaving.

IRINA: That's easy to understand. (*Pause.*) Our city is emptying out now.

TUZENBACH: (*Glancing at his watch.*) Darling, I'll be right back.

IRINA: Where are you going?

TUZENBACH: I have to go into the city for . . . to say goodbye to my friends.

IRINA: That's not true . . . Nikolay, why are you so distracted today? (*Pause.*) What happened yesterday near the theater?

TUZENBACH: (*With an impatient movement.*) In an hour I'll return and be with you again. (*Kisses her hands.*) My beloved . . . (*Looks into her eyes.*) Five years have passed since I've been in love with you, and I still can't get used to the idea that you seem to get more and more beautiful all the time. What charming, wondrous hair! What eyes! I'll take you away tomorrow, we'll work, we'll be rich, my dreams will come true. You will be happy. The only thing is, the only thing, you don't love me!

---

58. From Lermontov's lyric poem "The Sail" (1832).

IRINA: I can't help it. I'll be your wife, and I'll be faithful and obedient, but there's no love, what can I do! (*Cries.*) I've never been in love in my life. Oh, I dreamed so much about love, dreamed about it for a long time, days and nights, but my heart is like an expensive piano, which is locked up and the key is lost. (*Pause.*) You look worried.

TUZENBACH: I didn't sleep all night. There's nothing in my life so awful that it frightens me, only that lost key wrings my heart, doesn't let me sleep . . . Tell me something. (*Pause.*) Tell me something . . .

IRINA: What? What should I say? What?

TUZENBACH: Anything.

IRINA: Enough! Enough!

Pause.

TUZENBACH: Sometimes, for no reason at all, trifles, stupid little things suddenly take on new meaning. You used to laugh at them, you thought they were trifles, and you didn't have the time to stop and look at them. Oh let's not talk about this! I'm cheerful. It's as if I am seeing these maples, firs, and birches for the first time, and they're all looking at me with curiosity and they're waiting. What beautiful trees and actually, that's just how beautiful life should be near them! (*A shout: "Ayy! Yoo-hoo!"*) I have to go, it's time now . . . Look there, that tree has dried up, but it's still waving in the breeze with the others. So I think that if I die, I too will still participate in life in some way or other. Goodbye my darling . . . (*Kisses her hand.*) Your papers, the ones you gave me, are on my table, under the calendar.

IRINA: I'll go with you.

TUZENBACH: (*Alarmed.*) No, no . . . (*Walks away quickly, and stops along the avenue of trees.*) Irina!

IRINA: What?

TUZENBACH: (*Not knowing what to say.*) I didn't have any coffee today. Ask them to make me some . . . (*Exits quickly.*)

Irina stands lost in thought, then goes upstage and sits on the swing. Andrey enters with the baby carriage; Ferapont appears.

FERAPONT: Andrey Sergeyevich, these papers here aren't mine, you know, but government ones. I didn't think them up.

ANDREY: Oh, where is it, where did my past go, when I was young, cheerful, intelligent, when I dreamed and thought so elegantly, when the present and the future were lit up by hope? Why is it that, just as we begin to live, we become so boring, gray, uninteresting, lazy, indifferent, useless, unhappy . . . Our city has existed for about two hundred years, in it there are a hundred thousand inhabitants, and there is not one person, who is not exactly like the others, not one rebel, in the past or in the present, not one scholar, not one artist, not one person who is even a little bit noteworthy, who could inspire envy, or a passionate desire to emulate him. They only eat, drink, sleep, then die . . . They give birth to others who also drink, eat, sleep. And to stave off the boredom, they vary their lives a little with their disgusting gossip, vodka, cards, cheating, and the wives cheat on their husbands, and the husbands lie, pretending that they don't see anything, don't hear anything, and their overwhelmingly vulgar influence oppresses their children so much that God's spark of life is extinguished in them, and they become the same pitiful identical corpses as their mothers and fathers . . . (*To Ferapont, angrily.*) What do you want?

FERAPONT: What? Sign the papers.

ANDREY: I'm sick and tired of you.

FERAPONT: (*Giving him the papers.*) Just now, the porter from the government treasury was saying . . . He was saying that this winter in St. Petersburg, it was two hundred degrees below zero.

ANDREY: The present is repellent, but then, when I think of the future, how good that is! It's becoming so easy, such broad vistas are appearing in the distance, there's a light. I can see freedom, I can see that I and my children will be free from idleness, from kvas,[59] from roast goose stuffed with cabbage, from sleep after dinner, from petty sponging off others.

FERAPONT: It seems that two thousand people froze to death. The people, they say, are scared. Was that in St. Petersburg or in Moscow . . . I don't remember.

---

59. A dark, nonalcoholic beer made from black bread.

ANDREY: (*Seized with a tender feeling.*) My dear ones, my sisters, my wondrous sisters! (*Tearfully.*) Masha, my sister.

NATASHA: (*At the window.*) Who's talking so loudly out there? Is it you, Andryusha? You'll wake Sofochka up. *Il ne faut pas faire du bruit. La Sophie es dormée déja. Vous êtes un ours.*[60] (*Getting angry.*) If you want to talk, then give the carriage and the child to someone else. Ferapont, take the carriage from the Master!

FERAPONT: Yes madam. (*Takes the carriage.*)

ANDREY: (*Embarrassed.*) I'm talking softly.

NATASHA: (*Behind the window, rocking her little boy.*) Bobik! You're a rascal, Bobik! Bad Bobik!

ANDREY: (*Looking at the papers.*) All right, I'll look them over, and sign what needs signing, and then you can take them back to the Board . . .

He goes into the house, reading the papers; Ferapont pushes the carriage to the back of the garden.

NATASHA: (*Behind the window.*) Bobik, what do you call your mama? Darling, darling! And who's this? This is Aunt Olya. Say "Hello, Auntie Olya!"

Itinerant musicians, a man and a woman, enter playing a violin and a harp; Vershinin, Olga, and Anfisa come out of the house and they listen silently for a moment. Irina joins them.

OLGA: Our garden is like a public square. Everyone walks or rides through it. Nanny, give the musicians something!

ANFISA: (*Gives to the musicians.*) May God be with you, dear hearts. (*The musicians bow and leave.*) A bitter life! They don't play because their stomachs are full. (*To Irina.*) Hello, Arisha! (*Kisses her.*) Well, my child, let me tell you how I'm living now! How I'm living! At the high school, my treasure, Olyushka and I have a government apartment. The Lord has provided for my old age. Since I was born, sinner that I am, I never lived like this . . . A big apartment, the government's,

---

60. "One mustn't make noise. Sophie is already asleep. You are a bear" (ungrammatical French).

and I have a whole room to myself, and a little bed. And it's all the government's. I fall asleep at night, and, oh Lord, oh Mother of God, there's never been a happier person!

VERSHININ: (*Glancing at his watch.*) I have to go right away, Olga Sergeyevna. It's time. (*Pause.*) I wish you all the best, all the best . . . Where is Maria Sergeyevna?

IRINA: She's somewhere in the garden . . . I'll go look for her.

VERSHININ: Please do. I'm in a hurry.

ANFISA: I'll go and look too. (*Shouts.*) Oh Mashenka, yoo-hoo! (*Exits with Irina upstage.*) Yoo-hoo, yoo-hoo!

VERSHININ: Everything comes to an end. So we too must part. (*Looks at his watch.*) The city gave us something like a luncheon. We drank champagne, the mayor gave a speech. I ate and listened, but my heart was here with you . . . (*Looks around the garden.*) I've gotten used to you.

OLGA: Won't we ever see each other again?

VERSHININ: Most probably not. (*Pause.*) My wife and both little girls will stay here another month or two. Please if anything happens or if they need anything . . .

OLGA: Yes, yes, of course. Don't worry. (*Pause.*) Tomorrow there will no longer be a single military man in the city, only the memory will remain and, of course, for us a new life will begin . . . (*Pause.*) Nothing works out as we wish. I didn't want to be principal, but still I became one. That means we won't be in Moscow . . .

VERSHININ: Well . . . Thank you for everything . . . Excuse me, if I'm not so . . . I've talked so much, so very much, and for that forgive me, think kindly of me.

OLGA: (*Wiping her eyes.*) Why isn't Masha coming . . .

VERSHININ: What else can I say to you in parting? What can I philosophize about? . . . (*Laughs.*) Life is hard. Many of us imagine it to be blind and hopeless, but still, you must admit, life is becoming clearer and easier, and it's obvious that the time is not very far away when the light of understanding will shine. (*Looks at his watch.*) It's time for me, it's time! Formerly humanity was busy with wars, the whole of existence was full of campaigns, invasions, conquests, but now we have outgrown all that, leaving behind a huge void which must be filled with something. Humanity passionately searches for that something, and, of course, it will be found one day. Ah, but the sooner we find it the better! (*Pause.*) You know, if only we could add education to a love of work, and a love of work to education! (*Looks at his watch.*) But it's time for me . . .

OLGA: Here she comes.

Masha enters.

VERSHININ: I came to say goodbye . . .

Olga walks off to the side in order not to interfere with the goodbyes.

MASHA: (*Looking into his eyes.*) Goodbye . . .

A prolonged kiss.

OLGA: All right, all right . . .

Masha breaks into sobs.

VERSHININ: Write to me . . . Don't forget! Let me go . . . It's time . . . Olga Sergeyevna, take her, I'm already . . . It's time . . . I'm late . . . (*Moved, he kisses Olga's hand, then once more embraces Masha and exits quickly.*)

OLGA: All right, Masha! Stop, darling . . .

Kulygin enters.

KULYGIN: (*Embarrassed.*) Never mind, let her cry a bit, let her . . . My pretty Masha, my good Masha . . . You are my wife and I'm happy, whatever's happened . . . I'm not sorry, I don't blame you . . . Olga's my witness . . . We'll start life over again, as before, and I won't say a word, not a hint . . .

MASHA: (*Restraining her sobs.*) "On a curved seashore, a green oak, a golden chain upon that oak . . . a golden chain upon that oak . . ." I'm losing my mind . . . "On a curved seashore . . . a green oak . . ."

OLGA: Calm yourself, Masha . . . Calm yourself . . . Give her some water.

MASHA: I'm not crying now . . .

KULYGIN: She's not crying . . . She's a good, kind woman . . .

A faint, faraway shot is heard.

MASHA: "On a curved seashore, a green oak, a golden chain upon that oak . . . A green cat . . . A green oak . . ." I'm confusing it . . . (*Drinks the water.*) My life is a failure . . . I don't need anything now . . . I'm calm now . . . It's all the same . . . What does that mean, on a curved seashore? Why do these words go through my head? My thoughts are confused.

Irina enters.

OLGA: Calm yourself, Masha. Now that's a good girl . . . Let's go inside.

MASHA: (*Angrily.*) I won't go in there. (*Sobs, but suddenly stops herself.*) I won't set foot in the house, I won't go . . .

IRINA: Let's sit together for a while, even if we don't talk. I'm going away tomorrow after all . . .

Pause.

KULYGIN: Yesterday in the third-year class I took this false mustache and beard away from one of the little rascals . . . (*Puts on the mustache and beard.*) Just like the German teacher, no? . . . (*Laughs.*) Isn't it the truth? These boys are so funny.

MASHA: You really do look like the German teacher.

OLGA: (*Laughs.*) Yes.

Masha cries.

IRINA: All right, Masha!

KULYGIN: Very much like him . . .

Natasha enters.

NATASHA: (*To the maid.*) Well, Protopopov, I mean Mikhail Ivanovich, is sitting with Sofochka, so let Andrey Sergeyevich wheel Bobik around for a while. So many worries with children . . . (*To Irina.*) Irina, you're leaving tomorrow. What a pity! Stay with us for just one more little week. (*Seeing Kulygin, she screams; he laughs, and takes off the mustache and beard.*) Well, you really scared me! (*To Irina.*) I've gotten used to you, and parting with you, you know, is not easy for me! I'll tell Andrey to move into your room with his violin. Let him scratch away in there! And I'll put Sofochka in his room. A divine, wondrous child! What a little bitty girl! Today she looked at me with such big eyes and said "Mama!"

KULYGIN: A beautiful child, that's true.

NATASHA: That means that tomorrow I'll be alone here. (*Sighs.*) First of all I'll tell them to chop down that avenue of firs, then that maple there . . . It's so unattractive in the evening. (*To Irina.*) My dear, that belt doesn't suit you at all . . . It's tasteless . . . You should wear something brighter. And I'll tell them to plant flowers everywhere here, flowers, what a smell there'll be here . . . (*Sternly.*) Why was this fork left on this bench? (*Going toward the house, to the maid.*) Why was this fork left on that bench? I asked you. (*Shouts.*) Shut up!

KULYGIN: She's off again!

Offstage the music of a march can be heard; everyone listens.

OLGA: They're leaving.

Chebutykin enters.

MASHA: Our dear ones are leaving. Well, what of it . . . I wish them a good journey! (*To her husband.*) We must go home . . . Where are my hat and cape?

KULYGIN: I took them into the house . . . I'll get them right away. (*Exits into the house.*)

OLGA: Yes, now we can all go home. It's time.

CHEBUTYKIN: Olga Sergeyevna!

OLGA: What? (*Pause.*) What?

CHEBUTYKIN: Nothing . . . I don't know how to tell you. (*Whispers in her ear.*)

OLGA: (*In a fright.*) It can't be!

CHEBUTYKIN: Yes . . . The same old story . . . I'm exhausted, tormented, I don't want to talk anymore . . . (*Annoyed.*) Besides, it's all the same!

MASHA: What happened?

OLGA: (*Embraces Irina.*) This is a terrible day . . . I don't know how to tell you, my dear one . . .

IRINA: What? Tell me quickly, what? God help me! (*Cries.*)

CHEBUTYKIN: The Baron has just been killed in a duel . . .

IRINA: (*Crying softly.*) I knew, I knew . . .

CHEBUTYKIN: (*Upstage, sitting on a bench.*) I'm exhausted . . . (*Takes a newspaper out of his pocket.*) Let them cry . . . (*Softly sings.*) "Tar-rar-ra boom-dee-ay . . . Sit on a curb dee-ay . . ." It's all the same, isn't it?

The three sisters stand, hugging each other.

MASHA: Oh, how the music plays! They're leaving us, one of them has left forever, forever and ever. We're left alone to start our lives over again. We must go on living . . . Must go on living . . .

IRINA: (*Lays her head on Olga's chest.*) A time will come, when everyone will know what it's all for, what all this suffering is for, and there won't be any mysteries, but until then we must go on living . . . We must work, only work! Tomorrow, I'll leave alone. I'll teach in the school and I'll give my whole life to whomever may need it. It's autumn now, soon the winter will come, snow will cover everything, and I'll work, I'll work . . .

OLGA: (*Embraces both sisters.*) The music plays so cheerfully, so boldly, you feel like living! Oh my God! Time will pass and we'll go away forever, they'll forget us, forget our faces, our voices, and how many of us there were, but our suffering will turn into joy for those who live after us. Happiness and peace will come to the earth, and then they will remember us with a kind word and a blessing. Oh dear sisters, our lives are not yet ended. We will go on living! The music is playing so cheerfully, so joyfully, and it seems that after just a little more time we'll know why we are living, why we are suffering . . . If only we knew, if only we knew!

The music plays more and more softly; Kulygin, happy and smiling, carries the hat and cape; Andrey pushes the baby carriage, in which Bobik is sitting.

CHEBUTYKIN: (*Sings softly.*) "Tar-rar-ra boom-dee-ay . . . Sit on the curb dee-ay . . ." (*Reads the newspaper.*) It's all the same! All the same!

OLGA: If only we knew, if only we knew.

Curtain.

The Cherry Orchard

A Comedy in Four Acts

[When Chekhov wrote *The Cherry Orchard* in 1903, he was very ill; and yet, he considered his last play to be "not a drama at all, but a comedy; in places it's even a farce."[1] The Moscow Art Theatre premiered the play on what would be the author's last name-day, January 17, 1904. The production was directed by Konstantin Stanislavsky, who also played Gayev with wit. Olga Knipper played Lyubov Ranevskaya. The dramatic force of the production led the ill and consequently ill-tempered Chekhov to complain that Stanislavsky "ruined my play."[2] The English language premiere was in London in 1911; U.S. audiences saw the play first in Russian during the 1923 and 1924 Moscow Art Theatre tours and then in English in 1928. The translation that follows was created at the request of the Russian émigré director Lev Vainstein for a 1980 production at New York University's Tisch School of the Arts.[3] —SMC]

The Characters

Ranyévskaya, Lyubóv Andréyevna, a landowner. [Her first name means "love" in Russian. Her nickname is Lyúba. She is also called "Mámochka," a sweet form of "Mother," like "Mommy."]

Ánya, her daughter, seventeen years old. [Her nickname is Ánichka.]

Várya, Ranyevskaya's adopted daughter, twenty-four years old. [Varya is her nickname; her formal name is Varvára Mikháilovna.]

Gáyev, Léonid Andréyevich, Ranyevskaya's brother. [His nickname is Lyónya.]

Lopákhin, Yermoláy Alekséyevich, a merchant.

Trofímov, Pyótr Sergéyevich, a student. [His nickname is Pétya.]

Simeónov-Píshchik, Borís Borísovich, a landowner. [A *píshchik* is a sqeaking sound and a small whistle used to make the squeaking voice of a traditional Russian puppet.]

---

1. Chekhov to M. P. Lilina, September 15, 1903, in *Pis'ma* [Letters], vol. 11 (Moscow: Nauka, 1982), 248.

2. Chekhov to O. L. Knipper, March 29, 1904, in *Pis'ma* [Letters], vol. 12 (Moscow: Nauka, 1983), 74.

3. "[Carnicke's] *Cherry Orchard* is direct, easily accessible to young American students and mercifully free of all that blather that mucks up so much of the other versions that I know." James Parker, Professor of Theater, Virginia Commonwealth University, letter to the translator, May 8, 1986.

Charlótta Ivánovna, the governess. [Like Russian circus performers generally, her name is somewhat strange; she has a Germanic first name and a Russian patronymic.]
Yepikhódov, Semyón Panteléyevich, a clerk.
Dunyásha, the maid. [Her formal name is Avdótya Fyódorovna Kozoyédova; her last name means "the goat-eater."]
Firs, a footman, an old man of eighty-seven. [He has an old-fashioned first name; his formal name is Firs Nikoláyevich.]
Yásha, a young footman.
A passerby.
The station master.
A postal clerk.
Guests, servants.

The action takes place on the estate of L. A. Ranyevskaya.

Act I

A room which is still called the nursery. One door leads to Anya's room. Dawn, the sun will soon rise. It is May; the cherries are already in bloom, but in the garden it is cold; there is a morning frost. The windows in the room are closed. Dunyasha enters with a candle, and Lopakhin is holding a book.

LOPAKHIN: The train's arrived, thank God. What time is it?

DUNYASHA: Almost two. (*Puts out the candle.*) It's already light.

LOPAKHIN: How late was the train? Two hours at least. (*Yawns and stretches.*) I'm a fine one, the devil I am! I come here especially to meet them at the station and then oversleep . . . Dozed off in the chair. Damn! . . . You could have woken me up.

DUNYASHA: I thought you left. (*Listens.*) Listen, I think they're coming.

LOPAKHIN: (*Listens.*) No . . . They have to pick up the baggage and all that . . . (*Pause.*) Lyubov Andreyevna lived abroad for five years; I don't know what she's like now . . . She's a good person. An easy-going simple person. I remember when I was kid about fifteen, my late father—at that time he was a merchant, had a little store here in the country—he socked me in the face and I got a bloody nose . . . We came here to the yard for some reason and he was drunk too. I remember it like it was yesterday. Lyubov Andreyevna—she was still so young, so thin—she took me to the washstand, here in this very room, in the nursery. "Don't cry, little peasant," she said, "you'll heal before you marry . . ."[4] (*Pause.*) Little peasant . . . It's true, my father was a peasant, but now I have a white waistcoat, and yellow shoes. Still you can't make a silk purse out of a sow's ear . . . I've made myself rich, got a lot of money but if you think about it, sort it all out, a peasant's a peasant . . . (*Pages through the book.*) You see, I've just read this book and didn't understand a thing. I read and fell asleep.

Pause.

DUNYASHA: The dogs didn't sleep all night; they sense their masters are coming.

LOPAKHIN: What's wrong with you, Dunyasha, you're so . . .

DUNYASHA: My hands are trembling. I'll faint.

LOPAKHIN: You're so very delicate, Dunyasha. And you dress like a lady, even your hairdo. You musn't do that. You ought to remember your place.

Yepikhodov enters with a bouquet; he is dressed in a jacket and in brightly polished boots that squeak loudly; as he enters, he drops the bouquet.

YEPIKHODOV: (*Picks up the bouquet.*) Here, the gardener sent these. He says to put them in the dining room. (*Hands Dunyasha the bouquet.*)

LOPAKHIN: And bring me some kvas.[5]

DUNYASHA: Yes, sir. (*Exits.*)

YEPIKHODOV: There's a morning frost now, three degrees below freezing, but still the cherries are all in bloom. I cannot approve of our climate. (*Sighs.*) I cannot. Our climate cannot promote itself suitably. Look, Yermolay Alekseyevich, allow me to add that I bought myself these boots three days ago,

---

4. A common expression of consolation.
5. A dark, nonalcoholic beer made from black bread.

and I dare to assure you, they squeak so much, it's impossible. What should I grease them with?

LOPAKHIN: Stop it. You bore me.

YEPIKHODOV: Everyday something bad happens to me. But I don't complain, I'm used to it, I even smile.

Dunyasha enters, hands Lopakhin a glass of kvas.

YEPIKHODOV: I'll go. (*Stumbles over a chair which falls.*) There . . . (*As if in triumph.*) There, you see, excuse the expression, but this kind of circumstance by the way . . . It's simply amazing! (*Exits.*)

DUNYASHA: I will tell you, Yermolay Alekseyevich, that Yepikhodov proposed to me!

LOPAKHIN: Ah!

DUNYASHA: I don't know how to . . . He's a quiet person, but sometimes, when he starts to talk, you don't understand anything. It's nice, and full of feeling, only incomprehensible. I sort of like him. He loves me madly. He's such an unlucky person, everyday there's something. We tease him about it too, call him "Twenty-Two Troubles" . . .

LOPAKHIN: (*Listens.*) Listen, I think they're coming . . .

DUNYASHA: They're coming! What's wrong with me . . . I'm so cold all over.

LOPAKHIN: They're actually coming. Let's go meet them. Will she recognize me? We haven't seen each other in five years.

DUNYASHA: (*Excited.*) I'll faint . . . Oh, I'll faint!

> Two carriages are heard pulling up to the house. Lopakhin and Dunyasha quickly exit. The stage is empty. Noise begins in the neighboring rooms. Firs, leaning on a cane, hastily crosses the stage to meet Lyubov Andreyevna; he wears old-fashioned livery and a top hat; he mumbles something to himself, but it's impossible to make out a single word. The noise offstage gets louder and louder. A voice: "Let's go through here . . ." Lyubov Andreyevna, Anya, and Charlotta Ivanovna with a little dog on a chain, all of them dressed for traveling, enter; Varya enters wearing a coat and kerchief; Gayev, Simeonov-Pishchik, Lopakhin, Dunyasha carrying a bundle and an umbrella, and a servant with some bags all walk through the room.

ANYA: Let's go through here. Mama, remember what room this is?

LYUBOV ANDREYEVNA: (*Joyfully, through tears.*) The nursery!

VARYA: How cold it is! My hands feel numb. (*To Lyubov Andreyevna.*) Your rooms, the white room and the violet one, are just as you left them, Mamochka.

LYUBOV ANDREYEVNA: The nursery, my lovely beautiful room . . . I slept here when I was a baby . . . (*Cries.*) And now, I'm still like a baby . . . (*Kisses her brother, Varya, and then her brother again.*) Varya, you're just like you were before, you look like a nun. And I even recognize Dunyasha . . . (*Kisses Dunyasha.*)

GAYEV: The train was two hours late? How's that? How's that for management?

CHARLOTTA: (*To Pishchik.*) My dog eats nuts.

PISHCHIK: (*Surprised.*) Imagine that!

All exit except Anya and Dunyasha.

DUNYASHA: We waited up for you . . . (*Takes off Anya's coat and hat.*)

ANYA: I didn't sleep for four nights on the road . . . Now I'm frozen.

DUNYASHA: You left during Lent[6] and there was still snow on the ground, there was a frost, but now? My darling! (*Laughs and kisses Anya.*) I waited up for you, my joy, the light of my life . . . I'll tell you right now, I can't hold it back a minute longer . . .

ANYA: (*Languidly.*) Always something . . .

DUNYASHA: Just after Holy Week,[7] the clerk Yepikhodov proposed to me.

ANYA: You always talk about the same thing . . . (*Fixing her hair.*) I've lost all my hairpins . . . (*Very tired; even staggers.*)

DUNYASHA: Well I don't know what to think. He loves me, loves me so!

---

6. The forty-day period of fasting that precedes the resurrection of Christ on Easter Sunday, according to Christian tradition.

7. The seven-day period just before Easter, which includes Good Friday, when Christ was crucified.

ANYA: (*Glancing through the door to her room, gently.*) My room, my windows, as if I had never left. I'm home! Tomorrow morning I'll get up and run out into the orchard . . . Oh if only I could sleep! I didn't sleep the whole way, my worrying tired me out.

DUNYASHA: Three days ago Pyotr Sergeyevich got here.

ANYA: (*Joyously.*) Petya!

DUNYASHA: He's sleeping in the bathhouse, staying there too. "I'm afraid," he says, "to embarrass them." (*Looking at her pocket watch.*) I should wake him up, but Varvara Mikhailovna told me not to. "Don't wake him up," she said.

Varya enters, at her waist a ring of keys.

VARYA: Dunyasha, make some coffee, quick . . . Mamochka is asking for coffee.

DUNYASHA: Right away. (*Exits.*)

VARYA: Well thank God you're back. You're home again. (*Caressing her.*) Darling, you're back. My pretty one's back!

ANYA: I've been through so much.

VARYA: I can imagine!

ANYA: I got there during Holy Week. It was so cold then. Charlotta talked the whole way and kept doing her magic tricks. Why did you tie me down with Charlotta? . . .

VARYA: You couldn't go alone, dear. At seventeen!

ANYA: We got to Paris, it was cold, there was snow. I speak awful French. Mama was living on the fifth floor, and when I went to see her, she had some French ladies visiting her, and an old priest with a little book. It was smoky and uncomfortable. And suddenly I felt sorry for Mama, so sorry. I hugged her head, pressed her hands, and couldn't let go. Then she kept hugging me and crying . . .

VARYA: (*Through tears.*) Don't tell me, don't tell me . . .

ANYA: She'd already sold the summer house near Mentone.[8] She had nothing left, nothing. And I didn't have a kopeck left either. We almost didn't get back. But Mama didn't understand! We

---

8. A town on the Mediterranean coast of France.

sat down to eat at the station, and she ordered the most expensive thing, and tipped each waiter a ruble. Charlotta did the same. And Yasha ordered a full portion for himself, too. It was just awful. You know Yasha is Mama's footman now. We brought him back with us too . . .

VARYA: I saw the scoundrel.

ANYA: Well, how are things going? Did you pay the interest?

VARYA: With what.

ANYA: My God, my God . . .

VARYA: In August the estate will be sold . . .

ANYA: My God . . .

LOPAKHIN: (*Looks in at the door and moos.*) Moo-oo . . . (*Exits.*)

VARYA: (*Through tears.*) If only I could give it to him . . . (*Threatens with a fist.*)

ANYA: (*Embraces Varya, softly.*) Varya, did he propose to you? (*Varya shakes her head no.*) But I'm sure he loves you . . . Why don't you talk it over with each other? What are you waiting for?

VARYA: I just think nothing will come of it. He's always busy; he has no time for me . . . He pays no attention. So to hell with him! It's hard for me seeing him . . . Everybody talks about our wedding, everybody congratulates me, but actually there's nothing there; it's all like a dream . . . (*In another tone of voice.*) You have a brooch like a bee.

ANYA: (*Sadly.*) Mama bought it. (*Goes toward her room, talking gaily like a child.*) And I flew over Paris in a big balloon.

VARYA: My dear one's back, you're back! My pretty one's back!

Dunyasha has entered with the coffee pot and makes coffee.

VARYA: (*Standing near the door.*) I fuss with the housework, dear, all day long, but still I dream. If only we could marry you to a rich man, then I'd feel calm. I would go to the local hermitage,[9] then to Kiev . . . To Moscow. And I would walk from holy place to holy place . . . Just walk and walk. How splendid!

---

9. A secluded retreat for a holy person, similar to a monastery or convent.

ANYA: The birds are singing in the orchard. What time is it now?

VARYA: It must be close to three. You should go to sleep, darling. (*Leads Anya into her room and exits.*) How splendid!

Yasha enters with a lap robe and a traveling case.

YASHA: (*Crosses the stage, daintily.*) Can one walk through here, mademoiselle?

DUNYASHA: I didn't recognize you, Yasha. How you've changed while you were abroad!

YASHA: Hmmm . . . And who are you?

DUNYASHA: When you left, I was still . . . (*Measures her height from the floor.*) Dunyasha, Fyódor Kozoyédov's daughter. You don't remember!

YASHA: Hmmm . . . a juicy little cucumber! (*Glances around and then embraces her; she cries out and drops a saucer. Yasha quickly exits.*)

VARYA: (*At the door, annoyed.*) What's happening here?

DUNYASHA: (*Through tears.*) I broke a saucer . . .

VARYA: That's a good sign.

ANYA: (*Coming out of her room.*) We should warn Mama that Petya's here . . .

VARYA: I told them not to wake him up.

ANYA: (*Meditatively.*) Six years ago Father died, a month later, our brother Grísha drowned in the river, a cute little seven-year-old boy. Mama couldn't bear it, and left, left without looking back . . . (*Sighs.*) How I understand her, if only she knew! (*Pause.*) And Petya Trofimov was Grisha's teacher, he might remind her . . .

Enter Firs; he wears a jacket and a white waistcoat.

FIRS: (*Goes to the coffee-maker, fussily.*) The mistress will have a bite to eat in here . . . (*Puts on white gloves.*) Is the coffee ready? (*Sternly to Dunyasha.*) You! Where's the cream?

DUNYASHA: Oh, my God . . . (*Exits quickly.*)

FIRS: (*Fusses over the coffee-maker.*) Ugh, you nincompoop . . . (*Mumbles to himself.*) She's come back from Paris. The master went to Paris once . . . by horse . . . (*Laughs.*)

VARYA: What's that, Firs?

FIRS: What is it you wish? (*Joyfully.*) My lady has come back! I waited up! Now I can die . . . (*Cries with joy.*)

Enter Lyubov Andreyevna, Gayev, and Simeonov-Pishchik. Pishchik wears a long pleated Russian coat, made from soft material, and loose Turkish trousers. Gayev motions with his hands and his body as if he were playing billiards.

LYUBOV ANDREYEVNA: How does it go? Let me remember . . . Yellow ball off the side! A rebound to the center!

GAYEV: Cut to the center![10] Once, you and I, sister, slept in this very room and now I'm fifty-one years old, strange as it may seem . . .

LOPAKHIN: Yes, time flies.

GAYEV: How's that?

LOPAKHIN: Time, I say, flies.

GAYEV: It smells of Patchouli[11] here.

ANYA: I'm going to sleep. Good night, Mama. (*Kisses her mother.*)

LYUBOV ANDREYEVNA: My beloved child. (*Kisses Anya's hands.*) Are you glad to be home? I can't seem to collect myself.

ANYA: Goodnight, Uncle.

GAYEV: (*Kisses Anya's face and hands.*) God be with you. How much you look like your mother! (*To his sister.*) Lyuba, at her age, you looked exactly like this.

---

10. Addicted to the game of billiards, Gayev uses its jargon throughout the play. He plays a version called carom billiards with three balls; wooden cue sticks manipulate the balls on a cloth-covered table with raised and cushioned sides. More familiar in the United States is the version called pocket billiards (or pool). Significantly, billiards uses indirection and angles to hit balls around the table, a kind of action that mirrors the oblique and often passive-aggressive interaction among Chekhov's characters.

11. A powerfully aromatic oil made from an East Indian plant.

Anya gives her hand to Lopakhin and to Pishchik; exits, closing the door behind her.

LYUBOV ANDREYEVNA: She's very tired.

PISHCHIK: The road, of course, was long.

VARYA: *(To Lopakhin and Pishchik.)* Well, gentlemen? It's nearly three, time to pay your respects.

LYUBOV ANDREYEVNA: *(Laughs.)* You're still the same, Varya. *(Draws Varya toward herself, and kisses her.)* I'll drink my coffee, then we'll all go. *(Firs puts a pillow under her feet.)* Thank you. You're like family. I've gotten used to coffee. I drink it day and night. Thank you, my sweet old man. *(Kisses Firs.)*

VARYA: I'll look to see if they brought in all the things . . . *(Exits.)*

LYUBOV ANDREYEVNA: Is it really me sitting here? *(Laughs.)* I feel like jumping, waving my arms. *(Covers her face with her hands.)* But what if I'm only asleep! God can see I love my homeland, love it tenderly, I couldn't look out of the train, cried the whole way. *(Through tears.)* However, I must drink my coffee. Thank you, Firs, thank you, my sweet old man. I'm so glad that you're still alive.

FIRS: Day before yesterday.

GAYEV: He's hard of hearing.

LOPAKHIN: I have to go now, at five o'clock in the morning I have to leave for Khárkov.[12] Damn it! I wanted to look at you, talk to you . . . You're still such a splendid woman . . .

PISHCHIK: *(Breathing heavily.)* Even more beautiful . . . Dressed in the Parisian fashion . . . Can't help falling for you, come what may . . .

LOPAKHIN: Your brother here, Leonid Andreyevich, says that I am a boor and a peasant, but it's all the same to me. Let him say what he wants. I only want you to trust me as you did before, to look at me with your surprising, touching eyes as before. God have mercy! My father was your father's and

---

12. An important cultural and mercantile center in the northeastern part of the Ukraine, with a university that dates from 1805; railroad transportation made it a hub for trade.

grandfather's serf, but you, particularly you, have done so much for me that I can forget all that. I love you like my own family . . . More than my family.

LYUBOV ANDREYEVNA: I can't sit still, I'm in no condition . . . (*Jumps up and walks about in high agitation.*) I won't survive this joy . . . Laugh at me, I'm stupid . . . My own dear cupboard . . . (*Kisses the cupboard.*) My little table . . .

GAYEV: While you were away, the nurse died.

LYUBOV ANDREYEVNA: (*Sits down and drinks coffee.*) Yes, God rest her soul. They wrote me.

GAYEV: And Anastásia died. Petrúshka,[13] the cross-eyed one, left me and went to live in town with the police officer. (*Takes a box of fruit-drops out of his pocket, sucks on one.*)

PISHCHIK: My daughter Dáshenka . . . sends you her regards . . .

LOPAKHIN: I want to tell you something pleasant, happy. (*Looks at his watch.*) I'm going now. I don't have time to chat . . . Well, so, I'll just say two or three words. You already know that the cherry orchard is to be sold to pay your debts. The auction is set for August 22nd. But don't worry, my dear one, sleep easy, there is a way out . . . Here is my plan. Pay attention now! Your estate is located only thirteen miles from town, and the railroad runs close by, so if the cherry orchard and the land near the river were cleared for small plots and leased for summer houses, then you would have at the least twenty-five thousand rubles a year income.

GAYEV: Excuse me, but that's nonsense!

LYUBOV ANDREYEVNA: I don't quite understand you, Yermolay Alekseyevich.

LOPAKHIN: You could get at the least twenty-five rubles a year for every two-and-a-half-acre plot, and if you advertise now, I guarantee you that by autumn you won't have one free scrap of land, everything will be snapped up. In short, congratulations, you are saved. The site is wonderful, the river is deep. But you'll have to tidy it up, of course, clear the land . . . For example, you'll have to take down the old structures, like this

---

13. The nickname for Pyotr and a popular Russian puppet that uses the *pishchik* whistle as its voice.

house, which isn't really needed now, and cut down the old cherry orchard . . .

LYUBOV ANDREYEVNA: Cut it down? Darling, forgive me, but you don't understand at all. If there's anything in the county you can point to as interesting, even remarkable, it can only be our cherry orchard.

LOPAKHIN: The only remarkable thing about this orchard is that it is very big. You get cherries only once every two years and then you can't get rid of them, nobody buys them.

GAYEV: But this orchard is so remarkable, it's even mentioned in the encyclopedia.

LOPAKHIN: (*Looking at his watch.*) If we don't think of anything or come to any conclusion, then on August 22nd, both the cherry orchard and the whole estate will be sold at auction. Make up your minds! There's no other way out, I swear to you. None, none.

FIRS: In the old days, about forty or fifty years ago, they dried the cherries, soaked them, marinated them, boiled them into jam, and they used to . . .

GAYEV: Be quiet, Firs.

FIRS: And they used to send off cartloads of dried cherries to Moscow, and to Kharkov. There was money then! And the dried cherries were so soft, juicy, sweet, fragrant . . . They knew the way to do it . . .

LYUBOV ANDREYEVNA: And where is the "way to do it" now?

FIRS: Forgotten. No one remembers.

PISHCHIK: (*To Lyubov Andreyevna.*) What's it like in Paris? How is it? Did you eat frogs?

LYUBOV ANDREYEVNA: I ate crocodiles.

PISHCHIK: Imagine that . . .

LOPAKHIN: Until now there were only masters and peasants in the country, but now these summer folk have appeared. All the cities, even the smallest ones, are surrounded by summer houses now. And it's safe to say that in twenty-five years the summer folk will multiply surprisingly fast. Now they only drink tea on their porches, but maybe they will take to cultivating their acres, and then your cherry orchard will be happy, rich, luxuriant . . .

GAYEV: (*Annoyed.*) What nonsense!

Enter Varya and Yasha.

VARYA: Here, Mamochka, there are two telegrams for you. (*Chooses a key and with a jingle opens an old-fashioned cupboard.*) Here they are.

LYUBOV ANDREYEVNA: From Paris. (*Tears them up without reading them.*) I'm finished with Paris . . .

GAYEV: Do you know, Lyuba, how old this cupboard is? A week ago I took out the bottom drawer, looked at it, and saw a date burned into it. This cupboard was made exactly one hundred years ago. How's that? Ah? Maybe we should celebrate its centennial. An inanimate object, but still, however you look at it, a cupboard for books.

PISHCHIK: (*Surprised.*) A hundred years . . . Imagine that! . . .

GAYEV: Yes . . . Quite something . . . (*Feeling the cupboard.*) Dear respected cupboard! I salute your existence, which has been directed for over one hundred years toward the glorious ideals of goodness and justice. Your silent appeal to fruitful labor has not weakened during the course of one hundred years, sustaining courage (*Through tears.*) and faith in a better future through generations of our family and engendering in us ideals of goodness and social consciousness.

Pause.

LOPAKHIN: Yes . . .

LYUBOV ANDREYEVNA: You're still the same, Lyonya.

GAYEV: (*A little confused.*) Straight to the right corner! Cut to the center! . . .

LOPAKHIN: (*Looking at his watch.*) Well, it's time for me to go.

YASHA: (*Hands Lyubov Andreyevna her medicine.*) Perhaps you should take your pills now.

PISHCHIK: You shouldn't take medications, darling one . . . Does no good, does no harm . . . Give it here, please . . . Madam. (*Takes the pills, blows on them, places them in his mouth, then washes them down with kvas.*) There!

LYUBOV ANDREYEVNA: (*Frightened.*) You've gone mad!

PISHCHIK: I took all the pills.

LOPAKHIN: What a glutton! (*All laugh.*)

FIRS: His excellency came to see us during Holy Week and ate half a bucket of our cucumbers . . . (*Mumbles.*)

LYUBOV ANDREYEVNA: What is he talking about?

VARYA: He's been mumbling for three years now. We're used to it.

YASHA: Senility.

Charlotta Ivanovna, in a white dress, very thin, straight-laced, with a lorgnette hanging at her waist, crosses the stage.

LOPAKHIN: Forgive me, Charlotta Ivanovna, I haven't had the chance to say hello to you. (*Tries to kiss her hand.*)

CHARLOTTA: (*Pulling her hand away.*) If I allow you to kiss my hand, then you'll want to kiss my elbow, then my shoulder . . .

LOPAKHIN: It's not my day today. (*All laugh.*) Charlotta Ivanovna, show us a trick!

LYUBOV ANDREYEVNA: Charlotta, show us a trick!

CHARLOTTA: Not now. I want to go to sleep. (*Exits.*)

LOPAKHIN: In three weeks we'll see each other again. (*Kisses Lyubov Andreyevna's hand.*) Goodbye for now. It's time to go. (*To Gayev.*) Goodbye. (*Exchanges kisses on the cheeks with Pishchik.*) Goodbye. (*Gives his hand to Varya, then to Firs and to Yasha.*) I don't want to leave. (*To Lyubov Andreyevna.*) If you think about the summer houses and decide to do it, then let me know, and I'll get you a loan of fifty thousand. Think it over seriously.

VARYA: (*Angrily.*) Go, if you're going!

LOPAKHIN: I'm going, I'm going . . . (*Goes.*)

GAYEV: Boor! Well, *pardon* . . . Varya's going to marry him. He's Varya's *beau*.[14]

VARYA: Don't talk, Uncle, about unnecessary things.

---

14. "Pardon me"; "boyfriend" (French).

LYUBOV ANDREYEVNA: What's wrong, Varya? I would be happy for you. He's a good person.

PISHCHIK: A person, to tell the truth . . . most worthy . . . and my Dashenka also says that . . . She says various things. (*Snores, but immediately wakes up.*) But all the same, madam, allow me . . . a loan of two hundred and forty rubles . . . Tomorrow I must pay the interest on my mortgage . . .

VARYA: (*Frightened.*) We've nothing, nothing!

LYUBOV ANDREYEVNA: I really do have nothing.

PISHCHIK: It'll turn up! (*Laughs.*) I never lose hope. You see, just when I thought everything was lost, ruined, then lo and behold, the railroad went through my land and . . . They paid me for it. And then, too, something else might happen, if not today, tomorrow . . . Maybe Dashenka will win two hundred thousand . . . She has a lottery ticket.

LYUBOV ANDREYEVNA: The coffee's drunk, now we can go to bed.

FIRS: (*Brushes off Gayev's clothes and scolds.*) You put on the wrong trousers again. What am I going to do with you?

VARYA: (*Softly.*) Anya's asleep. (*Quietly opens the window.*) The sun's up already, it's not cold. Look, Mamochka, what wonderful trees! My God, the air! The starlings are singing!

GAYEV: (*Opens the other window.*) The orchard is all white. You didn't forget, Lyuba? There's that long avenue of trees that lies so straight, just like a taut belt. It shines on moonlit nights. Do you remember? You didn't forget?

LYUBOV ANDREYEVNA: (*Looks out the window into the orchard.*) Oh my childhood, my purity! I slept in this nursery, looked from here out into the orchard, happiness awoke with me every morning, and the orchard was just the same then, nothing has changed! (*Laughs from joy.*) All, all white! Oh my orchard! After a dark rainy autumn and a cold winter, you're still young, full of happiness. Heavenly angels have not deserted you . . . If I could take this heavy stone off my chest, and off my shoulders, if I could forget my past!

GAYEV: Yes, and the orchard will be sold to pay the debts, strange as it may seem . . .

The Cherry Orchard, Act I

LYUBOV ANDREYEVNA: Look, our late mama is walking in the orchard . . . in a white dress! (*Laughs from joy.*) It's her!

GAYEV: Where?

VARYA: God be with you, Mamochka!

LYUBOV ANDREYEVNA: No one's there, I imagined it. On the right, as the path turns toward the gazebo, there's a little white tree that's bent over, it looks like a woman . . .

Trofimov enters in a shabby student uniform and glasses.

LYUBOV ANDREYEVNA: What an amazing orchard! Masses of white flowers, blue sky . . .

TROFIMOV: Lyubov Andreyevna! (*She looks around at him.*) I only want to pay my respects and then I'll leave. (*Kisses her hand warmly.*) I was told to wait until morning, but I didn't have enough patience.

Lyubov Andreyevna looks at him, confused.

VARYA: (*Through tears.*) This is Petya Trofimov . . .

TROFIMOV: Petya Trofimov, Grisha's former teacher . . . Have I changed so much?

Lyubov Andreyevna embraces him, and quietly cries.

GAYEV: (*Embarrassed.*) Enough, enough, Lyuba.

VARYA: (*Cries.*) I told you, Petya, that it could wait until tomorrow.

LYUBOV ANDREYEVNA: My Grisha . . . my little boy . . . Grisha . . . my son . . .

VARYA: What can we do, Mamochka. It's God's will.

TROFIMOV: (*Softly, through tears.*) Don't, don't . . .

LYUBOV ANDREYEVNA: (*Quietly cries.*) My little boy died, drowned . . . For what? For what, my friend? (*More quietly.*) Anya's asleep in the next room, and I'm talking so loudly . . . Making noise . . . What's the matter, Petya? Why have you lost your looks? Why have you gotten so old?

TROFIMOV: In the train an old woman called me a "shabby lord."

LYUBOV ANDREYEVNA: You were such a young boy then, a good-looking student, and now your hair is thin, glasses. Are you really still a student? (*Goes toward the door.*)

TROFIMOV: I'll probably be an eternal student.[15]

LYUBOV ANDREYEVNA: (*Kisses her brother, then Varya.*) Well, let's go to sleep. You've gotten old too, Leonid.

PISHCHIK: (*Following her.*) That means it's time to sleep now . . . Oh, my gout.[16] I'll stay here for the night . . . Perhaps then, Lyubov Andreyevna, dear heart, tomorrow morning, bright and early . . . Two hundred and forty rubles . . .

GAYEV: Always talking about his own problems.

PISHCHIK: Two hundred and forty rubles . . . have to pay the interest on my mortgage.

LYUBOV ANDREYEVNA: I don't have any money, dear friend.

PISHCHIK: I'll give it back, darling . . . a trivial sum . . .

LYUBOV ANDREYEVNA: Well, all right, Leonid will give it to you . . . Give it to him, Leonid.

GAYEV: I'll give it to him all right!

LYUBOV ANDREYEVNA: What's to be done, give it . . . He needs it . . . He'll give it back.

Lyubov Andreyevna, Trofimov, Pishchik, and Firs exit. Gayev, Varya, and Yasha are left on stage.

GAYEV: My sister is not yet unused to squandering her money. (*To Yasha.*) Go away, lad, you smell like a henhouse.

YASHA: (*With a smirk.*) And you, Leonid Andreyevich, are just like you were.

GAYEV: How's that? (*To Varya.*) What did he say?

VARYA: (*To Yasha.*) Your mother's come from the country. She's been sitting in the servants' quarters since yesterday. She wants to see you . . .

---

15. Students with radical political leanings and liberal social ideas, such as Trofimov, were often suspended or expelled from schools by the tsarist government; they could even be exiled from the country.
16. A disease characterized by swelling of the joints in the legs.

YASHA: To hell with her!

VARYA: Ah, you should be ashamed!

YASHA: She's all I need now! She could have come tomorrow. (*Exits.*)

VARYA: Mamochka is the same as she ever was, hasn't changed a bit. If she had her way, she'd give everything away.

GAYEV: Yes . . . (*Pause.*) If they prescribe a lot of remedies for some sickness or other, it means that the sickness is incurable. I think, I strain my brain, I come up with a lot of remedies, a lot, but that means, in fact, that I don't have one. It would be good to receive an inheritance from someone, good to marry Anya to a very rich man, good to go to Yaroslávl and try our luck with our aunt the Countess.[17] Our aunt is very rich, after all. Very rich.

VARYA: (*Cries.*) If only God would help us.

GAYEV: Don't whine. Our aunt is rich, but she doesn't like us. In the first place, my sister married a lawyer, not a nobleman . . .

Anya appears at the doorway.

GAYEV: Didn't marry a nobleman, and you can't say that she exactly conducts herself virtuously . . . She's a fine, good, wonderful woman, I love her very much, but, however you allow for extenuating circumstances, you still have to admit that she's wanton. You can feel it in her every move.

VARYA: (*In a whisper.*) Anya's standing at the door.

GAYEV: How's that? (*Pause.*) That's odd. Something's gotten into my right eye . . . I'm not seeing well. And Thursday, when I was at the district court . . .

Anya enters.

VARYA: Why aren't you asleep, Anya?

ANYA: I can't fall asleep. I can't.

---

17. A city on the upper Volga River, founded in medieval times; it once served as Russia's capital. The fact that their aunt is a countess underlines the family's connection to Russia's royalty.

GAYEV: My little sweet. (*Kisses Anya's face, her hands.*) My child . . . (*Through tears.*) You're not my niece, you're my angel, you're everything to me. Trust me, trust me . . .

ANYA: I trust you, Uncle. We all love you, respect you . . . but my darling uncle, you should keep quiet, just keep quiet. What did you just say about my Mama, about your own sister? Why did you say that?

GAYEV: Yes, yes . . . (*Covers his face with his hands.*) It really is awful! My God! God, save me! And today I made a speech to the cupboard . . . So stupid! And only when I finished did I understand how stupid!

VARYA: It's true, Uncle, you should keep quiet. Just keep quiet.

ANYA: If you'll keep quiet, then even you will feel calmer.

GAYEV: I'll keep quiet. (*Kisses Anya's hands and Varya's hands.*) I'll keep quiet. But one thing about business. Thursday, I was at the district court, and well, a group gathered, we started to talk about this and that, one thing and another, and it seems that maybe I could arrange a loan on a promissory note in order to pay the interest at the bank.

VARYA: If only God would help!

GAYEV: Tuesday, I'll go and talk about it again. (*To Varya.*) Don't whine. (*To Anya.*) Your mama will talk to Lopakhin. He, of course, won't refuse her . . . And you, when you're rested, you'll go to Yaroslavl to your great aunt, the Countess. So that's what we'll do, from three sides—and it's in the bag! We'll pay the interest, I'm sure of it . . . (*Puts a candy in his mouth.*) On my honor, I'll swear by whatever you like, the estate won't be sold! (*Excitedly.*) I'll swear by my own happiness. Here's my hand. Call me a worthless, dishonorable man if I allow the auction to take place. By my whole being, I swear!

ANYA: (*A calm mood returns to her; she is happy.*) How good you are, Uncle, how smart! (*Hugs her uncle.*) I'm calm now! I'm calm! I'm happy.

Firs enters.

FIRS: (*Reproachfully.*) Leonid Andreyevich, don't you fear God! When will you go to sleep?

GAYEV: Right away, right away. You go along, Firs. It's all right, I'll undress myself. Well, children, lullaby and goodnight . . . The details tomorrow, and now, it's time to go to sleep. (*Kisses Anya and Varya.*) I'm a man of the eighties[18] . . . They don't value that decade much these days, and I can say that I have indeed suffered for my convictions during my life. Not for nothing does the peasant love me. A peasant should know! Should know what kind of . . .

ANYA: You're at it again, Uncle!

VARYA: Keep quiet, Uncle dear.

FIRS: (*Angrily.*) Leonid Andreyevich!

GAYEV: Coming, coming . . . Go to sleep! Off both sides to the center! I'll sink the white ball . . . (*Exits with Firs hobbling after him.*)

ANYA: Now I'm calm. I don't feel like going to Yaroslavl. I don't like my great aunt, but still I'm calm. Thanks to Uncle. (*Sits.*)

VARYA: You must sleep. I'll go. Oh, while you were away, something unpleasant happened here. In the old servants' quarters, you know, where only the old servants live, Yefímushka, Pólya, Yevstignéy,[19] and Karp too. They started letting all kinds of good-for-nothings spend the night—and I kept quiet. But then I heard a rumor that I ordered them to be fed only peas. From stinginess, you understand . . . And it's all Yevstigney's fault . . . All right, I thought. If they think that, just you wait. So I called for Yevstigney. (*Yawns.*) He came . . . "How is it" I say to Yevstigney . . . "that you're such a fool . . ." (*Looking at Anya.*) Anichka! . . . (*Pause.*) She's asleep . . . (*Takes Anya by the arm.*) Let's put you to bed. Let's go . . . (*Leads Anya.*) My darling is asleep! Let's go. (*They go.*)

Far beyond the orchard a shepherd plays on a pipe. Trofimov crosses the stage, and, upon seeing Varya and Anya, stops.

VARYA: Shh . . . She's asleep . . . asleep . . . Let's go, my own.

---

18. During the 1880s under the repressive reign of Alexander III, Russia's social reformers were unable to effect any significant changes; they could only improve living conditions among peasants in small, localized ways.
19. An old-fashioned name.

ANYA: (*Softly, half asleep.*) I'm so tired . . . Everywhere little bells . . . Uncle . . . dear, and Mama and Uncle . . .

VARYA: Let's go, my own, let's go . . . (*They go into Anya's room.*)

TROFIMOV: (*Tenderly.*) My sunlight! My spring!

Curtain.

Act II

A field. An old, lopsided, long-neglected chapel; near it a well. Big stones that apparently once were gravestones, and an old bench. The road to Gayev's manor house can be seen. On one side, poplars loom up darkly; that is where the cherry orchard begins. In the distance, a row of telegraph poles, and far, far away, on the horizon one can barely make out a big city, that can only be seen well in good, clear weather. Soon the sun will set. Charlotta, Yasha, and Dunyasha are sitting on the bench; Yepikhodov stands nearby and plays something sad on a guitar; all sit lost in thought. Charlotta wears an old peaked cap; she takes a gun from her shoulder and fixes the buckle on the strap.

CHARLOTTA: (*Deep in thought.*) I don't have a real passport, I don't know how old I am, but I think I'm quite young. When I was a little girl, my father and Mama went around to the fairs[20] and gave performances, very good ones. And I jumped the *salto mortale*[21] and did various tricks. And when Papa and Mama died, a certain German lady took me in and began to educate me. It was good. I grew up, then became a governess. But where I came from and who I am—I don't know . . . Who my parents were, whether they were even married . . . I don't know . . . (*Takes a cucumber out of her pocket and eats.*) I don't know anything. (*Pause.*) I feel so much like talking to someone . . . I don't have anyone.

YEPIKHODOV: (*Plays the guitar and sings.*) "What care I for the din of the world. What are friends or foes to me . . ."[22] How pleasant it is to play the mandolin!

---

20. Russian annual fairs featured puppet shows, dancing bears, circus acts, and theatrical presentations.
21. "Leap of death" (Italian).
22. A soulful ballad.

DUNYASHA: That's a guitar, not a mandolin. (*Looks in a pocket mirror and powders her nose.*)

YEPIKHODOV: For a man mad with love, this is a mandolin. (*Continuing the song.*) "If only my heart could be set aglow (*Yasha sings along.*) by requited love from thee!"

CHARLOTTA: These people sing so badly . . . Ugh! Like jackals.

DUNYASHA: (*To Yasha.*) But still, what happiness to have gone abroad!

YASHA: Yes, of course. I can't help but agree with you. (*Yawns and lights a cigar.*)

YEPIKHODOV: An understandable point. Abroad, everything long ago reached its full development.

YASHA: That goes without saying!

YEPIKHODOV: I am a well-developed person, I read various marvelous books, but somehow I can't understand the direction in which I personally feel like going, to live or to shoot myself, personally speaking. But just in case, I always carry a revolver on me. Here it is . . . (*Shows the revolver.*)

CHARLOTTA: I'm finished. Now I'm going. (*Puts the gun over her shoulder.*) You, Yepikhodov, are a very intelligent person and very frightening. Women must love you madly. Brrr! (*Goes.*) All these smart ones are still so stupid. There's no one for me to talk to . . . Always alone. Alone, I have no one and . . . And who I am, why I am, remains unknown . . . (*Exits slowly.*)

YEPIKHODOV: Personally speaking, not referring to other objects, I must express myself, by the way, on the subject that fate treats me without compassion, like a storm treats a small ship. If, let's say, I am mistaken, then why should I wake up this morning, let's take this as an example, I wake up, look down, and on my chest there's a frightening, gigantic spider . . . like that. (*Measures it with both hands.*) Or also, I take some kvas to drink, and look, there in the bottom of the glass is something most improper, something like a cockroach. (*Pause.*) Have you read the English historian, Buckle?[23] (*Pause.*) I would like, Avdotya Fyodorovna, to bother you a little with a word or two.

---

23. Henry Thomas Buckle (1821–1862), author of *History of Civilization* (1861), was popular among liberal thinkers in Russia.

DUNYASHA: Speak.

YEPIKHODOV: But I would like to speak with you in private . . . (*Sighs.*)

DUNYASHA: (*Embarrassed.*) All right . . . Only first bring me my wrap. It's near the cupboard . . . It's a little damp out here . . .

YEPIKHODOV: Yes, madam . . . I'll bring it, madam . . . Now I know what to do with my revolver . . . (*Takes the guitar and plays as he exits.*)

YASHA: Twenty-Two Troubles! A stupid person, just between us. (*Yawns.*)

DUNYASHA: God forbid he shoot himself! (*Pause.*) I've become so excitable, everything upsets me. When I was still a little girl, they brought me to live with the masters and now I'm unused to the simple life. Just look how softest-soft my hands are, like a lady's. I've become so tender, so delicate, well-bred, I'm afraid of everything . . . Frighteningly so. And Yasha, if you were to deceive me, I don't know what would happen to my nerves.

YASHA: (*Kisses her.*) My juicy little cucumber! Of course, every girl should rein herself in. What I dislike more than anything else, is a girl who behaves improperly.

DUNYASHA: I've fallen passionately in love with you, you're so educated, you can discuss everything. (*Pause.*)

YASHA: Yes, madam . . . In my opinion, it's like this: if a girl loves someone, then that means she's immoral. (*Pause.*) It's pleasant smoking cigars out in the fresh air . . . (*Listens.*) Someone's coming this way . . . It's the masters . . .

Dunyasha impulsively hugs him.

YASHA: Go home, as if you had gone for a swim in the river, go by that path there, or else they'll meet you and think that I was out here with you. I can't stand this.

DUNYASHA: (*Softly coughs.*) My head's spinning from your cigars. (*Exits.*)

Yasha remains; he sits down near the chapel. Enter Lyubov Andreyevna, Gayev, and Lopakhin.

LOPAKHIN: You must decide once and for all. Time will not wait for you. There's no point in questioning it. Do you agree to rent your land for summer houses or not? Answer in one word. Yes or no? Only one word!

LYUBOV ANDREYEVNA: Who's been smoking those revolting cigars here . . . (*Sits down.*)

GAYEV: Once they built the railroad, it became so convenient. (*Sits down.*) We ride into town and have lunch . . . Green ball to the center! I'd like to go home first, and play a game.

LYUBOV ANDREYEVNA: You'll have time later.

LOPAKHIN: Only one word! (*Pleadingly.*) Give me your answer!

GAYEV: (*Yawning.*) How's that?

LYUBOV ANDREYEVNA: (*Looks in her purse.*) Yesterday there was a lot of money, but today there's so little. My poor Varya feeds everybody milk soup to economize, and in the kitchen they eat only peas, but I waste money senselessly . . . (*Drops her purse and her gold pieces scatter.*) There, they're strewn all over the place . . . (*Annoyed.*)

YASHA: Allow me, I'll get them. (*Collects the change.*[24])

LYUBOV ANDREYEVNA: If you'd be so kind, Yasha. Why did I go out to lunch anyway . . . Your restaurant is wretched, with its music and tablecloths that smell of soap . . . Why do you drink so much, Lyonya? Why do you eat so much? Why do you talk so much? Today in the restaurant you talked a lot again, and none of it was to the point. About the seventies, about the decadents![25] And to whom? You talk to the waiters about the decadents!

LOPAKHIN: Yes.

GAYEV: (*Waves his hands.*) I'm incorrigible, that's obvious . . . (*Annoyed by Yasha.*) What's this, why are you always twirling about in front of me?

YASHA: (*Laughs.*) I can't help laughing when I hear your voice.

---

24. Following the Moscow Art Theatre's staging of this moment, actors playing Yasha often pocket coins as they collect them.
25. During the 1870s, before the reign of Alexander III, reformers known as Populists initiated major social changes in the education of the peasantry. Symbolist writers were derogatorily called decadents.

GAYEV: (*To his sister.*) It's either him or me . . .

LYUBOV ANDREYEVNA: Go away, Yasha, run along . . .

YASHA: (*Gives Lyubov Andreyevna her purse.*) Now I'll go. (*Hardly keeps from laughing.*) This minute . . . (*Exits.*)

LOPAKHIN: The rich Derigánov plans to buy your estate. He's going himself, personally, they say, to the sale.

LYUBOV ANDREYEVNA: And where did you hear that?

LOPAKHIN: They're talking about it in town.

GAYEV: Our aunt from Yaroslavl promised to send something, but when and how much we don't know . . .

LOPAKHIN: How much will she send? One hundred thousand? Two hundred thousand?

LYUBOV ANDREYEVNA: Well . . . Ten thousand . . . or fifteen, and for that we'll be grateful.

LOPAKHIN: Excuse me, I've never met such frivolous people as you, such unbusiness-like, strange people. I'm telling you plainly that your estate will be sold, and you simply don't understand.

LYUBOV ANDREYEVNA: What can we do? Teach us what?

LOPAKHIN: I teach you every day. Every day I tell you one and the same thing . . . Both the cherry orchard and the land by the river must be rented for summer houses. Do that now, immediately, the auction is on top of you! Understand? Once you decide, once and for all, that there should be summer houses, then you'll get all the money you need, and then you'll be saved.

LYUBOV ANDREYEVNA: Summer houses and summer folk—it's so vulgar, forgive me.

GAYEV: I completely agree with you.

LOPAKHIN: I'll either sob, or I'll yell, or I'll faint. I can't stand it! You're torturing me! (*To Gayev.*) You're an old woman!

GAYEV: How's that?

LOPAKHIN: An old woman! (*Starts to go.*)

LYUBOV ANDREYEVNA: (*Startled.*) No, don't go, stay, my dearest, I beg you. Maybe we can think of something.

LOPAKHIN: What's there to think of!

LYUBOV ANDREYEVNA: Don't go, I beg you. It's always more cheerful with you . . . (*Pause.*) I keep expecting something to happen like the house collapsing down around us.

GAYEV: (*Deeply lost in thought.*) A rebound to the corner . . . A spot to the center . . .

LYUBOV ANDREYEVNA: After all, we have sinned so much . . .

LOPAKHIN: What kind of sins could you have . . .

GAYEV: (*Places a fruit-drop in his mouth.*) They say I've eaten up my whole fortune in candy . . . (*Laughs.*)

LYUBOV ANDREYEVNA: Oh, my sins . . . I always squandered my money without holding back, like a madwoman, and I married a man who made no money, only made debts. My husband died of champagne—he drank terribly—and to my misfortune, I fell in love with another man, went off after him, and just then—this was my first punishment, a blow directly to the head—right here in the river . . . My little boy drowned, and I left for abroad, completely left, never to return, never to see this river again . . . I closed my eyes and ran, forgetting myself, and *he* followed me . . . so pitiless, so coarse. I bought a summer house near Mentone, because *he* got sick there, and for three years I knew no rest, day or night. The sick man tortured me, my soul dried up. Then last year, when the summer house was sold to pay the debts, I left for Paris, and there he robbed me, left me, went off with another woman. I tried to poison myself . . . so stupid, so shameless . . . And suddenly, something began to pull me back to Russia, to my homeland, to my little girl . . . (*Wipes away her tears.*) Oh Lord, Lord, have mercy, forgive me my sins! Don't punish me anymore! (*Takes a telegram out of her pocket.*) I received this today from Paris . . . He asks me to forgive him, he begs me to return . . . (*Tears up the telegram.*) I think I hear music from somewhere. (*Listens.*)

GAYEV: That's our famous Jewish orchestra, you remember. Four violins, a flute, and a double-bass.

LYUBOV ANDREYEVNA: It still exists? We should send for them and give a little party.

LOPAKHIN: (*Listens.*) I don't hear it . . . (*Sings softly.*) "For money the Germans will turn the Russians into French."[26] (*Laughs.*) What a play I saw at the theater yesterday, very funny!

LYUBOV ANDREYEVNA: There was probably nothing funny about it. You shouldn't be looking at plays, but look at yourself more often. How dull all your lives are, how much you talk about unnecessary things.

LOPAKHIN: That's true. I frankly admit, our lives are foolish. (*Pause.*) My father was a peasant, an idiot, didn't understand anything, didn't teach me anything, only beat me when he was drunk, and with a stick too. Actually, I'm a windbag and an idiot. I haven't learned anything, my handwriting is atrocious. I'm ashamed to have people see it. I write like a pig.

LYUBOV ANDREYEVNA: You need to get married, my friend.

LOPAKHIN: Yes . . . That's true.

LYUBOV ANDREYEVNA: To our Varya. She's a good girl.

LOPAKHIN: Yes.

LYUBOV ANDREYEVNA: She came to me from simple people, works all day long, and the main thing is that she loves you. Yes, and you've liked her for a long time too.

LOPAKHIN: Well? I'm not against it . . . She's a good girl. (*Pause.*)

GAYEV: They offered me a position in the bank. Six thousand a year . . . Did you hear?

LYUBOV ANDREYEVNA: Oh, you just stay put!

Firs enters; he carries a coat.

FIRS: (*To Gayev.*) Would you please put this on, sir. It's damp out here.

GAYEV: (*Puts on the coat.*) You bore me, old man.

FIRS: Never mind . . . You left this morning without telling me. (*Looks Gayev over.*)

LYUBOV ANDREYEVNA: How old you've gotten, Firs!

FIRS: Excuse me?

---

26. It was said that Russia took its government from the Germans and its culture from the French.

LOPAKHIN: She said, "How very old you've gotten!"

FIRS: I've lived a long time. They wanted to marry me off before your papa was even born . . . (*Laughs.*) When they set us free,[27] I was already a senior valet. But I didn't agree to freedom, stayed with the masters . . . (*Pause.*) I remember everyone was glad for some reason, but why they were glad, they didn't know.

LOPAKHIN: It was so very good in the old days. They flogged you at least.

FIRS: (*Who has not heard.*) I should think so. The peasants and the masters, the masters and the peasants, but now everything's mixed up, you can't understand anything.

GAYEV: Be quiet, Firs. Tomorrow I have to go into the city. I'm supposed to meet a certain general who can give me a promissory note.

LOPAKHIN: Nothing will come of it. And you won't pay the interest, don't worry.

LYUBOV ANDREYEVNA: He's delirious. There are no generals.

Enter Trofimov, Anya, and Varya.

GAYEV: Here come our dear ones.

ANYA: Mama's sitting over here.

LYUBOV ANDREYEVNA: (*Tenderly.*) Come here, come here . . . my own dear family . . . (*Hugs Anya and Varya.*) If only you both knew how I love you. Sit down next to me, right here. (*They sit down.*)

LOPAKHIN: Our eternal student always walks with the ladies.

TROFIMOV: It's none of your business.

LOPAKHIN: He'll soon be fifty years old, and he's still a student.

TROFIMOV: Cut out your stupid jokes.

LOPAKHIN: What's the matter, you freak, are you angry?

---

27. In 1861 Alexander II signed Russia's emancipation act, which abolished landowners' right to own "serfs," also called "souls." However, because no clear arrangements were made to redistribute land, freed serfs often found themselves destitute.

TROFIMOV: Just drop it!

LOPAKHIN: (*Laughs.*) If I may ask, what do you think of me?

TROFIMOV: This is what I think of you, Yermolay Alekseyevich: you are a rich man, soon you will be a millionaire. And, given the balance of nature, you are necessary, like the beast of prey who devours everything that gets in his way, that's how you are necessary. (*All laugh.*)

VARYA: Petya, you would do better to discuss the planets.

LYUBOV ANDREYEVNA: No, let's continue yesterday's conversation.

TROFIMOV: What was it about?

GAYEV: About taking pride in the fact that we are human beings.

TROFIMOV: Yesterday we talked for a long time, but we didn't get anywhere. In human pride, in your idea of it, there is something mystical. And maybe from your vantage point you're right. But when you analyze it simply, without overcomplicating it, what kind of pride can there be, what sense does it make, in light of the fact that human beings are by constitution physiologically weak, that in the vast majority of cases, people are coarse, unintelligent, deeply unhappy? One must stop admiring oneself. One must only work.

GAYEV: You'll still die.

TROFIMOV: Who knows? And what does that mean—you'll die? It may be that people have one hundred senses and that with death only the five known to us are destroyed, but the other ninety-five live on.

LYUBOV ANDREYEVNA: How intelligent you are, Petya! . . .

LOPAKHIN: (*Ironically.*) Extremely intelligent!

TROFIMOV: Humanity moves forward, perfecting its powers. Everything that seems unattainable now, will some day be within our grasp, comprehensible. Only now we must work, and with all our power help those who search for truth. Very few of us in Russia work now. The vast majority of the intelligentsia that I know, don't search for anything, don't do anything and aren't capable of labor. They call themselves the intelligentsia, but they talk to their servants like children, and talk to their peasants as if they were animals, they're poorly educated, don't read anything serious, do absolutely nothing, only talk about science, and understand very little about art. They're all so serious, they all have stern faces, they all talk about what's important, they philosophize, but meanwhile, before their very eyes, the workers eat disgustingly, sleep without pillows, thirty or forty in a single room, everywhere there's bedbugs, stench, dampness, immorality . . . So, apparently, all these good conversations we have, serve only to delude ourselves and others. Show me where the nurseries are that we talk about so much and so often. Where are the libraries? They're found only in novels, but they don't exist in fact. There's only filth, vulgarity, asiaticism[28] . . . I don't like, I'm afraid of these serious physiognomies, I'm afraid of serious conversations. It's better to keep quiet.

LOPAKHIN: Do you know, I get up at five o'clock in the morning, I work from morning to night, and I deal constantly with money, my own and other people's, and so I see what kind of people there are in the world. You only have to start to work at something to understand how few honorable, respectable people there are. One time, when I couldn't sleep, I thought, "Lord, you gave us vast forests, boundless fields, broad horizons, and living here, we really ought to be giants . . ."

LYUBOV ANDREYEVNA: Now you want giants . . . They're only good in fairy tales, otherwise they frighten you.

Yepikhodov crosses upstage and softly, sadly plays the guitar.

LYUBOV ANDREYEVNA: (*Lost in thought.*) There's Yepikhodov . . .

ANYA: (*Lost in thought.*) There's Yepikhodov . . .

GAYEV: The sun has set, ladies and gentlemen.

TROFIMOV: Yes.

GAYEV: (*Not loudly, but as if declaiming.*) Oh, nature, divine nature, you shine with an eternal radiance, beautiful and indifferent, you, whom we call Mother, contain within you both being and death, you give life and you destroy . . .

VARYA: (*Pleadingly.*) Uncle dear!

ANYA: Uncle, you're at it again!

---

28. A commonly used racial pejorative for Russians, whose vast country extends into Central Asia.

TROFIMOV: You'd do better to shoot the green ball to the center with a rebound.

GAYEV: I'll keep quiet, I'll keep quiet.

Everyone sits lost in thought. Silence. Only the quiet mumbling of Firs is heard. Suddenly there is a faraway sound, as if from the sky, the sound of a snapping string, sad.

LYUBOV ANDREYEVNA: What's that?

LOPAKHIN: I don't know. Somewhere far away in the mines a bucket broke loose. But somewhere very far away.

GAYEV: Maybe it's a bird of some kind . . . like a heron.

TROFIMOV: Or an owl.

LYUBOV ANDREYEVNA: (*Shudders.*) It's unsettling somehow!

Pause.

FIRS: Before the calamity it was like that. An owl screeched, and the sámovar[29] hissed without stopping.

GAYEV: Before what calamity?

FIRS: Before they set us free.

Pause.

LYUBOV ANDREYEVNA: Come, let's go, my friends. It's already evening. (*To Anya.*) You have tears in your eyes . . . What's wrong, my little girl? (*Hugs her.*)

ANYA: It's all right, Mama. It's nothing.

TROFIMOV: Someone's coming.

A passerby dressed in a worn white peaked cap and coat appears; he is a little drunk.

PASSERBY: Allow me to ask, can I cross through here to get to the station?

GAYEV: You can. Take this road.

---

29. A metal urn that boils water for making tea.

PASSERBY: I'm sincerely grateful to you. (*Coughing.*) The weather is excellent . . . (*Declaims.*) "Brother, my brother, you suffer . . . Go down to the Volga, whose moaning waters . . ."[30] (*To Varya.*) Mademoiselle, give a hungry Russian thirty kopecks . . . (*Varya is startled and cries out.*)

LOPAKHIN: (*Angrily.*) There's a limit to every impropriety.

LYUBOV ANDREYEVNA: (*Struck dumb.*) Take this . . . Here you . . . (*Searches in her purse.*) There's no silver . . . It's all the same, here's a gold piece for you . . .

PASSERBY: I'm sincerely grateful to you! (*Exits.*)

Laughter.

VARYA: (*Startled.*) I'm going . . . I'm going . . . Ah, Mamochka, there's nothing for the servants to eat at home, and you give him gold.

LYUBOV ANDREYEVNA: What can you do with me, I'm so stupid! When we get home, I'll give you everything, everything I have. Yermolay Alekseyevich, lend me some more! . . .

LOPAKHIN: I obey.

LYUBOV ANDREYEVNA: Let's go, ladies and gentlemen, it's time. And Varya, we've made a match for you. Congratulations!

VARYA: (*Through tears.*) Mama, you musn't joke about that.

LOPAKHIN: Ohmelia, get thee to a hermitage . . .[31]

GAYEV: My hands are trembling; I haven't played billiards in a long time.

LOPAKHIN: Ohmelia, oh, nymph, remember me in thy prayers!

LYUBOV ANDREYEVNA: Let's go, ladies and gentlemen. Soon it will be dinner time.

VARYA: He frightened me. My heart's pounding.

LOPAKHIN: Let me remind you, ladies and gentlemen: on August 22nd the cherry orchard will be sold. Think about that! . . . Think about it! . . .

---

30. These lines are from two different Populist poems from the 1870s: the first by Semyon Yakovlevich Nadson (1862–1887) and the second by Nikolay Alekseyevich Nekrasov (1821–1878).

31. Here and below are misquotations from Shakespeare's *Hamlet,* Act III, scene 1, when Prince Hamlet confronts and spurns Ophelia.

All exit except Trofimov and Anya.

ANYA: (*Laughing.*) Thanks to the passerby who frightened Varya, we're alone now.

TROFIMOV: Varya's afraid that we will suddenly fall in love with one another, so she follows us about all day long. With her narrow mind, she can't understand that we are above love. To avoid the petty and illusionary that interferes with our being free and happy, that is the goal and meaning of our lives. Forward! We are going irresistibly toward a bright star which shines in the distance! Forward! Don't lag behind, my friends!

ANYA: (*Clasping her hands.*) How well you speak! (*Pause.*) It's divine here today!

TROFIMOV: Yes, the weather is amazing.

ANYA: What have you done to me, Petya, that I don't love the cherry orchard as I did before? I loved it so tenderly, I thought there wasn't a better place in the whole world than our orchard.

TROFIMOV: All Russia is our orchard. The world is big and beautiful, and there are many wonderful places in it. (*Pause.*) Just think, Anya, your grandfather and great-grandfather, and all your ancestors were serf-owners, owners of living souls. So isn't it possible that behind each cherry tree in the orchard, behind each leaf, behind each trunk, there are human beings looking out at you? Isn't it possible that you could hear their voices? To own living souls—surely that has transformed all of you, those who lived before and those who live now, so that your mother, you, your uncle don't even notice that you are living in debt, at someone else's expense, at the expense of those people who weren't allowed to go further than your threshold . . . We lag behind by at least two hundred years, we have exactly nothing, no definite relationship to the past, we only philosophize, complain about boredom and drink vodka. Isn't it clear that to start to live in the present, we must begin to atone for our past, to finish with it? And only suffering can atone for it, only extraordinary, ceaseless labor. Remember that, Anya.

ANYA: The house in which we live has not been our house for a long time, and I'll leave, I give you my word.

TROFIMOV: If you have the keys to the household, throw them away, into the well, and leave. Be free like the wind.

ANYA: (*In ecstasy.*) How well you speak!

TROFIMOV: Believe me, Anya, believe me! I'm not yet thirty. I'm young, still a student, but I've already endured so much! As soon as it's winter, I'm hungry, sick, worried, poor like a beggar, and wherever fate has driven me, there I've gone! But still my soul has always, at every moment of the day and night, been full of inexplicable premonitions. I have a premonition of happiness, Anya! I can already see it . . .

ANYA: (*Lost in thought.*) The moon is rising.

Yepikhodov is heard still playing the same sad song on the guitar. The moon rises. Somewhere near the poplars, Varya looks for Anya and calls, "Anya! Where are you?"

TROFIMOV: Yes, the moon is rising. (*Pause.*) Happiness, too, is rising, getting nearer and nearer, I already hear its footsteps. And if we don't see it, don't know it, what of it! Others will see it!

The voice of Varya: "Anya! Where are you?"

TROFIMOV: It's Varya again! (*Angrily.*) It's revolting!

ANYA: Well then, let's go to the river! It's nice there.

TROFIMOV: Let's go. (*They go.*)

The voice of Varya: "Anya! Anya!"

Curtain.

Act III

A drawing room, separated from a hall by an archway. The chandelier is lit. The Jewish orchestra, the same one mentioned in Act II, is heard playing in the anteroom. Evening. They are dancing a grand rond *in the hall. The voice of Simeonov-Pishchik:* Promenade à une paire! *Entering into the drawing room: the first couple—Pishchik and Charlotta Ivanovna; the second—Trofimov and Lyubov Andreyevna; the third—Anya with a postal clerk, the fourth—Varya with the station* master, etc. Varya cries quietly and, while dancing, wipes away her tears. Dunyasha is in the last couple to enter. They all go through the drawing room, Pishchik yells: *Grand rond, balancez!* and *Les cavaliers à genoux et remerciez vos dames!*[32] Firs in a frock coat[33] brings in a tray with seltzer water. Pishchik and Trofimov enter the drawing room.

PISHCHIK: I'm full-blooded, but I've already had two strokes, so it's hard for me to dance. But, as they say, when in Rome, do as the Romans do. I'm as healthy as a horse. Concerning our origins, my late parent—what a joker he was, may he rest in peace—said that the ancient line of the Simeonov-Pishchiks comes down from that very same horse that Caligula seated in the senate[34] . . . *(Sits down.)* But then, the trouble is: there's no money! A hungry dog believes only in meat . . . *(Snores and then wakes up again.)* Same with me . . . I can only think about money . . .

TROFIMOV: There is actually something horse-like about your figure . . .

PISHCHIK: Well . . . A horse is a good animal . . . You can sell a horse . . .

In the neighboring room a billiard game can be heard. Varya appears in the hall, under the arch.

TROFIMOV: *(Teases Varya.)* Madame Lopakhin! Madame Lopakhin! . . .

VARYA: *(Angrily.)* "Shabby lord!"

TROFIMOV: Yes, I'm shabby, and proud of it!

VARYA: *(Having bitter second thoughts.)* We've hired musicians, but what can we pay them with? *(Exits.)*

TROFIMOV: *(To Pishchik.)* If you had used all the energy you spent all your life in pursuit of money to pay the interest on your

---

32. They are dancing a quadrille (similar to a square dance), and Pishchik is calling out the steps in French: "Promenade with your partner!"; "In a large circle, step from side to side!"; "Gentlemen, on your knees to thank your ladies!"

33. A man's dress jacket that is fitted at the waist and extends to the knees.

34. The ancient Roman emperor, Caligula (12–41), thought to be insane, mocked the Senate by making his horse a member.

loan, if you had used that energy for something else, then you probably could have moved the earth.

PISHCHIK: Nietzsche . . . the philosopher . . . the greatest, the most famous . . . a man with a huge mind, says in his essays, that you can make counterfeit money.[35]

TROFIMOV: You've read Nietzsche?

PISHCHIK: Well . . . Dashenka told me. And now I'm in such straits that I'm ready to make some . . . The day after tomorrow I have to pay three hundred and ten rubles . . . I've already got together one hundred and thirty . . . (*Feels his pocket, anxiously.*) The money's gone! I've lost the money! (*Through tears.*) Where's the money? (*Joyfully.*) Here it is, in the lining . . . I even broke out into a sweat . . .

Enter Lyubov Andreyevna and Charlotta Ivanovna.

LYUBOV ANDREYEVNA: (*Humming the lezginka.*[36]) Why is Leonid taking so long? What is he doing in town? (*To Dunyasha.*) Dunyasha, offer the musicians some tea . . .

TROFIMOV: The auction probably didn't take place yet.

LYUBOV ANDREYEVNA: The musicians came at the wrong time, and we gave a ball at the wrong time . . . Well, never mind . . . (*Sits and softly sings.*)

CHARLOTTA: (*Gives Pishchik a deck of cards.*) Here's a deck of cards for you. Think of a card, any card.

PISHCHIK: Got it!

CHARLOTTA: Now shuffle the deck. Very good. Give it to me, oh my dear *Herr* Pishchik. *Ein, zwei, drei!*[37] Now, take a look. The card is in your side pocket . . .

PISHCHIK: (*Pulls a card out of his side pocket.*) The eight of spades, that's exactly right! (*Surprised.*) Imagine that!

CHARLOTTA: (*Holds the deck of cards in her hand, to Trofimov.*) Tell me quick, which card is on top.

---

35. The philosopher Friedrich Nietzsche (1844–1900) saw Western civilization as *Beyond Good and Evil* (the title of his book from 1886).
36. A lively sword dance from the Caucasus.
37. "Mr. Pishchik"; "one, two, three" (German).

TROFIMOV: What? Well, the queen of spades.

CHARLOTTA: Here it is! (*To Pishchik.*) Well? Which card is on the bottom?

PISHCHIK: The ace of hearts.

CHARLOTTA: Here it is! (*Strikes her palm, the deck disappears.*) What beautiful weather we have today! (*A mysterious feminine voice, apparently coming from under the floor answers her: "Oh yes, the weather is splendid, my lady."*) You are so very nice, my pretty one, my ideal . . . (*The voice: "And you, my lady, I like you very much too."*)

STATION MASTER: (*Applauding.*) Madam the ventriloquist, bravo!

PISHCHIK: (*Surprised.*) Imagine that! My most charming Charlotta Ivanovna . . . I'm simply in love . . .

CHARLOTTA: In love? (*Shrugs her shoulders.*) Can you love? *Guter mensch aber schlecter musikant.*[38]

TROFIMOV: (*Clasps Pishchik on the shoulder.*) Just like a horse . . .

CHARLOTTA: Attention please, one more trick. (*Takes a lap robe off a chair.*) Here's a very pretty plaid, I would like to sell it . . . (*Shakes it out and holds it up.*) Doesn't anyone want to buy it?

PISHCHIK: (*Surprised.*) Imagine that!

CHARLOTTA: *Ein, zwei, drei!* (*Quickly raises the lap robe; behind it stands Anya to the amazement of all; she curtsies, runs to her mother, hugs her, and runs out into the hall.*)

LYUBOV ANDREYEVNA: (*Applauds.*) Bravo, bravo! . . .

CHARLOTTA: Now one more! *Ein, zwei, drei!* (*Raises the lap robe; behind it stands Varya, who bows.*)

PISHCHIK: (*Surprised.*) Imagine that!

CHARLOTTA: The end! (*Throws the lap robe to Pishchik, curtsies, and runs out into the hall.*)

PISHCHIK: (*Hurries after her.*) You are a sorceress . . . That's what you are! You are! (*Exits.*)

---

38. "A good man, but a poor musician" (German).

LYUBOV ANDREYEVNA: But Leonid's not back yet. What is he doing in town so long? I don't understand! Shouldn't everything there be finished by now? The estate is either sold or the auction didn't take place. Why prolong the suspense!

VARYA: (*Trying to calm her.*) Uncle bought it, I'm sure of it.

TROFIMOV: (*Mockingly.*) Sure.

VARYA: Our great aunt sent him her power of attorney to buy it and transfer the debt to her name. She did it for Anya. And I'm sure, with God's help, Uncle is buying it.

LYUBOV ANDREYEVNA: Your great aunt from Yaroslavl sent fifteen thousand to buy the estate in her name—she doesn't trust us—and that's not enough money to pay even the interest on the mortgage. (*Covers her face with her hands.*) Today my fate is decided, my fate . . .

TROFIMOV: (*Teasing Varya.*) Madame Lopakhin!

VARYA: (*Angrily.*) Eternal student! They've already thrown you out of the university twice.

LYUBOV ANDREYEVNA: Why are you angry, Varya? He teases you about Lopakhin, but so what? Marry Lopakhin, if you want. He's a good and interesting person. If you don't want to, then don't. No one's forcing you, darling . . .

VARYA: To be honest, Mamochka, I look upon this as a serious matter. He's a good person, I like him.

LYUBOV ANDREYEVNA: So marry him. Why wait? I don't understand!

VARYA: Mamochka, I can't propose to him myself! For two years now, everyone's been talking to me about him, everyone's talking but him. Either he keeps quiet or he jokes. I understand. He's getting rich, he's busy, he has no time for me. If there were some money, even a little, only a hundred rubles, I would quit everything, and move on somewhere. I'd go to a hermitage.

TROFIMOV: How splendid!

VARYA: (*To Trofimov.*) A student should be smart! (*In a softer tone of voice, with tears in her eyes.*) How ugly you've gotten, Petya! How old! (*To Lyubov Andreyevna, no longer crying.*) It's just that I can't live without something to keep me busy, Mamochka. I need to be doing something every minute.

Yasha enters.

YASHA: (*Barely holding back his laugher.*) Yepikhodov broke a billiard cue! . . . (*Exits.*)

VARYA: Why is Yepikhodov here? Who let him play billiards? I don't understand these people . . . (*Exits.*)

LYUBOV ANDREYEVNA: Don't tease her, Petya. You can see that she's miserable even without that.

TROFIMOV: But she's very eager to meddle in other people's business. All summer long she didn't give me or Anya any peace; she was so afraid a little romance would develop between us. What business is that of hers? And besides I've never given that impression, I'm far away from such vulgarity. We are above love!

LYUBOV ANDREYEVNA: And so then I must be below love. (*In great agitation.*) Why is Leonid not here? If only I knew whether the estate were sold or not? This trouble seems to me so unbelievable that I don't even know what to think, I'm in despair . . . I could scream right now . . . could do something stupid. Save me, Petya. Tell me something, tell me . . .

TROFIMOV: Whether the estate has been sold today or whether it hasn't been sold—isn't it all the same? It was finished long ago, there's no turning back, the path is overgrown. Be calm, dear soul. You don't need to deceive yourself, you need to look truth straight in the eye.

LYUBOV ANDREYEVNA: What truth? You can see what is true and what is not true, but I feel like I've lost my sight and can see nothing. You boldly decide how to answer all the important questions, but tell me, dear friend, isn't that because you're young, and because you haven't yet suffered through any one of those questions? You look boldly forward, but isn't that because you don't see, you don't expect anything frightening there, since life is still hidden from your young eyes? You're bolder, more honorable, deeper than us, but just think, be a tiny little bit more generous, and spare me. I was born here, after all, lived here with my father and mother, my grandfather . . . I love this house. Without the cherry orchard I wouldn't understand my own life, and if it must be sold, then sell me with the orchard . . . (*Hugs Trofimov, kisses him on the forehead.*) My son drowned here, after all . . . (*Cries.*) Pity me, my good, my kind friend.

TROFIMOV: You know that I sympathize whole-heartedly.

LYUBOV ANDREYEVNA: But you should say that differently, differently . . . (*Takes out a handkerchief, and a telegram falls to the floor.*) My soul feels so heavy today, you can't imagine. Here it's noisy, but my soul trembles with every sound, I'm trembling all over, but I can't go to my room, it's frightening to sit by myself in the quiet. Don't judge me, Petya . . . I love you, like my own son. I would gladly give you Anya's hand, I swear it, but dear friend, you must learn, you must finish your studies. You don't do anything, you let fate toss you from place to place, it's so strange . . . Isn't that true? Isn't it? And you must do something with that beard, so it will grow . . . (*Laughs.*) You're ridiculous!

TROFIMOV: (*Picks up the telegram.*) I don't want to be a beauty.

LYUBOV ANDREYEVNA: The telegram's from Paris. Every day I get one. Yesterday and today. That wild man is sick again, things aren't going well for him again . . . He begs me to forgive him, implores me to come back, and really I ought to go to Paris to be with him. You look so stern, Petya, but what can I do, my friend, what can I do, he's sick, he's alone, unhappy, and who's there to look after him, who'll keep him from making mistakes, who'll give him his medicine? And why should I hide it, or keep quiet about it? I love him, that's obvious. I love him, love him . . . It's a stone around my neck, and it's pulling me down to the bottom, but I love this stone, I can't live without him. (*Presses Trofimov's hand.*) Don't think badly of me, Petya, and don't tell me anything, don't tell me . . .

TROFIMOV: (*Through tears.*) Forgive me for my frankness, for God's sake, but didn't he rob you?

LYUBOV ANDREYEVNA: No, no, no, don't talk like that . . . (*Covers her ears.*)

TROFIMOV: But he's a scoundrel. And you're the only one who doesn't know it! He's a petty scoundrel, a nonentity . . .

LYUBOV ANDREYEVNA: (*Getting angry but controlling it.*) You are twenty-six or twenty-seven years old, and you're still a schoolboy in the second grade!

TROFIMOV: Let me be!

LYUBOV ANDREYEVNA: You must become a man, at your age you should understand those who love. And you yourself must love . . . You must fall in love! (*Angrily.*) Yes, yes! You have no purity, you're only a prude, a ridiculous freak, ugly . . .

TROFIMOV: (*In horror.*) What is she saying!

LYUBOV ANDREYEVNA: "I'm above love!" You're not above love, as Firs would say, you're just a "nincompoop." At your age not to have a lover! . . .

TROFIMOV: (*In terror.*) That's horrible! What is she saying?! (*Goes quickly toward the hall, holding his head in his hands.*) That's horrible . . . I can't stand it, I'm going . . . (*Exits but returns immediately.*) Everything is finished between us! (*Goes out into the anteroom.*)

LYUBOV ANDREYEVNA: (*Yells after him.*) Petya, wait a minute! You're ridiculous, I was joking! Petya!

He is heard quickly going down the stairs, then suddenly he falls down with a clatter. Anya and Varya cry out, and then laughter is heard.

LYUBOV ANDREYEVNA: What was that?

Anya runs in.

ANYA: (*Laughing.*) Petya fell down the stairs. (*She runs out.*)

LYUBOV ANDREYEVNA: What a freak Petya is . . .

The station master stands in the middle of the hall and recites "The Sinful Woman," a poem by A. Tolstóy.[39] *Everyone listens to him, but he has finished only a few lines when*

---

39. "The Sinful Woman" is a poem by Aleksey Konstantinovich Tolstoy (1817–1875), a cousin of the novelist. It tells the biblical story of the prostitute Mary Magdalene, who repents when she meets Jesus at a celebratory feast. In production, the first lines can be used:
    The lute resounds, the cymbals crash!
    Amidst the twirling dancers,
    Dressed in rich brocades, her dark eyes flash!
    Near the portal regally stand
    A pair of broken columns,
    Where flowers too are strewn . . .

waltz music is heard coming from the anteroom and the recitation breaks off. Everyone dances. Trofimov, Anya, Varya, and Lyubov Andreyevna come in from the anteroom.

LYUBOV ANDREYEVNA: Well Petya . . . Well, dear heart . . . Please forgive me. Let's dance . . . (*Dances with Petya.*)

Anya and Varya dance. Firs enters and places his cane next to the side door. Yasha also comes into the drawing room and watches the dance.

YASHA: What's up, Grandpa?

FIRS: Don't feel well. Before this, generals, barons, admirals used to dance at our balls, but now we send for a postal clerk and the station master, and even they don't feel much like coming. Somehow I've gotten weak. The late master, their grandfather, used to use sealing wax for all our diseases. I've been taking sealing wax every day now for about twenty years, or maybe more. Maybe that's why I'm alive.

YASHA: You bore me, Grandpa. (*Yawns.*) Hope you croak soon.

FIRS: Ah, you . . . nincompoop! (*Mumbles.*)

Trofimov and Lyubov Andreyevna dance into the hall, then into the drawing room.

LYUBOV ANDREYEVNA: Merci.[40] I'll sit for awhile . . . (*Sits down.*) I'm tired.

Anya enters.

ANYA: (*Excited.*) There was some man in the kitchen just now who said that the cherry orchard was sold today.

LYUBOV ANDREYEVNA: Sold to whom?

ANYA: He didn't say to whom. He left. (*Dances with Trofimov, and they exit into the hall.*)

YASHA: That was just some old man babbling. A stranger.

---

40. "Thank you" (French).

FIRS: And Leonid Andreyevich still isn't here, he didn't come back yet. He wore a light spring coat, and just you wait, he'll catch his death of cold. Ah, young and green!

LYUBOV ANDREYEVNA: I'll die right now. Go, Yasha, find out who it was sold to.

YASHA: But he left a long time ago, that old man. (*Laughs.*)

LYUBOV ANDREYEVNA: (*Slightly annoyed.*) Well, what are you laughing at? Why are you so happy?

YASHA: That Yepikhodov is very funny. An empty-headed person, Twenty-Two Troubles.

LYUBOV ANDREYEVNA: Firs, if they sell the estate, where will you go?

FIRS: Wherever you say, there I'll go.

LYUBOV ANDREYEVNA: Why does your face look like that? Are you ill? You should go to sleep, you know . . .

FIRS: Yes . . . (*With a smile.*) I'll go to sleep, and then without me who will serve, who will keep things in order? I'm the only one in the whole house.

YASHA: (*To Lyubov Andreyevna.*) Lyubov Andreyevna! Allow me to make a request of you, be so kind! If you go to Paris again, take me with you, do me this kindness. It's absolutely impossible for me to stay here. (*Looks around, in a whisper.*) I don't need to tell you, you can see for yourself, the country's uneducated, the people are immoral, then there's the boredom. In the kitchen they feed us atrociously, and then there's this Firs always walking around, mumbling various irrelevant things. Take me with you, be so kind!

Pishchik enters.

PISHCHIK: May I have the pleasure . . . of a little waltz, my most beauteous lady . . . (*Lyubov Andreyevna follows him.*) My charmer, I still need to borrow one hundred and eighty little rubles from you . . . I'll borrow . . . (*They dance.*) One hundred and eighty little rubles . . . (*They exit into the hall.*)

YASHA: (*Softly sings.*) "I wonder if you understand the beating of my heart . . ."[41]

41. From a popular ballad of the 1870s.

In the hall, a figure in a gray top hat and checked pants waves a hand and jumps. There are cries of "Bravo, Charlotta Ivanovna!"

DUNYASHA: (*Stops in order to powder her nose.*) The mistress told me to dance. There are so many cavaliers, but so few ladies, and now my head is spinning from the dances, my heart is pounding, Firs Nikolayevich. And just now the clerk from the post office said something to me that took my breath away.

The music quiets down.

FIRS: What did he say to you?

DUNYASHA: "You," he said, "are like a flower."

YASHA: (*Yawns.*) Ignoramus . . . (*Exits.*)

DUNYASHA: "Like a flower" . . . I'm such a delicate young girl, I love tender words so awfully much.

FIRS: You've got your head screwed on wrong.

Enter Yepikhovdov.

YEPIKHODOV: Avdotya Fyodorovna, you don't want to see me . . . I might as well be some kind of an insect. (*Sighs.*) Ah, life!

DUNYASHA: What do you want?

YEPIKHODOV: Undoubtedly, you are perhaps right. (*Sighs.*) But, of course, if you look at it from a point of view, if I may express myself this way, forgive me for my frankness, you have brought me to a state of mind. I know my own fortune, every day something bad happens to me, and I've been used to it for a long time now, and so I look at my fate with a smile. You gave me your word, and although I . . .

DUNYASHA: I beg you, let's talk about this later; leave me in peace now. Now I'm daydreaming . . . (*Plays with her fan.*)

YEPIKHODOV: Something bad happens to me every day, and if I may express myself, I only smile, I even laugh.

Varya enters from the hall.

VARYA: (*To Yepikhodov.*) You still haven't left, Semyon? What a disrespectful man you are, truly. (*To Dunyasha.*) Run along,

DUNYASHA. (*To Yepikhodov.*) You either play billiards and break the cues, or you walk around the drawing room like a guest.

YEPIKHODOV: You cannot, if I may express myself, you cannot reproach me.

VARYA: I'm not reproaching you, I'm telling you. You're the only one who knows why you walk from place to place, and don't attend to your business. We keep a clerk, but who knows what for.

YEPIKHODOV: (*Offended.*) About whether I work, whether I walk around, whether I eat, whether I play billiards, only people who understand and are older can judge.

VARYA: You dare to talk to me like that! (*Flaring up.*) You dare? You mean to say that I don't understand anything? Get out of here! This minute.

YEPIKHODOV: (*Losing his courage.*) I beg you to express yourself in a more delicate way.

VARYA: (*Losing her temper.*) Get out of here this minute! Out! (*He goes to the door; she follows him.*) Twenty-Two Troubles! Don't let me see your face! Don't let me hear your voice! (*Yepikhodov exits. His voice behind the door: "I'll complain about you . . ."*) Are you coming back? (*She takes the cane which Firs left near the door.*) Come on . . . Come on . . . Come on, I'll show you . . . Well are you coming? Are you coming? Then take this . . . (*She brandishes the cane and at the same time, Lopakhin enters.*)

LOPAKHIN: Thank you kindly.

VARYA: (*Angrily and mockingly.*) My fault!

LOPAKHIN: It's nothing, madam. I humbly thank you for your pleasant hospitality.

VARYA: Don't bother to thank me. (*Walks away, then looks around and asks gently.*) I didn't hurt you, did I?

LOPAKHIN: No, not at all. A huge bump's coming up, that's all.

*A voice in the hall: "Lopakhin's arrived!
It's Yermolay Alekseyevich!"*

PISHCHIK: (*Enters.*) A sight for sore eyes . . . (*Kisses Lopakhin.*) You smell of cognac, my dear, my darling. We've been making merry here too.

Lyubov Andreyevna enters.

LYUBOV ANDREYEVNA: Is it you, Yermolay Alekseyevich? Why did it take you so long? Where's Leonid?

LOPAKHIN: Leonid Andreyevich arrived with me, he's coming . . .

LYUBOV ANDREYEVNA: (*Excited.*) Well, what happened? Was there an auction? Tell me!

LOPAKHIN: (*Confused, afraid to destroy his own joy.*) The auction was over at four o'clock . . . We missed the train, had to wait until nine thirty. (*Sighs deeply.*) Ugh! My head is spinning a little . . .

Gayev enters; in his right hand he has some purchases, with his left he wipes away his tears.

LYUBOV ANDREYEVNA: Lyonya, what is it? Lyonya, what? (*Impatiently, with tears in her eyes.*) Quickly, for God's sake . . .

GAYEV: (*Doesn't answer her, only waves his hand; to Firs, crying.*) Here take this . . . There's some anchovies, Kerch herring[42] . . . I didn't eat anything today . . . How much I've suffered! (*The door to the billiard room is open; the striking of balls can be heard, and the voice of Yasha: "Seven and eighteen!" Gayev's expression changes; he's no longer crying.*) I'm awfully tired. Help me, Firs, to get undressed. (*Exits to his room, Firs following him.*)

PISHCHIK: What happened at the auction? Tell me!

LYUBOV ANDREYEVNA: Was the cherry orchard sold?

LOPAKHIN: It was sold.

LYUBOV ANDREYEVNA: Who bought it?

LOPAKHIN: I bought it. (*Pause.*)

---

42. A seafood delicacy from the Ukraine.

Lyubov Andreyevna is overcome; she would fall if she weren't standing near an armchair or table. Varya takes the keys from her belt, throws them on the floor in the middle of the drawing room and exits.

LOPAKHIN: I bought it! Wait a minute, ladies and gentlemen, be so kind, my head is swimming, I can't talk . . . (*Laughs.*) We got to the auction. Deriganov was there. Leonid Andreyevich had only fifteen thousand and Deriganov had already put down thirty thousand over and above the debt. I saw how the business stood, so I jumped in and put down forty . . . He put down forty-five. I made it fifty-five. You see he kept adding five thousand and I added ten each time . . . Well, it came to a finish. I put down ninety thousand over and above the debt, and it was mine. Now the cherry orchard is mine! Mine! (*Laughs out loud.*) My God, Lord in Heaven, the cherry orchard is mine! Tell me that I'm drunk, not in my right mind, that I've imagined all of this . . . (*Stamps his feet.*) Don't laugh at me. If my father and grandfather were to get up out of their graves and look at everything that's happened, how their Yermolay, their beaten, half-literate Yermolay, who ran around barefoot in the winter, how this very same Yermolay bought an estate, the most beautiful one in the whole world. I bought the estate where my grandfather and father were slaves, where they weren't allowed into the kitchen. I'm asleep, this is a mirage for me, it only seems to be . . . This is the fruit of your imagination, hidden by the darkness of the unknown . . . (*Picks up the keys, smiling tenderly.*) She threw down the keys, wants to show that she's no longer the housekeeper here . . . (*Jingles the keys.*) Well, it's all the same. (*The orchestra is heard tuning up.*) Hey musicians, play, I want to hear you! Everyone, come look at how Yermolay Lopakhin will take the axe to the cherry orchard, how the trees will fall to the ground! We'll build summer houses and our grandchildren and their grandchildren will see a new life . . . Music, play! (*The music plays. Lyubov Andreyevna lowers herself to a chair and bitterly cries. To her reproachfully.*) Why, why didn't you listen to me? My poor, good woman, you can't go back now. (*With tears.*) Oh if only all this would pass quickly, if only our incoherent, unhappy lives would change quickly!

PISHCHIK: (*Takes him by the arm, in a whisper.*) She's crying. Let's go into the hall, leave her alone . . . Let's go . . . (*Takes him by the arm and leads him into the hall.*)

LOPAKHIN: What happened? Music, play out clearly! Let everything be as I want! (*With irony.*) The new landowner is coming; the owner of the cherry orchard! (*Accidentally bumps into a table which almost knocks over a candelabra.*) I can pay for everything! (*Exits with Pishchik.*)

There is no one in the hall and drawing room except Lyubov Andreyevna, who sits huddled up, and weeps bitterly. The music plays softly. Quickly Anya and Trofimov enter. Anya goes to her mother and kneels in front of her. Trofimov remains at the entrance to the hall.

ANYA: Mama! . . . Mama, are you crying? My dear, kind, my good Mama, my beautiful Mama, I love you . . . I bless you. The cherry orchard is sold, it's gone, that's true, true, but don't cry, Mama, your life remains ahead of you, your good, pure soul remains . . . Come with me away from here, my darling, come! . . . We'll plant a new orchard, more luxurious than this one, you'll see, you'll understand, and joy, quiet deep joy will fill your soul, like the rays of the setting sun, and you'll smile, Mama! Come, darling! Come! . . .

Curtain.

Act IV

The set from the first Act. There are no curtains in the windows, or paintings on the walls, there is a little furniture remaining which is pushed to one corner, as if to be sold. There is a feeling of emptiness. Near the door to the outside and upstage there are suitcases, traveling bundles, etc. To the left, the door is open, and from there the voices of Varya and Anya are heard. Lopakhin stands and waits. Yasha holds a tray with glasses, filled with champagne. In the hallway, Yepikhodov ties up a box. Far offstage there is a rumbling. The peasants are saying goodbye. The voice of Gayev: "Thank you, my friends, thank you."

YASHA: The simple people have come to say goodbye. I am of the opinion, Yermolay Alekseyevich, they're a good people but they don't understand much.

The rumbling quiets down. Lyubov Andreyevna and Gayev enter from the hallway; she does not cry, but she is pale, her lips are trembling, she cannot speak.

GAYEV: You gave them your purse, Lyuba. You musn't do that! You musn't do that!

LYUBOV ANDREYEVNA: I couldn't help it! I couldn't help it! (*They both exit.*)

LOPAKHIN: (*At the door, after them.*) Please, I most humbly beg you! Have a drink to our goodbyes. I didn't think to bring any from town and I only found one bottle at the station. Please! (*Pause.*) What's wrong, ladies and gentlemen! Don't you want to? (*Walks away from the door.*) If I'd known, I wouldn't have brought it. Well, I won't drink any either. (*Yasha carefully puts the tray on the table.*) Drink up, Yasha, you at least have some.

YASHA: To those who are departing! Good luck to those who stay! (*Drinks.*) This isn't real champagne, I can assure you.

LOPAKHIN: Eight rubles a bottle. (*Pause.*) It's cold as hell here.

YASHA: They didn't light the fires, since we're leaving. (*Laughs.*)

LOPAKHIN: What's the matter?

YASHA: Just happy.

LOPAKHIN: Outside it's October, but it's as sunny and as quiet as summer. Good for building. (*Looking at his watch, at the door.*) Ladies and gentlemen, keep in mind that the train leaves in just forty-six minutes! That means, that in twenty minutes you have to leave for the station. So hurry up a bit.

Trofimov in a coat enters from the outside.

TROFIMOV: I think it's already time to leave. The horses are harnessed. The devil knows where my galoshes are. They're gone. (*At the door.*) Anya, my galoshes aren't anywhere! I didn't find them!

LOPAKHIN: And I have to go to Kharkov. I'll go with you on the same train. I'll spend the whole winter in Kharkov. I've been hanging about with you all this time and tormenting myself by staying away from my business. I can't live without work,

I don't know what to do with my hands. They hang about so strangely, as if they belonged to someone else.

TROFIMOV: We'll be leaving and so you can get back to your own useful work again.

LOPAKHIN: Have a quick drink.

TROFIMOV: I can't.

LOPAKHIN: So you'll be going to Moscow now?

TROFIMOV: Yes, I'll take them to town and tomorrow I'll go to Moscow.

LOPAKHIN: Yes . . . Well, the professors, no doubt, haven't been giving their lectures; they're probably all waiting for you to come back!

TROFIMOV: It's none of your business.

LOPAKHIN: How many years have you been studying at the university?

TROFIMOV: Why not think up something a little newer. That's old and flat. (*Looks for his galoshes.*) You know, we may never see each other again, so allow me to give you one piece of advice at parting: don't wave your arms! Get rid of that habit—waving your arms. And this too—building summer houses and counting on the summer folk to cultivate the land on their own—that's waving your arms too . . . But anyway, I still love you. You have fine, tender fingers, like an artist, you have a fine, tender soul . . .

LOPAKHIN: (*Hugs him.*) Goodbye, my friend. Thank you for everything. If you need it, let me give you some money for the road.

TROFIMOV: What for? I don't need it.

LOPAKHIN: But you don't have any!

TROFIMOV: Yes I do. Thank you. I got some for a translation. Here it is, in my pocket. (*Anxiously.*) But my galoshes aren't here.

VARYA: (*From the other room.*) Take these disgusting things! (*She throws a pair of rubber galoshes on stage.*)

TROFIMOV: Why are you angry, Varya? Hmmm . . . These aren't my galoshes!

LOPAKHIN: In the spring I planted two thousand seven hundred acres of poppies and now I've made forty thousand clear profit from them. But when my poppies were in bloom, what a picture that was! So as I said, I made forty thousand and that means I'm offering you a loan because I can. Why turn your nose up at it? I'm a peasant . . . I speak plainly.

TROFIMOV: Your father was a serf, mine—a pharmacist, but that doesn't necessarily mean anything. (*Lopakhin takes out his wallet.*) Put it away, put it away . . . Even if you gave me two hundred thousand, I wouldn't take it. I'm a free man. Everything that all of you, the rich and the poor, value so highly and dearly hasn't the slightest influence over me, it's like fluff blown around by the wind. I can get along without you, I can pass you by, I'm strong and proud. Humanity is going toward the highest truth, toward the highest happiness that is possible on earth, and I am in the front ranks.

LOPAKHIN: Will you get there?

TROFIMOV: I'll get there. (*Pause.*) I'll get there or I'll show others the way to get there.

The sound of the axe chopping down trees is heard in the distance.

LOPAKHIN: Well, goodbye, my friend. It's time to go. We turn our noses up at each other, but life passes us by unconcerned. When I work for a long time without a break, then my thoughts rest easier, and I think that I too know why I'm living. But, brother, how many people are there in Russia, who live without knowing why. Well, it's all the same, that's not what keeps things going. Leonid Andreyevich, they say, has taken a position, he'll work in the bank, six thousand a year . . . Only he probably won't stick to it, he's very lazy . . .

ANYA: (*At the door.*) Mama asks you not to cut the orchard while she's still here.

TROFIMOV: Really, have you no tact . . . (*Exits through the hallway.*)

LOPAKHIN: Right away, right away . . . These people, really. (*Follows Trofimov off.*)

ANYA: Did they take Firs to the hospital?

YASHA: I told them to this morning. I think they must have taken him.

ANYA: (*To Yepikhodov, who crosses through the hall.*) Semyon Panteleyevich, find out, please, if they took Firs to the hospital.

YASHA: (*Offended.*) I told Yégor to this morning. Why ask about it ten times!

YEPIKHODOV: Long-lived Firs, in my decisive opinion, is not fit to be mended. It is high time for him to join his forefathers. I can only envy him. (*Puts a suitcase down on a hatbox and crushes it.*) There, of course. Just as I knew. (*Exits.*)

YASHA: (*Sarcastically.*) Twenty-Two Troubles.

VARYA: (*Behind the door.*) Did they take Firs to the hospital?

ANYA: They took him.

VARYA: Why didn't they take the letter to the doctor with them?

ANYA: We'll have to send it on after them . . . (*Exits.*)

VARYA: (*From the neighboring room.*) Where's Yasha? Tell him his mother's come to say goodbye to him.

YASHA: (*Waves his arm.*) They are trying my patience.

Dunyasha has been fussing with the baggage the whole time; now, when Yasha is alone, she goes up to him.

DUNYASHA: If only you'd look at me for one more time, Yasha. You're leaving . . . forsaking me . . . (*Cries and throws her arms around him.*)

YASHA: Why cry? (*Drinks champagne.*) In six days I'll be in Paris again. Tomorrow we'll take the express train and off we'll go, you won't see us for the dust. I can hardly believe it. *Vive la France!*[43] . . . This isn't for me, I can't live here. Nothing to do about it. I've looked at these ignoramuses enough—I've had enough! (*Drinks champagne.*) Why cry? Behave yourself properly, and you won't cry.

DUNYASHA: (*Powders her nose, looking in a hand mirror.*) Send me a letter from Paris. After all, I loved you, Yasha, loved you so! I'm a tender creature, Yasha!

---

43. "Long live France!" (French).

YASHA: They're coming this way! (*Fusses over the suitcases, sings quietly.*)

Enter Lyubov Andreyevna, Gayev, Anya, and Charlotta Ivanovna.

GAYEV: We have to go. Only a little time left. (*Looking at Yasha.*) Who smells of herring?

LYUBOV ANDREYEVNA: In about ten minutes we'll go out to the carriages . . . (*Glances around the room.*) Goodbye, dear house, old grandfather. The winter will pass, then will come spring, and you won't be here anymore, they'll tear you down. How much these walls have seen! (*Kisses her daughter warmly.*) My treasure, you're shining, your eyes are sparkling like diamonds. Are you happy? Very?

ANYA: Very! A new life is beginning, Mama!

GAYEV: (*Happily.*) True, everything's very good now. Before the sale of the cherry orchard, all of us were so worried, we suffered, and then, when the question was finally decided, irrevocably, everyone calmed down, even became happy . . . I'm a banker now, now I'm a financier . . . Yellow ball into the center, and you, Lyuba, somehow you look better, no doubt about it.

LYUBOV ANDREYEVNA: Yes. My nerves are better, that's true. (*She is handed her hat and coat.*) I sleep well. Bring me my things, Yasha. It's time. (*To Anya.*) My little girl, we'll see each other again soon . . . I'll go to Paris, live there on the money which your great aunt from Yaroslavl sent to buy the estate. Long live your great aunt! But that money won't last long.

ANYA: Mama, you'll come back soon, soon . . . Isn't that true? I'll study and pass the high-school examination, and then I'll work and help you. Mama, we'll read all kinds of books together. Isn't that true? (*Kisses her mother's hands.*) We'll read on autumn evenings, we'll read a lot of books, and a new, miraculous world will open up before us . . . (*Daydreams.*) Mama, you'll come back . . .

LYUBOV ANDREYEVNA: I'll come back, my precious. (*Hugs her daughter.*)

Lopakhin enters. Charlotta quietly sings a little song.

GAYEV: Happy Charlotta, she's singing!

CHARLOTTA: (*Picks up a bundle and holds it to look like a baby wrapped in a blanket.*) My little baby, lullaby, lullaby . . . (*The baby's crying is heard:* "*Wa! Wa!* . . .") Quiet, my pretty one, my dear little boy. ("*Wa!* . . . *Wa!* . . .") I'm so sorry for you! (*She throws the bundle down.*) Please, find me a position. I can't stand it like this.

LOPAKHIN: We'll find something, Charlotta Ivanovna, don't worry.

GAYEV: They're all leaving us, Varya's going away . . . We're suddenly unnecessary.

CHARLOTTA: There's nowhere for me to live in town. I have to go away. (*Hums.*) It's all the same . . .

Enter Pishchik.

LOPAKHIN: The miracle of nature!

PISHCHIK: Oh, let me catch my breath . . . I'm tormented . . . My most respected friends . . . Give me some water . . .

GAYEV: Come for money, no doubt. Your humble servant, but I flee temptation[44] . . . (*Exits.*)

PISHCHIK: I haven't been to see you in a long time . . . My beauteous lady . . . (*To Lopakhin.*) You're here too . . . Glad to see you . . . A person with a huge mind . . . Take this . . . Here you are . . . (*Hands Lopakhin some money.*) Four hundred rubles . . . That leaves eight hundred forty that I still owe . . .

LOPAKHIN: (*Shrugs his shoulders in bewilderment.*) It's like a dream . . . Where did you get this?

PISHCHIK: Wait a minute . . . It's hot in here . . . The most unusual occurrence. Some Englishmen came to see me and found some kind of white clay on my land[45] . . . (*To Lyubov Andreyevna.*) And for you four hundred . . . You beautiful, amazing woman . . . (*Hands her money.*) The rest later. (*Drinks some water.*) Just now a certain young man in the train told me that a certain . . . a great philosopher advises you to jump off

---

44. A common saying when avoiding something unpleasant.
45. Soil rich in clay is difficult to cultivate, but can be mined for any number of manufacturing uses. The clay may also suggest the presence of oil.

the roof . . . "Jump!" he says, and that will solve everything. (*Surprised.*) Imagine that! Water! . . .

LOPAKHIN: Who are these Englishmen?

PISHCHIK: I leased them a piece of the land with the clay on it for twenty-four years. And now, excuse me, I have no time . . . I'll tell you later . . . I'm going to Znóikov . . . and to Kardamónov[46] . . . I owe everybody . . . (*Drinks.*) I just wanted to say hello . . . Thursday, I'll drop by . . .

LYUBOV ANDREYEVNA: We're leaving for town now, and tomorrow I'll be abroad . . .

PISHCHIK: What? (*Alarmed.*) Why to town? So that's why I see the furniture . . . suitcases . . . Well, it's nothing . . . (*Through tears.*) Nothing . . . People of great minds . . . these English . . . Nothing . . . Be happy . . . God will help you . . . Nothing . . . Everything on this earth comes to an end . . . (*Kisses Lyubov Andreyevna's hand.*) And if you hear rumor that my end has come, remember that . . . that very same horse, and say, "There was on earth a certain so and so . . . a Simeonov-Pishchik . . . May he rest in peace" . . . Wonderful weather . . . Yes . . . (*Exits greatly disconcerted, but immediately returns and says at the door.*) Dashenka sends her regards! (*Exits.*)

LYUBOV ANDREYEVNA: Now we can go. I'm leaving with two worries. The first—Firs is sick. (*Looking at her watch.*) We still have five minutes.

ANYA: Mama, they already took Firs to the hospital. Yasha sent him this morning.

LYUBOV ANDREYEVNA: My second worry is Varya. She's used to getting up early and working, and now without her work she's like a fish out of water. She's getting thin, getting pale, and she cries, poor thing . . . (*Pause.*) You know very well, Yermolay Alekseyevich, that I've dreamed . . . of giving you Varya's hand, and it seemed obvious to everyone that you would marry her. (*Whispers to Anya, then nods to Charlotta; both exit.*) She loves you, you're fond of her, and I don't know, I don't know why you avoid each other. I don't understand!

LOPAKHIN: I have to admit I don't understand it either. It's all so strange somehow . . . If there's still some time, I'm ready right

---

46. These two names mean "heatwave" and "cardamon."

now . . . Let's finish this off immediately, and be done with it. But without you I feel that I won't propose.

LYUBOV ANDREYEVNA: Excellent. After all, you only need a minute. I'll call her right now . . .

LOPAKHIN: There's champagne at the ready, too! (*Looking at the glasses.*) They're empty, someone's drunk it all. (*Yasha hiccups.*) That's what you'd call really lapping it up . . .

LYUBOV ANDREYEVNA: (*In a lively manner.*) Wonderful. We'll leave you . . . Yasha, *allez!*[47] I'll call her . . . (*At the door.*) Varya, drop everything and come here. Come on! (*Exits with Yasha.*)

LOPAKHIN: (*Looking at his watch.*) Yes . . . (*Pause.*)

Behind the door, a stifled laugh, whispers, finally Varya enters.

VARYA: (*Examines the baggage for a long time.*) It's strange, I can't seem to find . . .

LOPAKHIN: What are you looking for?

VARYA: I packed it myself and I can't remember where.

Pause.

LOPAKHIN: Where are you going now, Varvara Mikhailovna?

VARYA: Me? To the Ragúlins . . . I agreed to look after the household for them . . . A housekeeper, I guess you'd say.

LOPAKHIN: Is that in Yáshnevo? That's about forty-three miles. (*Pause.*) So life in this house is finished . . .

VARYA: (*Examining the baggage.*) Where can it be . . . Maybe I put it in the trunk . . . Yes, life in this house is finished . . . There won't be anymore . . .

LOPAKHIN: I'm going to Kharkov right now . . . on the same train. A lot of business there. I'm leaving Yepikhodov here on the property . . . I've hired him.

VARYA: Well!

---

47. "Go!" (French).

LOPAKHIN: Last year at this time it had already snowed, if you remember, and now it's quiet, sunny. Only it's cold . . . Three degrees below freezing.

VARYA: I didn't look. (*Pause.*) Besides, our thermometer is broken.

Pause. A voice at the door from outside: "Yermolay Alekseyevich! . . ."

LOPAKHIN: (*As if he had been waiting for this call.*) Right away! (*Exits quickly.*)

Varya sits on the floor, puts her head on a bundle tied up with a scarf, and quietly sobs, The door opens, Lyubov Andreyevna enters cautiously.

LYUBOV ANDREYEVNA: Well? (*Pause.*) We must go.

VARYA: (*No longer crying, wipes her eyes.*) Yes, it's time, Mamochka. I'll make it to the Ragulins today, if I don't miss the train . . .

LYUBOV ANDREYEVNA: (*At the door.*) Anya, put on your coat!

Anya enters, then Gayev, Charlotta Ivanovna; Gayev wears a warm cloth coat with a hood. Servants and coachmen come in. Yepikhodov fusses near the baggage.

LYUBOV ANDREYEVNA: Now we can be on our way.

ANYA: (*Joyfully.*) On our way!

GAYEV: My friends, my dears, my darling ones! In forsaking this house forever, how can I keep quiet, how can I refrain from expressing at parting, those feelings which now fill my whole being . . .

ANYA: (*Pleadingly.*) Uncle!

VARYA: Uncle dear, it's not necessary!

GAYEV: (*Despondently.*) Yellow ball, rebound to the center . . . I'll keep quiet . . .

Enter Trofimov, then Lopakhin.

TROFIMOV: Well, ladies and gentlemen, time to leave!

LOPAKHIN: Yepikhodov, my coat!

LYUBOV ANDREYEVNA: I'll sit down for one minute.[48] I feel as if I've never seen what the walls of this house are like, what the ceilings are like, and now I look at them with such a thirst, with such tender love . . .

GAYEV: I remember when I was six years old, on Trinity Sunday,[49] I sat at this window and watched my father walk to church . . .

LYUBOV ANDREYEVNA: Are the things ready?

LOPAKHIN: It seems so. Everything's set. (*To Yepikhodov, putting on his coat.*) Make sure, Yepikhodov, that you keep everything in order.

YEPIKHODOV: (*Talks in a hoarse voice.*) Rest easy, Yermolay Alekseyevich!

LOPAKHIN: What's wrong with your voice?

YEPIKHODOV: I just drank some water and swallowed something.

YASHA: (*With contempt.*) Ignoramus . . .

LYUBOV ANDREYEVNA: We'll go and not a soul will be here . . .

LOPAKHIN: Not until spring.

VARYA: (*Pulling an umbrella out of a bundle in a way that looks as if she were going to hit someone; Lopakhin pretends that he is afraid.*) What are you . . . What . . . I didn't mean to . . .

TROFIMOV: Ladies and gentlemen, let's go to the carriages . . . It's time! The train's coming soon!

VARYA: Petya, here they are, your galoshes, near this suitcase. (*With tears in her eyes.*) How dirty they are, how old . . .

TROFIMOV: (*Putting on the galoshes.*) Let's go, ladies and gentlemen!

---

48. Before leaving for a journey, Russians customarily sit for a few moments. This custom invokes good luck for the trip and for a safe return.
49. In the Christian calendar, this day falls one week after Pentecost, when the Holy Spirit visited Christ's apostles as a tongue of flame. Pentecost is fifty days after Easter.

GAYEV: (*Greatly embarrassed, afraid of crying.*) The train . . . The station . . . A spot to the center, the cue ball rebounds to the corner . . .

LYUBOV ANDREYEVNA: Let's go!

LOPAKHIN: Everyone's here? No one's left in there? (*Locks the side door on the left.*) The things are staying in here so we have to lock up. Let's go! . . .

ANYA: Goodbye, house! Goodbye, old life!

TROFIMOV: Hello, new life! . . . (*Exits with Anya.*)

Varya glances at the room and exits without hurrying. Yasha and Charlotta with her dog exit.

LOPAKHIN: So then, until spring. Let's go out this way, ladies and gentlemen . . . Until next time! . . . (*Exits.*)

Lyubov Andreyevna and Gayev remain together. They seem to have been waiting for this, and throw their arms around each other, but hold back their sobs, crying quietly, afraid to be heard.

GAYEV: (*In despair.*) My sister, my sister . . .

LYUBOV ANDREYEVNA: Oh, my sweet, my tender, my beautiful orchard! . . . My life, my youth, my happiness, goodbye! . . . Goodbye! . . .

Voice of Anya, happily calling: "Mama! . . ."

Voice of Trofimov, happily, excitedly: "Yoo-hoo! . . ."

LYUBOV ANDREYEVNA: The last time I'll look at the walls, the windows . . . Our late mother loved to walk around this room . . .

GAYEV: My sister, my sister! . . .

Voice of Anya: "Mama! . . ."

Voice of Trofimov: "Yoo-hoo! . . ."

LYUBOV ANDREYEVNA: We're coming! . . . (*They exit.*)

The stage is empty. A key is heard locking the door, then the carriages are heard leaving. It becomes quiet. In the silence the dull sound of the axe cutting the trees is heard, sounding lonely and sad. Footsteps are heard; Firs appears at the door to the right. He is dressed, as always, in a jacket and a white waistcoat. On his feet he wears slippers. He is sick.

FIRS: (*Approaches the door, tries the doorknob.*) Locked. They left... (*Sits on the divan.*) Forgot about me... It's nothing... I'll sit here a while... I'll bet Leonid Andreyevich didn't put on the fur coat, but went out in the cloth coat... (*Sighs worriedly.*) And I didn't see to it. Young and green! (*Mumbles something that cannot be understood.*) Life has passed by as if it were never lived... (*Lies down.*) I'll lie down a while... You don't have your strength now, do you? Nothing's left, nothing... Ah you... Nincompoop!... (*Lies still.*)

A distant sound is heard, as if coming from the sky—the sound of a snapping string, dying away, sad. The silence descends and only the faraway sound of the axe chopping the trees in the orchard is heard.

Curtain.

A Selected Bibliography in English

Biographies of Anton Chekhov

Callow, Phillip. *Chekhov, The Hidden Ground: A Biography.* Chicago: Ivan R. Dee, 1998.

McVay, Gordon. *Chekhov: A Life in Letters.* London: Folio Society, 1994.

Rayfield, Donald. *Anton Chekhov: A Life.* New York: Henry Holt, 1997.

Simmons, Ernest J. *Chekhov: A Biography.* Chicago: The University of Chicago Press, 1962.

Collections of Chekhov's Stories, Letters, and the Complete Plays

Benedetti, Jean, trans. and ed. *The Moscow Art Theatre Letters.* New York: Routledge, 1991. [Includes letters by and to Chekhov, Knipper, Nemirovich-Danchenko, Stanislavsky, and other members of the Moscow Art Theatre company.]

———, trans. and ed. *Dear Writer, Dear Actress: The Love Letters of Anton Chekhov and Olga Knipper.* Hopewell, NJ: Ecco Press, 1997.

Chekhov, Anton. *The Selected Letters of Anton Chekhov.* New York: Farrar, Straus, 1955.

———. *The Undiscovered Chekhov: Forty-Three New Stories.* Translated by Peter Constantine. New York: Seven Stories Press, 1998. [Includes very early stories, usually excluded from anthologies.]

———. *Stories.* Translated by Richard Pevear and Larissa Volokhonsky. New York: Bantam Books, 2000.

———. *The Complete Plays.* Translated and edited by Laurence Senelick. New York: W. W. Norton, 2006. [Includes all of Chekhov's plays and their multiple revisions.]

Garnett, Constance, trans. and ed. *Letters of Anton Chekhov to Olga Knipper.* New York: Blom, 1968.

Karlinsky, Simon, and Michael Henry Heim, trans. and eds. *Anton Chekhov's Life and Thought: Selected Letters.* Berkeley: University of California at Berkeley Press, 1975.

Critical Studies on Chekhov's Dramaturgy

Adler, Stella. *Stella Adler on Ibsen, Strindberg, and Chekhov.* Edited by Barry Paris. New York: Alfred A. Knopf, 1999.

Allen, David. *Performing Chekhov.* New York: Routledge, 2000.

Barricelli, Jean-Pierre, ed. *Chekhov's Great Plays: A Critical Anthology.* New York: New York University Press, 1981. [Includes essays by major scholars.]

Beckerman, Bernard. "Dramatic Analysis and Literary Interpretation: *The Cherry Orchard* as Exemplum." *New Literary History: A Journal of Thought and Interpretation* 2:3(Spring 1971): 391–406.

———. "The Artifice of 'Reality' in Chekhov and Pinter." *Modern Drama* 21(1978): 153–61.

Bentley, Eric. "Craftsmanship in *Uncle Vanya*," in *In Search of Theatre.* London: Dennis Dobson, 1954.

Blair, Rhonda. "Translation, Image, Action and Chekhov's *The Seagull*," in *The Actor, Image and Action: Acting and Cognitive Neuroscience.* New York: Rouledge, 2008.

Bloom, Harold, ed. *Anton Chekhov: Bloom's Major Dramatists.* Bromall, PA: Chelsea House, 2000. [This anthology includes biographical information, plot summaries of the plays, and critical essays by various authors.]

Brustein, Robert. "Anton Chekhov," in *The Theatre of Revolt.* Boston: Little, Brown, 1964.

Carnicke, Sharon Marie. "Stanislavsky's Production of *The Cherry Orchard* in the U.S." in J. Douglas Clayton, ed., *Chekhov Then and Now: The Reception of Chekhov in World Culture.* New York: Peter Lang, 1997. [An anthology of interesting essays.]

———. "Translating Chekhov's Plays Without Russian, or The Nasty Habit of Adaptation" in Michael C. Finke and Julie de Sherbinin, eds., *Chekhov the Immigrant: Translating a Cultural Icon.* Bloomington, IN: Slavica, 2007. [A collection of articles.]

Clyman, Toby W., ed. *A Chekhov Companion.* Westport, CT: Greenwood Press, 1985. [A collection of articles by major scholars.]

De Maegd-Soëp, Carolina. *Chekhov and Women: Women in the Life and Work of Chekhov.* Bloomington, IN: Slavica, 1987.

Emeljanow, Victor. *Chekhov: The Critical Heritage.* Boston: Routledge and Kegan Paul, 1981.

Finke, Michael C. *Seeing Chekhov: Life and Art.* Ithaca: Cornell University Press, 2005.

Gilman, Richard. *Chekhov's Plays: An Opening into Eternity.* New Haven: Yale University Press, 1995.

Gottlieb, Vera, and Paul Allain, eds. *The Cambridge Companion to Chekhov*. Cambridge: Cambridge University Press, 2000. [An anthology of critical articles.]

Gottlieb, Vera. *Chekhov and the Vaudeville: A Study of Chekhov's One Act Plays*. New York: Cambridge University Press, 1982.

———, trans. and ed. *Anton Chekhov at the Moscow Art Theatre: Illustrations of the Original Productions*. New York: Routledge, 2005. [A book of wonderful photographs.]

Jackson, Robert Louis, ed. *Chekhov: A Collection of Critical Essays*. Englewood Cliffs, NJ: Prentice-Hall, 1967. [Includes essays by major scholars from Russia.]

Koteliansky, S.S., ed. *Anton Tchekhov* [sic]*: Literary and Theatrical Reminiscences*. New York: Haskell House, 1974.

Levin, Irina, and Igor Levin. *Working on the Play and the Role: The Stanislavsky Method for Analyzing the Characters in a Drama*. Chicago: Ivan R. Dee, 1992. [Uses *The Cherry Orchard* to describe acting technique.]

Loehlin, James, N. *Chekhov: The Cherry Orchard*. Cambridge: Cambridge University Press, 2006.

Magarshack, David. *Chekhov as a Dramatist*. New York: Hill and Wang, 1968.

McVay, Gordon. *Chekhov's* Three Sisters. London: Bristol Classical Press, 1995.

Nemirovitch-Dantchenko [sic], Vladimir. *My Life in the Russian Theatre*. Boston: Little, Brown, 1937.

Peace, Richard. *Chekhov: A Study of the Four Major Plays*. New Haven: Yale University Press, 1983.

Pervukhina, Natalia. *Anton Chekhov: The Sense and the Nonsense*. New York: Legas, 1993. [An excellent study of Chekhov's use of humor and absurdity.]

Pitcher, Harvey J. *The Chekhov Play: A New Interpretation*. New York: Barnes and Noble, 1973.

———. *Chekhov's Leading Lady: A Portrait of the Actress Olga Knipper*. New York: F. Watts, 1980.

Rayfield, Donald. *Chekhov's* Uncle Vania *and* The Wood Demon. London: Bristol Classical Press, 1995.

———. *Understanding Chekhov: A Critical Study of Chekhov's Prose and Drama*. Madison: University of Wisconsin Press, 1999.

Reid, John McKellor. *The Polemical Force of Chekhovian Comedies: A Rhetorical Analysis*. Lewiston, NY: Edwin Mellen Press, 2007.

Senelick, Laurence. *Anton Chekhov*. New York: Grove Press, 1985.

———. *The Chekhov Theatre: A Century of the Plays in Performance.* New York: Cambridge University Press, 1997.

Stanislavski [sic], K. S. *My Life in Art.* Translated by J. J. Robbins. New York: Theatre Arts Books, 1948. [This is the classic translation.]

———. *My Life in Art.* Translated by Jean Benedetti. New York: Routledge, 2008.

Stelleman, Jenny. *Aspects of Dramatic Communication: Action, Non-Action, Interaction.* Amsterdam: Rodopi, 1992. [Includes discussion of Chekhov and two other Russian dramatists: the symbolist A. Blok and the absurdist D. Kharms.]

Styan, J. L. *Chekhov in Performance: A Commentary on the Major Plays.* New York: Cambridge University Press, 1971.

Tait, Peta. *Performing Emotions: Gender, Bodies, Spaces, in Chekhov's Drama and Stanislavski's Theatre.* Aldershot, UK: Ashgate, 2003.

Tulloch, John. *Chekhov: A Structuralist Study.* Totowa, NJ: Barnes and Noble, 1980.

Valency, Maurice. *The Breaking Sting: The Plays of Anton Chekhov.* New York: Schocken Books, 1983. [A classic study of Chekhov's drama.]

Wellek, René, and Nonna D. Wellek, eds. *Chekhov: New Perspectives.* Englewood Cliffs, NJ: Prentice-Hall, 1984. [An anthology of major critical essays.]

Worall, Nick, ed. *File on Chekhov.* New York: Methuen, 1986. [A concise and useful chronology of information.]